YOUR HANDBOOK
OF EVERYDAY LAW

YOUR HANDBOOK OF
EVERYDAY
LAW

FIFTH EDITION

George Gordon Coughlin, Jr.

HarperPerennial

A Division of HarperCollins*Publishers*

HarperCollins books may be purchased for educational, business, or sales promotional use. For information, please write: Special Markets Department, HarperCollins Publishers, Inc., 10 East 53rd Street, New York, NY 10022.

FIRST EDITION

Designed by C. Linda Dingler

Library of Congress Cataloging-in-Publication Data

Coughlin, George Gordon.
    Your handbook of everyday law / George Gordon Coughlin, Jr. -- 5th ed.
        p.   cm.
    Rev. ed. of: Your introduction to law. 4th ed. c1983.
    Includes index.
    ISBN 0-06-271572-0 — ISBN 0-06-273240-4 (pbk.)
    1. Law — United States — Popular works. I. Coughlin, George Gordon. Your introduction to law. II. Title.
KF387.C6 1993
    349.73 — dc20
    [347.3]   93-25283

93 94 95 96 97 ❖/RRD 10 9 8 7 6 5 4 3 2 1
93 94 95 96 97 ❖/RRD 10 9 8 7 6 5 4 3 2 1 (pbk.)

CONTENTS

FOREWORD
TO FIRST EDITION

This fine tool for self-education of Americans about the nature of their law should be welcomed throughout the land. The challenges to our democratic way of life in the last generation have made it increasingly clear that one of the glories of our society is its independent legal system. Too many of us are only dimly aware of the fact that it is the existence of the rule of law which provides part of the assurance and stability of expectation upon which our economy is based. No person or entity, including the government, is powerful enough to trample on the rights of the weakest of our citizens while he has access to the courts and an advocate to press his case. There are occasional failures of justice, but they are relatively rare and becoming rarer. It is the law's fairness and protection that prevents democracy from degenerating into a dictatorship of transient majorities. The self-respect and confidence engendered by the concept of equality before the law has permitted in this country an astounding outpouring of creativity and energy responsible for much of our riches and for our leadership of the free world.

The need for laymen in a democracy to learn about the law is based on more than their civic responsibility to understand the system which they ultimately control. A legal system can operate effectively only if most people follow its precepts willingly. Law can operate as the great teacher and civilizer, regulating day-to-day activities peacefully, only if those whose conduct should be guided by it know what is expected of them. For example, many of the finer aspects of criminal law, as in the rules of self-defenses, are based upon an analysis of deterrence. But it is absurd to work out a calculus of deterrence considering such questions as whether a man attacked can be, or should be, forced to retreat under the threat of criminal punishment if he kills his attacker, when the public is not aware of an obligation to retreat. Equal and unbiased administration of the law requires the assumption that all men know the law, and, for most purposes, ignorance of the law is no excuse. Yet to enforce the law against a person who thought he was acting properly may be cruel and harsh. The only effective escape from the dilemma lies in a sustained effort to teach the public its legal rights and responsibilities.

Recognizing that no man can call himself truly educated unless he understands our legal system, many of our best universities are providing courses in law for those who will not be lawyers. This text will prove useful to such students. It will also be helpful to teachers and advanced students in high school. The adult who wishes a short home reference on some of law's fundamentals and pitfalls, which he can read and understand without an instructor's aid, will welcome it. Finally, this book should assist people from abroad who want an overview of our legal system. In short, the author has created a work valuable to a wide spectrum of people.

The abstractions and complexities have been reduced to concrete and readily understandable pithy hypotheticals and summaries easily grasped by any layman. Cutting cleanly to the essence of each topic permits insights into our legal system that sometimes escape even the advanced student of law who is too close to the detail to see the broader structure.

Both substantive law, defining our rights and obligations vis a vis each other and our government, and procedural law, regulating the method of vindicating those rights and enforcing those obligations in courts of law, are covered. The author, recognizing that any living institution can be no better than the men who administer it, has described the bench and bar and suggested the importance of their training and aspirations as guardians of justice.

George Coughlin is particularly well qualified to write broadly on the law. His meticulous schooling and early training in one of the best of New York's large law firms, as well as his judgment, warmth, and fine character, quickly made him a leader among lawyers. In a relatively small but vital city in upstate New York, he has met almost every kind of legal problem brought by people from all sectors of our society.

Like all fine lawyers who practice in the grand style, much of the author's energy has been devoted to improvement of the law. Thus, when it was necessary to completely revise New York's civil procedure, he was appointed to the small committee assigned the task of study and drafting. He served with full and unstinted devotion for years when scores of time-consuming meetings and advance preparation cut heavily into his practice and home life. A conservative in the best sense of the word, the fervor of his demand for change when it promised improvement had great weight with the legislature that adopted the new practice. Numbered among his many other activities have been those for the bar association which resulted in modernization of the corporate law in New York.

This book, then, is written by a student and skilled practitioner of the law who brings to it an almost unique understanding of what the law is and how justice is administered in the United States. But more than knowledge is here. The work reflects the deep love for the law of one committed to its profession.

JACK B. WEINSTEIN[1]

[1]Judge of the United States District Court for the Eastern District of New York.

Written for the first edition of this book, published in 1960, when the author was a Professor of Law at Columbia University's School of Law.

PREFACE TO
FIRST EDITION

Everyone in a democracy should familiarize himself with the laws regulating his daily life. Obviously, he cannot know all the law, but he should know the fundamentals for his own protection.

In ancient Greece and Rome, small boys were obliged to commit to memory the laws of their countries. In our country, students must become familiar at least with the basic law of the land, and immigrants are required to learn some of the basic tenets of the law before being naturalized. Both naturalized and native-born citizens would greatly benefit, however, from learning more about the practical workings of our public and private laws, for in a democracy there is a fiction that people are "presumed to know the law." Actually, few do.

Our laws are complex, but our civilization is so interwoven with complexities that the laws cannot be made simple. After forty years of legal practice, I have attempted to clarify some of the law's workings in an effort to help the layman to better understand legal fundamentals and procedures. This book only scratches the surface of the subject. Neither it nor any single volume can state the law as a whole.

My efforts here do not constitute a law-made-easy book or a do-it-yourself book. (Do it yourself, unless you are trained in the law, and you are headed for trouble.) The idea of "every man his own lawyer" is a foolish one, as foolish as expecting every man to be successful as his own surgeon, dentist, or electrical engineer.

The aim of this book is to stimulate the lay person's interest in the elementary principles by which we must all live, in the rules which govern our American society. Read this book, then, for self-protection, education, and sharpened awareness of when you need legal advice.

GEORGE G. COUGHLIN
1960

This publication is designed to provide accurate and authoritative information in regard to the subject matter covered. It is sold with the understanding that the publisher is not engaged in rendering legal, accounting or other professional service. If legal advice or other expert assistance is required, the services of a competent professional person should be sought.

—from a Declaration of Principles jointly adopted by a Committee of Publishers and Associations on Bar Cooperation and the American Bar Association's Standing Committee on Unauthorized Practice of Law.

1

THE LEGAL PROFESSION

The rules that govern our complicated civilization are known as law. Law is interpreted and administered by lawyers. Because they are the stewards of the rights and obligations of all citizens, they are public servants and make a unique and fundamentally important contribution to American society.

It is hard to keep track of the legal profession. The United States has more lawyers than any other country in the world. The number of lawyers in the United States is fast approaching 750,000, practically 70 percent of the world's lawyers. It is difficult to count the number of "lawyers" in the world because a "lawyer" is defined differently in each country.

THE AMERICAN LAWYER: ETHICS AND SERVICE

The standards of the American lawyer are high. He or she must meet rigid character and educational requirements in order to become a member of the legal profession, and in daily work he or she must conform to a rigorous code of principles and practice.

Despite the high character of lawyers and the great trust that has been placed in them in public office and private life, it is possible to find many persons who believe that lawyers do not tell the truth (or distort it), that they are paid to lie. This is not true. A lawyer is sworn to be loyal to his client, but this loyalty does not include the obligation to manufacture false testimony or to permit bribery or perjury. Elihu Root, one of the greatest public servants in American history, stated, "For every detractor, we find a thousand men and women who trust their lawyers implicitly in their most intimate and vital affairs, with the frankness and confidence of personal friendship, and who are justified in their trust."

Complaints against lawyers are said to stem from complaints against the administration of justice. The primary end of law is justice, and every citizen feels he knows what is just. He would like to be able to go to court and tell his story without having to employ a lawyer. But when two or more individuals have a dispute, each one has a different idea of what constitutes justice. Instead of solving their dispute with violence, they are compelled by the law to resolve their differences in court; in order to do this, each one needs to hire a lawyer to explain the complicated laws involved in their dispute.

Although in every profession there are dishonest, unethical practitioners, fewer than one percent of practicing lawyers have been found guilty of crimes or unethical conduct. Most lawyers have great personal integrity and live up to the high standards of ethics imposed upon them by their profession.

The Organized Bar

The term *organized bar* refers to members of bar associations as distinguished from lawyers as individuals. A bar association generally is established for the purpose of advancing the science of law and promoting the administration of justice and upholding the standards of the legal profession.

In 1870 the Association of the Bar of the City of New York was organized. Almost immediately the association came in conflict with the Tweed Ring (a corrupt organization which then dominated New York politics). An investigation it had recommended resulted in the impeachment of two judges and the resignation of a third. This action played an important part in the downfall of the Ring and established public confidence in that bar association.

The American Bar Association (ABA) was organized in Saratoga Springs, New York, in July 1878. Today, after many struggles and a reorganization, the ABA is a potent force in upholding and defending the United States Constitution and in promoting the public good. The work of the ABA is broken down into various subjects and is handled by sections. The sections embrace the following fields: administrative law, antitrust law, corporation, banking and business law, criminal law, family law, individual rights and responsibilities, insurance negligence and compensation law, international and comparative law, judicial administration, labor relations law, legal education and admission to the bar, local government law, natural resources law, patent, trademark, and copyright law, public contract law, public utility law, real property, probate and trust law, and tax law. Each state has its own bar association, as do large cities and many counties.

The organized bar actively polices its own ranks. Bar associations of the United States have successfully resisted pressure, political or otherwise, to go easy on those lawyers against whom disciplinary measures should be taken.

Ethics and Discipline in the Profession

Dean John H. Wigmore, one of America's great legal writers, once said,

This living spirit of the profession, which limits it yet uplifts it as a livelihood, has been customarily known by the vague term "legal ethics." An apprentice must hope and expect to make full acquaintance with this body of traditions as his manual of equipment, without which he cannot do his part to keep the law on the level of a profession.[1]

The term *legal ethics* has been defined as "that branch of moral science which treats of the duties which a member of the legal profession owes to the public, the court, his professional brethren, and his client."[2]

In his authoritative book, *Legal Ethics*,[3] Henry S. Drinker examines the four duties of a lawyer. In discussing a lawyer's obligation to the public, Drinker says that just criticisms of the bar are the unwillingness of lawyers to expose their colleagues' abuses and the reluctance of judges to disbar, suspend or even publicly reprimand such lawyers. He attributes much of the public suspicion of lawyers to the realization that most of the abuses of which lawyers are guilty could be eliminated if the bar and the courts were constantly alert and willing to do their full duty in this regard. Drinker cites the Canons of Professional Ethics (now superseded by the Rules of Professional Conduct), which places upon lawyers the obligations (to endeavor) to prevent political considerations from outweighing judicial fitness in the selection of judges, to represent the poor and the indigent, and the duty not to stir up litigation. (The solicitation of automobile accident and negligence claims, "Ambulance chasing," is an example of stirring up litigation.)

For years the bible on the subject of ethical conduct in the legal profession was the Canons of Professional Ethics, which had its origin in 1887. Over the years the ABA and the bar associations of the various states have struggled with the problem of wording of ethical obligations of lawyers.

In 1970 a new set of rules known as the Code of Professional Responsibility was established, but there were many dissenters who were dissatisfied with some of the wording of the code, so a new study was instigated on the subject of ethics, which wound up in 1984 with a new set of rules known as "The Model Rules of Professional Conduct." The new name uses the word "rules" instead of the words "canons" or "code." The model Rules of Professional Conduct furnish a new set of guidelines for ethical conduct by lawyers, but they are not effective until adopted by the individual bar associations or other governing bodies of the individual states. A few state bar associations have adopted the new rules, but the procedure seems lengthy and time consuming, and it will be some years before we can say that all fifty states within the United States have uniform standards of ethics. The model Rules of Professional Conduct list various ethical problems which lawyers face and outline lawyers' obligations and responsibilities with regard to the public.

Practice and procedure for disciplining lawyers varies from state to state. In almost all jurisdictions, however, anyone may file a complaint concerning a lawyer's misconduct. Most state bar associations and many city and county associations have grievance committees, which are charged with receiving and investigating complaints, making preliminary findings, and, if they warrant it, referring complaints to the appropriate court. The court rules on the lawyer's conduct and may suspend him from practice or even disbar him. In some states court proceedings are instituted and conducted by the attorney general of the state or by the county attorney.

A lawyer may be suspended from practice or disbarred if his conduct indicates that he cannot be trusted to advise and act for clients and also in those cases where his conduct indicates that he would cast serious reflection on the dignity of the court and on the reputation of the profession if he were allowed to continue to practice.

Bar associations are striving for stricter adherence to the model Rules of Professional Conduct. The question is whether greater adherence should be brought about by educational processes or through harsher disciplinary actions. Surveys throughout the country indicate that in some areas disciplinary action is more or less futile, for only the most brazen violations are prosecuted, and grievance committee members are often too lenient with offenders.

The difficulty of disciplinary action has been increased by differing interpretations and applications of the old Canons of Ethics among grievance and ethics committees throughout the United States, although, generally, the interpretations made by the committee of the American Bar Association are considered the most authoritative. It appears, then, that a more widespread understanding of the model Rules of Professional Conduct should be attempted by education (advising new members of the ethical standards of the profession) and by publicity (making the public aware of the high standard of the bar).

U.S. Supreme Court Ruling That Lawyers May Advertise

In 1977 the U.S. Supreme Court ruled that the prohibition of advertising by lawyers violated the free speech provision of the First Amendment of the Constitution. The Court held that lawyers may not be subject to a "blanket suppression" of advertising, but said that the bar associations of the various states should regulate and lay down guidelines for lawyer advertising.

Legal Aid and Other Services

Legal aid is the organized effort of a bar association and the community to provide the services of lawyers free or for token charges to persons who cannot afford to pay attorneys' fees. The aim of legal aid is that no citizen because of his financial hardship be denied protection and benefits under the law. This goal has been achieved in substantial measure in the large cities; in smaller cities, however, there is much to be accomplished in providing legal assistance to the indigent. The enlightened attitude of the organized bar has been responsible for the great increase in the number of legal aid offices established.

In determining eligibility for legal aid, family income, health, property ownership, and similar factors are considered. The Legal Aid Society of New York sets up this test: "Could a competent private attorney be found to take the case for whatever fee the case might yield?" If one would take the case, then the society refers the person seeking assistance to a private attorney. A large part of legal aid work is devoted to tasks of counseling, mediation, and drafting papers.

The term *legal aid* does not include the private donation of free service to deserving people by lawyers. Again, organized legal aid should not be confused with the *assignment by the court of counsel* to represent a needy person in a criminal case. In this situation, the lawyer's compensation is fixed by the court and is paid by the state. In addition, certain communities support the so-called *public defender* system; the public defender is paid by the state to defend indigent persons accused of crimes.

Some states are more aggressive in their defense of the poor. For example, in New Jersey the office of the Public Advocate and Public Defender has a staff of 380 lawyers, of which 330 defend the poor and fifty who monitor utility rates and look out for the physically and mentally ill, prison inmates, homeless, and ordinary citizens. Since its establishment in 1974, the Office of Public Advocate and Public Defender has taken on some legal matters which many of the department's critics, mostly public officials, have no trouble endorsing. However, other states, as well as the federal government, have been somewhat less aggressive.

Legal aid should also not be confused with *lawyer reference plans,* through which bar associations bring persons needing legal advice into contact with lawyers who are willing to serve them for modest fees.

Pro Bono Work

Pro bono, shortened from *pro bono publico*, a Latin phrase meaning "for the public good," is a phrase that lawyers use to describe volunteering their time, energy, and experience to increase the legal services for the poor. *Pro bono* work can either take the form of representing an indigent client or of working for a charitable organization.

In recent years many state bar associations have begun more aggressively to assert that which many individual lawyers have recognized for years; that they owe a responsibility to the predicament of a poor person with a legal problem; that they owe a duty to society to work for the public good. Some bar associations, usually on a voluntary basis, are asking lawyer-members for details on the amount of their *pro bono* work done. For example, a former chief judge of the New York State Court of Appeals (who also was chief administrative judge) proposed a mandatory *pro bono* requirement. (The New York State Bar Association has undertaken a two-year study, during which time *pro bono* work is on a voluntary basis.)

THE AMERICAN LAWYER: TRAINING AND SPECIALIZATION

In colonial days—and even in the nineteenth century—so-called attorneys were tutored minor court officers, such as deputy sheriffs, clerks, and justices, who fostered litigation for petty court fees. Gradually, however, a system of legal training began to develop.

Legal Education in the United States

In the early days of our republic lawyers studied the works of the leading authorities in Europe and England, particularly the *Commentaries on the Laws of England* by the English jurist Sir William Blackstone (1723–80). Blackstone's influence is said to have resulted in the establishment of chairs of law at several American universities; yet the main education of lawyers remained for some time in office apprenticeships.

Lawyers of the last century were still reluctant to accept the idea of university training. They clung to the belief that legal education was nothing more than the mastering of a craft, the skills for which had to be passed on from the practitioner to the novice. Supreme Court Justice Joseph Story criticized the narrowness of the legal instruction at that time and pointed to the need for knowledge of the principles of law and broad study liberalized by acquaintance with philosophy and the wisdom of ancient and modern times.

The first university school of law was founded at Harvard in 1815; Yale followed in 1826 with its law school. In 1850 there were fifteen university law schools in the United States, and thirty-one in 1870.

Today there are over 170 law schools, with about 120,000 students, of whom roughly forty percent are women (compared with about 1,000 women in law schools in the early 1950s). For example, there were 381 students admitted to the 1992 entering class at the University of Virginia Law School, of whom 145 were women. This profile closely parallels national statistics.

In 1870, Dean Christopher C. Langdell of Harvard established the case method, a system of teaching law through the study of actual cases and judicial decisions. Only a few law schools then recognized and applied the use of the textbook method of teaching, but today the case system is used in almost every well-recognized law school in the country.

High Standards of Modern American Law School

In 1921, the ABA, led by such men as Elihu Root and William Howard Taft, recommended that all law colleges require of students the following conditions for admission to the bar: (1) at least two years of college study before attending law school; (2) at least a three-year course in law school; (3) full-time attendance at law school and instruction by full-time teachers; and (4) examination by public authority (that is, graduation from law school should not automatically determine fitness for admission to the bar).

In 1923, the ABA published its first list of approved law schools. It became apparent, however, that it was impossible to evaluate the qualifications of law schools without personal inspection. In 1927, advisers of the American Bar Association began inspecting law schools and assisting them with their problems. They also began urging the state and local bar associations to adopt the ABA standards for admission to the bar. As a result of these activities, law schools in 1952 increased to three the number of years of acceptable college study necessary for admission.

Postadmission Legal Education

A century ago, when a lawyer completed his legal education and was admitted to the bar, he assumed that his schooling was over. The modern lawyer, on the other hand, appreciates the need for continuing his legal education. Keeping up with current reading is not sufficient.

Various organizations such as the American Law Institute, the Practicing Law Institute, and state and local bar associations give regular postadmission courses of instruction. Each year the Practicing Law Institute conducts courses for thousands of lawyers through Saturday forums, summer sessions, home study programs, and published monographs. In addition, the American Law Institute supervises postadmission legal education programs on a national level.

This type of postadmission legal education is known among lawyers as "continuing legal education" (CLE). Many states today require, either on a voluntary or a mandatory basis, that a lawyer complete a specified number of hours of CLE to "keep his pencils sharp."

Specialization

Today there is a trend in states to allow lawyers to hold themselves as "specialists" in certain fields. For example, in Florida, upon completion of certain CLE courses, a lawyer may hold him or herself out as a "specialist" in, for example, trust and estate law.

There are both proponents and opponents of this trend. The proponents contend that the consumer (the potential client) may better be able to find a lawyer who is knowledgeable in her or his particular problem area. The opponents believe that they may amount to false or misleading advertising.

Classification of Lawyers

The four main fields in which lawyers serve are: (1) private practice of the law, (2) government service, (3) direct employment by private business, and (4) employment by labor unions. More than 75 percent of the total number of lawyers in the United States are in private practice. Unlike English lawyers, who are either solicitors (office lawyers) or barristers (courtroom lawyers), all American lawyers are licensed to be both office and courtroom lawyers.

Private practitioners may be grouped in scores of classifications, of which the following are typical, but not coequal: general practitioners, office, trial, patent, tax, corporation, real estate, or estate lawyers. A lawyer employed by a business firm may be counsel for the corporation (sometimes designated as "house counsel") or a member of the law department of the particular firm.

Lawyers serving the government directly may be employed at the federal, state, or local level.

The so-called labor lawyer may work either for private industry or for labor unions. In the early days of the labor movement in this country, there was some prejudice against lawyers who represented unions. The stigma has gradually disappeared, and the integrity of the labor lawyer is now recognized.

Lawyers may also be district attorneys, public defenders, law enforcement officers, or work as staff members in the judicial branch of a government, or they may be judges, legislators, mayors, or governors.

The Work of the Average Practitioner

What, then, are the everyday activities of the American lawyer? It has been said that the work of the lawyer is

to be a wise counselor,

to be an advocate,

to work toward the improvement of the profession,

to answer calls to public office, and

to help form public opinion.

Whether he practices alone, in partnership, or as a member of a law firm, he may perform, for example, any or all the following tasks:

He may assist clients in the purchase, sale, leasing, and mortgaging of houses, buildings, and other real estate;

he may give advice through estate planning, preparing wills, and handling general estate matters;

he may also give advice concerning the tax consequences (including income, estate, and gift taxes) of certain proposed transactions and prepare federal and state tax returns;

he may advise business people about the advantages and disadvantages of the different forms of business organization, selecting the form that would be most advantageous in a particular circumstance;

he may continue this sort of activity by organizing partnerships, corporations, and other forms of business and by preparing all the documents needed for purchasing and doing business in various situations;

he may provide counsel in labor relations cases, including such matters as union negotiations, union contracts, minimum wages, and labor laws in general;

he may handle negotiations for the settlement of controversies;

when negotiations fail, he may institute legal proceedings to recover damages for wrongful acts or for the enforcement of legal rights or, when representing a person or persons against whom legal proceedings have been started, enter defense in behalf of the person or persons sued;

he may advise and defend those accused of crimes; he may attempt to reconcile estranged husbands and wives and, if necessary, institute or defend legal proceedings for divorce, separation, or annulment; he may prepare documents of every conceivable kind for his clients;

he may appear before administrative tribunals and legislative bodies.

SELECTION OF A LAWYER

Before engaging a lawyer, one should carefully check his qualifications, experience, and reputation. One's lawyer should be a person of character and integrity, the lawyer in his community that one would most trust.

If the individual has a special type of legal problem, he should consider lawyers experienced in that particular field. If, for example, he wants to have a will drawn, he should choose a lawyer who specializes in the handling of estate matters. He may also want to ask his banker or a reliable merchant or the president of the local bar association for assistance in selecting a lawyer experienced in a particular area of law.

Beware of lawyers who are guilty of unethical practices. For instance, it is unethical for a lawyer to solicit automobile accident cases. A person who will not conform to the rules of his own profession is not to be trusted and, of course, should not be employed or retained.

Most experienced lawyers apply the principles of preventive law to many problems and, when feasible, encourage the settlement of controversies out of court, for litigation is costly and time consuming. These lawyers know that the real service they can render their clients is keeping them from going to court, even though their fees are smaller when certain types of cases are settled out of court. For example, many lawyers try to reunite estranged couples or to prevent families from being broken up by divorce or annulment.

Once an individual has selected a lawyer, he should decide about consulting or retaining (employing) the person. In consulting a lawyer, an individual simply goes to the lawyer's office for advice. Consulting an attorney does not obligate him to give the attorney the case. When an individual retains a lawyer, however, he does put his problem in the lawyer's hands.

Determination of Lawyers' Fees

When a prospective client consults a lawyer he should expect to pay him a fee for his advice. Many individuals are under the false impression that one visit to a lawyer for advice would cost a great deal. Actually, consulting a lawyer costs no more than a consultation with a physician. A lawyer's consultation fee may range from $10 to $200 or more, depending on the complexity of the case, the amount of time spent with the client, the amount of research involved in obtaining the answer to the problem, the lawyer's experience and standing in his profession, and the size of the community in which he practices. It is sensible for the client to ask the lawyer in advance what the consultation fee will be.[4]

There are several methods of paying a lawyer, if he is retained to handle a particular case. Probably the two most widely used means for paying legal fees are the contingent fee and the flat fee.

In a *contingent fee arrangement*, the client and the lawyer agree that the lawyer is willing to handle the case for a percentage—for instance, one-third—of what is obtained in settlement of the case or through litigation. Payment under the contingent fee agreement is conditioned on success; that is, the fee is paid only if the lawyer wins the case. If he fails, the client pays nothing except the out-of-pocket expenses the lawyer has advanced for his client.

The former Code of Professional Responsibility had this to say on the subject of contingent fees:

Contingent fee arrangements in civil cases have long been commonly accepted in the United States in proceedings to enforce claims. Because of the human relationships involved and the unique character of the proceedings, contingent fee arrangements in domestic relation cases are rarely justified. Public policy properly condemns contingent fee arrangements in criminal cases. The fundamental reason for the use of contingent fee contracts is to assist those who have no funds with which to hire lawyers. Under certain circumstances clients prefer contingent fee plans because they do not have to pay fees if the cases are lost; lawyers like them because they are generally rewarded with larger fees when their cases are successful. A contingent fee arrangement is not the only one under which a lawyer will handle a case, as many people seem to believe. A client may reject the contingent fee plan. If an individual feels that his case is a sure thing, that it will never go to trial (and thereby incur the high trial expenses), he simply may wish to pay the lawyer a flat fee for his time and advice. The payment of a flat fee does not depend on the outcome of the case: The client has to pay the fee–win, lose, or draw.

The former Code of Professional Responsibility set forth the following factors as guides for determining the reasonableness of lawyers' fees:

1) The time and labor required, the novelty and difficulty of the questions involved, and the skill requisite to perform the legal service properly;
2) The likelihood, if apparent to the client, that the acceptance of the particular employment will preclude other employment by the lawyer;
3) The fee customarily charged in the locality for similar legal services;
4) The amount involved and the results obtained;
5) The time limitations imposed by the client or by the circumstances;
6) The nature and length of the professional relationship with the client;
7) The experience, reputation, and ability of the lawyer or lawyers performing the services;
8) Whether the fee is fixed or contingent.

These principles are basic guidelines, which survive many changes in the model Rules of Professional Conduct.

NOTES

[1] Albert P. Blaustein, et al., *The American Lawyer* (Chicago: University of Chicago Press, 1954), p. 240.

[2] Francis Rawle, ed.. *Bouvier's Law Dictionary* (St. Paul, Minn.: West Publishing Co., 1914).

[3] Henry S. Drinker, *Legal Ethics* (New York: The William Nelson Cromwell Foundation and Columbia University Press, 1955), pp. 59–64.

[4] Bar associations in more than 250 communities of the United States have lawyer reference plans, so that a person who needs the advice of a lawyer may phone the local bar association, which then will refer the prospective client to a local lawyer (knowledgeable in a particular field). The prospective client will be told in advance the lawyer's fee for the conference. (The average fee is $25 for a half-hour consultation.)

2

THE COURT SYSTEM IN THE UNITED STATES

Once a question of law has been deliberately examined and decided in the United States, it is binding on the courts within the jurisdiction; this is the principle of *stare decisis*. Under the American court (or English court) system (and unlike civil and other systems), this doctrine is considered indispensable to the administration of justice. Although it is in general bound by this doctrine along with the lesser courts, the U.S. Supreme Court sometimes upsets precedents and establishes a new principle. Its decisions are binding on all other courts.

TYPES OF COURTS

A *court* is a place where justice is administered. It may consist of a judge and a jury or only a judge and a clerk, or it may be a tribunal including a number of judges. The words *judge* and *court* are sometimes loosely interchanged, but they are not necessarily synonymous.

A *term of court* is the period fixed by law for the holding of court sessions. Although each state legislature has the power to set the schedule, very often the designation of time for holding court sessions is left to the court itself. Terms of court may be regular or special; the latter are held for a special purpose, usually for the hearing of nonjury cases.

Courts of Original and Appellate Jurisdiction

Jurisdiction[1] has been defined as the authority of a court to hear and determine a case. A *court of original jurisdiction* is one in which a legal proceeding is first started. A *court of appellate jurisdiction* is one that reviews cases removed by appeal from a lower court.

Courts of Law and Courts of Equity

A *court of law* is one which administers justice according to the principles and the forms of common law. A *court of equity* is one which administers justice according to the rules and principles of equity. (The term *equity* is a survival from ancient English times, when litigants felt the harshness and rigidity of the common law and, therefore, appealed to the king's chancellor for special consideration, [justice] based on equitable principles.) Many states have abolished the distinction between courts of law and equity.

Courts of Record and Courts Not of Record

A *court of record* was originally defined as one where the acts and judicial proceedings were enrolled permanently on parchment. Today, a court of record may be defined as a superior court that keeps a permanent record of its proceedings and that may have power to fine or imprison. A *court not of record* is an inferior court that has no power to fine or imprison and that does not record proceedings.

Civil and Criminal Courts

Civil courts are those which are established to decide disputes between persons in their private capacity, whether they be individuals, partnerships, or corporations. Sometimes civil courts decide disputes between private persons and governments or between branches of the government. Criminal courts are those established for the determination and punishment of felonies and misdemeanors.

THE FEDERAL JUDICIAL SYSTEM

The Constitution of the United States provides that "the judicial power of the United States shall be vested in one Supreme Court and in such inferior courts as the Congress may, from time to time, ordain and establish." Judges in federal courts are appointed for life and can be removed only if impeached for gross misconduct by the House of Representatives and convicted by the Senate. The federal judicial system consists of the following courts:

The *Supreme Court* of the United States, holding sessions in Washington, D.C., and consisting of nine judges, is the court of final resort. It hears appeals on federal questions from circuit courts or the highest state courts, but it hears only such cases as it deems necessary to the public interest.

Courts of appeal, one for each of eleven circuits in the United States, are courts of appellate jurisdiction. Each court of appeal has five or six judges. These courts were formerly called circuit courts of appeal, hence, are sometimes now referred to as "circuit courts."

District courts have been set up in each of the fifty states and the District of Columbia; there are ninety-three in all. Each of these courts, as a rule, has jurisdiction over a state or part of a state.

The *court of claims* is the court in which suits against the government of the United States are heard.

There also are other specialized federal courts, which handle, for example, only tax matters, customs matters, trademarks, service marks and patents, admiralty matters, etc.

THE STATE JUDICIAL SYSTEMS

Each of the fifty states is to a great extent a law unto itself, because each of the original thirteen colonies insisted that it had the right to run its own internal affairs. Legal authorities differ in their opinions about whether the legislature or the courts should determine the detailed rules governing the conduct of legal actions and proceedings. In certain states the powers to make rules are vested in the legislature; in others, the courts, by convention of judges, adopt specific rules for legal procedure.

State judicial systems consist of the following courts:

Courts of original jurisdiction, as indicated above, are those in which a legal action or a proceeding may be started. Courts exercising original jurisdiction may be divided into two groups: those of general or superior jurisdiction and those of limited, inferior, or special jurisdiction.

Courts of general or superior jurisdiction have different names in the various states. In some states they are called circuit courts; in other states they are called district courts, superior courts, or courts of common pleas. In some states, all courts of record are consolidated into one court. (See list of courts by state at the end of this chapter.)

Courts of special, limited, or inferior jurisdiction are not set up uniformly in the state judicial systems. Some states have special courts to handle the estates of deceased persons; these are often called probate courts, orphans' courts, or surrogates' courts. A few states have courts of claims that have jurisdiction over claims against the state, although in many cases states cannot be sued. Almost all states have special courts, such as juvenile court, courts of crimes, police courts, domestic relations courts, courts of tax appeals, justice courts, municipal courts, and city courts.

Most Suits Brought at State Level

When does an aggrieved person bring his suit in a federal court, and when does he bring his suit in a state court? In almost all cases, a person seeking justice brings his suit in a state court in the state in which he lives.

In order for the suit to be brought in a federal district court, it is necessary to show that the suit would be between citizens of different states or between a citizen and an alien, or that the suit involves a question arising under the laws or Constitution of the United States (called a federal question), and also that in civil cases the amount involved is at least $50,000. Federal courts also have jurisdiction over admiralty, maritime, bankruptcy, patent, copyright, postal, internal revenue, and a variety of other matters. When the suit has been brought before a federal court, and if after a federal district court has made a final decision a litigant still feels that justice has not been served, he may appeal to the court of appeals. The decision of the court of appeals is final, unless appealed to the U.S. Supreme Court.

Sometimes an irate litigant may say that he will carry his case to the U.S. Supreme Court, and he may desire very strongly to do so. This does not mean, however, that he is entitled to have his case heard there. Many thousands of cases are heard in the United States every year, but only a few hundred get to the Supreme Court. In a few very special cases, the Supreme Court will issue what is known as a *writ of certiorari*, which is a writ requiring a lower court to furnish the records of a case to a higher court; in this way, the case will be brought before it, and it will review the decision of the Court of appeals or another lower court.

Jurisdiction of State Courts

In order for a case to be properly brought in a state court, the court must have (1) jurisdiction of the subject matter of the action and (2) jurisdiction of the parties to the lawsuit. A state court action may involve an injury to a person or to property, a breach of contract, the determination of title to real estate, or a score of other matters.

Generally, jurisdiction is acquired by the court of the state where the claim (called in law the "cause of action") arose. The theory is that all other elements being equal, the place where the cause of action accrues determines jurisdiction, but in practice this is regarded as a platitude with many exceptions.

In bringing suit the first thing to determine is whether an action is local or transitory. A *transitory action* is one which may be brought in any state regardless of where the cause of action arose. Almost everywhere actions for damages, personal injury, property damage, or for breach of contract are regarded as transitory actions. Certain other actions are regulated by state statutes and are called *local actions*. For example, the law of Pennsylvania gave abutting landowners the right to sue a canal company for injuries to property resulting from the overflow of the canal; this was held to be a purely local action. Most actions involving real estate may be brought only in the state (and, perhaps, county) in which the real estate is located.

A number of states require litigants in disputes involving trifling amounts to bring their suits in inferior courts. Hence, cases involving less than a specified amount (for instance, $500) may not be brought in a superior court. In most states constitutional and statutory provisions restrict the jurisdiction of lesser courts (such as justice courts, municipal courts, county courts) to certain specified amounts. For example, if a particular city court is limited in jurisdiction to cases involving not more than $1,000, and if a suit is brought in that court for $9,000, the case is dismissed because the court does not have jurisdiction of the subject matter.

An essential requirement in the action is that the court obtain jurisdiction of the parties: Without jurisdiction of the parties, the court is powerless to settle a legal controversy. Broadly speaking, in order for the court to obtain jurisdiction over a defendant or a lawsuit, it is necessary that the defendant be personally present within the state so that he may receive service of a summons or other court process. (See Chapter 3 for proceedings in commencement of actions.)

There is, however, a broad class of exceptions that allows state courts jurisdiction in an action against a nonresident if he happens to be within the state or if he voluntarily submits to the jurisdiction of the court. If the nonresident has real or personal property within the state, the court may acquire jurisdiction by issuing an attachment on the property within the state. In most states where the defendant owns real property that is the subject of the action, the court may serve the nonresident defendant by "substituted service" or "service by publication." (Substituted service may be by a court order that requires the defendant owning property within the state to be served by mail and also by publication of a notice in the newspapers in the area where his property is situated.)

Then, there is a special class of cases concerning nonresident motorists passing through a state, who are generally deemed to have appointed the secretary of state of the state where an accident takes place to be their agent and, thus, receive service of summons in behalf of nonresidents.

Conflicts in Court Jurisdiction

Fortunately, considering the hundreds of thousands of court cases, there are relatively few cases where there is a conflict of jurisdiction among the courts of several states or between the state and federal courts. There is a basic rule of comity between states, which helps eliminate many conflicts among the laws of several states. (*Comity* is the recognition that one state gives to the laws of another; it is not a matter of right, but rather a matter of courtesy and good will.) Therefore, the court in one state generally will recognize proceedings of the court of another state, and when the courts of one state have first taken jurisdiction of a controversy, the courts of a second state will usually not interfere.

On the other hand, a federal court will interfere and assert its proper jurisdiction when a state court has acted in a matter given by the U.S.

Constitution or the federal statutes to the protection of the federal courts. In other words, state courts cannot invade a field that has been given by federal law to its own courts. For example, the state courts have no jurisdiction in admiralty cases or in matters arising under the patent or copyright laws of the United States nor in bankruptcy matters, interstate commerce, nor matters affecting the property or territory of the United States.

In 1948 Congress enacted the Federal Tort Claims Act (FTCA), which contained many special provisions, including the waiving of immunity of the United States against suits. There is an exception to this immunity, however, in the case of service men's claims against the government. The Supreme Court has barred suits against the government for torts arising out of military service.

Civilian courts should defer to military tribunals; that is, civilian courts should not interfere with military matters which are being handled by military courts. Criminal jurisdiction of the military courts is limited to crimes which have a connection with the military service. In other words, if a man is accused of theft and the theft is committed off the military base, then the military courts have no jurisdiction. However, there seems to be some flexibility to this rule because the courts have held that the sale or use of drugs off the base may be handled by the military courts because the use of drugs is of vital concern to the military branch of our government.

COURTS OPEN TO THE PUBLIC

The U.S. Supreme Court has held that the public and the press have access to courtrooms while trials are in progress. Although the Supreme Court could find no express constitutional provision giving the press or the public the right of access to criminal trials, the court found that the freedom of speech and freedom of the press provisions of the U.S. Constitution made it implicit that the public and the press should have access to criminal trials. Hence, the trial judge does not have unlimited discretion in the absence of the unusual circumstances to close the court room to the press or to the public.

It has been a growing trend in the courts, both in the federal court system and in the various state court systems, to allow television cameras in the courtroom during the course of the trial.

Courts of Original Jurisdiction and Appellate Courts

STATES	APPELLATE COURTS	COURTS OF ORIGINAL JURISDICTION*
Alabama	Supreme Court (Supreme Court has original jursidiction and also appellate jurisdiction in appeals from certain lower court cases), Court of Appeals	Circuit Courts, County Courts, District Courts
Alaska	Supreme Court, Court of Appeals	Superior Court and District and Magistrate Courts
Arizona	Supreme Court, Court of Appeals	Superior Courts
Arkansas	Supreme Court	Circuit Courts, Chancery Courts, County Courts, Common Plea Courts
California	Supreme Court, District Court of Appeals (Intermediate Appellate Court)	Superior Courts
Colorado	Supreme Court, Court of Appeals	District Courts, Superior Courts, County Courts
Connecticut	Supreme Court	Superior Courts
Delaware	Supreme Court	Court of Chancery, Superior Court, Courts of Common Pleas
Florida	Supreme Court, District Court of Appeals	Circuit Courts, County Courts
Georgia	Supreme Court, Court of Appeals	Superior Courts, County Courts
Hawaii	Supreme Court of Hawaii, Intermediate Appellate Court	Circuit Courts, District Courts
Idaho	Supreme Court, Court of Appeals	District Courts
Illinois	Supreme Court, Appellate Courts	Circuit Courts, County Courts
Indiana	Supreme Court, Court of Appeals	Superior Courts, Circuit Courts
Iowa	Supreme Court, Court of Appeals	District Courts
Kansas	Supreme Court, Court of Appeals	District Courts, County Courts

* In most states, there also are courts dealing with specialized problems, such as a court having charge only of wills, trusts, and estates (called probate, orphans', or surrogate's courts); courts dealing with family and domestic problems (sometimes called domestic relations courts, family courts, or juvenile courts); courts dealing with claims against the municipalities or the states (sometimes called claims courts, city courts, mayors' courts, or magistrates' courts). This last type of court is of limited jurisdiction, particularly as to the dollar amount of the claims that the court can handle; it is usually not a court of record, meaning that no official record or transcript is kept of its proceedings.

Courts of Original Jurisdiction and Appellate Courts (*continued*)

STATES	APPELLATE COURTS	COURTS OF ORIGINAL JURISDICTION*
Kentucky	Supreme Court, Court of Appeals	Circuit Courts, Quarterly Courts, District Courts, County Courts
Louisiana	Supreme Court of Louisiana	District Courts
Maine	Supreme Judicial Court of Maine	Superior Courts, State District Courts
Maryland	Court of Appeals, Court of Special Appeals	Circuit Courts of Counties, District Courts
Massachusetts	Supreme Judicial Court, Appeals Court	Trial Court (Superior Court Department, District Court Department, etc.)
Michigan	State Supreme Court, State Court of Appeals	Circuit Courts, District Courts
Minnesota	Supreme Court of Minnesota	District Court of Minnesota
Mississippi	Supreme Court	Circuit Courts, Chancery Courts, County Courts
Missouri	Supreme Court of Missouri, Court of Appeals	Circuit Courts
Montana	Supreme Court of Montana	District Courts
Nebraska	Supreme Court of Nebraska	District Court, County Courts
Nevada	Supreme Court of Nevada	District Courts of Nevada
New Hampshire	New Hampshire Supreme Court	Superior Court, District Court
New Jersey	Supreme Court	Superior Court, County Court, County District Courts
New Mexico	Supreme Court, Court of Appeals	State District Courts
New York	Court of Appeals, Appellate Divisions of the Supreme Court	Supreme Court, County Courts
North Carolina	Supreme Court of North Carolina, Court of Appeals	Superior Courts, County Courts
North Dakota	Supreme Court	District Courts, County Courts
Ohio	Supreme Court of Ohio, Courts of Appeals	Courts of Common Pleas
Oklahoma	State Supreme Court, Court of Criminal Appeals, Court of Appeals	District Courts, County Courts

Courts of Original Jurisdiction and Appellate Courts (*continued*)

STATES	APPELLATE COURTS	COURTS OF ORIGINAL JURISDICTION*
Oregon	Supreme Court of Oregon, Court of Appeals	Circuit Courts, County Courts, District Courts
Pennsylvania	State Supreme Court	State Superior Court, Commonwealth Court, Common Pleas Court
Rhode Island	Supreme Court	District Courts, Superior Courts
South Carolina	Supreme Court, Court of Appeals	Circuit Courts, County Courts
South Dakota	Supreme Court	Circuit Courts, County Courts
Tennessee	Supreme Court of Tennessee, Court of Criminal Appeals, Court of Appeals	Chancery Courts
Texas	Supreme Court of Texas, Court of Civil Appeals, Court of Criminal Appeals	District Courts, County Courts
Utah	Supreme Court	District Courts
Vermont	Supreme Court	Superior Courts, Court of Chancery, District Courts
Virginia	Supreme Court	Circuit Courts
Washington	Supreme Court, Court of Appeals	Superior Courts
West Virginia	Supreme Court of Appeals	Circuit Courts, County Commissions
Wisconsin	Supreme Court, Court of Appeals	Circuit Courts, County Courts
Wyoming	Supreme Court of Wyoming	District Courts, County Courts

This continues to be a subject of contentious debate between the courts and the media; usually, the trial judges, operating under strict guidelines, have limited discretion to bar TV cameras and photographers. For example, in certain criminal cases, the faces and identities of the jurors (and sometimes the witnesses) cannot be photographed or disclosed.

Small Claims Courts

Most states have small claims courts. Therefore, when anyone has a dispute involving minor damages, such as irreparable damage to a suede coat at the dry cleaners, a bungled job by a carpenter, an unpaid bill by a customer, the customary advice is to take the conflict to the small claims court.

That court was established in most states during the depression and was based upon the concept originally set forth in ancient Greece that small claims court permits the lay person to bring a relatively minor dispute directly before the judge for an immediate decision. This saves lawyer's fees—although you can hire a lawyer if you wish—and the long wait in the regular court system. The average filing fee is $25, although it may vary from state to state.

These days, most of the allowable claims are not so small. For instance, the maximum amount that can be collected in New York in small claims court was originally capped at $50. The limit now is $2,000. In Alaska, California, Georgia, New Mexico, and Pennsylvania, it was recently raised to $5,000. In urban areas of Tennessee, it has been extended to $10,000. In New Jersey, it is $1,500.

Cases can usually be heard within a month of filing the initial petition. Therefore, in most cases, small claims court can be convenient and fast. However, it is no easier to win a case there than in regular court, unless your argument is prepared very carefully. Consequently, before filing an application or petition, it is wise to think calmly about whether the case is viable. You need to have suffered a loss that someone is legally liable to make good. You will need documentary evidence to support your claim.

A retired judge of the New York State Small Claims Court said that in his experience, the most serious mistake made by claimants is failing to bring along documentary evidence. The key to convincing the judge, he said, is to "tell your story concisely and clearly" and to back it up with pertinent papers (estimates, bills, receipts, warranties, photographs, letters of opinion and ordinances, etc.). He also said a critical point not to be overlooked is "keep it short." Rehearsals can help. Spending a couple of hours observing in court prior to your court appearance can make you less nervous; you also may be able to pick up some good ideas.

The person(s) you are suing also must have the ability to pay. Any defendant worth suing should have a steady income and/or real property such as a home or a place of business. Suing a fly-by-night contractor who works out of the back of his truck is probably a waste of time; such defendants are often "judgement proof."

NOTE

[1]There is perhaps no word in legal terminology so frequently used in a general and a vague sense as the word *jurisdiction*. There are many kinds of jurisdiction, among them territorial, civil, and criminal, plus jurisdiction over the person, jurisdiction over property, and many others.

3

COURT PROCEDURE: LEGAL WRONGS AND REMEDIES

It is a fundamental principle of law that for every wrong (the violation of a right), there is a remedy. The subject of rights and wrongs embraces the entire subject of human relations.

RIGHTS AND REMEDIES

When new cases arose under recognized principles during the formative period of the common law, it was necessary to find new remedies to fit them. Throughout the centuries of common law, both in England and in this country, the maxim "wherever there is a right, there is a remedy" has been an ideal to which the law aspires. It cannot be said that in all ways the law has lived up to this ideal; admittedly, the best the law has done is to strive for perfection.

Actions, Suits and Special Proceedings

In a court of law, an *action* or *suit* is a proceeding by which one party prosecutes another for the enforcement or protection of a right or for the prevention of a wrong. In a civil action, one sues to enforce a private right or redress a private wrong. Through a *criminal action*, an individual or the state sues to redress a public wrong.

Common-Law Forms of Action

Many states have preserved common-law forms of action which are highly technical and labeled with Latin or obscure phrases. Among these are the following:

Action of assumpsit is brought to recover damages for a breach of simple contract.

Action of covenant is brought to recover for a contract under seal.

Action in trespass is a suit to recover for direct injury.

Action on the case is brought for indirect injury.

Action in trover is a suit for interfering with or converting the goods of another.

Action in detinue is brought for the recovery of specific chattels.

For example, although Pennsylvania and New Hampshire have retained common-law forms of action, they are gradually being liberalized by court rules and statutes.

Most states have adopted "codes of civil procedure," or "practice acts," that abolish the distinction between the different common-law forms of action and provide for one single form of civil action.[1]

Forms of Equity Action

In the early days of the common law in England, the various forms of common-law actions were found to be too inflexible to fit many human demands. Therefore, when the legal maxim "wherever there is a right, there is a remedy" could not otherwise be satisfied, an appeal was made to the king's chancellor, who then would set up a court of chancery to mete out justice in the case. This court became known as a *court of equity*.

As with a common-law action, the form of an equitable action is often significant. It is important to determine, for example, whether the action is brought in the "law side" or the "equity side" of the court. Many states say that in effect the distinction between actions in law and suits in equity has been abolished, but that the substantive rules governing legal actions and equitable actions are preserved.

Actions of a legal nature include, among others, action for the recovery of a money judgment, action for breach of contract, and action for damages for personal injuries. Actions of an equitable nature include, among others, action for an accounting, action for the specific performance of a contract, action to enforce a trust, and action for an injunction.

Commencement of Actions

Procedural matters vary greatly among the states. In many jurisdictions, an action is commenced when a summons or other writ is issued or served. Some states follow the federal rule that an action is commenced with the filing of a complaint in the office of the clerk of court; in other states, the summons must be served by the sheriff or another officer of the court and also filed with the court; in still other states, the summons may be served by any person, who is not a party to the action and is over eighteen years of age. Service of a paper means that the paper is delivered to and left with the person to be notified.

Statutes of Limitations

Most legal actions have to be brought within time limits known as statutes of limitations. The time within which legal actions may be brought varies from a few months to ten years, according to the type of action and the state where the claim arises. Furthermore, in order to decide whether the action is begun within the proper time limits, it is necessary to determine at just what time a cause of action accrued. A cause of action is a claim that can be enforced; hence, a "good" cause of action is a valid claim. Recently, some states have literally interpreted statutes of limitations by saying that the statute of limitation does not start to run until the plaintiff discovers the act of wrongdoing complained of.

Examples of the operation of statutes of limitations follow:

Sam Bufort was struck by an automobile in Columbus, Ohio, on January 10, 1986. On January 20, 1988, Sam commenced an action in an Ohio court to recover damages for bodily injury. Sam cannot succeed in his lawsuit because in Ohio an action for bodily injury must be commenced within two years from the date of the injury.

In Texas, actions on contracts in writing must be brought within Four years from the time of accrual of the cause of action. On July 14, 1975, Robert Wayman brought suit on a contract entered into in Texas for the sale of merchandise; he claimed that on July 15, 1971, the man who agreed to sell him the merchandise failed to deliver the goods and so broke the contract. The action was timely brought and within the statute of limitations.

(See the end of this chapter for the various state statutes of limitations.)

Pleadings

Pleadings are written statements constituting a plaintiff's (the person who instituted the action or suit) cause of action or a defendant's (the person against whom the action or suit is brought) ground of defense. They are allegations in writing of what is claimed on one side or denied on the other. The function of pleadings is to define the issues in the case for the court and for the opposing party (a litigant in an action or a suit); it also gives that party the opportunity to prepare to meet the issues raised at the trial (the judicial hearing held for the purpose of deciding on the issues in a case).

The federal Rules of Practice expound the concept that it is no longer necessary in pleadings to set forth facts but necessary only to state a claim. The current theory is that the facts may be developed later; all an adversary needs to know is that the claim is being made. This is sometimes called "notice pleading."

In most jurisdictions there is a trend away from the old common-law forms of pleadings. The codes and practice acts enacted in the various states have abolished certain technicalities of the common-law systems, thus simplifying legal pleadings.

Complaint or Declaration

In common law the plaintiff's first pleading was known as a *declaration*; under the modern codes and practice acts, it is variously referred to as a *complaint* (or *petition*, or *statement*). A complaint begins with the title of the action, identifying the plaintiff and the defendant, designates the court where the action is brought, and tells the story of the claim in legal form. The complaint usually includes the residence of the parties, a statement of the plaintiff's claim of grievance, the basis for the defendant's legal liability, and a request for damages or another remedy.

Plea or Answer

If the defendant desires to contest the claim of the plaintiff, he must file a *plea* or *answer* admitting or denying the various claims set forth in the complaint or declaration. The answer or plea may also state separate, affirmative defenses or a counterclaim (a claim introduced by the defendant in opposition to the plaintiff's claim).

Replication or Reply

The pleading after the answer is the *replication* or *reply*. Its purpose is to give the plaintiff an opportunity to answer the new material, such as a counterclaim, set forth in the defendant's answer.

Demurrer

When the pleading is served in an action and one party does not believe that the pleading is sufficient at law, he is then given an opportunity to make a motion or application to the court to this effect: "It is not necessary to go to trial because even assuming that all my adversary says is true, he still does not have a good case." Such an application is called a *demurrer*, or a testing of the sufficiency of the pleading.

Bill of Particulars

When a party to a lawsuit wants more specific information concerning a claim set forth in his adversary's pleading, he may require his adversary to furnish more specific details in a *bill of particulars*. An example of such an instance follows:

Foley sues Jennings, claiming in his complaint that Jennings ran into and damaged Foley's automobile to the extent of $600. Jennings demands a bill of particulars requiring the make, model, year, and mileage of the automobile, a list of the automobile parts which were damaged in the accident, and, if the automobile was repaired, a copy of the repair bill and any other pertinent information.

Pretrial Proceedings

Court calendars are so clogged with lawsuits that in some metropolitan centers the courts are from three to five years behind in the trial of litigated matters; however, in recent years, great strides have been made in procedural reform and especially in connection with pretrial proceedings.

Pretrial proceedings include the discovery of evidence, the inspection of documents before trial, application to the court for the granting of judgment before trial, and pretrial conferences.

Disclosure Proceedings

Proceedings for the discovery of evidence before trial and the inspection of documents and the like are known as *disclosure*, or discovery proceedings. Generally, such proceedings take the form of examinations before trial (EBT). Lawsuits in which both parties are examined before trial are more apt to be settled out of court, or if they go to court their trials are apt to be shorter than those suits in which no pretrial examinations take place. At first, there was much resistance to reforms in court procedures which permitted unlimited examinations before trial. Such examinations were called "fishing expeditions," designed to delay or frustrate judicial process. Currently, there is the feeling that all facts should be disclosed before trial so that the trial itself will not be (as it might have been in the past) a surprise or a game of wits and strategy.

Summary Judgments

The remedy for deciding a case on affidavits without the necessity of a trial is called *summary judgment*. If the court is satisfied from the affidavits or the documents presented that there is no dispute concerning the facts but simply a question of interpretation of those facts, then judgment may be entered for either party. An example of summary judgment before trial follows:

The Excelsior Bank sues Fred Applebottom on a $1,000 note. In response to the complaint, Applebottom has his lawyer file an answer alleging that the vice president of the bank made a verbal agreement with Applebottom that he would not have to pay the note for three years after it was due. Instead of waiting until the case was reached for trial, the bank makes an application to the court for summary judgment, saying that the vice president never made the agreement claimed and that because he had no authority to make the agreement (even if he had made it), it is void. The court upholds the bank, says that there is no reason for delay, and grants summary judgment in favor of the bank against Applebottom.

Pretrial Conferences

Originally, *pretrial conferences* were designed merely as a means whereby the trial judge could shorten trials by having the attorneys in lawsuits narrow the issues and agree on certain facts. However, pretrial conferences have become a means of settling cases without going to trial at all. In these conferences, the judge meets with the attorneys for the parties to a lawsuit (and sometimes with the parties themselves) and concentrates with them on reaching a common ground for settlement. An example of the workings of a pretrial settlement conference follows:

Webster sues the Valley Lumber Company for personal injuries resulting from a collision between Webster's automobile and the lumber firm's truck. Webster claims that as a result of a broken hip suffered in the accident, he will not be able to work again for the rest of his life and that he should be paid $500,000 for his injuries.

The lumber company carries liability insurance, and the attorney for the insurance company (defending the lawsuit) claims that the accident was caused by Webster's intoxication and that the lumber company should not pay anything; but, in order to dispose of the litigation, his firm will pay $50,000. A pretrial settlement conference is arranged before the trial judge, who confers first with the attorneys for both parties, then separately with each of them, and later with the plaintiff and the plaintiff's attorney. The judge points out to the plaintiff and his attorney that he is satisfied (1) that there was serious doubt as to Webster's sobriety at the time of the collision and (2) that there would be reliable proof in two years' time that Webster will recover completely. As a result of the pretrial settlement conference, the case is settled out of court for $100,000.

TRIAL BY JURY AND BY JUDGE

The distinguishing feature of the English and American systems of law is the *trial by jury*. When a case is tried in front of a jury, it is up to the jury to decide what are the facts in the case—in other words, to decide who is telling the truth. It has been said that in a jury trial there are two sets of judges: the jurors, who are judges of the facts, and the judge on the bench, who is the judge of the law.

Some persons think that in a jury trial a judge is nothing more than a glorified referee. This is not so. Throughout a jury trial the judge must decide all questions of law, all questions concerning whether or not evidence should be received, and whether or not there is sufficient evidence to permit the case to be decided by a jury. When a case is tried without a jury before a judge, arbiter, or commissioner, one of the latter occupies a dual role: He is the presiding officer who must guide the trial and, at the same time, he is the finder of the facts.

Every experienced lawyer knows that most lawsuits are won or lost before they are heard in court. Thus, good lawyers prepare cases carefully, undertaking exhaustive research and investigation, before they go into the courtroom. They interview and take statements from all available witnesses; they ascertain what witnesses are likely to be called by the other side and find out all they can about them. They plan strategy in the handling of the case, decide whether expert witnesses should be called (such as physicians, engineers, chemists, architects, or others who have special knowledge of the subject matter of the suit), read books and articles on the subject, meet with the witnesses time and time again, and prepare witnesses for courtroom pitfalls, including the questions which might be asked by opposing lawyers. As a result of thorough preparation, the lawyer knows the strong and weak points of the case and is thus able to serve his or her client well.

In getting his case ready, the experienced lawyer may also prepare a trial memorandum of law to be handed up to the court at the outset of the trial. Although some assume that the judge is the fountainhead of law and endowed with complete knowledge of it, he or she is, in actual fact, just a lawyer who has been elevated to the bench to preside at trials. As such, he welcomes these memoranda.

Selection of the Jury

The *petit* or *trial jury* serves in the trial of a civil or criminal case. It consists usually of twelve jurors and sometimes of alternate jurors, who replace other jurors in emergencies.

A petit jury (consisting of either 6 or 12 jurors,[2] depending on the particular court) is drawn from a large jury panel (varying in size from 25 to 300 or more citizens, depending on the size and activity of the court). The panel is chosen by a jury commissioner or other public officer. In most states the names of the jurors are drawn from the jury panel by lot; then the prospective jurors take their places in the jury box, and the lawyers examine them about their acquaintanceship with the parties, interest in the case, and prejudices or predispositions. In federal courts, the judge may also ask questions of the prospective jurors to determine whether or not they will be impartial.

A prospective juror is often perplexed by the questions a lawyer asks in determining if the juror should be selected to serve in the case. Sometimes he is resentful of a lawyer's questions concerning his private affairs. He should realize, however, that the average lawyer is only trying to discover if the prospective juror has a pet notion or prejudice that might influence his judgment of the case.

If an attorney decides that he or she does not want a particular juror to sit in the case, he exercises a challenge in an attempt to have the juror excused. Challenges are of two kinds: challenges for cause and peremptory challenges.

A *challenge for cause* may be granted when the court rules that the prospective juror, by reason of blood relationship, pecuniary interest in the outcome of the case, or other prejudice, may not look at the case objectively and, thus, may not make an impartial juror. Challenges for cause are unlimited in number.[3]

A *peremptory challenge* is one which may be made without giving any reason for it. Generally in each state lawyers may make only a limited number of peremptory challenges in one case. The peremptory challenge (when within the number allowed by lot) is automatically granted, and the court does not have to approve it.

In selecting jurors lawyers are guided by experience and intuition. The appearance and behavior of a prospective juror and the way he or she answers questions help the lawyer to determine whether or not the person would be favorably disposed to the lawyer's side of the case.

For example, a lawyer representing a plaintiff who is suing for damages for personal injuries would like to have as jurors persons who would be sympathetic toward an injured person and willing to give a generous verdict. But a lawyer representing the defendant in a personal injury case would like to have as jurors individuals who would be apt to bring in a miserly verdict. Although the court is interested in seeing that a fair and impartial jury is selected, each litigant wants a jury that will favor his side.

According to a 1991 report on the civil (but not criminal) jury system, jurors should be allowed to be more active participants in the trial. The report was prepared by the Brookings Institution and the litigation section of the American Bar Association.

The study summarizes the results of a three-day conference during which practicing lawyers, judges, and law professors submitted papers and discussed the problems. Some of the recommendations include the following:

- Courts should permit more extensive use of visual exhibits, including videotapes of trial testimony and computer demonstrations.
- The rules of evidence should be simplified, reflecting confidence in the ability of jurors to evaluate what they hear in court as intelligently as what they hear outside it.
- Lawyers and judges should apprise jurors more regularly and explicitly, through periodic instructions, statements, and summations, about the nature and direction of the trial.
- Juries of twelve members, rather than six, should be used to assure greater predictability and discourage obstructionism by individual jurors.
- Major improvements should be made in the treatment and pay of the 5.6 million Americans called to jury duty each year, a process in which, some jurors conclude, judges and lawyers are treated like sacred cows and jurors like cattle.

Opening Statement

Lawyers for the parties make *opening statements*, that is, each lawyer outlines to the jury his version of the facts and explains his theory of the case. The opening statement is not an argument; its purpose is to inform the jurors of the nature of the case so they will understand the evidence as it is presented.

Direct Examination and Cross-Examination of Witnesses

Under the English and American systems of law, it is believed that the search for truth can best be conducted by opposing attorneys who (1) call as witnesses those people who claim to know something about the particular case and (2) bring out the testimony of the witnesses by questioning them. (In many European countries, only the judge can interrogate the witnesses.)

Briefly, the *direct-examination procedure* in an American court is as follows: Each witness is called before the clerk of the court or the judge and is required to take an oath that the testimony he gives in the courtroom will be the truth. This is known as swearing a witness. Each witness is first examined by the lawyer who called him. His testimony is produced by a combination of the lawyer's questions and his answers. In obtaining the testimony, the lawyer is not supposed to ask questions that suggest to the witness the response desired. Such leading questions can be objected to by the opposing lawyer.

Much has been written and said about the skills of the trial advocate and the art of *cross-examination*. Nevertheless, most trial lawyers agree that there is as much skill required in the direct examination of witnesses as there is in the cross-examination of them. In direct examination, it is especially important, however, that the attorney be adept at getting witnesses to tell their stories naturally and convincingly.

The purpose of cross-examination is to test the truth or falsity of the testimony given by an opposing witness. If it is skillfully employed, cross-examination can expose falsehoods and reduce exaggerated statements to their true proportion. However, young lawyers are constantly warned against too much cross-examination, for it can bring out harmful testimony or give the witness an opportunity to reinforce his direct testimony.

Documentary Evidence

Documents, such as correspondence, deeds, maps, photographs, diagrams, and miscellaneous memoranda and writings, often are important as evidence. Documents to be offered as evidence in a suit are referred to as *exhibits for identification*. Once they are received in evidence, they are exhibits and may be read or shown to the jury. For example:

The attorney for the plaintiff in a lawsuit wishes to introduce in evidence five letters written by the defendant and also the contract entered into by the plaintiff and defendant. First, he asks the court stenographer to have the five letters marked "Exhibits A, B, C, D, E for identification"; then he asks the court stenographer to have the contract marked "Exhibit F for identification." Next, he shows the exhibits for identification to an appropriate witness and proves the signature and the mailing of the letters and the delivery of the contract. After that he offers the exhibits in evidence. When the exhibits are received in evidence, the stenographer crosses out the words "for identification," and the letters and contract become Exhibits A, B, C, D, E, F in the case.

Objections, Exceptions and Motions to Strike

The trial of a lawsuit is an inquiry into a dispute to determine where justice lies. Rules of evidence have been developed over the years to determine what testimony would best assist the court and the jury in deciding the truth of the matter in controversy.

Observers in court are often confused by the number of objections made by lawyers, but under the rules of evidence objections may be necessary to preserve the rights of a party to a lawsuit. Thus, when one party to a lawsuit offers evidence that is inadmissible under the rules of evidence, the other party must object if he wishes to keep such evidence out of the case. Generally, a lawyer who fails to object to evidence waives all claims as to its inadmissibility.

An example of proper objection follows:

In a suit brought by Wright against Gillespie to recover damages for breach of contract, Wright is questioned by his lawyer about a conversation he had with his neighbor concerning the subject of the contract. Gillespie's lawyer properly objects on the ground that the conversation is "hearsay and not binding on my client." The court sustains the objection.

Blanket objections on the ground that proposed evidence is "incompetent, immaterial, irrelevant, and improper" are outdated. In current practice, an objection pinpoints for the court the precise reason why the lawyer feels the proposed evidence is improper.

The purpose of an exception is to give the trial court notice that an attorney does not agree to a ruling. Attorneys rarely take exceptions when it is obvious to the court that a ruling is adverse. In such an instance the attorney is more likely to make his position known to the court by objections or by other means.

A motion to strike out evidence may sometimes be granted by the court (1) when evidence was apparently proper when it is received but is subsequently shown to be objectionable; (2) when evidence is admitted with the understanding that it will be ruled on at a later stage of the proceedings; (3) when evidence is admitted subject to later consideration by the court of a motion to strike out; (4) when a witness makes a voluntary statement or testifies without a question being asked of him; or (5) when an answer is not responsive to a question.

Recent Codification of Rules of Evidence

There is probably no more technical branch of law than the law of evidence, which was hammered out over hundreds of years of English and American common law. In an attempt to simplify the rules, Congress in 1975 enacted federal "Rules of Evidence" to be followed by the federal trial courts. Some states have enacted separate rules of evidence, attempting to follow the principles laid down in the federal rules. (See Chapter 27 for further discussion.)

Expert Witnesses and the Hypothetical Question

Expert witnesses are permitted by the rules of evidence to give their opinions regarding scientific and technical matters and concerning case and effect. Such opinions are not permitted from ordinary witnesses. The expert, by reason of his special training and experience, is deemed qualified to assist the court and jury in arriving at a determination of the facts. Medicine, engineering, and the sciences are the most common fields from which experts are required to provide testimony.

A *hypothetical question* is used when the expert witness called is not personally familiar with the facts in the case. The hypothetical question includes all the testimony on a given point. The expert is asked to base his opinion on the assumption that the testimony in the question is true.

Here is an example of an abbreviated hypothetical question:

Dr. Atlas, assume that a man forty-eight years old, who had previously enjoyed excellent health, was employed in a factory on a day when the temperature was about 94°F. Assume further that this man was engaged in lifting heavy barrels of sand which weighed from 400 to 500 pounds each and that the barrels were heavier and larger than any he had previously lifted on the job. Assume that he had been doing this work for about five hours, and that about three o'clock on the afternoon in question this man suddenly fell to the floor and died five minutes later. Assume further that a post-mortem examination of the man revealed an aorta ruptured about six inches from where it entered the heart. Assuming, Doctor, the foregoing statements to be true, what is your opinion concerning whether or not the work of lifting the barrels was a probable cause of the man's death?

Recently, courts in some jurisdictions have held that an expert witness may be asked his opinion directly, instead of having to give it as an answer to a hypothetical question.

Final Argument to the Jury

A party to a lawsuit has the right to have his case fully and fairly argued to the jury. The judge, exercising reasonable discretion, may limit the length of the *final argument* to the jury. This argument is popularly called "summation" or "summing up."

The plaintiff's attorney makes his opening statement first, but sums up last. The theory is that the party having the burden of proof should present the last argument to a jury in order to demonstrate that he has sustained his burden of proof.

Great latitude is given attorneys in summation. They are permitted to draw all reasonable inferences from the evidence. They may comment fairly on the testimony of witnesses or argue, to the jury, that some witnesses should not be believed. In summing up, lawyers are not permitted to go outside of the evidence and discuss facts which have not been proved, nor may they resort to appeals to passion or to prejudice.

The Court's Charge to the Jury

The court's *charge to the jury* advises the jury regarding the law applicable in the case and aids the jury in understanding the case and in reaching a just conclusion and verdict. It is the function of the judge to decide the law applicable to the case; it is the function of the jury to decide the facts after the judge has instructed them concerning the law.

The judge's charge can be divided roughly into four parts: (1) a statement of what the case is about, what each side contends, and, sometimes, even a brief outline of the testimony on both sides; (2) the general rules of law applicable to lawsuits, that is, what tests should be applied by the jury in passing on the weight of testimony, what is meant by "burden of proof," "interested witnesses," "false testimony," "opinion evidence," and so forth; (3) the law that should be applied to the particular case being considered by the jury; and (4) the form the jury verdict should take.

At the conclusion of the court's charge to the jury, any party may object to or except to portions of the court's charge. Any party may also request that additional instructions be given to the jury.

Verdict of the Jury

The ultimate verdict of the jury (or decision of the court) must be based on the evidence. As lawyers and judges constantly remind juries, they must decide a case "not on what the lawyers say, but solely on the evidence presented."

A *verdict* is the answer of the jury concerning the issues in a case. Verdicts are of two kinds—general and special. A *general verdict* is one by which the jury makes an overall decision on the issues in a case. A *special verdict* is one by which the jury answers a request made to it to decide on a particular question of fact; the special verdict leaves the ultimate decision of the case to the judge.

A general verdict in a personal injury accident case might be: "We find a verdict in favor of the plaintiff for xx dollars," or, "We find in favor of the defendant," or, "No cause of action" (meaning a verdict in favor of the defendant).

A special verdict might take the form, "We find that Bailey was an employee of Brown at the time of the accident," or, "We find that Mary was the common-law wife of Roberts."

APPEALS

In American law an essential right of an aggrieved person in a legal proceeding is review of a court decision by a superior or appellate court. The right to appeal derives from English law. Review by a higher court was obtained by means of a writ of error, which directed the judge in the lower court to send the record "of the case to the appellate court," where it was examined in order to correct any errors in the proceedings. Most American states have abolished the writ of error, and an appeal proceeding is initiated by the filing of a notice of appeal.

The person who appeals to a higher court is called the *appellant* or the plaintiff in error. The person in favor of whom the judgment or decree in the lower court was rendered is known as the *appellee*, respondent, or defendant in error.

General Appellate Procedure

In some states a case may be completely retried in a higher court, but this is the exception rather than the rule. For the most part an appeal involves (1) the filing of a notice of appeal; (2) the preparation of a record on appeal, which contains a typewritten, photocopied, or printed record of all the proceedings in the lower court; (3) the preparation and filing of typewritten or printed "briefs" that outline the reasons (points of law) why the decision of the lower court should be reversed and that furnish information to the appellate court and opposing counsel, and (4) the oral presentation of arguments by counsel for both parties before the appellate court, which generally consists of three or nine judges (three to seven judges in many appellate courts and nine in the U.S. Supreme Court).

Technicalities of an Appeal

Not every decision or order of a court may be appealed.

In some states appeals are permitted only in certain types of cases or certain types of decisions. Some state laws restrict appeals action to final judgments, orders, or decrees and require a litigant who is dissatisfied with orders and decisions of the court at various stages of the case to await the final decision before he may appeal. (The legislature in each state may authorize an appeal from a court decision or public officer or board or commission.)

Sometimes appeals are permissible only to an intermediate appellate court, and the proceedings end there. In other cases the decision of the intermediate appellate court may be appealed to a higher and final appeals court. The decision of the appellate court may determine that the court below committed procedural error or error in the admission of evidence, either of which requires a new trial; or the appellate court may decide the case once and for all by its own decision.

Preserving Rights for an Appeal

Not every alleged error will be reviewed by an appellate court. An appellate court does not have the power to review questions which were not raised nor properly preserved for review in the trial court. The reason for this almost universal rule, which requires the points at issue to be raised in the court below, is to give the opposing party the opportunity to correct the alleged error or to furnish necessary proof in the court below.

The most common example of the necessity for raising points in the lower court is in the matter of objections or exceptions. By raising an objection, counsel tells the court and his adversary that he does not think the evidence should be considered. Generally speaking, errors concerning the admission of evidence should not be reviewed in the appellate court unless proper objections were made in the trial court.

The objection must be timely; it ordinarily must be made during the trial and in time to allow the alleged error to be avoided or corrected. An exception, another form of objection, is used to challenge the correctness of a ruling or decision of the trial court so that the ruling or decision may be corrected by the judge himself. An objection is normally made before the court's ruling or decision, and an exception is made after the court rules.

Time for Taking and Perfecting an Appeal

The time within which an appeal must be taken to a higher court and perfected is regulated by statute; of course, the appeal should be taken (varying from ten to ninety days) and also perfected within the prescribed statutory periods. In some jurisdictions, an appeal must be taken at the term of court in which the decree or order appealed from is entered. There is no relief when a person is late in taking an appeal, and the other party cannot consent to an appeal in order to confer jurisdiction on the appellate court.

Perfecting an appeal includes filing the notice and filing the record and briefs.

Under some state laws an appeal is taken as a matter of right. In other states the appellant must first apply to the appellate court and obtain permission for the appeal. The theory in such a case is that the appellant must convince the appellate court that there is a unique or novel question of law involved that ought to be reviewed by the appellate court.

State Time Limitations in Years for Commencement of Actions

	TORTS											CONTRACTS		
	Personal injuries	Property damage	Wrongful death	Libel	Slander	Assault and battery	Malpractice	Malicious prosecution	False imprisonment	Trespass or conversion	Suit or judgment of court of record	Oral	Under seal	Written, Not under seal
Alabama	2	2	2	1	2	6	2	2	2	6	20	6	10	6
Alaska	2	2	2	2	2	6	2	2	2	6	10	6	10	6
Arizona	2	2	2	1	1	2-6	2-6	1	1	2	5	3-4	6	4-6
Arkansas	3-4	3	3-4	3	1	1	2	5	1	3	10	3	5	4-5
California	1	1-3	1	1	1	1	1-3	1	1	3		2	4	4
Colorado	6	6	2	1	1	6		6	1	3	6	6	6	3-6
Connecticut	2	2	2	2	2	3	1-2	3	3	3	25	3	6	6
Delaware	2	2	2	2	3	2	2-3	3	3	3		3	20	3-6
Florida	4	3-4	2	2	2	4	2	4	4	4	20	4	5	5
Georgia	2	4	2	1	1	2	2	2	2	4	10	4	20	6
Hawaii	2	2	2	2	2	2	2-6	6	6	6	10	4	6	4-6
Idaho	2	3	2	2	2	2	2	4	2	3	6	4	5	5
Illinois	2	5	2	1	1	2	2-10	2	2	5	20	5	10	10
Indiana	2	2	2	2	2	2	2	2	2	6	10	6	10	4-10
Iowa	2	5	2	2	2	2	2	2	2	5	20	5	10	10
Kansas	2	2	2	1	1	1	2	1	1	2	5	3	5	4-5
Kentucky	1	5	1	1	1	1	1	1	1	5	15	4-5	15	4-15
Louisiana	1	1	1	1	1	1	1	6	1		10	3-10	10	3-10
Maine	6	6	2	2	2	2	2		2	6	20	6	20	4-10
Maryland	3	3	3	1	1	1	3	3	3	3	12	3	12	3-4
Massachusetts	2-3	2-3	2-3	3	3	3	3	3	3	3	20	6	20	4-6
Michigan	3	3	3	1	1	2	2	2	2	3	10	6	6	4-6
Minnesota	6	6	3-6	2	2	2	2	2	2	6	10	6	6	4-6

State													
Mississippi	6	6	1	1	1	2–6	1	1	6	7	1–3	6	6
Missouri	5	5	2	2	2	2	2	2	5	10	5	10	4–10
Montana	3	2	2	2	2	3–5	3	2	2	10	5	8	4–8
Nebraska	4	4	1	1	1	2	1	1	3	4	4	5	4–5
Nevada	2	3	2	2	2	2–4	4	2	6	6	4	6	4–6
New Hampshire	3–6	6	3–6	3–6	3–6	6	6	6	6	20	6	20	4–6
New Jersey	2	6	1	1	2	2	6	6	6	20	6	16	4–6
New Mexico	3	4	3	3	3	2	3	3	4	14	4	6	4–6
New York	3	3	1	1	1	2½–3	1	1	3	20	6	6	4–6
North Carolina	3	3	1	1	1	2–3	3	1	3	10	3	10	3–4
North Dakota	6	6	2	2	2–6	2	6	2	6	10	6	6	4–6
Ohio	2	2	1	1	1	1	1	1	4	21	6	4–15	4–15
Oklahoma	2	2	1	1	1	2	1	1	2	5	3	5	5
Oregon	2–3	6	1	1	2	2–5	2	2	6	10	4–6	6–10	4–6
Pennsylvania	2	2	1	1	1	2–6	2	2	2	6	4–6	6–20	4–6
Rhode Island	3	10	10	1	10	3–10	10	10	10	20	10	20	4–10
South Carolina	6	6	2	2	2	6	6	2	6	10	6	20	6
South Dakota	3	6	2	2	2	6	6	2	6	20	6	20	4–6
Tennessee	1	3	1	6 mos.	1	1	1	1	3	10	4	6	4–6
Texas	2	2	2	1	2	4	4	2	2	10	4	4	4
Utah	4	3	1	1	1	2–4	4	1	3	8	4	6	4–6
Vermont*	3*	3	3	1	6	3	6	3	6	8	6	8	4–6
Virginia	2	5	1	1	3	2	6	1	5	10	3	5	4–5
Washington	3	3	2	2	3	3	3	2	3	6	3	6	4–6
West Virginia	2	2	2	2	2	3	3	2	2	10	5	10	4–10
Wisconsin	3	6	2	2	2	3	2	2	6	20	6	6	6
Wyoming	4	4	1	1	1	2–4	1	1	4	10	8	10	10

* Injuries sustained in skiing 1 year; all others, 3 years.

NOTES

[1]Civil or Roman law, rather than the common law, forms the basis of practice in Louisiana.

[2]The number of jurors is determined by each state's statutes (or by each city's ordinances). However, the U.S. Supreme Court has held—at least in the case of criminal trials—that a jury must consist of no less than six persons.

[3]The U.S. Supreme Court has circumscribed and limited the number of such challenges. The rulings have arisen in recent criminal cases, and were based upon a member of a minority having a constitutional right to jury duty.

4

CONTRACTS (TYPES)

A *contract* is a promise that creates a legal obligation. Most contracts are simple everyday affairs that are forgotten when completed and that cause no trouble.

An *express contract* is one in which the terms are specifically stated by the parties. An *implied contract* is one in which the terms are not expressly stated but are inferred by law from the acts of the parties and the surrounding circumstances.

A *contract under seal* is a written agreement with a seal attached. In ancient common law the seal was a piece of wax, wafer or other substance affixed to the written contract. Today printed scroll, sign, or impression is used in place of the wax or the word *seal* is printed or written opposite the signature. Sometimes the initials L.S. (for the Latin phrase *locus sigilli*, "place of the seal") are used in place of the seal. Nearly half of the states have abolished the distinction between sealed and unsealed writings, except in deeds and bonds. Today, the sealing of a document is no longer essential to its validity.

Void contracts are those that create no legal obligation. *Voidable contracts* are those that either party may have set aside by court action. Typical voidable contracts are those entered into by a minor and those brought about by fraud, mistake, or duress. An *executed contract* is one which has been carried out, and an *executory contract* is one which has not been completed.

ESSENTIAL ELEMENTS OF A CONTRACT

A contract need not be in writing to be binding. Only certain types of contracts must be in writing. For an oral or written contract to exist, however, there must be first an offer and then an acceptance of the offer; in some states there must also be "consideration," something given in return for a promise. There must be at least two parties to a contract. A contract should be complete: It should cover all the important acts to be performed by each party, and nothing should be left for future understanding or agreement—there should be a definite understanding of who is to do what and when and where and how.

There is an old saying, "An agreement to agree is no agreement." An example follows:

Mr. Black writes to Mr. White, "I will buy your house for $40,000. Just how much I will pay down and how much mortgage I will give you is something we must decide upon at a later date. Also, the time when the purchase will be completed is something that you and I must mutually agree upon." Mr. White writes back saying that they have a deal. There is no contract. They made nothing more than an unenforceable "agreement to agree."

There are many rules governing the subject of offers and acceptances; those discussed in the following sections are among the important ones.

OFFER

An *offer* is a promise that something will or will not happen.

Jones says to Smith, "This watch is yours if you will pay me $25 for it." As soon as Smith says yes to Jones, the offer, or promise to turn over the watch, has been accepted, and a contract has been made.

An *expression of intention* is not an offer. An offer should also be distinguished from preliminary negotiations.

Mr. Harsh writes to Mr. Loomis, "I am planning to sell my house for $400,000. I would really like to get rid of it." Loomis promptly writes an answering letter and says, "I will buy your house at the price stated in your letter." There is no contract, because Mr. Harsh simply expressed a plan or intention.

Definite Offer

An offer must be so definite in its terms that the parties can be certain about what is intended. If promises are indefinite concerning the time and the place of performance or in other material respects, they do not constitute valid offers.

Mr. Cohen promises to sell Mr. Levy certain goods, and Mr. Levy promises to buy the goods from him at cost plus "a nice profit." This promise is too indefinite to form a contract.

Mr. Hempel promises Mr. Smith to do a specified piece of work, and Mr. Smith promises to pay a price "to be mutually agreed upon." Since the only method of settling the price is dependent upon the future agreement of the parties, there is no contract.

On the other hand, an indefinite offer accepted by partial performance may sometimes create a contract.

Howard says to Bill, "I will employ you at $20 a day." This offer is too indefinite because it does not specify the length of time for which Howard will employ Bill. If, however, Bill works one or more days. Howard has created a contractual obligation to pay Bill $20 for each day's work.

Withdrawal of Offer

An offer may be withdrawn at any time before it is accepted. Withdrawal of the offer must be definite and positive.

Mr. Rall makes an offer by mail to Mr. Hall and subsequently by mail revokes the offer. Before receiving the revocation, Mr. Hall mails an acceptance. The revocation is too late.

Offers may be withdrawn if they can be considered to comprise parts of a series of separate contracts.

Mr. Brown offers to sell Mr. Gray five tons of coal a day and offers five tons at once. Mr. Gray accepts the offer. The five tons are furnished daily for a number of days; then Mr. Brown states to Mr. Gray that he revokes the offer. The revocation is good because each sale of five tons a day was a separate contract. If Mr. Brown's original proposal had been to sell to Mr. Gray five tons of coal daily during the period of two months, Mr. Brown could not revoke the contract once it was accepted.

Termination of Offer

For how long is an offer good, and how is an offer terminated? Generally, an offer is deemed to be terminated (1) when it has been rejected by the person to whom it was made; (2) by the lapse of the time specified or the lapse of a reasonable time when the offer is silent concerning duration; (3) by the occurrence of a condition laid down in the offer relating to termination or withdrawal; (4) by the death of the person necessary to carry out the contract; (5) by the destruction of the subject matter of the contract; (6) by revocation of the person making the offer.

ACCEPTANCE

One party to a contract must accept the offer made by the other party or parties if there is to be a contract. Acceptance is the act of assenting by word or by conduct to the offer made.

Conditions of Acceptance

If an offer attaches conditions of acceptance, those conditions must ordinarily be met. If the offer prescribes only the time, place, or manner of acceptance, another method of acceptance that is just as good may be satisfactory.

Mr. Crane writes Mr. Vickers, "I must receive your acceptance by return mail." Mr. Vickers sends a telegram, which arrives even more quickly than the mail would, and the contract is made.

Mr. Gay makes an offer to Mr. Sour and adds, "Send a messenger with an answer to this address by twelve o'clock." Mr. Sour comes himself before twelve o'clock and accepts. There is a contract.

If Mr. Gay had said to Mr. Sour, "You must accept this, if at all, by coming in person to my office at ten o'clock tomorrow morning," Mr. Sour would have had to comply strictly with that method of acceptance.

Means of Acceptance

If a person making an offer specifies or authorizes the means by which the acceptance is to be made and the person making the acceptance uses that method, the contract is complete.

Mr. Miller makes an offer to Mr. Gifford by mail stating, "Telegraph your answer." Mr. Gifford promptly telegraphs an acceptance. The telegram never reaches Mr. Miller, but there is a contract as soon as the telegram is released to the telegraph company.

When an offer has been rejected, it ceases to exist. Once the offer has been rejected, the person to whom the offer is made cannot change his mind and later accept the offer. A counteroffer is considered to be a rejection of the original offer.

Mr. Hartwig offers to sell Mr. Gordon the Hartwig farm for $500,000. Mr. Gordon counters, "I will pay you $290,500 for the farm." Hartwig promptly rejects this offer. Then Gordon writes, "Now I will accept your offer to sell for $500,000." Too late! The counteroffer of $290,500 wiped out the offer of $500,000 and, thus, there is no contract.

Hartwig makes the same offer to Gordon and Gordon replies, "Will you take less?" and Hartwig answers, "No." Within five days, Gordon accepts Hartwig's $300,000 offer, and the contract is made.

Obviously, an offer terminates at the time specified, but if no time is specified, it is said to terminate at the end of a "reasonable time." What is a reasonable time? That depends on the nature of the contract and other circumstances. Thus, a reasonable time is often a matter of common sense.

A newspaper offers a reward for information leading to the arrest and conviction of a murderer. Mr. Citizen, intending to obtain the reward, gives the requested information two months after publication of the offer. There is a contract.

Mr. Adams sends Mr. Boston an offer by telegram to sell soybean meal, which at the time is subject to rapid fluctuations in price. One week later Mr. Boston accepts the offer. Mr. Adams says, "Too late." Undoubtedly Mr. Adams's position would be upheld in court.

Mr. Cook sends Mr. Warter an offer by mail to sell a piece of land. After three days Mr. Warter sends an acceptance. No doubt Mr. Warter's acceptance would be good, and a valid contract would be created.

Consideration

Although the rule has been relaxed in some states, generally a contract must be supported by consideration. Bearing in mind that a contract is essentially a promise, consideration is something given in return for a promise. It does not necessarily have to have monetary value. Consideration will support a promise if the condition of the promise is that the person to whom it is made agrees to do something in return or to refrain from doing something.

Mr. Ames promises his nephew that if he will go to college and complete his course, he will pay him $10,000. The nephew receives a college degree and has a valid contract claim against his uncle.

In the average case the consideration does have a dollars-and-cents value, but this is not necessary.

When one says to the owner of a garage, "I will pay you $150 if you will make my car run properly," the undertaking by the garage owner of the job is sufficient consideration for the promise.

It is not necessary that the person making the promise be benefitted by the consideration.

A father promises to pay his son the sum of $500 if the son does not use intoxicating liquor until he reaches the age of 25 years. The forbearance by the son of his legal right to use intoxicating liquors is sufficient consideration.

Written as well as oral promises generally require consideration, but some states have reconsidered consideration; that is, they have changed the rules of the common law in order to provide that the majority of written contracts are presumed to have valid consideration.

WRITTEN CONTRACTS

In 1677 the English Parliament passed a law providing that no suit or action could be brought on certain contracts unless a note or memorandum thereof in writing was signed by the party to be charged with an obligation. This law became known as the Statute of Frauds, and its purpose was to close the door to numerous fraudulent and perjurious claims that existed as contracts when there was nothing in writing to support these claims.

During the past 300 years, the Statute of Frauds has been qualified and varied by state legislatures and courts in many ways. For example, partial performance of a contract that would otherwise be unenforceable under the Statute of Frauds makes it enforceable. The Statute of Frauds has been adopted in one form or another in nearly all the states.

The requirement that contracts be in writing applies to:

1) conveyances or agreements to convey interests in lands (real estate)
2) the undertaking or guaranty to perform the obligations of another person
3) a contract that by its terms is not to be performed within a specified period of time (generally one year)
4) an agreement to create a trust in land (real estate)
5) a lease of land, except a lease for a specified period (in most states, less than one year; in a few states, three years)
6) a contract for the sale of goods of a specified value (in most states, over $500).

Assignment of Contracts

Contracts may be "assigned" or transferred, except in the following cases: (1) the transfer is prohibited by the contract, (2) the contract requires personal or special services, or (3) substitution of a new party to the contract would be contrary to the spirit of the contract.

Mr. Briggs, an excellent house painter, in consideration of the sum of $4,300, agrees to paint Mr. Tuttle's house during the month of May. In April, Mr. Briggs moves to another state and assigns the contract to another painter. The assignment is not valid.

Mr. Wade contracts to sell his house to Mr. Ware. Mr. Ware assigns the contract to Mr. Smith. The assignment is good.

Lord Bromfield makes a contract with Smithers for Smithers to serve Lord Bromfield as a valet. Smithers signs and delivers to Jones a paper reading, "I assign to Jones my rights under my contract with Lord Bromfield." Jones acquires no right to act as valet to Lord Bromfield. The contract is too personal to assign.

Interpretation of Agreements

In court a lawyer may object to testimony, saying, "I object to any attempt to vary the terms of a written contract by *parol evidence*." In making the objection, the lawyer refers to the rule that written contracts ordinarily speak for themselves, and the parties are not permitted to give verbal testimony to show that a different meaning was intended. There are, however, exceptions to this rule.

Parol evidence may be admitted (1) to establish the meaning of ambiguous provisions of the contract or (2) to prove facts rendering the agreement void because of illegality, fraud, duress, mistake, or insufficiency of consideration.

Illegal Contracts

Contracts which have for their purpose or object the violation of law are illegal and will not be enforced.

Cook entered into a written agreement with Phillips to lend him $1,000 at a usurious rate of interest. Because the agreement called for an unlawful act, it was held invalid.

The Excelsior Factory made a contract with the Heart Company for Heart to build stairways and exits which were known by both parties not to be in compliance with the state building codes. The Excelsior Factory agreed to pay $15,000 for the work instead of the $25,000 the job would cost if the stairways were built in compliance with the codes. The executives of the Excelsior Company changed their minds and decided not to go through with the contract. Heart sued. The court held that the contract was illegal and that it would not enforce a contract in violation of laws designed to protect human safety.

A party to an illegal contract cannot ask a court to assist him in carrying out a plan that would be in violation of a statute or an established principle of law. The courts have applied this principle not only to contracts involving the commission of a crime but also to contracts involving a civil wrong or a contract that is contrary to public policy or public morals.

Joe, a professional boxer, made a contract with two managers that violated the state laws regulating the amount of the managers' fees and the duration of the contract. The court held the contract was void and unenforceable.

Hanes agreed to conceal and withhold evidence in the trial of Rudd's son, who was charged with stealing money. In return for the agreement, Rudd gave Hanes a six-months' promissory note for $5,000. At the end of the six months Rudd did not pay. Hanes sued. The court said there could be no recovery because giving the promissory note was part of the plan to do an illegal act.

Breach of Contract

A breach of contract is the nonperformance of any contractual obligation. A contract may be entirely or partially breached.

The Sloan Automobile Agency agrees to sell Mr. Post an automobile, and Mr. Post agrees to pay $15,000 on delivery. The Sloan Agency tenders the automobile to Mr. Post, but Mr. Post refuses without justification to accept delivery. Mr. Post has committed a breach of contract.

Mr. Green, a tile worker, contracts to point up the brick front of Mr. Wilson's apartment house and to do the work carefully. Mr. Green does a sloppy, unskilled job and, thus, commits a breach of contract.

Remedies for Breach of Contract

When a contract is broken, the person who is damaged may sue for breach of contract; in such a suit ordinary, traditional remedies for breach of contract are (1) recovery of damages in a court of law or (2) specific performance. Damages means a sum of money awarded as compensation for injury. Damages may be nominal when the harm caused by the breach is insubstantial. Ordinary damages are called compensatory damages, that is, damages for substantial injury.

The Blanford Automobile Agency sells an automobile for $4,000 to Mr. Rubin, who has already found a purchaser who will pay $4,500 for the car. If the Blanford Agency fails to deliver the machine in accordance with the contract, Mr. Rubin can recover for his expected profit of $500. If Mr. Rubin had no such definite purchaser, he could only recover the difference between the market price of the automobile and the contract price of the automobile.

Sometimes the granting of money damages would be an inadequate remedy for the contract breached, so a court will say to the party who has breached the contract, "You are commanded to carry out the contract that you entered into; if you do not do so, you will be guilty of contempt of court and go to jail." This is called specific performance.

Mr. and Mrs. Foster saved for years to buy their dream house. They entered into a written contract with Mr. Ruther to buy his house for $30,000. Then Mr. Ruther changed his mind and said. "I guess I won't sell." A court would say, "Dollars-and-cents damages would be an insufficient remedy. You agreed to sell the house to Mr. and Mrs. Foster, and you must go through with the deal."

Fine Print in Contracts

The U.S. Supreme Court in recent decisions has held that any waiver of constitutional rights must be "voluntary, intelligently, and knowingly" made and that the waiver clause must be conspicuous in the contract to meet the requirements of the Uniform Commercial Code (see Chapter 21). Although the field of consumer protection has only been scratched in connection with the law of contracts, legal scholars predict that fine print clauses in contracts between parties of unequal economic status and bargaining power are on the way out and will not be enforced by the courts in the future.

Constitutional Restriction on Impairment of Contracts

The U.S. Constitution provides that no state may pass a law impairing the obligation of contracts. This clause in the constitution was somewhat of a dead letter until recently. However, the U.S. Supreme Court has recently held that the states under the guise of social or economic legislation may not impair the obligation of contracts. Thus, in a sense, the Supreme Court has resurrected the contract clause of the Constitution.

5

INTENTIONAL HARMS
TO PERSONS
AND PROPERTY

This chapter concerns a branch of the law of torts. A *tort* is a civil wrong, other than a breach of contract, for which one may have remedy in the form of an action for damages. In order to be charged with legal responsibility for a tort, one must be at fault, that is, guilty of an intentional wrong or of negligence.

This chapter deals with intentional wrongs to persons and property; negligent wrongs are discussed in Chapter 8. In law neither hostile intent nor harmful design is necessary to constitute an intentional act. A person may be liable for doing something even though he meant it to be nothing more than a good-natured practical joke or thought he honestly believed he would not injure anyone. In law a person intends to do something when he has the simple desire to bring about an immediate result.

INTENTIONAL INTERFERENCE WITH PERSONS

Interference with persons includes assault, battery, illegal confinement, false imprisonment, and words or acts causing mental suffering.

(Defamation, involving the law of libel and slander, is another type of intentional wrong and is treated in Chapter 7.)

Assault and Battery An assault does not involve physical contact with another person; a battery does.

What Constitutes Assault? When one intends to inflict harm on another and puts the other person in fear of injury, one may be liable for assault.

Mr. Litton threatens to strike his neighbor with a club. Bystanders intervene and prevent Litton from striking his neighbor. The mere threat of bodily harm is sufficient to make Litton liable to his neighbor for assault.

Even though the intent is only to scare and not to cause bodily harm, the one threatening the action may be liable for assault if the person threatened believes he will be injured.

Rococco, an expert knife thrower, intending to frighten but not hit, throws a knife at Baldy, his friend, who is standing against a building. Baldy fears that he will be injured by the knife. Rococco is technically liable for assault.

Personal hostility is not necessary to make a person liable for assault.

Harry, intending to play a joke on Jim, disguises himself as a thug, accosts Jim on a lonely road, and, pointing an unloaded pistol at him, says, "Stick 'em up." Harry is liable to Jim for assault.

What Constitutes Battery? Any intentional, harmful, unprivileged contact with another person is a battery and may give rise to legal liability. As in the case of assault, it is not necessary that the battery be inspired by personal hostility or the desire to injure the other person.

Blackie, a practical joker, tricks his friend Joe. Blackie's intention was only to throw Joe off balance and embarrass him to the amusement of friends who were standing nearby. Instead, Joe did not recover his balance and was thrown against a picket fence, lacerating and bruising his arm. Blackie is liable to Joe even though Blackie had no hostility toward Joe.

Moreover, the courts have held that well-meaning but unauthorized surgical operations may give rise to a cause of action of battery.

Mr. Ingalls employs Dr. Jones to operate on the septum of his nose. During the course of the nose operation, Dr. Jones removes Mr. Ingalls' diseased tonsils. Because the tonsillectomy was unauthorized, in a suit the court awards damages against Dr. Jones.

Injuries Inflicted in Self-Defense

If one should inflict injury on another person in self-defense, one would not be liable (1) if he believed that the other person intended to injure him; (2) if the bodily harm was not intended or not likely to cause death or serious bodily injury; and (3) if he believed that the injury about to be done to him could be prevented only by infliction of injury on the other person. As Justice Oliver Wendell Holmes said, "Reasoned reflection cannot be demanded in the face of an uplifted revolver."

Butchman, known to be a desperate character, has threatened to shoot Senko on sight, and Senko knows it. Butchman comes into the room where Senko is standing and reaches into his pocket. Senko mistakenly believes that Butchman is about to shoot him and knocks Butchman down. Senko is not liable to Butchman.

The law does not permit infliction of injury as a punishment or in retaliation for a past aggression or as a warning.

Harvey strikes Dewey with a cane. Dewey disarms Harvey. Dewey is not then privileged to inflict a beating upon Harvey.

Little Joe throws a snowball at Mr. Brown, hitting Mr. Brown in the eye and causing severe pain. Mr. Brown is not privileged to inflict a beating on Joe, either as punishment or as a warning against similar misconduct in the future.

The question of whether excessive force may be used in self-defense frequently arises. The answer is that the person attacked may use only reasonable means to stop the attack.

Edson attempts to slap Taft's face. Taft can prevent Edson from doing so by pushing him away or leaving the room or locking the door or even confining himself, but Taft is not privileged to beat and inflict serious injuries on Edson. A person is privileged to knock another down if the latter threatens him with violence. But the one attacked is not privileged to knock his attacker down if he knows that to do so may kill him.

Jones threatens to slap McDonald's face. Although he knows that Jones is suffering from heart disease and that the slightest shock to Jones may prove fatal, McDonald picks up a cane and strikes Jones several times. McDonald has abused his privilege of self-defense; he had no right to use such violent means to resist Jones's threat of slight harm.

In recent years, there has been a judicial trend to review—and sometimes accept—defenses based upon psychological factors. Consider the following example:

Sally had been the victim of physical abuse from her husband, John, for a number of years. One day, during a beating by John, Sally shot him. During her trial for his murder, she asserted a defense based on psychological grounds. The court allowed the jury to consider this ground of self-defense.

Defense of Land as Self-Defense

Bodily harm may be inflicted on another in order to prevent intrusion on one's land or property. In other words, defense of land may be a form of self-defense.

During a family automobile tour in the country, the Shavers stop to admire Mr. Lint's apple orchard and to gather fruit. Mr. Lint may use such reasonable force as is necessary to expel the Shavers from his farm.

However, as in defense against personal harm, a possessor of land or property is not privileged to expel an intruder if he knows that the intruder's condition or surrounding circumstances are such that expulsion would be likely to cause death or serious bodily harm.

Beatrice comes to the railroad station to take a train. She finds that it has already departed. The station master permits Beatrice to remain in the station until late at night. At closing time he forces her to leave, ejecting her into a violent sleet and ice storm. She goes out in search of a hotel and catches pneumonia. The stationmaster may be liable to Beatrice.

Owners of land and property are privileged to use mechanical devices to protect their land and property.

For example, a property owner may close off his lawn with a barbed-wire fence to prevent neighbors from taking a shortcut across it. The property owner is not liable if the neighbor uses a shortcut without the landowner's permission and scratches himself on the barbed-wire fence. On the other hand, a landowner may not charge his fence with electric voltage strong enough to electrocute an animal or a person.

The use of electrically charged fences to confine or exclude animals is generally permissible providing the voltage is mild.

Illegal Confinement

Illegal confinement is a broad term including any confinement by physical barriers or by force or by threats of physical force.

Illegal confinement may be committed by any person whether or not he claims to have legal authority. A person may be liable to another if he causes the other to be illegally confined.

Just before the lunch hour, Mr. Grant sends his clerk into a cold-storage vault to take inventory. Then he locks the door of the vault during the lunch hour. Mr. Grant is liable for the illegal confinement of his clerk.

Some authorities call any illegal confinement "false imprisonment," but the modern and more easily understood viewpoint interprets false imprisonment as one phase of the general subject of illegal confinement. Usually *false arrest* is committed by someone who asserts he has the legal authority to arrest or to imprison. In false imprisonment it makes no difference whether or not the illegal act is inspired by malice or by personal hostility. The first of the two examples which follow illustrates false arrest; the second, false imprisonment.

Mr. Jameson, a private citizen, obtains a policeman's uniform and badge. He accosts Mr. Dickerman saying, "I arrest you." Dickerman, believing Jameson to be a policeman, submits to the arrest. Jameson is liable for illegal confinement of Dickerman.

Sharp exhibits to Montgomery an invalid warrant for Montgomery's arrest. Montgomery, after inspecting the warrant, concludes it must be valid and submits to the arrest. Sharp takes Montgomery into custody (and is liable for false imprisonment).

False arrest and false imprisonment should be distinguished from *malicious prosecution*, the groundless institution of criminal proceedings. A person may be guilty of false arrest even though there was a formal compliance with the requirements of law, such as swearing out a valid warrant for arrest. Liability in malicious prosecution depends on proof of malice and an absence of probable cause for conviction as well as a termination of the proceeding in favor of the person who is criminally prosecuted.

WORDS OR ACTS CAUSING MENTAL OR EMOTIONAL DISTRESS

Emotional distress may be brought about in many ways. The victim of an intended physical injury almost always suffers at least temporary emotional or mental stress. Emotional or mental distress may simply be the desired result of one person's action or attack on another.

There is a growing tendency for the courts to recognize liability for inflicting intentional mental or emotional disturbances, even though unaccompanied by physical injury.

In the past, New York courts have held that mental or emotional injuries, standing alone, were so vague that it would be against public policy to permit money recoveries; this "type of injury could be feigned without detection and to permit recovery would result in a flood of litigation." Pennsylvania has held that to allow such claims "would open a Pandora's box."

In 1962, however, the New York Court of Appeals, in a 4 to 3 decision, overruled a sixty-year-old precedent and now allows recovery for emotional or mental injuries, even though there is no physical contact, if the injured person was within the "zone of danger" of physical injury. California has gone one step further by allowing a dollars-and-cents recovery for the emotional stress, for example, that a mother suffered in witnessing an injury to her child.

California courts seem to be the leaders in cases expanding Rules of tort liability. For years it has been the rule that the plaintiff may recover for emotional distress only when accompanied by physical injury. Now the California Supreme Court has held that emotional distress may form the basis of a cause of action even though such distress is not accompanied by physical injury.

INTENDED EMOTIONAL DISTRESS

The majority of the states still adhere to the time-honored rule that no matter how evil the intention of the one causing the emotional or mental disturbance, there is no legal liability simply for causing a person mental or emotional distress unless it is accompanied by physical injury.

Miss Simpson, as a joke, tells her friend that an ordinary dance to which she is invited is a fancy dress dance. The friend goes to the dance in a masquerade costume. Realizing the situation at the dance, the friend is humiliated. Miss Simpson is not liable.

Mr. Corey tells Mr. Ditmore, his enemy, that his neighbors believe him to be guilty of gross immoral conduct. Mr. Ditmore so worries over this that he becomes ill. Mr. Corey is not liable to Mr. Ditmore.

Emotional Distress Resulting from Illegal Acts

One who commits an illegal act may be liable for damages resulting from mental or emotional distress incident to other damages which are recoverable. This is an exception to the broad rule that an act that simply causes emotional distress results in no legal liability. The reasoning for the exception seems to be based on situations in which the wrongdoer's crime or flagrant violation of human or property rights results in mental or emotional damage for which he should be held responsible.

A hotel-keeper breaks into a room occupied by his two guests, Mr. Seltzer and his wife, and accuses them (wrongly) of not being married and orders them to leave the hotel. The hotel-keeper is not only liable for the invasion of the Seltzers' privacy and breach of his obligation to them as a hotel-keeper but is also liable for the humiliation and emotional suffering caused the Seltzers by his unlawful acts.

Emotional Distress and Common Carriers

Common carriers, such as railroads, are obligated to provide the public with comfortable, safe, and courteous service. A special rule makes common carriers liable to the public for offenses resulting from the insulting conduct of employees. Common instances that created the need for this special rule are the case of a conductor who wrongfully accuses a passenger of not paying his fare, the case of a passenger who has paid his fare but who is ejected from the train or otherwise treated as though he had not paid, the case of a trainman who uses insulting language to one who is slow in leaving the train, and so on.

INTENTIONAL INTERFERENCE WITH PROPERTY

Interference with persons discussed in the preceding section differs from intentional interference with property, which is concerned with *trespass* and *conversion.*

Trespass

Trespass is a technical invasion of property (real estate) rights. One who intentionally and without consent enters on the land of another is liable to the owner as a trespasser regardless of whether any harm has been done. The same technical trespass may apply if the person throws or places on land anything that does not belong there.

Lewis intentionally throws a pail of water against his neighbor's house. Lewis is a trespasser.
Egbert drives a stray horse from his pasture into the pasture of his neighbor. Egbert is a trespasser.
Wilcox erects a dam across a stream thereby causing the water to back up and flood Smithfield's land. Wilcox is a trespasser.

An intrusion is not restricted to the surface of the earth but may be anything above or below the land in question.

Biggs erects a house on the border of Lounsberry's land. The eaves of the roof overhang Lounsberry's land. Biggs is a trespasser.
Hinkleman strings a telephone wire across the corner of Harrison's land. This is a trespass.[1]

Damage Resulting from Trespass

Technical trespass may not be of serious consequence in the ordinary case, but it becomes important when damages result to the owner of the land.

Lowey, without permission, decides to do a little amateur welding in McCabe's blacksmith shop. In order to do so he lights a fire in the forge, but before leaving he takes precautions to make sure that the fire is out. However, a high wind brings the fire to life again, and the fire burns down the shop. Lowey is liable to McCabe for the loss of his shop.

Trespass by Mistake

One who intentionally enters the land of another, under the mistaken belief that he is entitled to the possession or ownership of the land or that he has consent or privilege to enter the land, may be liable as a trespasser.

The X Mining Company, having mistaken the location of its boundary, takes coal from Mr. Abbott's land. The mining company is liable to Abbott although the mistake was reasonable.

Mr. Cady employs a surveyor of recognized ability to survey his land. The survey shows that he owns a particular strip of land. He tills the land and prepares it for cultivation. It turns out that the survey is wrong and that the land belongs to his neighbor, Mr. Christian. Cady is liable to Christian for trespassing.

Accidental Trespass

The situation in the case of a completely accidental and nonintentional trespass on land is different from the intentional, though mistaken, trespass. It does not result in legal liability.

Mr. Felter is driving his automobile along the street when he suddenly has a heart attack. He loses control of the automobile and it runs up on Mr. Goodman's property, damaging his lawn. Mr. Felter is not liable to Mr. Goodman.

Conversion

The subject of trespass is real property; here we will discuss the subject of conversion, personal property. *Conversion* may be committed (1) by intentionally taking property from its owner; (2) by intentionally destroying or altering property; (3) by using property without permission; (4) by disposing of property without permission by sale, lease or in other ways; or (5) by refusing to surrender another's property on demand.

Intentionally Taking Another's Property

Personal property may be improperly taken from the possession of another by open or obvious means or may be taken by fraudulent schemes or devices.

While his neighbor Amboy is on vacation, Bird walks over to Amboy's garage and "borrows" his lawnmower. Bird has no legal right to do this and is liable for the conversion of Amboy's lawnmower.

Beck, representing himself as a garage man, goes to the King home and tells Mrs. King that her husband has authorized him to take the King automobile to have it repaired. Through this fraudulent device Beck secures the automobile for a day's pleasure and later returns it to the King garage. Beck is liable for conversion of the automobile.

Destruction or Alteration of Property

One who is legally entitled to possession of property but who does not own it has no right to alter or destroy it; if he does so, he commits the legal wrong of conversion. The rule is clear in the destruction of property, but sometimes disputes arise when the form of the property is altered, rather than destroyed, for its identity may be lost when altered.

Examples of acts altering property are sawing logs into lumber, making of grapes into wine, and manufacture of cloth into clothing.

Using Property without Owner's Permission

When a person lawfully comes into possession but not ownership of property, he has no right to use it without the permission of the owner. If he does so, he may be liable for conversion.

Before Morgan goes to Florida for a month, he stores his automobile in Brennan's garage. Every Sunday Brennan uses the car to take his family for a ride. Brennan is liable to Morgan for conversion of the automobile.

Groves sends his tuxedo to Cleaner to be pressed and cleaned. Cleaner wears the suit to a social event. Groves finds out and recovers damages from Cleaner for converting the suit to his own use.

Disposing of Property without Owner's Permission

A person who is legally entitled to possession but not ownership of property may be guilty of conversion if he delivers it to another with the intention of transferring an interest in it. Conversion results when the sale, lease, gift, or other transfer of property is made without permission of the owner.

Jane loans her emerald ring to Margaret for an indefinite period. Margaret keeps it for several years. She finally treats it as her own and one day in a generous mood makes a gift of the ring to Helen. Margaret is liable for converting the ring to her own use.

Scott borrows money from Belcher, who pledges negotiable bonds as security for the loan. Before the loan is due Belcher sells the bonds. Belcher is liable for conversion for the improper sale of the bonds.

Refusal to Surrender Property on Owner's Demand

When one in possession of property refuses to surrender it to the owner, he is liable for conversion. If the demand for the surrender of the property is unreasonable, or if the delivery is held up because of doubt about the proper claimant, there is no liability for conversion.

Johnson, who has stored his furniture at the Excellent Warehouse, demands delivery of the furniture at midnight. Excellent tells Johnson that it will not deliver the furniture at midnight but that the furniture will be available to Johnson at a reasonable hour in the morning. Excellent Warehouse is not liable to Johnson for conversion.

Manhouser ships goods to Bush. Bush presents to the railroad company a bill of lading for the goods and demands immediate delivery. The railroad informs Bush that the goods will be delivered as soon as it is satisfied that he is really Bush. Bush becomes angry and sues the railroad for conversion. The railroad is not liable, and Bush loses the suit.

NOTE

[1]For liability of landowner for injuries sustained by trespasser, see Chapter 8.

6

MALPRACTICE

MEDICAL MALPRACTICE

In recent years a storm has been brewing about medical malpractice insurance. Physicians threatened to strike because of the large insurance they had to carry as protection against malpractice suits. In a few sections of the country they did strike. The medical profession and the public are at odds. Physicians continue to fear huge jury verdicts. Insurance companies very often make large settlements rather than risk large jury verdicts. Doctors blame insurance companies and the legal profession.

In recent years there has been legislative action in the field of medical malpractice. The legislatures of some states have provided for the establishment of underwriting associations as a means of alleviating the malpractice crisis. Some legislatures require all malpractice insurance companies to join a pool to offer medical malpractice insurance to doctors. Other state laws have sought to reduce medical liability verdicts. Ohio, for example, established a ceiling of $200,000 for a single case, while Louisiana and Indiana imposed a $500,000 maximum verdict.

Some states allow the admission of evidence showing collateral sources of payment (for example, accident insurance, Social Security, Workers' Compensation or other employee benefits). Some states set up machinery to discourage frivolous or weak claims by providing that claims must first be submitted to a "screening panel." The findings of the panel may be admissible as evidence in court. Other states are experimenting with arbitration. If either party refuses to accept the arbitration board's decision, the case can go to court, and the arbitration panel's decision is admissible as evidence. Some states recently have abolished the "screening panel."

OTHER PROFESSIONAL MALPRACTICE

Today architects, lawyers, accountants, and other professionals are being held to a stricter level of liability and responsibility. It is not uncommon for malpractice suits to be brought—and to succeed—against other professional persons.

For example, in a few states, if a realtor does not disclose to his or her client defects in the prospective property, that realtor may be held accountable. In a limited number of other states, an insurance agent has been held accountable in damages if that agent has not fully explained the substance and alternatives in an insurance policy. This type of claim is sometimes referred to as an errors and omissions claim or an officers and directors' liability claim.

Legal Malpractice

Lawyers who perform professional services in a negligent or in an incomplete manner often are successfully sued by their clients. The era when lawyers would not testify as a witness against other lawyers, who were defendants in malpractice suits, is long past.

Today, the organized bar attempts to police its lawyer-members. For example, the New York State Bar Association recently has published a list of hints about malpractice and its prevention:

1) Do not promise or predict any specific outcome or dollar recovery.

2) Before performing any services, explain to your client the amount of fees or basis for computing them. Any fee contract between attorney and client arranged after representation has begun may be challenged by the client.

3) Maintain detailed and complete time records for all services rendered, including hours and description of services. When appro-

priate, bill your client periodically and explain the basis for your charges.

4) Do not ignore the client. Inform the client by periodic status reports. If there are long periods of delay, explain the reason for inactivity. Send copies of pleadings and self-explanatory letters and return telephone calls.

5) Keep your client advised of any serious problems that have developed. Do not minimize risks that may be involved in the proceedings. Where there are alternative strategies or options that involve risks, inform your client and let the client choose which of the strategies should be allowed.

6) Take no material action that may prejudice your client without express consent. Do not settle the cause, agree to judgement, or release or dismiss the case without your client's consent.

7) Avoid representing parties with conflicting interests (including parties to a divorce). Disclose any prior representation that may appear to affect the quality or extent of representation. Disclose any personal or adverse interest you may have in the matter being represented.

8) Preserve the client's confidence.

9) Develop a system that will assure compliance with all deadlines, statutory limitations, law and motion matters, trial setting dates, and other dates that must be remembered.

10) Confirm all oral instructions or important conversations with your client by letters.

11) Do not talk down to your client. Your general attitude and rapport with your client are vital.

12) Do not overstate the strength of your case.

13) Do not associate other counsel or refer to a specialist without your client's consent.

14) Do not undertake representation in matters beyond your experience or ability without securing assistance or associating other counsel.

15) Do not criticize your client's former lawyer without being fully apprised of all material facts.

16) Do not reveal that you carry malpractice insurance. Retain all your policies, primary and excess, especially those written on an occurrence basis.

17) Do not attempt to defend your own malpractice claims.

7

DEFAMATION OF CHARACTER

Character may be defamed in law in two ways: by libel or by slander. *Libel* consists of the publication of defamatory matter in the form of written or printed words or pictures, caricatures, statues and so forth in letters, circulars, petitions, newspapers or books. A libel may be published by broadcasting or telecasting, by means of radio or television, if the speaker or the actor reads or follows a prepared script or written notes. *Slander* consists of the publication of defamatory matter by spoken words, gestures, and so on.

DETERMINING A DEFAMATION OF CHARACTER

When is a communication defamatory? It is defamatory when it tends to harm the reputation of another, to lower his esteem in his community, to cause persons to stop associating or dealing with him, or to expose a person to scorn, ridicule, or contempt. One can defame another by questioning his personal morality or integrity or by branding him with a loathsome disease that would cause people to shun him. Examples of defamatory statements or acts follow:

A newspaper publishes a statement that a certain department store is conducting dishonest business or is in financial distress.

Miss Smith states that Miss Jones, while posing as a dressmaker, is really the mistress of a prominent citizen.

Mr. Roberts draws and circulates a caricatured figure labeled "murderer." The figure is easily recognized as Mr. Edwards.

A tells his friends that X, the neighborhood druggist, consorts with dope peddlers.

A woman tells her friends that a certain market sells contaminated meat.

Although decency and courtesy require us to speak well of the dead, there is no legal liability to the estate of a deceased person for defaming the deceased's reputation.

One who falsely and without justification publishes defamatory material about a corporation or a partnership is liable to the firm.

The Jones Newspaper Company publishes an article charging that a life insurance company has fraudulently issued stock. The newspaper has defamed the life insurance company and would be liable in a suit for damages.

The Smith Newspaper Company publishes a statement that a law firm is composed of shysters who are devoid of honesty and fair dealing. The firm and the individual members of the firm have been defamed and may sue separately for damages.

DETERMINING PUBLICATION OF DEFAMATION

What constitutes *publication* of defamatory matter? In law, publication of defamatory matter is the communicating of the defamation, intentionally or carelessly, to a person other than the one defamed. Thus, three people must be involved to establish publication. Examples of an unpublished and a published defamation follow:

Harry and Joe are in the woods on a hunting trip. Harry accused Joe of murder. There is no one else in the vicinity to hear the accusation. Harry has not published a slander.

McDonald, during his lunch hour, tells his fellow employee that his neighbor, Wilson, a teller in the bank, has been caught dipping into the till and that the bank is going to turn him over to the authorities. McDonald has published a slander.

TYPES OF DEFAMATORY COMMUNICATION

The general types of defamatory communication are statements of fact and expressions of opinion.

Statements of Fact

Statements of fact which amount to defamation consist of accusing a person of a particular act and, thus, exposing that person to scorn, ridicule, contempt, or jeopardizing his business or financial reputation. The example immediately above and the one below illustrate this point.

Cooley writes a letter to his friends accusing Spencer, an amateur golfer, of accepting money for playing in exhibition matches. A number of persons understand that by so accepting money for playing golf, Spencer has forfeited his amateur standing. In making the alleged statements of fact, Cooley has defamed Spencer.

Expressions of Opinion

Defamation may consist of opinions expressed with reference to facts either known or undisclosed. Defamation consists of implying that another has been guilty of reprehensible conduct. If you call a person a thief or a murderer, you imply that he has stolen or murdered. As a result, the majority of newspapers are very careful in characterizing the conduct of others.

Harwood writes an article for a newspaper in which he refers to Cahill as a traitor and a "second Benedict Arnold." Harwood has defamed Cahill.

RULES FOR LIBEL AND SLANDER

When Libel Is Actionable Per Se

Almost any published libel is actionable per se, regardless of whether special harm has been caused. The person defamed may recover nominal damages and thus be vindicated. Common forms of libel which are actionable *per se* are those which accuse persons of crimes, immoral conduct, improper conduct in business or profession, dishonesty, and so on.

A newspaper publishes a false article stating that Harmon has "jumped his board bill." The newspaper is liable to Harmon without any proof of special harm to Harmon.

Margaret, a beneficiary of an estate, writes her sister that their cousin, Herbert, the executor of the estate, has been spending estate funds for his own personal gain and has been investing some of the estate funds in his own personal business. Margaret has published a libel that is actionable per se.

Cuphbert circulates a memo to his business associates warning them not to use the sevices of Boothbay, a certified public accountant, because "he is drunk half the time, runs around with notorious women, and is not to be trusted." When Boothbay sues Cuphbert for libel, he does not have to prove special damages.

Robert writes his brother that he is disgusted with Dr. Cuttem, a surgeon, because "he is money crazy, more of a businessman than a doctor, and operates on people at the slightest excuse, whether or not they need surgery." Dr. Cuttem has a libel claim against Robert.

DEFAMATION OF CHARACTER

When Slander Is Actionable Per Se

Through the years the courts have handed down rules distinguishing slander from libel and providing for the special treatment of it. How absurd it is to have a law making people responsible for all libel but responsible for slander in only four situations. The need for reform is obvious when a person may be sued for writing a postcard saying that someone is dishonest, but he may go scotfree for saying the same thing to an audience of a thousand persons.

Slander (generally the spoken word) that results in no special harm is actionable per se only in the following four cases:

1) When one who falsely and without justification publishes a slander to suggest that another has been guilty of a criminal offense that would be (a) chargeable by indictment and (b) punishable by death or imprisonment, he is liable for slander without proof of special damage.

   McGillacuddy falsely states to McDonald, "Gunther has served time in state prison." Gunther may sue McGillacuddy for slander and recover nominal damages even though he cannot show any special harm resulting from the slander.

   Donovan says to Wilbur, "Gunther is the type of man who would commit murder at the slightest provocation." Donovan has not charged Gunther with the crime and is not liable for slander.

2) When one who falsely and without justification publishes a slan-

der which suggests that another has an existing loathsome disease, he is liable, even though there is no proof of special harm.

Jones tells Smith that Brown has venereal disease. Jones is liable to Brown without proof of damages.

3) When one accuses another of improper conduct of a business or profession, he is liable without proof of special harm.

Fisher accuses Smith, a bricklayer, of being a hypocrite. He has not committed slander per se.

Fisher accuses lawyer Jones of being ignorant and incompetent and says that he neglects his clients, spending his time in gambling and drinking. He has committed slander per se.

Cutts calls Vincent, a dry-goods store operator, insolvent. He is liable for slander per se.

4) When one impugns unchastity to a woman, he is liable for slander without proof of special harm.

Herman tells Stanley that Julia is unfaithful to her husband. Herman is liable for damages to Julia.

Proving Special Damages

When slander does not enter within the four categories enumerated above, it is necessary to prove special harm. The special harm must be a specific money or material loss that the injured person can show, such as losing his job.

A priest falsely and without justification says that a merchant had been excommunicated from his church. The merchant loses a large number of customers and can prove that his loss stems from the priest's words. The priest is liable to the merchant.

Mary falsely and without justification tells Helen that Beatrice is a vulgar gossip. Helen, though previously a very good friend of Beatrice, stops speaking to her. Mary is not liable to Beatrice without proof of resulting special harm.

Republication of Slander or Libel

One who repeats or republishes defamatory matter is just as liable as if he had originated it.

Sarah tells Mary that their neighbor, Mrs. Blackstone, is a kleptomaniac and has been found guilty of shoplifting. Mary repeats this to her bridge club. Mary is guilty of republishing a slander.

Each time an article is republished a fresh wrong is committed. Thus, a newspaper is liable if without justification it republishes false and defamatory statements, even though it names the author and the paper in which the statements first appeared.

A newspaper syndicate supplies a defamatory article to each newspaper using its service. Each paper that prints the article has published a libel and may be sued.

The *Centerville Herald* prints a libelous article and says that the article has been copied from the *Boston Times*. The fact that it originated elsewhere is no excuse: Reprinting it is libel. The fact that a mistake has been innocently made or that the person republishing the libel or slander did not intend defamation is no excuse.

DEFENSES TO ACTIONS FOR LIBEL OR SLANDER

There are several defenses to actions for libel and slander; among them are truth, consent, and privilege.

Truth

Truth is always a defense to libel or slander.

Bertram moves to Syracuse, New York, and there opens a real estate brokerage office. Harold, an old acquaintance, recognizes Bertram and writes a letter to a friend saying that Bertram is a proven crook and cannot be trusted. It turns out that Bertram was previously convicted of embezzlement under a different name and had a bad reputation in Nevada, his home state. Harold was justified in reviling Bertram because the statements he made about him were true.

A mistaken belief in the truth of the matter published, although honest and reasonable, is not a defense.

Miss Bonam applied for a teaching position at a private school for girls. The headmistress, in processing Miss Bonam's application, received a report from a reliable investigation agency that Miss Bonam had been discharged from another school for immoral conduct. The headmistress prepared a detailed report to a committee of the school trustees stating that in her opinion Miss

Bonam was unfit to hold the teaching position. The report of the investigation agency turned out to be untrue. Although the headmistress of the school acted in good faith in making her report to the committee, she is legally responsible for libeling Miss Bonam.

Consent

A good defense is the consent of the person who claims to have been defamed to the publication of the defamatory matter.

A school teacher is summarily discharged by the school board. The teacher demands that the reason for his dismissal be made public, and the president of the school board publishes the reason. The reason turns out to be defamatory, but because the teacher consented to the publication he does not have a case.

Privilege of Those Performing Public Functions

Certain public officials and others charged with the performance of public functions are said to be privileged, or free from liability for libel or slander. Judges or judicial officers in the performance of their duties, lawyers, witnesses, and jurors, during the course of judicial proceedings, and members of Congress or of state legislatures in the performance of their legislative functions are privileged and cannot be held responsible for libel or slander.

Senator Kleghorn, from the floor of the state senate, charged that Governor Broomfield was a dishonest grafter and was stealing from the public treasury. The governor challenged the senator to repeat such slander outside the walls of the senate. The senator declined and confined his defamatory remarks to the privileged legislative halls.

Circuit Judge Buffim, in sentencing Harry S. for the crime of treason, called him a "Judas Iscariot" and "a traitor to his flag and his country"; these judicial pronouncements were broadcast over the radio and appeared in the press. It later turned out that Harry S. was convicted on perjured testimony, and he was subsequently freed. Thereafter he sued Judge Buffim for slander. The judge was not liable, because his remarks as a judicial officer are privileged.

Husband and Wife

A husband or wife is absolutely privileged to publish to his or her spouse false and defamatory matter concerning a third person. This exception to the rule undoubtedly came from the old common-law concept that a husband and his wife were, in law, one person. Today the rule has a practical application: When one spouse tells the other some scandalous slander about a neighbor, the scandal, up to that point at least, has not been broadcast.

Fair Comment

The interests of society require that matters of public interest should be the subject of frank and open comment, criticism, and discussion without fear of liability for libel or slander; hence, the law says that fair comment is a matter of right. The question occasionally arises, "Is the comment fair and reasonable?" Sometimes comment or criticism goes beyond the bounds of fairness and becomes a matter of personal malice or spite.

A comment is said to be fair when it is (1) based on facts; (2) truly stated; (3) free from charges of improper or dishonorable motives on the part of the person whose conduct is criticized; or (4) an honest expression of opinion or belief.

Mere exaggerations, irony, wit, or sarcasm will not render the comment defamatory.

A congressman voted against the Lend-Lease Bill in the House of Representatives in February 1941. As a result, a newspaper in an editorial charged that the congressman was giving aid to the agents of Hitler and Mussolini and asked the congressman if he wanted to be classed as a Quisling. The congressman brought suit for libel. The court held that the editorial was fair comment and hence free from liability.

But, when comment or criticism is motivated by malice, the privilege of fair comment is lost.

A newspaper critic refers to a college lecturer as illiterate, uncultivated, coarse, and vulgar. The critic also says that the professor is sensational, absurd, foolish, and a literary freak. In a libel suit the court holds that the critic went beyond the limits of fair comment and indulged in a personal attack that exposed the professor to public contempt, shame, and ridicule. The court held the newspaper to be responsible.

The defense of fair comment should not be confused with the privilege of making a fair and true report of legislative, judicial, or legal proceedings. A defendant in a libel suit may show by way of defense that he was just reporting a public proceeding or divulging to the public (by way of newspaper report, for example) matters that are on file in a public office and open to inspection by the public.

Different Rules for Public Figures

The Supreme Court in recent years has changed the basic law of libel by protecting freedom of the press under the First Amendment of the Constitution. In the decision of *The New York Times v. Sullivan* (1964), the Court held that a public official may not recover damages for libel against a newspaper unless the public official can prove that the defamatory statement was published with malice—that is, with knowledge that the statement was false or with reckless disregard of whether it was false or not. The Court, in overturning the libel award, held that "even erroneous allegations of fact require protection to provide sufficient room for effective discussion of public affairs." To that end, the court established rules for public figures who are plaintiffs in libel actions. For example, to recover they must prove with "convincing clarity" that the defendant knew the offending statement was or probably was false—so-called "actual malice." The court reviewed the constitutional character of freedom to criticize governmental and other public officials and to engage in uninhibited and robust debate on public issues. Later the Supreme Court extended the protection of *The New York Times* ruling by holding that news media are protected in making otherwise libelous statements against private individuals where the defamatory statements involve issues of "public or general concern."

A radio station in reporting on a crackdown on pornographers referred to a magazine as "obscene" and said that the publisher was engaged in the "smut literature racket." The Court rejected the publisher's suit for libel saying that the radio station was discussing "an issue of public concern."

DAMAGES FOR LIBEL OR SLANDER

As indicated before, the victim of a libel or slander that is actionable without proof of special harm may recover "at least nominal damages." Nominal damages usually are a trivial sum, such as six cents. But a person who has been the victim of libel or slander may also recover compensatory damages for the value of the loss suffered. The injured person may also show special harm resulting from the libelous publication.

Cato falsely and without justification writes a letter to Raedes' employer telling him that Raedes is a radical labor agitator and a bad influence on other employees. As a result, Raedes is discharged and may recover damages from Cato for the injury to his reputation and may also recover for the loss of his employment.

Hapgood falsely and without justification, in the presence of another, charges Lemon, a merchant, with using false weights and measures, as a result of which Lemon's business drops off noticeably. Lemon may recover from Hapgood damages for loss of reputation and loss of business.

Facts which tend to restrict or limit the amount of damages are sometimes called "matters in mitigation of damages." Such facts include (1) publication, (2) bad reputation of the plaintiff, and (3) proof that the defendant acted with proper motives and a belief in the truth of what he said. These three factors have reduced damages, but they do not limit or restrict basic liability for libel or slander. Proof of proper motives or belief in the truth of the slander or the libel would not prevent a verdict in favor of the person libeled or slandered, but it could be a factor considered by the jury in determining the amount of the damages. In determining the amount of an award for general damages, the jury should consider the character of the plaintiff and his standing in the community together with the effect the language used may have had on his reputation.

In order for a published retraction to mitigate damages, it must be published at least with equal prominence.

The *Press* falsely accuses Dr. Smith of constant intoxication. The article is printed on page one of the *Press*. It later publishes a retraction of the original—and false—article that appears on page 35, in an inconspicuous location. Such a retraction would not mitigate damages.

On its evening newscast, a TV station falsely reports that a certain manufacturer uses recycled, defective steel. Upon learning of the falsity of its report, the TV station retracts the libel on the same evening newscast, devoting an equal amount of time to the retraction. This would help to reduce, or mitigate, damages.

8

NEGLIGENCE

Negligence is a branch of the law of torts. *Tort* is a term applied to a miscellaneous group of private or civil wrongs, excluding breach of contract, for which courts provide remedies in the form of actions for damages. A negligent act is a careless or reckless one rather than an intentional harm. It is the omission of a duty that should have been performed or the performance of an act that should not have been done. A person is negligent when he fails to use the care that a reasonable person would use in the same circumstances. The criterion is: How would a reasonable person act?

FACTORS AFFECTING NEGLIGENCE CLAIMS

In a negligence claim a person must generally prove (1) that the person against whom the claim is made had a duty and was negligent and (2) that he himself was not guilty of even negligence contributing to the accident.

Duty

A person suing another for negligence must prove that a duty actually devolved on the second person. Duty may be imposed by statute, by court decisions or by circumstances peculiar to the situation. A duty may also be assumed; that is, one may offer to perform a particular act and then may perform it negligently.

Contributory Negligence

Contributory negligence is the want of ordinary care which contributes to an accident. Contributory negligence may result from the failure of the person claiming damages to use the care which a reasonable person would have used to avoid danger, or it may result from his voluntarily exposing himself to danger. The latter, sometimes called "assumption of risk," will defeat a recovery in a negligence action.

The rule of contributory negligence is: If the claimant (one who seeks damages) is guilty of any negligence which contributes to his own injury, he has no claim.

Fredericks is injured in an accident in which he himself is 10 percent to blame. Even though his own negligence contributes only slightly to the accident. he is not permitted to recover for his injuries.

The rule of contributory negligence has been criticized for its harshness, for it may absolutely bar recovery for damage against the person most to blame.

Comparative Negligence

Forty-five states and territories (Alaska, Arizona, Arkansas, California, Colorado, Connecticut, Delaware, Florida, Georgia, Hawaii, Idaho, Indiana, Iowa, Kansas, Kentucky, Louisiana, Maine, Massachusetts, Michigan, Minnesota, Mississippi, Missouri, Montana, Nebraska, Nevada, New Hampshire, New Jersey, New Mexico, New York, North Dakota, Ohio, Oklahoma, Oregon, Pennsylvania, Puerto Rico, Rhode Island, South Dakota, Texas, Utah, Vermont, Virgin Islands, Washington, West Virginia, Wisconsin and Wyoming), and in certain cases, the federal courts, apply the rule of comparative negligence, through which an injured person is not barred from recovering damages when he is guilty of contributory negligence. The amount of damages recovered, however, is reduced in proportion to the amount of negligence of the claimant. The determination of the extent of the claimant's negligence is left to the court and jury.

Many of these forty-five states and territories have adopted a "modified comparative fault rule," in some form, under which the plaintiff's (the claimant's) fault must be less than the defendant's fault in order for the plaintiff to recover.

Egan is injured in the Stone Company's store. The case is submitted to a jury in Wisconsin, which has the rule of comparative negligence. The jury finds that the Stone Company was negligent, that the amount of the damages suffered by Egan was $100,000, and that Egan's own negligence contributed to his injury in the proportion of 25 percent. Therefore, judgment is rendered in favor of Egan against the Stone Company for 75 percent of the total injury, or $75,000.

Doctrine of Last Clear Chance

A person who has negligently exposed himself to injury may nevertheless recover from a negligent wrongdoer if the latter was aware of the claimant's helplessness and could have, had he chosen to, avoided injuring him. This doctrine of last clear chance is based on the principle that even when the plaintiff is negligent, the defendant should be charged with liability if by exercising care he might have avoided the consequences of the plaintiff's negligence.

The following is a classic illustration:

Caspar, knowing that the motor in his ancient automobile often sputters and stalls, drives onto a railroad crossing where his automobile stalls in front of an approaching train. If the railroad engineer has ample opportunity to discover Caspar's stalled automobile, and yet fails to use reasonable caution in stopping the train before it hits the automobile. Caspar, or his surviving relatives, may recover damages against the railroad under the doctrine of last clear chance.

NEGLIGENCE CLAIMS IN AUTOMOBILE ACCIDENTS

Public streets are for everyone's use, but in using public property one must conduct himself in a manner that will not cause injury to others. Thus, one who drives an automobile on public streets must do so in a reasonable manner and with that degree of care which a prudent person would use under the circumstances.

There are certain statutes governing the use of automobiles on the streets, such as laws fixing the speed limit and laws requiring vehicles to be in good mechanical condition (to have passed state inspection). A violation of one of these statutes may be the proximate cause of an injury and hence actionable negligence. Common sense and good judgment are necessary in obeying these regulations, too. For instance, although the speed limit may be thirty miles per hour in a certain area, one cannot always drive at that speed in that locality without fear of negligence, for the street at a particular moment may be so crowded or so icy that twenty miles per hour might be a reckless and excessive rate of speed.

Pedestrians also have certain duties in the use of the streets. A pedestrian jaywalking (crossing against traffic lights or between intersections) or failing to heed a siren timely blown or in rural areas walking on the wrong side of the road or failing to look for approaching vehicles may be just as responsible as the driver of the automobile that hit him. Moreover, the pedestrian's negligence may prevent him from recovering for his injuries.

Automobile Accident Claims

Who is at fault in an automobile accident is usually a question of fact depending upon particular conditions and circumstances at the time and place of the accident. As traffic has increasingly jammed our highways, so also have lawsuits arising out of automobile negligence actions jammed the court calendars in our metropolitan areas. In these court cases the injured persons (the plaintiffs) sue car owners and drivers (the defendants); 90 percent of these car owners and drivers are insured by liability insurance companies, which furnish legal counsel to defend suits.

Automobile Liability

Although there are a number of other kinds of automobile insurance with special benefits (such as medical payments, collision, and comprehensive insurance), the basic type of automobile insurance of concern is liability insurance, which protects the insured against the claims of others. In a liability policy the insurance company agrees to pay for all damages which the owner of the car may become legally obliged to pay, as a result of ownership, maintenance, or use of the automobile. This type of insurance is based on legal liability.

Determining Legal Liability

The rule of contributory negligence in auto accident cases continues to apply in six of the fifty states: Alabama, North Carolina, South Carolina, Tennessee, Virginia, and Maryland, and the District of Columbia. In order for a claimant in these states and district to have a good claim, she or he must be prepared to prove (1) that the person against whom the claim is made was negligent (which negligence was the cause of the accident) and (2) that the claimant was not guilty of any negligence that contributed to the accident.

If the *driver* (rather than the owner) of the automobile is negligent, is the car owner still responsible (legally liable)? And under such circumstances, can the injured person collect from the insurance company? The legislatures in some states have passed special laws making the car owner responsible in such cases for the driver's negligence, but in most states the owner of a motor vehicle is liable only for his own negligence and not for the driver's. In the absence of a special law passed by the legislature, the car owner, when not present in the car at the time of the accident, is liable for injuries sustained by another *only* if the car is being driven by his agent or employee.

In California, Florida, Idaho, Iowa, Michigan, Minnesota, Nevada, New York, and Rhode Island, the car owner is liable for the operation of an automobile if it is driven with the permission or consent of the owner.

Saber of Binghamton, New York, lends his automobile to a neighbor. The neighbor runs into a pedestrian, who makes a claim against Saber. Saber is held responsible by reason of Section 59 of the Vehicle and Traffic Law of the State of New York, which makes the owner liable for the operation of a vehicle when it is being used "with the permission, either express or implied, of such owner."

In Connecticut, Massachusetts, New Jersey, Oregon, Rhode Island, Tennessee, Virginia, and West Virginia, the law imposes liability on the owner and presumes that at the time of the accident the automobile was being driven by an authorized agent or someone who had the owner's consent. This presumption is called a rebuttable presumption—that is, the owner can show that the presumption is contrary to the facts.

The *family purpose doctrine* exists in sixteen states: Alaska, Arizona, Colorado, Connecticut, Georgia, Kentucky, Michigan, Nebraska, Nevada, New Jersey, North Carolina, North Dakota, Oregon, Tennessee, Washington, and West Virginia. This doctrine makes the head of the family liable for the negligence of a member of the family while driving the family car. The rule is said to be necessary because not all family members may be financially responsible.

Mr. Rathbun of Detroit, Michigan, owns a Buick, which his son, Robert, drives to a high school dance. Owing to his own negligence, Robert is involved in an accident, and his high school classmates make claims against Mr. Rathbun. These claims are sustained under the family purpose doctrine, even though the son was not driving the car on his father's business. Mr. Rathbun's insurance company has to pay the claim because of Mr. Rathbun's legal liability.

Imposing responsibility, or legal liability, on the owner, whether imposed by the state legislature or through case law, is a growing trend.

Types of Automobile Accident Claims and Means of Settlement

Automobile accident claims may be treated under various headings, such as claims for personal injuries, death claims, and property damage claims, and in a different type of classification, claims of passengers and pedestrians.

Personal Injury Claims

There is no absolute yardstick for measuring the dollars-and-cents value of human suffering or personal injuries. A personal injury claim is worth only the amount for which it can be settled or the amount the jury will award. In a personal injury case, insurance adjusters will usually pay an amount based on the following factors: (1) special damages, that is, out-of-pocket expenses, such as doctors', nurses', and hospital fees and lost earnings; (2) an amount for the person's pain and suffering; and (3) an amount to compensate for permanent injury and disability.

Bodecker is struck by a car and suffers a broken leg. He makes what the doctors call an uneventful recovery with no permanent disability. He is laid up for six weeks and then returns to work. His medical bills and loss of income total $13,750. The insurance company values the claim at $50,000 and pays it.

Loss of Consortium

In legal actions brought by a husband against a third person for causing injury to his wife, he can recover for loss of "consortium," that is, his wife's services and companionship. Until 1950, only the husband could recover for loss of consortium. Now, due to women's emancipation laws, the rule has been changed in nineteen states. Today, consortium is defined by the courts to include not only loss of support or services, but also such elements as love, companionship, affection, society, sexual relations, solace, and more.

Mr. M was completely paralyzed from his waist down as a result of an elevator accident. His wife brought a suit for loss of consortium against the elevator company for negligence based on her claim that her husband would spend the rest of his life as an invalid. The New York Court of Appeals overruled previous law and recognized a cause of action for consortium in the wife, "thereby terminating an unjust discrimination under New York law."

Formerly, loss of consortium meant a spouse's claim for loss of the society and companionship of his or her spouse during a physical injury. Now the Massachusetts Supreme Court has extended the rule to include children's claims for loss of parental society.

In the Massachusetts case, a small boy's father was paralyzed from the neck down when the defendant's load of wood fell on him. The Massachusetts court changed the rule in that state by allowing a recovery by the children of the paralyzed man. The injury was so severe that the children were deprived of the society and companionship of their father. Whether the courts of other states will follow the lead of the Massachusetts court is a big question. In some state courts they allow not only children to sue for loss of consortium of a parent, but also allow parents to sue for loss of consortium of their children who are injured in a serious accident.

DEATH CLAIMS

In most states the amount that can be recovered for "wrongful death" resulting from an automobile accident usually is limited to the pecuniary loss to the family. Thus, the relatives of the deceased are limited to proving a dollars-and-cents loss, mental anguish, or loss of the companionship of the decedent. In a few states recovery in death cases is not limited to pecuniary loss, and Alabama allows punitive damages. Kansas and Tennessee allow damages for mental anguish, loss of companionship, and so forth.

Irrespective of the earnings after the decedent or the relationship of the survivors to the decedent, eight states limit the amount of damages that can be recovered in certain death claims (wrongful death actions), as in the table on page 89.

Property Damage Claims

When an owner claims damages to his car, is he responsible for the negligence of the driver? The answer is that generally the owner as a claimant is chargeable with the negligence of the driver (1) if the driver is the employee of the owner; (2) if the owner is in the car and has the right to control it; (3) if the owner knows that the driver is reckless, unskilled, intoxicated, or otherwise unfit to drive; or (4) if the owner permits the use of his car with the knowledge that it is unsafe or defective. In some states the absentee owner rule permits the owner to recover damages although the driver is partially to blame for the accident, providing (1) the owner was not in the car at the time of the accident and (2) the driver was not the owner's agent or employee.

In New York, Parker loans his car to Beeman; Beeman collides with a car owned and driven by Nutley. The accident was caused by the joint negligence of Beeman and Nutley. Because Parker was not in the automobile at the time of the accident, he is not responsible for Beeman's negligence. He sues Nutley and recovers for damages to his automobile.

The average insurance adjuster does not like to settle an automobile property damage claim for more than the amount of the auto repair bill, but the owner of an automobile may legally recover for the difference between the market value of the automobile immediately before and immediately after the accident, where that depreciation represents the true damage to the automobile.

Again, most insurance companies discourage claims for loss of use of the vehicle during the time it is being repaired, but the loss of use of the automobile during repair can be an element of damage; if the owner insists, he can recover in court the rental value of the car pending its repair.

Maximum Recovery Against State

STATE

Colorado (liability of employer for employee) $3,000–$10,000 (if deceased left neither spouse, minor child, nor dependent parent; otherwise, $150,000 per person or $400,000 per accident)

Kansas $100,000 (limitation on amount recoverable for intangibles, such as mental anguish, suffering, or bereavement)

Maine $75,000 (limitation on amount recovery for loss of consortium, including damages for emotional distress)

Maryland in all personal injury actions after July 1, 1986, there is a $350,000 limit for non-economic damages, including pain and suffering and loss of consortium. Limited waiver on state sovereign immunity in tort claims, only to extent of insurance coverage. (Personal injury action includes statutory wrongful death action.)

Massachusetts $4,000 (for death actions or injuries suffered because of defect in highway or building); limit of $4,000 when government responsible for repairing of same)

New Hampshire $50,000 (unless deceased left a widow, widower, child or children, father or mother, or relative dependent on deceased, in which case there is no limitation)

Oregon $50,000 (noneconomic damages limitations; damages may not exceed $500,000. Non-economic damages includes subjective, nonmonetary losses, such as pain, suffering, emotional distress, injury to reputation, and loss of consortium.)

South Carolina $4,000 to $500,000 (a claimant can sue for wrongful death if action could have been brought for bodily injury damages had death not ensued)

(Recovery per person for single occurrence against a private person or corporation is $250,000 with a total recovery not exceeding $500,000. No punitive damages are available.)

(In an action against a municipal corporation, recovery is limited to $4,000)

(In an action against a charitable corporation, such as a charitable hospital, recovery is limited to $200,000)

Passengers' Claims

In nine states (Alabama, Georgia, Virginia, Arkansas, Illinois, California, Indiana, Florida, and Nebraska) passengers' claims come under "guest statutes," which prevent a guest passenger from recovering for injuries unless his host is guilty of willful and wanton misconduct, gross negligence, or intoxication. (In Georgia only gross negligence need be proved.)

The appeals courts in Idaho and Iowa have held that their guest statutes were unconstitutional. The Kansas legislature repealed its guest statute.

The number of states requiring that the host-driver be found liable for some form of "gross, wanton or willful" misconduct is decreasing with each passing year.

Some regard the guest statutes as harsh, because in a large number of cases they prevent guest passengers from recovering for their injuries. Those favoring the guest statutes claim that they prevent collusion between car owners and their passengers, who are often friends and relatives and who attempt to frame cases against insurance companies. Nineteen states entirely ignore guest statutes and support the common-law rule of ordinary negligence.

Pedestrians' Claims

Although a right-of-way is never absolute, it often has an important bearing on the claims of pedestrians injured in highway accidents. In over forty states, pedestrians have the right-of-way on crosswalks or at intersections in the absence of traffic lights. Generally, motor vehicles have the right-of-way between intersections of streets and on highways. In effect, the law says that crosswalks are for pedestrians, and in the middle of the block automobiles have the right-of-way. The following is an actual court case:

A pedestrian was seriously injured while crossing the street three feet north of the center of the crosswalk. The court said it was the duty of the pedestrian to maintain such a lookout as was reasonably necessary to enable her to yield the right-of-way to the automobile. The pedestrian did not do so and was guilty of negligence that contributed to her injuries and defeated a recovery in court.

NO-FAULT AUTO INSURANCE

The discussion in the preceding pages about automobile negligence claims is based on the so-called fault system. If we do wrong to someone, we are at fault and hence have to pay damages.

If we drive an auto carelessly and injure someone, we are legally liable and have to pay the person injured or the owner of property damaged by our carelessness (negligence). Automobiles are such an important part of our lives, and the risk of injury and damage to others is so great, that we have to insure against legal liability based on fault. Hence auto liability insurance is carried by nearly every automobile owner.

In the past sometimes the determination of legal liability in auto accidents required going to court with long delays. Our court calendars have become clogged with auto accident cases. Delays and legal technicalities caused public dissatisfaction, resulting in a proposed no-fault system of insurance. Politicians, lawyers, insurance companies, and legislators have debated the merits and weaknesses of no-fault proposals.

No-fault insurance has caught public imagination. To many it seems the answer to public dissatisfaction. Its opponents say we will regret its adoption by many states and that auto accident victims will be the losers. Nineteen states have adopted no-fault plans: Arkansas, Colorado, Connecticut, Delaware, Florida, Georgia, Hawaii, Kansas, Kentucky, Maryland, Massachusetts, Michigan, Minnesota, New Jersey, New York, North Dakota, Oregon, South Carolina, and South Dakota, including the District of Columbia and Puerto Rico. Pennsylvania recently repealed its no-fault law, and Utah has held that the law only applies to personal injury claims.

Under the fault system that exists in the other thirty-one states, if you are injured in an auto accident, you may recover damages from the person or persons who are legally to blame for the accident. Then liability insurance companies for those people pay you. Of course, if you were to blame for the accident, you cannot collect from anybody. If no-fault insurance applies, then you can collect your medical bills and lost wages (economic loss) from your own insurance company, no matter who is to blame for the accident. Like other professions and all specialized fields of activity, the insurance industry has its own vernacular, which can make simple explanations sound complicated. For example, insurance people refer to no-fault payments as "first-party benefits" because (according to insurance explanations) they are paid directly to the injured person by his own insurance company. These first-party benefits may only be 80 percent of lost earnings and are reduced by workmen's compensation and Social Security disability benefits paid to the injured person.

Each of the state no-fault laws is different, although someday they may be uniform. Each state puts a different limit on the amount that your insurance company pays you. Some states put the limit at $5,000, some states at $2,000, and New York (requiring the largest amount) at $50,000.

Under no-fault, ordinarily you cannot sue the other party for damages resulting from the accident unless your medical expenses exceed a specified amount (varying from $400 to $1,000, depending on the law of your particular state) or unless you sustain a fractured bone, permanent injury, or disfigurement. Each state law is different from the others. The lack of uniformity in state laws on no-fault may lead Congress to pass a federal no-fault plan. Check with your insurance agent and ask that the no-fault requirements of your state be explained if it has such a law.

Example of No-fault Plan in One State

The Insurance Department of New York state explains the benefits and outlines the highlights of the New York plan, adopted February 1, 1974. It brings about:

1) Prompt payment of economic losses to persons injured in auto accidents, regardless of fault, be they motorists, passengers, or pedestrians.
2) Elimination of most lawsuits for bodily injury arising out of auto accidents in New York state, thereby easing the burden on the courts.
3) Insurance premium savings for New York motorists.

An automobile owner automatically receives basic no-fault auto insurance from his insurance company in the form of a special indorsement to be attached to his present policy. Supplemental benefits also may be bought.

In the event of an accident, the insurance company that issued a policy on a particular car will pay no-fault benefits to injured occupants of that car and to pedestrians injured by that car.

The Basic Benefits New York law requires that each registered motor vehicle (other than a motorcycle) be insured for up to $50,000 per person in economic losses to an injured driver and passengers of that vehicle, and to pedestrians injured by it, because of an accident in New York state. The benefits may be less than the injured person's actual economic loss, as is explained below. For example, only 80 percent of lost earnings is paid, and benefits would be reduced by a deductible, if there is one, and by workmen's compensation and social security disability benefits, if any. Within the overall limit, the basic no-fault benefits are as follows:

1) All reasonable and necessary medical and rehabilitation expenses.

2) Lost earnings up to $1,000 a month for three years, less 20 percent because the benefit payments, unlike earnings, will not be taxable.

3) Up to $25 a day for a year for other reasonable and necessary expenses incurred because of an accident, such as the cost of hiring a housekeeper to perform the services of an injured housewife.

About Property Damage

The new no-fault law has no effect on present property damage coverages or financial requirements. Claims for damages to your vehicle still will be covered by your own collision or comprehensive insurance policy, if you have one. As in the past, if another motorist is at fault in an accident, you may file a claim against him for property damage. Therefore, each car owner still must buy property damage liability insurance to protect himself against being sued.

The Right to Sue

Under a typical no-fault plan, you, as an accident victim, would retain the right to sue a negligent driver for personal injury losses in certain cases:

1) For your medical expenses and other economic losses to the extent they exceed the no-fault benefit levels required by law.

2) For "pain and suffering," if you suffer serious injury, which includes a permanent injury, significant disfigurement, a serious fracture, or an injury needing medical treatment with a total value of more than $500.

3) For injury resulting in death.

As previously noted, you retain the right to sue a negligent driver for property damage.

For Bodily Injury Protection

Because accident victims will retain the right to sue a negligent driver for personal injury losses in certain cases, and for property damage in all cases, you, as an auto owner, still may be sued in certain cases. Therefore, you still are required to carry minimum liability insurance (usually bodily injury limits of $10,000 per person and $20,000 per accident and a property damage limit of $5,000). As in the past, you have the choice of buying higher liability insurance limits.

Out-of-State Protection

Most other states, and the Canadian provinces, require that visiting motorists, including New York auto owners, meet certain minimum insurance requirements. Depending on the state or province, that may be some form of basic no-fault insurance or minimum amounts of the traditional liability insurance, or both.

Rapid Benefit Payment

Your losses will be paid as they are incurred: as medical bills are received and earnings would be paid. The insurance company is required to make payment within three days after you supply proof of loss. If the company fails to do so, it must pay 2 percent interest per month on the unpaid amounts and reasonable legal fees if it was necessary for you to retain a lawyer in order to collect a valid claim.

Objections to No-Fault Insurance

Opponents of no-fault insurance refused to accept the verdict of the legislatures of the states that adopted it. Those opponents tested various aspects of the constitutionality of the no-fault statutes.

The first constitutional objection was that the legislature took away from individual plaintiffs "vested property rights." The courts rejected that argument.

The second objection was that when legal remedies are taken away from victims of automobile accidents, the legislature must provide an adequate substitute for the legal remedy removed. In some courts the argument was raised that the legislature cannot abrogate a common law cause of action without providing an adequate substitute. The courts also rejected that argument, holding that it cannot be known whether a victim will recover anything at all from a lawsuit; his own negligence might play a role in contributing to his injuries and he might not be able to prove fault on the part of the defendant.

The third objection raised in court tests was that the "threshold" provision of the no-fault laws prevented injured people from recovering anything for pain and suffering. The courts, however, said that while the plaintiff could not recover for pain and suffering if he failed to meet the threshold test, he would not in a lawsuit be able to recover anything if his negligence contributed to the injury complained of.

A fourth objection was that the no-fault statutes violated the equal protection provisions of the U.S. Constitution. Some statutes required coverage for only certain types of vehicles and discriminated among motor vehicle owners and among accident victims. This objection was also overruled by the courts. One court held: "There is a reasonable basis upon which the legislature may exclude these types of vehicles (taxis, motorcycles, buses, and commercial vehicles) from coverage of the Act. Merely because the legislature has seen fit to remedy a perceived evil in one area, it is not compelled to extend that remedy to all areas in which it might be applied."

A fifth objection was that the statutes discriminated against the poor, who receive less expensive treatment than the rich. The "threshold" provision requires that a certain amount be expended for medical treatment before a person can sue. The court said: "No merit to this claim."

No-fault opponents succeeded on one point. They successfully contended that the provisions of the law which allowed suits for pain and suffering only upon the showing of an appropriate type of injury were arbitrary and unconstitutional because some very serious injuries did not fall within any of the specified categories. A Florida court said that the category of injuries described as a "fracture to a weight-bearing bone or a compound comminuted displaced or compressed fracture" was not a valid classification. This meant that a person who suffered a broken toe, for example, would be allowed to sue for his pain and suffering only if the fracture were considered a permanent injury.

Illinois and New Hampshire found in favor of the opponents of the no-fault statutes and decided that certain provisions of the law took away from claimants the right to a trial by jury. These provisions were held unconstitutional.

A PRACTICAL ALTERNATIVE TO NO-FAULT INSURANCE

A professor at the University of Virginia Law School has been an early champion of "no-fault" insurance. Professor Jeffry O'Connell says that thirteen cents of every insurance premium dollar is spent on fighting over legal liability in accidents, but that only twenty-three cents of every insurance dollar is awarded to the tiny number of victims for pain and suffering.

Under his proposed no-fault system, drivers would have the choice of either sticking with their present liability insurance coverage, or buying cheaper no-fault policies. The no-fault policies would guarantee compensation for economic losses up to the limits of the coverage. Any insured person could buy as much coverage as he wishes.

There are those who object to the plan, including plaintiffs' trial lawyers, and including Ralph Nader, the consumer advocate. He wants no part of any change giving drivers a financial incentive to limit their rights in court.

Professor O'Connell says that the best hope for giving drivers a choice lies within Washington, through federal legislation. However, conservatives are leery of federal legislation that requires states to do anything in particular about automobile insurance.

Dram Shop Rule

The Dram Shop Rule imposes liability on anybody (a liquor store proprietor, a tavern owner, a bartender, the host or other person serving liquor) who serves liquor to a person who is obviously intoxicated or likely to be intoxicated, who causes injury to another person because of the intoxication. At least thirty-eight states have laws incorporating the Dram Shop Rule or Principle.

NEGLIGENCE CLAIMS AGAINST OWNERS OR TENANTS OF REAL ESTATE

A person who maintains, controls, and operates a building must do so in such a way as not to cause injury to those lawfully within the premises. If a defective condition exists—such as torn doormats, worn staircases or stair railings, accumulations of refuse, weak ceilings or roofs, or damaged flooring—and a person is injured thereby, the owner of or person in control of or manager of the building is liable. One who constructs a building must likewise do so in such a manner as not to injure other persons. A landlord relinquishes control of those parts of the premises he lets (leases, rents), but may be required by statute to keep them in repair. Those portions of the premises which are used by all or most of the tenants, such as hallways, vestibules, or plumbing or heating equipment, are under the control of the landlord.

There are distinctions among the various people who use certain premises. To *invitees* (those who are in the building at the express or implied invitation of the landlord or tenants), the landlord owes care and good judgment in maintaining and managing the property. Another class of persons that the landlord permits to enter the premises is *licensees*, those people who are lawfully in the building on their own business. Still another class of persons that enters the building is *trespassers*; such persons enter the premises without permission of any kind.

Rule Concerning Trespassers

In cases of negligence to trespassers, the general rule is that the owner or tenant of real estate is not liable for harm to trespassers even if his property is in an unsafe condition. This is because our economic system is based on private ownership, and the courts have considered it a sound policy to allow a person to use his own land in his own way without the burden of watching for and protecting those who come on the land without permission.

In order to catch foxes and other small animals, Bly places traps on a tract of woodland that he owns. A trespasser on the land catches his foot in one of the animal traps and is injured. Bly is not liable to the trespasser even though he could have posted signs in the woods warning trespassers of the danger of the traps.

There are three main exceptions to the rule that a landowner is not liable to a trespasser. These exceptions involve discovery or knowledge of the trespassing and "attractive nuisance."

Discovery of Trespasser

If the presence of the trespasser is discovered and the landowner (or tenant) has an opportunity to avoid injury to the trespasser and fails to do so, he may be liable for injuries sustained by the trespasser.

Joe Carlisle, while trespassing upon the right-of-way of the XYZ Railroad Company, walks through a deep cut only wide enough to permit the passage of a single train. The engineer of an approaching freight train sees Joe but thinks that Joe has enough space to get out of the way of the train. The engineer misjudges the space, and Joe is struck down. The railroad company is liable because, even though he was a trespasser, the engineer knew of Joe's presence and should have stopped the train (used reasonable care) before it hit him.

Knowledge of Frequent Trespassing

When the land owner (or tenant) knows that trespassers frequently intrude upon a particular part of his property, he is required to exercise reasonable care in avoiding injury to trespassers.

The RST Railroad Company knows that many inhabitants of Collarville constantly use a part of the railroad right-of-way as a shortcut to their homes. The path they have worn is so close to where the tracks curve sharply that it is dangerous to use while trains are passing. Aridale is walking along the path when an electric locomotive of the railroad company zooms around the curve at high speed in the same direction. Aridale is hit and seriously injured. The railroad company is liable to Aridale for damages.

Attractive Nuisance

The courts in about two-thirds of the states have adopted the rule that a landowner is liable for bodily harm to trespassing children if they are injured by some structure or artificial condition maintained on land, providing the landowner knows that (1) the place is one where children are likely to trespass, (2) the condition or object is attractive to children, (3) the children are attracted to the object, and (4) the owner fails to use reasonable care and the children are not contributorily negligent. The following is an illustration of this doctrine of attractive nuisance:

The Florida and Mexico Railroad Company maintains a turntable at a point on its unfenced land close to a highway that young children constantly cross. The railroad knows the children are in the habit of playing on the turntable, but a simple locking device, which would make it difficult for the children to set the turntable in motion, is never installed. One day the children set the turntable in motion, and one of them is caught in it and seriously hurt. The railroad company is liable for the injury to the child.

The courts of a number of leading industrial states have rejected the doctrine of attractive nuisance as a piece of sentimental humanitarianism that places undue burden on landowners and industry. On the other hand, in those jurisdictions which have refused to recognize the doctrine, resistance to it is lessening and the courts sometimes establish legal liability in favor of a child trespasser.

Rule Concerning Licensees

A landlord ordinarily is not liable to a licensee. The distinction between liability to licensees and trespassers is that to the licensee the landlord owes no duty of active care, whereas to the trespasser he owes only the duty of not intentionally inflicting injury on him. A landowner or tenant is liable for injuries caused to licensees only if (1) he knows his land is dangerous and that it involves an unreasonable risk to licensees or (2) he invites or permits licensees to use the land without first having taken reasonable care to make the condition safe or without warning the licensees of the danger.

A landowner or anyone in possession of land, such as a tenant, would be liable for injuries to a social guest only if he is aware that a dangerous condition imperils his guest.

If, in the example given below, John had not known about the dangerous condition of the bridge, he would not be liable to Jim because his duty is only to warn of known dangers. But a landowner owes his guest no absolute duty to prepare a safe place for his coming, nor to inspect his land to uncover possible dangers.

John invites his friend Jim to have dinner with him at his country place. John knows that a bridge in his driveway over which Jim must pass is dangerous but that the condition is not apparent. John has not warned Jim. The bridge gives way under Jim's car causing him serious harm. John is liable to Jim.

Rule Concerning Business Visitors

The basic distinction between the landowner's (or tenant's) duty to a social guest and to a business visitor is that the landowner (or tenant) must take reasonable care to discover dangerous conditions on the premises and either make them safe or warn his business visitor of the dangerous conditions; to the social guest or the licensee, the landowner is responsible only for disclosing to his guest dangerous defects which happen to be known to him.

Since in our country the business guest receives greater protection than the social guest, there seems to be a fundamental obligation that the possessor of land owes to one from whom he expects to derive a profit or economic benefit. The courts are very liberal in defining a business visitor and have held that customers, those who attend a free lecture or meeting or who enter a place of amusement on a pass, those who go into a store to use a telephone or into a bank to change a bill or go with the owner of an automobile to get his car at a parking lot or garage are all business visitors. Once a building is open to the public, anyone who has a legitimate reason for entering the premises is regarded as a business visitor. A business visitor does not actually have to engage in a commercial transaction, such as making a purchase in a store. But, theoretically, anyone who comes into a store merely to loaf or to get out of the rain is not a business visitor: to be a business visitor he must be on a legitimate errand in the store.

Although the rule concerning business visitors is liberal, there are limitations. There is no liability for harm resulting from dangerous conditions about which the owner or tenant does not know or which an inspection would not uncover. But if he knows of or creates the dangerous condition, liability may ensue.

Jane enters a supermarket and bruises her leg and ruins her stockings on a crate of produce that the department head has been slow in cleaning up. Jane is a business visitor, and the store is liable for the failure to use reasonable care in providing a safe passageway for her.

Drummer, a guest at the Valley Hotel, is injured when he turns a corner in a slippery corridor where the cleaning people are mopping up. He may recover from the hotel because its employees failed to warn him of the slippery floor.

NEW TRENDS REGARDING TRESPASSERS, LICENSEES AND INVITEES

We have stated the rules of liability of a property owner to trespassers, licensees, and business and social invitees that are accepted by most American courts. However, there is a trend on the part of courts to depart from those classifications as being ill-suited to an industrial, urban society. These later interpretations hold that the label or classification of an entrant on another's property is not important. The test, they say, should be: (1) Did the owner of the property know of the dangerous condition? and (2) Did he take steps to correct it?

Liability of Landlords under Leases to Persons Injured on the Property

Although a landlord usually is not liable for bodily injuries sustained by his tenant or others owing to a dangerous condition which develops *after* the tenant takes possession. The four conditions which are exceptions to this rule are discussed below.

1) Preexisting Conditions or Covenant to Repair

   The landlord is subject to liability for bodily injuries caused to his tenant or others if a condition of disrepair existed before the tenant took possession or if the landlord agreed by covenant in the lease or otherwise to keep the premises in repair.

   Carter leases an apartment to Smith, with the agreement that he will keep it in good repair if Smith notifies him of such need. Smith notifies Carter that the dining room ceiling needs repairing. One night the ceiling falls and injures guests of the Smiths. Carter is liable if he had ample time to make the repairs.

2) Inherent Defect in Leased Premises

   A landlord who conceals from his tenant a condition involving risk of bodily harm to persons coming onto the land is subject to the liability for whatever harm results.

   In leasing a dwelling to Simkins, Roberts conceals the fact that termites have weakened supporting floor beams of the house. Simkins, on taking possession, gives a housewarming party, during which the floor gives way, throwing everybody into the cellar. Roberts is liable to Simkins and his guests.

3)   Use of Premises by Large Number of Persons

A landlord who leases real property for use by a large number of persons may be subject to liability for bodily injuries caused by a dangerous condition existing when the tenant took possession if the landlord knows of this condition and realizes that there might be unreasonable risk to patrons of the tenant.

The Island Amusement Company leases its baseball park to the Eagle Baseball Club for the season. The lease contains a covenant by the tenant to make necessary repairs. Two months after the Eagle Club takes possession, a section of the bleachers collapses, injuring a spectator. The collapse was caused by rotted supports, which a reasonable inspection would have disclosed to either owner or lessee. The Island Amusement Company is liable to the spectator, in spite of the baseball club's covenant to repair the premises.

4)   Retention of Control of Part of Premises

A landlord who leases part of a building and retains in his possession another part that the tenants are entitled to use is liable to his tenants or others for injury caused by a dangerous condition in the part of the premises in his control.

Scrooge leases apartments in a six-family apartment house. A tread on one of the steps of the common stairway of the apartment house is loose and needs repairing. While descending the stairway, one of the tenants catches her foot on the broken tread, falls and breaks her ankle. The landlord is liable to the woman for failure to repair the stairway.

NEGLIGENCE CLAIMS AGAINST PERSONS SUPPLYING PROPERTY FOR USE OF OTHERS

A manufacturer or seller of merchandise is required to conduct his business so as not to injure consumers. This applies to articles for human consumption as well as to other products.

Manufacturers

A manufacturer who fails to exercise reasonable care in the manufacture of merchandise may be subject to liability for bodily harm resulting from his negligence.

The Royal Motor Co. incorporates in its automobile defective wheels made by the Disc Wheel Co. Desmond buys one of the cars through an independent distributor. While he is driving it, a wheel collapses, and the car swerves and hits and injures Applebaum. Desmond and Applebaum can recover damages from the Royal Motor Co., the Disc Wheel Co., and the distributor.

Sellers of Merchandise

The American courts have almost entirely broken away from the old rule of *caveat emptor* ("let the buyer beware"), by which the seller of merchandise assumed no responsibility for defects in the merchandise. Today, it is the seller's well-established duty to make sure that the merchandise cannot harm the buyer. Moreover, the liability of a seller to a buyer for negligence is largely superseded by the strict liability for breach of warranty. Nowadays most storekeepers practically guarantee to the buyer the quality and safe condition of goods. The provisions of the Uniform Commercial Code (see Chapter 21) supersede to a great extent the rules of negligence concerning claims made directly by a buyer against a seller. In every sale of merchandise there is an implied warranty made by the seller to the buyer that the goods are of merchantable quality and suitable to the purpose for which sold.

Mrs. Stevens buys from a hardware store an insecticide bomb and places it on the shelf in her kitchen. It explodes, and Mrs. Stevens is injured. The hardware store that sold Mrs. Stevens the insecticide bomb is liable for her injuries, even though it had no knowledge of the defective condition of the bomb. If Mrs. Stevens sues, the hardware store must in turn seek recourse from the manufacturer of the bomb.

A U.S. court of appeal has ruled that regulatory approval of a product largely shields the product's makers from lawsuits seeking damages for injuries to users. The ruling also bars more aggressive state regulation on lawsuits based on state law.

Although the case only applies to an FDA approval of a medical device, other courts may apply the same reasoning (and shield) to federal regulatory approval of an array of products. This could sharply curtail suits by plaintiffs who allege "negligent design" on "failure to warn of side effects."

Strict Liability

The legal doctrine of strict liability is rapidly expanding. It means that an injured person may recover against the manufacturer or seller of an inherently dangerous or defective product even though the manufacturer was not negligent and even though the injured person had no dealings or legal relationship with either the manufacturer or the seller.

The courts of many states have been liberal in recognizing the rule of strict liability as a means of providing greater consumer protection. Examples of products to which strict liability applies are foodstuffs, items intended for bodily use (such as cosmetics), automobiles, building supplies, and drugs.

This rule applies even though the seller has used all possible care in the preparation and sale of the product; the injured party in making a claim does not have to prove that the seller was negligent.

An electric hot water heater exploded and substantially destroyed a house. The trial court held that several components of the heater were defective and malfunctioned, and it held the manufacturer liable for damage to the house.

Formerly, people using dynamite or other explosives for blasting were immune from damage claims of neighboring property owners provided that rocks or other material were not cast upon the damaged premises. In 1893 a court stated, "Public policy is promoted by building up of towns and cities and improvement of property. Any unnecessary restraint on freedom of action of a property owner hinders this." Most states have changed this rule and hold a blaster absolutely responsible for vibration damage caused to neighboring property, even though the blaster is not negligent.

In 1969 the New York State Court of Appeals overturned the 1893 rule and granted an award of damages to a garage owner whose property was wrecked by a dynamite blast about 125 feet away. This is part of the modern concept of absolute liability without proof of negligence.

Nuisance

Nuisance is a term that has been involved in much legal confusion. There are two types: A *public nuisance* is one of a miscellaneous group of minor criminal offenses that obstruct or cause inconvenience or damage to the public. A *private nuisance* is unreasonable interference with the interests of an individual in the use or enjoyment of land. Such nuisance requires substantial harm, as distinguished from a trespass, which may consist of a mere technicality. A nuisance may be intentional or negligent, or it may result from an unusually hazardous activity for which the law imposes strict liability. The term is vague and has been applied indiscriminately to such inconveniences as a foul smell coming from a manufacturing plant and a cockroach found in food. A nuisance used to be considered an independent tort or legal wrong, but today there is no liability for nuisance unless an individual's rights have been intentionally invaded or one has been negligent or has been engaged in an unusually hazardous activity.

STRUCTURED SETTLEMENTS

As jury verdicts and judgments have increased, a new development in personal injury claims has come into use; it is known as a "structured settlement." A structured settlement may occur in a case of very serious injuries or death where it is not practical or necessary to make one payment to cover all damages; hence, for example, the structured settlement may be for $2 million, with a lump sum payment of $750,000 and the balance spread over a period of years. Generally, defendants (particularly insurance companies) can better finance structured settlements, and the injured party may be better off with staggered payments over a specified time period.

9

WILLS

A will is a written instrument by means of which a person makes provision for the disposal of his property to take effect upon his death. A will has no legal effect on property mentioned in the will until the death of the testator.

Unless he is a lawyer, no one should draw his own will. The old saying, "A man who acts as his own lawyer has a fool for a client," is certainly true for the person who attempts to draw his own will. When an individual becomes aware of the complicated problems connected with settling the estates of deceased persons, he usually realizes the need for a will.

NECESSITY FOR MAKING A WILL

Unless a person is positive that he is going to die a pauper, he should make a will. The one to consult in drawing a will is neither the person in the stationery store who sells printed forms for wills nor an accountant, nor a banker, nor a so-called estate planner, but a lawyer.

Too many persons assume that "the law takes care of things without a will." The laws of the states do provide for distribution of an individual's property on his death, but not always in the manner he would have preferred. (See the discussion of descent and distribution, pp. 134–135.) In one state the deceased's wife may receive one-third of his estate and his one-year-old baby may get two-thirds if he dies without leaving a will. According to the laws of another state, a man who dies without a will and leaves most of his property in real estate may actually leave his widow only one-third of the life use of the real estate. In still another state, a man may die *intestate* (without a will), and his widow may be shocked to find that outside of $5,000 she will receive only one-half his property and his parents, though wealthy, will receive the other half.

Too often, married persons believe that they can avoid the necessity for making a will by having all property jointly held. However, there are reasons, among them tax pitfalls, why jointly owned property does not adequately solve all estate problems.

MAKING A VALID WILL

The privileges of making a will, or "speaking after death," is extended by law to persons who have reached the age of maturity and who are of sound mind: The person making the will must understand the nature and purpose of the will and the nature and extent of the property bequeathed. All wills except nuncupative wills must be written. All property owned by a *testator* (a man who makes a will) or a *testatrix* (a woman who makes a will), regardless of its nature or location, may be disposed of in a will.

TYPES OF WILLS

A *holographic will* is one that the testator writes, dates, and signs entirely in his own handwriting. Roughly half of the states recognize holographic wills as valid for various limited purposes.

A *nuncupative will* is one declared orally by the testator in his last illness or in contemplation of death and is generally limited to soldiers in actual service or seamen at sea. It is not required to be in writing nor to be formally attested. Most states limit nuncupative wills to a small amount of personal property varying from $50 to $500 in value. Where recognized, the oral will must be reduced to writing within a very short time (from three to thirty days) after it is spoken and must also be very quickly admitted to probate. A nuncupative will is so restricted in scope that it is not practical and should not be attempted. Thus, it is advisable to see a lawyer and have a will drawn in the proper way.

Although joint, mutual, and reciprocal wills are discussed by legal writers, these types of wills are used infrequently and are only of passing interest. A *joint will* is a single testamentary instrument containing the wills of two or more persons and jointly executed by them. *Mutual wills* are the separate wills of two or more persons that are reciprocal in their provisions and are generally executed in accordance with an agreement between these persons to dispose of their property to each other or to third persons in a particular manner. (The agreements relating to mutual wills and the execution of mutual wills themselves are full of technical pitfalls, and for that reason are seldom resorted to.) *Reciprocal wills* are those in which each of two or more testators makes a testamentary disposition in favor of the other or others.

Essentials of a Valid Will

The requisites of a valid will are that it be an instrument in writing (except in the case of a nuncupative will); that it be executed as prescribed by the statute of the particular state; that it be intended as a will by the person making it; that it dispose of the person's property (to take effect) after his death; and that it be revocable during the lifetime of the maker.

The test of whether or not a particular instrument disposing of property is a will (as distinguished from a deed, mortgage, contract, bond, bill of sale, or trust instrument) is whether the person making the instrument intended it to take effect upon his death and to be revocable until that time. The validity of a will is generally determined by the law of the state of the testator's last domicile (the place that he intended to be his permanent residence). When real estate is disposed of by a will, its validity is determined by the law of the place where the real estate is located.

Form and Content of a Will

It is usually not necessary that any particular form or particular words be used in making a will; the form is not so important as the intent of the testator. The will must be worded with sufficient clarity to enable the court to determine from the will itself just what the testator intended.

Execution of a Will

A will must be executed with all the formalities relating to signatures, witnesses, and the like required by the laws of the state. The purpose of the statutory requirements for the execution of wills is to guard against mistake, undue influence, fraud, or deception.

Generally, it is essential to the validity of a will that it be signed by the testator. The use of a mark by the testator sometimes will suffice. Few states' statutes require no more than that the will be in writing and be signed. In such cases it does not matter where the testator's signature is placed—it may be in the margin or at the top of the page—as long as it is clearly intended to be the signature to the will. Other state statutes require that the signature be at the end of the will; so strict is the rule in these states, that if the signature is in the middle or at the side or any place but the physical end (bottom) of the will, the will may be held invalid.

The attestation and subscription by witnesses, where required, must be in accordance with the requirements of the statute. Some states require two witnesses, others three. Some states require that the execution be notarized. The witnesses should be disinterested persons, not beneficiaries. Witnesses should attest and sign at the request of the testator, who should make it known that the instrument to be executed by him is his last will and testament. Making it known that this instrument is a will is called "publication" and is required by many states. Most states require the testator to sign the will in the presence of the witnesses and the witnesses to sign in the presence of the testator and of each other. The witnesses may also sign a certificate known as an "attestation clause," declaring the truth of the facts and circumstances attending the execution of the will. Such a certificate is useful and customary, but it is not essential to the validity of the will.

Legatees and Devisees

A gift of personal property in a will is called a *legacy* or *bequest*. The person who receives such a gift is called a *legatee*. A gift of real estate in a will is called a *devise*. The person who receives a gift of real estate is called a *devisee*.

Disinheritance of Husband or Wife or Relatives

A testator may disinherit his relatives and in a very few states his wife; a testatrix may likewise disinherit her relatives, but rarely her husband. There is a popular notion that in order to disinherit a child or other close relative, the maker of a will must give the child one dollar or a token gift. This is not literally true. The requirement of the law is that the testator know or is aware of who are the natural objects of his bounty. In drawing a will, some lawyers feel that it is wise to mention the relatives who are disinherited and, sometimes, to give a tactful reason for disinheritance (in the belief that tact is required, because otherwise the disinherited relative may become indignant and contest the will).

Although children usually may also be disinherited, most states provide that children who are born after the making of a will but before the death of the testator inherit as though there were no will, unless it appears that the testator intended otherwise.

Some states still use the common-law rights of dower and curtesy (see p. 135) and provide that even though a husband or wife be disinherited, he or she may still have these rights. Such rights, however, are often vague and unsatisfactory. In most states the surviving spouse, if dissatisfied with the provisions of the will, may within a short time after it is probated file a notice of election to take the same share to which he or she would be entitled under law if his or her spouse had died without leaving a will.

Limitations on Charitable Bequests. Although 46 states have no specific limitations on charitable bequests, a handful of states have specific limitations either limiting the proportion of the estate that may be given to charity or voiding the bequest if made within a specified time period prior to death. For example, under Florida law such a bequest may be voided if the will is executed less than six months before death unless the same or similar bequest was made in an earlier will.

Age requirements. In forty-seven states a person must be eighteen years of age in order to make a will. In the balance of the states, the age requirements vary: in Wyoming, it is nineteen; in Georgia, it is fourteen; in Louisiana, it is sixteen. However, there are exceptions; for example, in Idaho, Iowa, Nebraska, New Hampshire, and South Carolina, a lawfully married minor may make a will, and in Indiana and Texas, a minor who is a member of the armed forces may make a written will.

Number and Age of Witnesses. All states require that there be witnesses to a written will (other than a holographic will). The vast majority of states require at least two witnesses; however, Vermont, for example, requires three witnesses.

The age requirement of the witness varies; usually the witness must be eighteen years of age, although many states simply require that the witnesses be "competent." Of course in those state permitting a person under eighteen to make a valid will, usually the witness also may be under eighteen years of age.

It is recommended that there be three witnesses to a will, in the event of the death or unavailability of one of them.[1]

Laws of Louisiana Governing Wills. The law of Louisiana is based on Roman law, as codified in the French and Spanish Civil codes. It is unique particularly in the field of estate law. For example, Louisiana has the law of "forced heirship." Prior to 1991 children could never be deprived of their right to inherit. (A 1991 amendment creates three very limited exceptions to this rule.) When there are children of the deceased, only the following portions of the estate may be disposed of by will: Three-fourths if there is one child and one-half if there are two or more children. Although other heirs may be excluded by a mere omission or disinherited without cause, a forced heir may only be deprived of the forced portion or "legitime" by specific disinherison for legal cause. A child may be disinherited if (without later having been forgiven) he has (1) struck or raised his hand to strike the parent; (2) been guilty toward the parent of cruelty, of a crime or grievous injury; (3) attempted to take the life of either parent: (4) accused the parent of any capital crime except high treason; (5) having the means to afford it, refused sustenance to a parent; (6) neglected to take care of a parent who became insane; (7) refused if able to afford it to ransom a parent when detained in captivity; (8) used any act or violence or coercion to hinder a parent from making a will; (9) having the means, refused to become surety for a parent in order to take time out of prison; (10) being a minor, married without the consent of his or her parents; (11) been convicted of a felony authorizing life imprisonment or death as a penalty; and (12) failed without just cause to communicate with parent for two years. The testator must express the reason he disinherits the child. A forced heir who is denied his right to his full forced portion has the right to reduce the excessive donations at the death of the donor. This right is not available to the forced heir's creditors but is available to his trustee in bankruptcy. (In effect since July 1, 1990, only children under age 23 and children subject to being interdicted will be "forced heirs.")

WILLS, STATE BY STATE

State	Holographic (Handwritten Unwitnessed)	Effect of Testamentary Gift to Attesting Witness	Validity of Will Executed Outside of State	Incorporated by Reference
Alabama	Not valid, unless its execution complies with the law of the place where the will was executed or testator was domiciled at time of execution or at time of death	Will is not invalid because the will is signed by an interested witness	Will is valid if executed in compliance with Alabama law or if its execution complies with the law, at the time of the execution, of the place where the will is executed or with the law of the place where, at the time of execution or the time of death, the testator is domiciled	Any writing in existence when a will is executed may be incorporated by reference
Alaska	Valid	Will is not invalid because the will is signed by an interested witness	Will executed outside of state in accordance with law of place where executed has same force as if executed in accordance with law of state	No limitation
Arizona	Valid	Will is not invalid because the will is signed by an interested witness	Ancillary probate generally necessary. Valid if valid in state where executed. May be informally probated.	Any writing in existence when a will is executed may be incorporated by reference if will manifests this intent sufficiently to permit its identification. In addition, a will may refer to a written statement or list to dispose of items of tangible personal property.
Arkansas	Valid, but must be established by the evidence of three disinterested witnesses	Does not invalidate will, unless the will is also attested to by two qualified disinterested witnesses, and interested witness forfeits so much of the provision made for him as exceeds his intestate share	Will executed outside state in manner prescribed by law of place where executed or by law of testator's domicile is valid	Any writing in existence when will is executed may be incorporated by reference if the language of the will manifests that intent. Also a written list to dispose of certain items of tangible personal property. This must either be in the handwriting of the testator or signed by him.
California	Valid	Will is not invalid. If there are two other disinterested witnesses, the interested witnesses may take the devise.	A written will is valid if its execution complies with: (1) the provisions of California law; (2) the law at the time of execution of the place where the will is executed; or (3) the law of the place where at the time of execution or at the time of death the testator is domiciled	A writing in existence when a will is executed may be incorporated in the will
Colorado	Valid	Will is not invalid because will is signed by interested witness	If executed according to Colorado law, complies with law of place where at time of execution or death testator is domiciled	Any writing in existence when will is executed. Tangible personal property may be disposed of by written statement or list referred to in will if in handwriting of testator or signed by testator.
Connecticut	Not valid if executed in Connecticut. Valid if made outside of state and according to the laws of the state or country where executed.	Void unless witness or spouse is an heir of the testator, or unless will is legally attested without such witness's signature	Valid if executed in compliance with laws of state or country where executed	—

State				
Delaware	Void	Valid	Valid if executed in compliance with law of place where executed	Writing may be incorporated by reference if document in existence (even though later amended). Writings related to the disposition of tangible personal property may be incorporated by reference, so long as the writing is signed by the testator or handwritten by him.
District of Columbia	Not recognized	Void except if the witness legatee may take intestate share	Must be executed in accordance with D.C. law to be admitted to probate in District of Columbia	Permits "pour-over" to a preexisting trust or a contemporaneously executed trust agreement
Florida	Not recognized. However, if will refers to a separate writing signed by the testator, sufficient to dispose of items of tangible personal property.	Will is not invalid because signed by an interested witness	A will (other than a holographic or nuncupative will) executed by a nonresident is valid. Valid at the time of execution under the place of execution.	Permitted if writing is in existence at the time the will is executed also; a separate writing which is referenced in a will can dispose of tangible personal property and may be disposed of by separate writing
Georgia	Not recognized	Witness is competent, but legacy or devise is void	Valid if in conformity with Georgia law. However, foreign will bequeathing Georgia personalty must be executed and attested under laws of the state or country of testator's residence at death to be probated in Georgia	Permitted as long as documents were in existence before execution of will and description is sufficiently clear to leave their identity free from doubt
Hawaii	Not recognized except for foreign wills admitted to probate	Interest does not disqualify a person as a witness, nor does it invalidate the will	Written will valid if execution complies with law at time of execution of place where executed, or law at time of execution of testator's domicile or residence	Any writing in existence when a will is executed may be incorporated by reference if the language of the will manifests this intent
Idaho	Valid	Will is not invalid because the will is signed by an interested witness	A written will is valid if executed in compliance with Idaho law, or if its execution complies with the law at the time of execution of the place where the will is executed or the law of the place where at the time of execution or at the time of death the testator is domiciled	Writing in existence when a will is executed may be incorporated by reference
Illinois	Not valid	Interested witnesses are deprived of any interest under will, except so much as does not exceed amount witness would be entitled to were will not established, but not so deprived if the will is duly attested by two other witnesses	Valid if executed in accordance with law of Illinois, of testator's domicile or of place of execution	Permitted if paper in existence when the will is executed and reasonably identified
Indiana	Not valid	Subscribing witness whose testimony is required to prove will may only take intestate's share.	Valid if executed in accordance with law of place of execution, or with law of domicile of testator at time of execution or at time of death	Permitted, if in existence at the time of execution of will, provided the will clearly identifies the writing. (Trust may be subsequently amended.)
Iowa	Not recognized, except if executed outside Iowa and valid in the state of execution	If interested witness essential, limited to share by intestate succession	Valid if executed in accordance with law of place of execution or law of domicile	Permitted, if writing (trust) in existence before or concurrently with the will. Tangible personal property may be bequeathed by separate writing dated and signed by testator.

State	Holographic (Handwritten Unwitnessed)	Effect of Testamentary Gift to Attesting Witness	Validity of Will Executed Outside of State	Incorporated by Reference
Kansas	Not recognized	Void except as to intestate's share	Valid if executed in accordance with law of Kansas, place of execution or testator's residence at death	May incorporate as a separate list disposing of personal property. Must be signed by testator. May be in existence at time of death and may be altered by testator after preparation. May adopt by reference any paper or document in existence at time of execution of will.
Kentucky	Recognized	Bequest void as to attesting witness. Also void as to spouse of attesting witness, except as to extent of intestate share.	Will executed with required formalities by a resident may be executed anywhere	Reference in a will to a later writing in regard to disposition of personal property has been held valid. Will to identify the trust which is the subject of a devise.
Louisiana	Recognized. Must be wholly written, dated and signed in the testator's hand.	Except for witnesses to a mystic testament, the legacy to the witness will be declared a nullity	Valid	Prohibited
Maine	Valid	Does not affect validity of will, and an interested witness may take under the will	Valid if executed in accordance with the law at the time of the execution of the place where the will is executed, or of the law of the place where at the time of death the testator is domiciled	Any writing in existence when a will is executed may be incorporated by reference
Maryland	Valid if entirely in handwriting of testator and signed outside the U.S. while serving in the armed services until one year after discharge (if still possessing testamentary capacity)	Valid	Valid if in writing, signed by testator and executed according to law of place where executed, or of testator's domicile or of Maryland	Terms of any writing in existence when will executed
Massachusetts	Not recognized	Gift to subscribing witness or to spouse of such witness is void unless there are two other competent witnesses	Valid if executed in accordance with the law of domicile or place of execution	Any document in existence may be incorporated by reference
Michigan	Valid	Subscribing witness may not take under will unless there are two other competent witnesses except as to intestate's share	Will is valid if executed in compliance with the laws of the state, or with the law at the time of execution of the place where the will is executed, or with the law of the place where at the time of execution or at the time of death the testator is domiciled	A writing in existence when a will is executed may be incorporated by reference
Minnesota	Not recognized	None	Will valid if in accordance with the law of place of execution	Any writing in existence when a will is executed may be incorporated by reference. A will also may refer to a written, signed statement to dispose of tangible personal property.
Mississippi	Recognized	Void if will cannot be proved without testimony of such witness; nevertheless, the witness may take his intestate's share	Valid	Bequest to revocable trust is valid

Missouri	No provision	Will not invalidated because attested by an interested witness, but interested witness shall, unless will is also attested by two disinterested witnesses, forfeit excess of intestate share	Will is valid if executed in compliance with the laws of this state, the laws, as of time of execution, of the place where the will is executed or the laws of the place where, at the time of execution or the time of the testator's death, the testator is domiciled	A devise or bequest may be made by will to a revocable trust which is identified in the will. Items of tangible personal property may be effectively bequeathed by a signed list referenced in the will.
Montana	Valid	Void unless there are two other competent witnesses, but may take intestate's share	Valid if executed in accordance with law of place where executed or where domiciled	Any "writing" in existence at the making of a will may be incorporated by reference, as may be a "separate writing," signed by testator, in existence at death, disposing of tangible personal property
Nebraska	Valid	Interested witness may testify. If there is at least one disinterested witness, provisions for interested witnesses will stand; however, if all witnesses are interested, each is limited to his intestate share, if any.	Written will is valid if valid at time and place of execution or place where at time of execution or time of death testator is domiciled	Any written existence whether or not written trust is identified or whether trust is amendable or revocable
Nevada	Valid	Void unless there are two other competent witnesses	Valid if in writing. Valid where executed or where testator was domiciled.	Written list of items of tangible personal property, not otherwise specifically disposed of by will. In certain instances, the terms of a trust may be incorporated.
New Hampshire	Not recognized	Void, unless there are other witnesses	Valid if executed in accordance with place where executed	No recognition of extraneous writings unless formal will requirements are met
New Jersey	Valid	Gift is valid	Valid if executed in compliance with law of place where executed or with law of place where at time of execution or at time of death the testator was domiciled	A signed statement or list may dispose of tangible personal property
New Mexico	Not recognized	None	Valid if executed in accordance with law of place where executed, where testator is domiciled at time of execution or at the time of his death	A will may refer to a written list to dispose of items of tangible personal property if writing either in handwriting of testator or signed by him. A devise or bequest may be made to the trustee of a trust established or to be established.
New York	Valid if made by mariner at sea, member of armed forces engaged in conflict, etc.	Void if will cannot be proved without testimony of such witness, but witness may receive intestate share	Will valid if executed in accordance with law of New York, the place of execution or the testator's domicile (either at time of execution or death)	Pour-over to existing inter vivos trusts permitted
North Carolina	Valid	Void unless there are two other disinterested witnesses	Will valid as to personal property if executed in accordance with the law of place of execution. As to real property, valid only if executed in accordance with law of North Carolina.	No comprehensive statutory provision but incorporation is a general practice
North Dakota	Valid	Will not invalid because signed by an interested witness	Written will valid if execution complies with the law at the time of execution in the place where the will is executed or law of the place where at the time of execution or time of death the testator is domiciled	Any identifiable writing in existence when the will is executed

State	Holographic (Handwritten Unwitnessed)	Effect of Testamentary Gift to Attesting Witness	Validity of Will Executed Outside of State	Incorporated by Reference
Ohio	Not recognized	Void unless there are two other witnesses, except to the extent of any intestate share of the witness	Valid if executed in accordance with law in force at time of execution in jurisdiction where executed, or law in force in Ohio at time of death or law in force in jurisdiction where testator was domiciled at time of death	An existing document may be incorporated
Oklahoma	Recognized	Void unless there are two other witnesses, but may take intestate's share	Valid if executed according to law of place where made or place of testator's domicile	Separate document may be incorporated into will in existence at time
Oregon	Not recognized	Will attested by an interested witness is not thereby invalidated	Lawfully executed if in writing, signed by or at the direction of the testator and otherwise executed in accordance with the law of Oregon (at the time of execution or at the time of death of the testator); or (domicile of the testator at the time of execution or at the time of his death); or (the place of execution at the time of execution)	May incorporate documents in a will if intent clear in the will
Pennsylvania	Valid	None	Valid if executed in compliance with Pennsylvania law or law of testator's domicile either at the time of execution of will or at time of death	Although there is no statutory authority for incorporation by reference, a devise or bequest may be made to a revocable trust before, concurrently with or after the execution of the will.
Rhode Island	Not recognized except as to soldier or seaman who may dispose of personal estate by holographic will	Void	Valid where executed in manner required by place of execution or of testator's domicile	Devise or bequest may be made to a revocable trust in existence when will executed. No other statutory authority for incorporation by reference.
South Carolina	Not recognized	Void, but such witness or spouse of such witness would be entitled to any intestate share	—	A written document in existence may be incorporated by reference
South Dakota	Valid	Void, unless two other subscribing witnesses. If witness whose share is voided, entitled to intestate share	Valid if executed in accordance with law of place where made or testator's domicile	Doctrine of incorporation is recognized
Tennessee	Valid, if proved by two witnesses	Void except for intestate share, unless there are two disinterested witnesses, and then fully allowed	Valid if executed in accordance with law of place where made or law of testator's domicile at time of execution	Documents then in existence referred to in will
Texas	Valid	Void except for intestate share not exceeding value unless corroborated by a disinterested witness	Valid if valid under Texas law	A writing in existence or document may be incorporated in or made a part of a will by reference
Utah	Valid	Does not invalidate will or provision, but witness who is a legatee or devisee is ordinarily limited to intestate share	A written will is valid if it complies with Utah's requirements for execution, or if it complies with the law at time of execution of the place where executed or of the law of the place where at the time of execution or at the time of death the testator is domiciled	Any writing in existence when a will is executed may be incorporated by reference if the language of the will manifests this intent and describes the writing sufficiently to permit its identification

State			
Vermont	Void except as to heir at law who attests will, or spouse of attesting heir at law, unless there are three other competent witnesses	Valid if executed in accordance with law of place where made or with law of testator's domicile	Trust established or to be established by a third person whether or not amendable, and if identified in the testator's will and executed before or concurrent with the execution of the will, may be incorporated by reference
Virginia	Valid if proved by two disinterested witnesses	Place of execution immaterial if testator is Virginia domiciliary and will meets Virginia requirements	Devise or bequest to educational, charitable or eleemosynary trust may incorporate by reference any written matter or existing document
	Gift is valid (except to prove handwriting of a holographic will, no person is incompetent as a witness because of interest).		
Washington	Not recognized	Valid if executed in accordance with law of place where made or of the testator's domicile	Any existing document may be incorporated by reference. A separate writing in the handwriting of or signed by the testator may be used to dispose of tangible personal property
	Gift void unless there are two other competent witnesses; if void, witness may still receive intestate share		
West Virginia	Recognized	Valid as to personal property if executed according to law of domicile; valid as to real property only if valid in state	An existing document may be incorporated by reference
	Void except for intestate's share		
Wisconsin	Not recognized	A will is validly executed if it is in writing and executed in accordance with the law of the place where the will is executed or the law of the place where the testator is domiciled at the time of execution of the will	Will may incorporate the language of another existing document by reference
	Will is not invalidated but, unless the will is also signed by two disinterested witnesses, interested witness or spouse may only receive an intestate share		
Wyoming	Recognized	A will is valid in Wyoming if it meets Wyoming requirements for execution, or execution complies with law at the time of execution of place where executed or execution complies with law of place where at time of execution or at time of death testator is domiciled, has a place of abode or is a national	Doctrine of incorporation by reference for pre-existing documents
	No subscribing witness may derive any benefit from the will unless there are two disinterested and competent witnesses, but if the witness would be an heir in intestacy, the witness may receive the lesser of intestate share or bequest in the will		
Virgin Islands	Void unless two other competent witnesses; however, witnesses entitled to intestate share	—	—
	If made by soldier or sailor in actual military or naval service, valid if reduced to writing within one year of discharge, if of testamentary capacity		

Factors Invalidating a Will

A will is invalid when the person making the will was incompetent to do so, when fraud or undue influence was exercised upon the testator, or when the formal statutory requirements for execution were not fulfilled.

A person is incompetent to make a will when he or she is under the lawful age or suffering from a mental disability, both of which may prevent him from understanding the nature and purpose of a will and from comprehending generally the nature and extent of his property and from recollecting his relationship with the natural objects of his bounty. The mental capacity of testators has been questioned in numerous cases. Despite this, no particular degree of mental capacity has been established. The existence of mental capacity or incapacity must be determined from the facts and circumstances in each case.

Fraud, mistake, or undue influence is a ground of objection to the validity of a will. In order to invalidate a will, fraud must be such as to induce the testator to make a disposition of his property that he would not otherwise have made, and he must actually be deceived. Mistakes that will defeat the intention of a testator, such as errors concerning what the will contains, are invalidating.

Undue influence is a common ground for avoiding a will. The improper influence must so overpower and subjugate the mind of the testator that it destroys his free will and makes him express the will of another rather than his own. The courts have said that it is impossible to define with precision what constitutes undue influence. Mere influence over a testator is not sufficient to invalidate a will. It has been said that the essential elements of proof of undue influence are (1) a susceptible testator (such as an aging, ill, or infirm person); (2) another's opportunity and effort to exert improper influence; (3) an effort for an improper purpose; (4) the fact that the improper influence was exercised or attempted; and (5) the result showing the effect of the unlawful influence.

In most states, when a beneficiary in a will is also witness to a will, the bequest or devise to the witness becomes invalidated. The witness forfeits the provision in the will for his benefit, unless he is a blood relative; then he may still take the share that would be his under law if there were no will.

In a few states the voiding of a devise or bequest is extended to a spouse if he or she is an attesting witness. Some states insist that the bequest to the subscribing witness be void unless there are two (or in some states three) competent additional witnesses by which the will can be proved.

Proving a Will or Probate

The mere existence of a will may mean nothing, for it may not be a valid will, or it may not be the last will. Also, it may have basic defects, which prevent it from ever being used as a will. The term *probate*, as applied to wills, means the proof and establishment of the validity of a will.

Whenever the executor (or the beneficiaries) wishes to establish the validity of a will, he institutes in a proper court a probate proceeding—an application to establish a document as the authoritative, final, and official will of the deceased person. The probate of a will is a judicial proceeding in which the heirs (those persons who would inherit the decedent's property if there were no will) receive notice that the will has been filed in court and that the court will be asked to establish it as the valid will of the decedent. The heirs are required at this time (or, in some states, within a specified period of time after the application for probate) either to consent to or to oppose the probate. They are given this opportunity to be heard, to say whether they have any objections to the probate, or to show cause in court why the will should not be admitted to probate. Only heirs or next of kin or beneficiaries under a prior will may oppose the probate proceeding.

If the probate is not contested, the judge of the probate court will hear the testimony of the witnesses to the will concerning its proper execution; then, if the will complies with the statutory requirements, it will be admitted to probate. If the will and the probate proceedings are contested, the court conducts a hearing and decides whether or not there are valid legal objections to the will.

Interpreting and Construing Wills

Often the meaning of a will, the intention of a testator, is ambiguous; sometimes there are questions concerning the identification of property and persons. Whenever he desires, an interested party may ask the probate court to *construe* and *interpret* a will. In a construction proceeding it is the court's duty first to examine the will and then, if possible, to determine its meaning. (The court must be careful not to remake or rewrite the will according to its idea of equity and justice.) In some cases the court also takes evidence to aid in construction of a will. By applying the rules of construction and taking evidence, the court seeks to uncover and interpret the intention of the testator and, if it is not contrary to an established law or to public policy, to give the intention effect.

Updating a Will

The time lag between execution of a will and the testator's death often creates serious problems because the family facts are so different at the time of execution from what they are at the time of death. The only remedies for such problems are intelligent estate planning and a continual, periodic change of wills as needed to bring them up to date.

Revoking a Will

A will may be revoked by an act of the testator or by operation of law. In order to revoke a will, the testator must have the same mental capacity as is required to make a will: He must be mentally competent. (A person may make a will while he is in full possession of his mental faculties and thereafter suffer a mental incapacity that prevents him from making a valid revocation of his will.)

A testator may revoke his will (1) by a subsequent writing that may be a later will or a codicil; (2) by an instrument other than a will containing an express declaration of absolute revocation; or (3) by mutilation, cancellation, or destruction of the will. Mutilation, cancellation, or destruction may be by tearing, cutting, burning, obliterating, or other physical means and may be done under the testator's direction, with his consent, or in his presence.

In many states a will cannot be revoked by a subsequent written instrument unless it is executed with the same formalities as a will. In some states certain changes in the condition or circumstances of the testator may work a revocation of his will by implication of wills. In other jurisdictions the doctrine of implied revocation has been abolished. Examples of revocation by operation of law, where permitted, are marriage and the birth of children. State laws differ greatly on the question of whether a marriage revokes a will.

Some states provide that if a testator remarries and has *issue* (children) of the marriage, the will is revoked unless a provision is made for the new mate and children. In other states a will is not revoked by a subsequent marriage; still other states provide by statute that a will is revoked by marriage, unless the will expressly states that it was made in contemplation of the marriage.

GIFT OF PART OF A HUMAN BODY AFTER DEATH

In recent years, over twenty-five states have adopted the Uniform Anatomical Gift Act, which permits a person by will, card, or other document to give upon his death all or part of his body to some hospital, physician, or research or educational institution.

Sarah Smith has always been interested in problems of blind people. She goes to a lawyer, who puts in her will a clause that reads: "Immediately upon my death, I give both of my eyes to Empress Hospital for the Blind." She tells her family, executor, friends, and the hospital what she has done. She carries a card that reads, "I have given my eyes to the Empress Hospital for the Blind. Please notify the hospital of my death." She signs the card with two witnesses to her signature.

TRUSTS

A will may give one's property outright to a specified legatee or devisee, or it may set up a trust and give the income from the trust fund to a specified beneficiary during his life or until he reaches a certain age. Under a trust, legal title to property is given to a person (called the *trustee*) who is directed to administer the trust (manage, invest, and control the property) for the benefit of another party (beneficiary) called the *cestui que trust*. A trust created in a will is called a *testamentary trust*. A trust created by a person during his lifetime is called a *living trust* or an *inter vivos trust*.

A beneficiary of a trust may have a vested or contingent interest in a trust. An interest is *vested* when it is fixed, certain, absolute, and not subject to defeat by a future uncertain event. An interest is *contingent* when it depends on the happening of an event that may or may not take place. One who receives income from a trust is called *an income bene-*

ficiary and, if circumstances warrant, may be called the *life beneficiary*. One who receives the property after the termination of the trust is called a *remainderman*.

DURATION OF A TRUST

The rule against perpetuities was founded on a public policy that disapproved of tying up property for an unreasonable length of time. As a result of this rule no trust was good unless it ended twenty-one years after the life of a person who was alive at the time of the creation of the trust. The life of that person was referred to as a "life in being" when the trust was created.

The common-law rule against perpetuities in this country is limited by most states to "lives in being at the time of the creation of the trust" plus twenty-one years. The "lives in being" rule means that John Jones may provide in his will that at the time of his death his property shall be put in trust, that the income shall be paid to his wife during her lifetime, that on her death it may be paid to John Jones's daughter, and on the daughter's death the principal of the trust shall be paid to the daughter's children. The duration of the trust is then measured by the lives of John Jones's wife and his daughter. The trust terminates legally on the death of his daughter. If, however, John Jones should provide that the trust should continue during the life of his daughter's grandchildren and those grandchildren were not "in being" at the time of John Jones' death, the trust would be invalid because it would violate the rule against perpetuities.

ACCUMULATION OF TRUST INCOME

When a minor is a beneficiary to a trust, the income from the trust, instead of being paid to him, may be accumulated until he reaches the age of eighteen or twenty-one. On the other hand, no accumulation is permitted for an adult beneficiary. The income generally must be paid to the adult beneficiary at once.

Furthermore, the trust may provide that the income be paid to a beneficiary until the happening of a certain condition. Thus, a trust may be terminated according to the desires of the person setting up the trust upon the remarriage of a widow, the marriage of a beneficiary, or a similar condition.

Living Trusts

In recent years, *living trusts*, referred to by lawyers as *inter vivos trusts*, have become more popular. The assets of a living trust need not go through probate. However, they are ordinarily subject to estate taxes. A living trust also has the advantage of confidentiality; usually, no public record is made of the assets of the trust.

Unless the living trust is a *"stand-by"* trust, the assets must be in the name of the trustee at the time that the trust is made or thereafter. Many persons consider this vehicle a substitute for a will. However, you still may need a will.

Living Wills and Health Care Proxies

In recent years a national debate has raged over the "right to die." In 1990, the U.S. Supreme Court issued its first "right to die" decision in a case involving a young girl named Nancy Cruzan. The Supreme Court considered whether under the U.S. Constitution Nancy Cruzan would have a right to compel the hospital to withdraw life-sustaining treatment for her.

Although the court recognized that a competent individual may refuse medical treatment, it concluded that an individual state could apply clear and convincing evidence standard in proceedings where a guardian seeks to have nutrition and hydration withheld from a person diagnosed to be in a persistent vegetative state (PVS). The Court did not establish a federal standard as to how that right may be exercised; rather, it permits each state to establish procedures limiting the methods of exercising the rights of a patient who is incompetent.

Through the use of living wills or health care proxies (which lawyers call "durable powers of attorney for health care"), a person today can preserve his or her desire to have either nutrition and hydration continued or have it discontinued. However, these instructions must clearly evidence the person's wishes. All lawyers have found an increase in their clients' interest in these documents since the Supreme Court decision in the *Cruzan* case.

Practically all states have "living will" statutes and all states do have durable power of attorney statutes. It is often said that lawyers are apt to say, "Everyone should have a will." Lawyers also should recommend that some sort of written "advance directive" be prepared for purposes of medical decision making.

Lawyers who are experts in estate planning say that the durable powers of attorney (or health care proxy) for health care remains the best and most flexible instrument to express one's wishes regarding the withholding or withdrawing of life-sustaining medical treatment. Unlike living will statutes, which apply only to patients who are terminally ill, the durable power can address the full range of medical problems (for example, strokes, heat attack, brain cancer, etc.). People may desire more aggressive medical care in certain circumstances. A durable power of attorney thus also may delegate a broader range of medical decisions to a third party.

It appears from the reading of the *Cruzan* decision, that at least five members of the Supreme Court would have voted to recognize surrogate decision making if a durable health care power of attorney had been well-drafted. It is essential that the durable health care powers of attorney be as specific as possible. In addition, if a person has some specific health risks in mind (such as stroke, heart attack, cancer, Alzheimer's, etc.), then that person should specifically mention them and the various forms of treatment used for such conditions that he or she wants to permit or to reject.

The American Bar Association (ABA) and the American Medical Association (AMA) recently issued a joint statement after the U.S. Supreme Court decision, in which it was stated that the *Cruzan* case highlights the fact that health care decision making by surrogates works best when the individual has acted in advance of incapacity. These mechanisms, sometimes referred to as "advance directives," are now recognized in most statements in the form of either "Living Will laws" or "Health Care Power of Attorney laws."

Although it is advisable to have such a document prepared at the time that a person has made a will, for any number of reasons it may not be possible or practicable to do so.

In such circumstances, a competent person faced with a "right to die" should write down his or her wishes in a "to who it may concern" memorandum, date it, sign it, and have it witnessed, if possible. Such a writing is more than likely to pass the "clear and convincing test" laid down by the U.S. Supreme Court.

This type of "to whom it may concern" memorandum—although useful as evidence of one's intent—is not legally binding unless it complies with the state statute regarding the formalities of execution.

The New York State Legislature recently adopted a new law called the New York Health Care Proxy Law, which allows you to appoint someone you trust to make decisions regarding your medical care. If, like Nancy Cruzan, you are subsequently declared by your doctor to be in a permanent vegetative state (PVS), then your health care agent can, if he or she is aware of your wishes, make decisions regarding artificial nutrition and hydration.

Even with the Health Care Proxy Law, the living will could still be used as a statement of a person's intentions without delegating any decision-making authority.

A sample health care proxy or durable power of attorney for health care, which can be used in such an emergency situation, follows. However, living wills and "health care proxies" should be drawn preferably with the help of an estate planning lawyer.

LIVING WILL AND HEALTH CARE PROXY

(1) I, _____ , residing at _____ hereby appoint _____
_____
      (name, home address and telephone number)
as my health care agent to make any and all health care decisions for me, except to the extent that I state otherwise. This proxy shall take effect when and if I become unable to make my own health care decisions. The determinnation of whether I can make my own health care decisions shall be made by my attending physician.

(2) Optional instructions: I direct my agent to make health care decisions in accordance with my wishes and limitations as stated below, or as he or she otherwise knows:

  (a) I direct my agent to authorize the withholding or withdrawal of treatment that serves only to prolong the process of my dying, if I should be in an incurable or irreversible mental or physical condition with no reasonable expectation of recovery.

  (b) I direct that treatment be limited to measures to keep me comfortable and to relieve pain, including any pain that might occur by withholding or withdrawing treatment. I DO WANT MAXIMUM PAIN RELIEF.

(c) If I am in an incurable or irreversible mental or physical condition with no reasonable expectation of recovery, I feel especially strongly about the following forms of treatment:

(i)   I do not want cardiac resuscitation.

(ii)   I do not want mechanical respiration.

(iii)   I do not want artificial nutrition or hydration (tube feeding).

(iv)   Other treatment (specify): _____

(d) Other instructions: _____

_____

These instructions reflect my firm and settled commitment described above. These instructions express my legal right to refuse treatment.

(3) Name of substitute or fill-agent if the person I appoint is unable, unwilling or unavailable to act as my health care agent:

_____

_____

(name, home address and telephone number)

(4) Unless I revoke it, this proxy shall remain in effect indefinitely, or until the date or conditions stated below. This proxy shall expire (specific date or conditions, if desired): _____

(5) Signature _____

Address _____

Date _____

Statement by witnesses (must be 18 or older)

I declare that the person who signed this document is personally known to me and appears to be of sound mind and acting of his or her own free will. He or she signed (or asked another to sign for him or her) this document in my presence.

Witness 1 _____

Address _____

Witness 2 _____

Address _____

NOTE

[1]The author gratefully acknowledges the gracious cooperation of the American College of Trust and Estate Counsel in permitting the reprint of the foregoing table in an abridged format. This partial summary is based upon the opinion of the various Fellows of the American College of Trust and Estate Counsel. Neither the College nor the individual reporters assume any responsibility for the accuracy of the information. The study was most recently updated (in October 1989) and compiled by George Gordon Coughlin, Jr.

10

ESTATES OF DECEASED PERSONS

A decedent's estate must be managed by someone, whether or not the decedent leaves a will. When the decedent leaves a will, he names this person, the *executor*, in the will. The executor must carry out all the responsibilities of the administration of an estate, enumerated below, and, in addition, he must scrupulously carry out the terms of the will. When the deceased does not leave a will, the estate is managed by an *administrator*, who may be the surviving spouse, or another person appointed by the court. An *administrator with the will annexed* is a person appointed by the court to administer an estate when the executor dies or fails to qualify. The entire property left by a decedent is called the *gross estate*. The balance of the estate remaining after making provision for taxes, administration expenses, and legacies is called the *residuary estate*.

DUTIES AND RIGHTS OF EXECUTOR OR ADMINISTRATOR

An executor or administrator is known in law as a "fiduciary" or "the legal representative of an estate." Most rights, duties, and privileges of a legal representative of an estate apply with equal force to an executor and to an administrator.

The legal representative must be honest, diligent, and vigilant in administering the affairs of the estate. He is not an insurer of the assets of the estate and will not in all cases be liable for loss that may result from his acts. He is, however, required to use that intelligence and that degree of care and diligence in the management of the estate that a reasonably prudent businessman would employ in the management of his own affairs.

Among the powers of the legal representative of an estate are the following:

1) He may take the assets of the estate into his possession. (Legal possession may not mean physical possession but rather actual control over the assets.)
2) He may sell and liquidate personal property and convert the assets of the estate into cash.
3) He may pay debts and funeral and administration expenses.
4) He may distribute the estate to the beneficiaries.

Taking Possession of Assets

The legal representative not only takes the assets into his possession but he must also obtain full information regarding the assets. He must examine all the belongings of the decedent, his account books, safety deposit box, and other books and papers. He must inspect every scrap of paper found in the possession of the decedent. Moreover, he must investigate assets carefully to determine their value, for claims which appear to be uncollectible may prove to be collectible, and stocks and bonds that seem to have little or no value may turn out to be of considerable value.

He should prepare a complete inventory of the decedent's assets as soon as possible.

A good example of the requirement that the executor shall reduce assets to his possession is the simple matter of bank accounts and cash belonging to the decedent. The legal representative of the estate must open a bank account in the name of the estate and must transfer the decedent's bank accounts to his own name, as executor or administrator. He may, but is not always required to, put the estate monies into an interest-bearing bank account. Because he may be called on to make frequent payments in the administration of the estate, a checking account may be the most practical type of account.

The problems of taking possession of assets are many. The legal representative should have the ownership of the decedent's stocks and bonds transferred to the name of the estate. He should collect the proceeds of life insurance and other types of insurance policies. If the decedent was a member of a partnership firm, he may have to have the interest of the deceased partner determined according to law and proceed with liquidation of the partner's interest. If the decedent owned real property, the legal representative may under certain circumstances be permitted to manage or sell the real estate. He should set aside certain property authorized by law as a "set-off" to the heirs and then make an inventory of all assets in the estate.

The cardinal sin of a legal representative is the commingling of estate funds with his own individual funds. In reducing estate monies to his possession, the legal representative must keep the funds and the property received separate from his own personal funds and property. No investment should be made nor funds deposited with any bank or corporation in the individual name of the legal representative. He must make sure that all funds are deposited in his name as executor or as administrator.

Keeping Records

It is important for the legal representative to keep proper accounts of the disposition of the funds and the property of the estate. He must keep a record of all receipts and disbursements in order to be prepared to make a final account of his stewardship. The keeping of books and records is so important that in the case of sizeable estates the legal representative may employ a bookkeeper or an accountant to keep books for him. Although a small estate cannot be taxed with this expense, it is necessary in a small estate, too, that proper books of account and records be kept.

Sale of Assets and Payment of Claims

In order that he may be able to pay creditors and distribute the estate to beneficiaries, the executor or administrator may have to sell the assets of the estate. Converting the assets into cash is one of his primary duties. Generally, in order to satisfy the decedent's debts, resort is had first to personal property and then to real estate. Very often it is necessary to get authority from the probate court in order to sell real estate.

In complying with his duty to ascertain and pay the debts of the decedent, the legal representative may sometimes have a notice published in a newspaper directing creditors to present their claims. Even if all creditors do not present their claims, the legal representative cannot ignore knowledge of just debts owed by the deceased to other persons. It is his duty to treat all persons interested in the estate fairly and to give all persons the information necessary so that they may present their claims in the proper manner. After claims are presented, the legal representative must investigate them and satisfy himself that they are valid. If he doubts the validity of a claim, he will have to present the matter to the probate court, which then will determine whether a particular claim should be accepted or rejected.

Many interesting questions are raised in connection with claims for actual or alleged services rendered to the decedent. Frequently, persons who have performed services for others (often close relatives) demand payment after the death of the one for whom the services were rendered. While the decedent was alive, there may have been no thought in anyone's mind that services were being performed for compensation; sometimes they seemed to be willingly performed for loved ones. This assumption does not prevent the presentation of a claim after the person's death. If the legal representative thinks that the decedent had no intention of paying for such services, it is his duty to contest the claim.

Inheritance and Estate Taxes

Today, an important aspect of estate administration is the filing of estate tax returns. There are two basic kinds of inheritance and estate taxes: state and federal. (In some instances taxes are imposed by states, other than the state of domicile, in which the decedent owned property.)

State and federal income tax returns are relatively straightforward documents compared with inheritance and estate tax returns. Estate tax returns contain many details, such as schedules of real estate, stocks and bonds, mortgages, notes, contracts, cash and insurance, jointly owned property, and miscellaneous property; they may also contain schedules regarding transfers made in contemplation of death, schedules concerning powers of appointment (involving a right or control that the decedent had over property owned by others), schedules of property previously taxed, schedules of funeral and administration expenses, charitable, public, and similar gifts and bequests, debts of the decedent, and schedules concerning the beneficiaries.

In an estate tax proceeding, the appraisal of the assets is the basis for the tax on the property. The valuation of the assets of an estate is frequently difficult. For example, although there is generally no problem in valuing the stock of publicly owned corporations, which are traded on recognized stock exchanges, it is often a problem to evaluate the stock of family-owned corporations when there are no records of recent sales of the stock.

If the decedent died after 1986, a federal estate tax return does not have to be filed unless the gross value of the estate exceeds $600,000. The federal estate tax return must be filed within nine (9) months after the date of the decedent's death, and any federal estate tax becomes due at that time. As a result of recent law changes, no matter what the value of the decedent's estate, all assets of the decedent that pass to his or her surviving spouse will not be subject to tax at the time the surviving spouse dies. This is known as the "unlimited marital deduction."

The $600,000 exemption generally is decreased by the value of any *intervivos* gifts exceeding $10,000 in each year ($20,000 if the spouse joins in the gift). Unless the gift is an outright gift, it may not qualify for the $10,000 annual exclusion.

The legal representative of an estate may employ agents and others to assist him with the administrative work of the estate and may employ attorneys to advise him about his rights and duties. In most cases, those employed by the legal representative for this purpose are entitled to compensation from estate funds. Whenever the legal representative feels that a charge for legal services is not proper, he may ask the probate court to determine the amount to be allowed to the representative for counsel fees.

Distribution to Beneficiaries

After all the foregoing steps have been taken and after all inheritance and estate taxes have been paid, the legal representative is ready to distribute the assets of the estate to the beneficiaries. Although some states set a goal of distribution within six or seven months from the time of the appointment of the executor or administrator, such a goal is in most instances unrealistic. When a federal estate tax return is required, the Internal Revenue Service usually takes a minimum of one year to audit it. This year, added to the 9 months allowed for preparation and filing of the federal estate tax return, means that estates of more than $600,000 are very difficult to distribute completely before at least two years after the decedent's death. In response to public criticism that it takes too long to settle an estate, legislatures in many states have adopted the Uniform Probate Code, which simplifies the process of probate and estate administration.

Commission of Legal Representatives

The compensation of a legal representative is generally based on the size of the estate; it is fixed by law in each state and varies from state to state. The compensation is awarded by the court and is known as a *commission*. Rates of commission range from 1-1/2 to 5 percent. The higher rates of commission are awarded on estates that are relatively small.

Judicial Approval of Legal Representative's Accounts

After he has completed his duties, the legal representative should file with the probate court an account setting forth all assets that he has received, all debts and administration expenses that he has paid, and showing the balance on hand for distribution.

The accounting is the final act of the legal representative; it discharges his responsibility to the estate. In this proceeding, he accounts for his acts in administering the affairs of the estate, and the court directs the manner in which the assets remaining in the legal representative's control are to be distributed. Additional questions, such as contested creditors' claims and also matters of interpreting and construing a will, which have been saved for submission to the probate court during the accounting proceeding, may be finally determined. Occasionally, when the legal representative has been lax in distributing the estate, the beneficiaries may compel an accounting and distribution of the estate.

Settlement of Estate without Accounting

When there are no disputes between the parties, an estate may be settled by written agreement rather than by an accounting proceeding. In such a case, the executor sets forth in the agreement what he has accomplished: the assets that have been collected; the debts, inheritance taxes, and administration expenses that have been paid; the amount on hand for distribution; and the share to which each distributee is entitled. Then the consenting parties acknowledge receipt of their respective distributive shares and release and discharge the legal representative from all legal liability and responsibility for his acts.

INHERITANCE WITHOUT A WILL

When a decedent leaves a valid will, he directs the disposal of his property; he determines which of his relatives and friends shall be his beneficiaries. When, on the other hand, an individual dies *intestate* (leaving property without having directed its disposition by will), his property is disposed of under the inheritance laws of the state in which he resided, that is, by the rules of descent and distribution and in some cases by dower and curtesy.

When a person dies intestate, his wife or her husband or children or nearest relative applies to the court for the appointment of an administrator to manage the estate. Once the administrator has been appointed, the management of the estate proceeds under the direction of the court in a manner similar to an estate disposed of by will.

DESCENT AND DISTRIBUTION

The right to inherit property when there is no will is governed by the laws of descent and distribution in each of the states. *Descent* refers to the handing down of real property (real estate) by inheritance on the death of an owner who dies intestate. *Distribution* means the allocation to heirs of the personal property of an individual who dies intestate after the payment of debts and charges against the estate. These laws of descent and distribution are diverse and difficult to reconcile, for they represent the varying views of the lawmakers in the fifty states concerning how property should be inherited by blood relatives when the decedent does not leave a will. The National Conference of Commissioners on Uniform State Laws has been successful in promoting uniformity among the laws of the states on more than thirty subjects, but has been unable to accomplish the same for the laws of descent and distribution.

DOWER AND CURTESY

Strictly speaking, the rules of dower and curtesy are not part of the law of descent and distribution; yet, if they were not discussed here, it would be difficult to understand the disposition of estates made by those states which retain the common-law rules of descent and distribution and also the rights of dower and curtesy. Such a state may disinherit a spouse from any interest in real estate on the death of the other spouse, except for rights of dower and curtesy.[1]

Dower is the interest that a wife has in her husband's real estate, but this only becomes effective on the death of her husband. Frequently, dower is a life interest in one-third of the real estate owned by the husband at the time of his death; that is, the widow has the right to the use or the right to the income from one-third of her husband's real estate (at the time of his death) for as long as she lives.

More than half the states have abolished the right to dower, but it has been retained in others. In New Jersey and Oregon, the widow has the life use of one-half of her husband's interest in real property. In Alabama, the widow is entitled to one-half of her husband's interest in real estate when he leaves no lineal descendants (children or grandchildren); when he does, the widow receives one-third of the real estate.

Curtesy is the interest that a husband has in his wife's real estate effective on the death of his wife and provided a child has been born to the marriage. Seven states (Kentucky, Illinois, Maryland, New Hampshire, North Carolina, Ohio, and Wisconsin) give a husband, in place of the curtesy right, the same right of dower as a wife.

RULES OF DESCENT AND DISTRIBUTION

The rules for descent and distribution concern the six major areas covered in the ensuing paragraphs.

Real and Personal Property

The modern trend among the states has been to eliminate the distinction in the treatment of inheritance rules for real and personal property. The term "heirs" once referred to those who inherited real property, and "next of kin" referred to those who inherited personal property; in many states the terms are now used interchangeably to cover persons entitled to take both real and personal property. Missouri is typical of those states that have modernized laws of descent and distribution and have thus eliminated a distinction between real property and personal property. Tennessee, on the other hand, has one set of involved rules for the descent of real property (involving distinctions within distinctions concerning whether the real property was acquired from a parent or another ancestor by gift, devise, or descent) and another set of rules for the distribution of personal property (eliminating the requirement concerning whether or not the property was acquired from a parent or an ancestor).

Community Property States

Community property is that owned by a husband and wife in marital partnership. Eight states (Arizona, California, Idaho, Louisiana, Nevada, New Mexico, Texas, and Washington) are community property states. Although their laws vary, some useful generalizations can be made. In these states, all property, except property owned by either the husband or wife before the marriage or thereafter acquired by gift, bequest, devise, or descent, becomes community property. Under some community property systems, and despite the provisions of a will, on the death of a husband or wife one-half of all the community property passes to the surviving spouse; the other half is subject to disposition by will. Thus, the surviving spouse has a vested right in and automatically inherits one-half of the community property whether or not there is a will. The surviving spouse may or may not benefit further under the provisions of the will disposing of the other half of the property.

These rules are complex. As a general rule, upon the death of a spouse, one-half of the community property belongs to the surviving spouse and the decedent may dispose of the balance without restriction. If the spouse died without a will (intestate), under the laws of some community property states, the other one-half would go to the children, even if there is a surviving spouse.

However, there are differences between the laws of these states. The following examples illustrate the lack of uniformity even among community property states:

In Washington the rule is that either spouse may dispose of one-half of the community property by will and the remaining half automatically goes to the surviving spouse.

Nevada and New Mexico have one rule for the death of the wife and another rule for the death of a husband. When the wife dies, the entire community property vests in the husband without the necessity of estate administration. When the husband dies, one-half of the community property vests in the wife and the other half is subject to disposition by the husband's will.

In Texas, when either party dies, all the community property goes to the survivor, if there is no surviving child (or children); if there is a child or children or grandchild or grandchildren, the surviving spouse takes one-half and the children or grandchildren inherit the other half.

Surviving Spouse and Blood Relatives

The prevailing principle in many states is that the surviving spouse shares the inheritance with the children. Other heirs and next of kin take possession of property in the following order: (1) children and descendants of deceased children, (2) parents or surviving parent, (3) brothers, sisters, or issue of deceased brothers or sisters, (4) other next of kin of equal degree.

The pattern of inheritance without a will varies. Each state legislature has established a statutory system which may—at one time—have been appropriate and fair for residents of that state.

It is worthwhile to compare the treatment of widows, children, and other relatives by the rules of descent and distribution in two neighboring states, Connecticut and New York:

In Connecticut, the surviving spouse takes $50,000 plus one-half of the estate, and the child or children take the other half. If issue of the deceased are not issue of the surviving spouse, then the estate is divided equally between the issue and the surviving spouse. If there is no child or descendants of a child but there is a surviving parent (or parents) of the deceased, the widow takes $50,000 plus three-fourths of the remainder of the estate. If there is neither child nor descendant of a child nor parent, the widow takes the entire estate.

Under New York law, a surviving spouse takes one-third of the estate if the decedent leaves descendants, but when the decedent leaves only one child (or representatives of a predeceased child), the surviving spouse takes one-half. If the deceased leaves no children or grandchildren but leaves a parent, the surviving husband or wife takes $25,000 and one-half of the estate. If the deceased leaves no parents, the surviving husband or wife takes all the estate.

Relatives of Half Blood and of Whole Blood

There are different rules among the states concerning whether collateral relatives of the half blood (such as a half-brother) share equally with collateral relatives of the whole blood. Most states provide that there is no distinction and that relatives of the half blood receive the same treatment as relatives of the whole blood. The other states (at this writing Florida, Georgia, Kentucky, Maryland, Massachusetts, Mississippi, Missouri, North Dakota, South Dakota, Texas, Virginia, Washington, and Wyoming) limit the inheritance of relatives of the half blood so that either (1) they take half as much as collateral relatives of the whole blood, or (2) relatives of the whole blood receive inheritances in preference to relatives of the half blood.

Illegitimate Children

Most of the states provide that illegitimate children inherit property from their mothers but not from their fathers. Florida, Minnesota, Nebraska, Nevada, New Mexico, Oklahoma, Oregon, South Dakota, Utah, Vermont, and Wisconsin laws make an illegitimate child an heir of the natural father if the latter has acknowledged paternity in writing. Some states require that the writing be witnessed, and other states require that the paternity be formally acknowledged before a notary public.

In order for an illegitimate child to be an heir of the putative father, Kansas and Utah require that the paternity simply be recognized and acknowledged by the father, without specifying the way in which such recognition or acknowledgment should be made. Alabama has a law permitting a father to make his bastard child legitimate by a written declaration made before two witnesses and filed in the probate office in the county of his residence.

Colorado, Maine, Missouri, New York, Pennsylvania, Rhode

Island, South Carolina, Texas, Virginia, Washington, West Virginia, and Wyoming provide that if the parents of an illegitimate child marry each other, the child inherits from both parents as though legitimate. In addition to intermarriage, Arizona, Connecticut, Illinois, Mississippi, Ohio, and Washington add the requirement of written recognition of the child by the father. Indiana, New York, Oregon, and Wisconsin also grant inheritance to a child from his father when he has been adjudged in court to be the father of the child.

Iowa grants inheritance from the father when paternity has been proved. Oregon, the most liberal state in this matter, treats illegitimates the same as legitimates under inheritance law.

Escheat

If after the lapse of a certain time no heirs claim the estate of a deceased person, it passes to and becomes the property of the state (or another unit of government). This is the doctrine of *escheat*. It exists in all fifty states, but the time limit in which after discovered heirs may bring proceedings in order to recover escheated property varies from three to seven years.

Certain states have provided interesting variations of the doctrine of escheat:

North Carolina provides that when there are no heirs, the estate escheats to the University of North Carolina.

Illinois directs that escheated property goes to the county where the decedent died.

South Carolina provides that the property goes to the township in which the decedent lived.

Pennsylvania, South Dakota, Tennessee, Utah, and Wisconsin earmark escheated property for common school funds.

NOTE

[1]In eight western states, the Community Property system replaces common law interests such as dower and statutory right to take a portion of a deceased spouse's separate estate. When a couple moves from one state to another state, and then one spouse dies, the "migrating couple's" estate planning becomes involved. Generally, the question of what law governs depends on where the property was accumulated.

11

COMMERCIAL PAPER

Commercial paper is a broad term that includes drafts (bills of exchange), promissory notes, checks and other negotiable instruments for the payment of money. To be negotiable, commercial paper must be transferable by indorsement or delivery without the consent of the debtor and must make the person to whom the instrument is endorsed or transferred the complete owner of the commercial paper. Negotiability is not, however, essential to its validity. Nonnegotiable commercial paper may be considered a valid contract.

LAWS GOVERNING COMMERCIAL PAPER

The use of commercial paper grew with the expansion of international trade. But the legal remedies of the courts in the past were inadequate to settle the merchants' disputes arising in international trade. Merchants settled their own disputes through informal tribunals, which they themselves convened. The mercantile customs which grew out of these tribunals eventually gained legal sanction and became known as the Law Merchant.

Credit and negotiable instruments are widely used in modern business and their use is governed mainly by two laws. The first is the Uniform Negotiable Instruments Law (a replacement and a codification of the Law Merchant), which was prepared in 1896 by the commissioners on uniform state laws. It was adopted by a few states in 1897 and eventually by all the states.

All of the states (except Louisiana) now have repealed the Negotiable Instruments Law and have substituted the second important contemporary law affecting commercial paper, the *Uniform Commercial Code*. The latter is a law sponsored jointly by the American Law Institute and the National Conference of Commissioners on Uniform State Laws. It covers the law of commercial paper and also nearly every phase of business activity, including sales and banking and commercial transactions.

NATURE OF NEGOTIABILITY

Commercial paper is a form of contract. Negotiability is that characteristic of certain commercial paper that permits it to be transferred by endorsement or delivery. Ordinarily a contract is transferred by a written instrument of assignment, but the owner of a negotiable instrument simply needs to write his name on it. If it is payable to bearer, the person who is in possession of commercial paper, he needs only to hand it to the new owner.

Importance of Negotiability

It is very important to determine whether a particular paper is negotiable because the law gives negotiable paper special treatment, and in doing so protects "innocent holders" (also referred to as "bona fide holders" or "holders in good faith"; see pp. 149–150). Negotiable bills, checks, and notes represent money and are intended to pass from hand to hand as money. Paper, if negotiable, may be transferred without notice to the debtor.

The person to whom a nonnegotiable instrument or contract is transferred takes it subject to all the original agreements, understandings, and defenses available between the original parties to the instrument; but a transferee of negotiable paper takes it free from all previous agreements, understandings, and defenses.

The consideration for a negotiable instrument is presumed, while the consideration for nonnegotiable paper must ordinarily be proved.

Tests of Negotiability

All five of the following tests for negotiability must be met:

1) The instrument must be in writing and signed by the maker or drawer (the person who originally signs a bill of exchange). It may be handwritten, typed, stamped, printed, and so on. The signature must be intended and must be a name, initials, mark, or trade or assumed name; it, too, may be handwritten, typed, printed, mechanically reproduced, and so on.

2) The instrument must contain an unconditional promise or order to pay a certain sum of money. A promise or order for payment should be distinguished from a mere request or acknowledgment of a debt. For example:

Leslie borrows $100 from Fisher and signs a paper as follows: "I hereby acknowledge receipt of the sum of $100, which sum I have borrowed of you and must be accountable for." The paper signed by Leslie is not a negotiable instrument and may not be transferred by indorsement or delivery.

If the instrument is conditional, then it is not negotiable.

Gray gives to Brown his promissory note: "I promise to pay to you the sum of $2000 payable on September 1, this year, provided you make your summer camp at Black Lake available to me." The instrument is conditional and hence is not negotiable.

3) The instrument must be payable on demand or at a fixed or determinable time in the future.

An instrument is payable on demand if it says so in those words or equivalent words, such as "on presentation" or "on sight," or if a person takes or endorses it after it is due.

In order to be negotiable, a bill or note or other instrument must be due and payable at a time that is either definite or is morally certain to occur. Such certainty must exist at the time the instrument is made.

John Tucker receives a sizeable inheritance and feels a moral obligation to support his Aunt Marie. John signs a promissory note reading, "I promise to pay to my Aunt Marie Tucker the sum of $10,000 at such time as she may need same for her support." The fact that the note was payable on the happening of an uncertain event (that she should need financial support) prevents the note from being negotiable.

Charlie borrows $3,500 from his Uncle Herbert, to help defray the expense of his college education. Charlie gives his uncle his promissory note, which reads, in part, as follows: "I promise to pay to Herbert Brown the sum of $3,500, payable at the rate of $100 per month with interest at the rate of 5 percent per annum, the first payment to be made one month after I obtain a permanent position after graduating from engineering school." This note, though enforceable between the parties, is not a negotiable instrument because the time of payment is uncertain.

And, even though an uncertain event on which a note or bill is payable occurs, the instrument is not thereby made negotiable.

4) The instrument must be payable to order or to bearer. The requirement of the Uniform Commercial Code that a note be "payable to order" means that the draft or note or other commercial paper must be payable to the order of a designated person, not just to the person. Otherwise, the instrument must be payable to bearer or its equivalent (cash, petty cash, and so on).

(Look carefully at a check and read the words, "pay to the order of"; these words make the check negotiable. Making a check payable to "cash" is the same as making it payable to bearer.)

5) In the case of a draft, the *drawee* (the person upon whom the draft is drawn and who becomes liable as soon as he accepts the bill of exchange) must be named or otherwise indicated with certainty. If the drawee is not definitely identifiable, the instrument is not negotiable even though valid.

Rowe draws a draft that reads: "To whomever may be my employer six months after date: pay to the order of Jonathan Jones the sum of $5000, and charge to my account." The bill of exchange, not containing a definite drawee, is not negotiable.

COMMON TYPES OF NEGOTIABLE INSTRUMENTS

Negotiable instruments or commercial papers are either orders or promises to pay money. There are many different types of negotiable instruments; common among them are promissory notes, bills of exchange, bank drafts, checks, paper money, bonds, trade acceptances, and municipal warrants.

There are, in addition, certain quasi-negotiable documents which do not call for the payment of money and, thus, are technically not negotiable instruments, but which have other qualities of negotiability under the Uniform Commercial Code. These quasi-negotiable documents are stock certificates, bills of lading, and warehouse receipts.

Promissory Notes and Similar Negotiable Instruments

A *promissory note* is a written promise by one person to pay to another or to bearer a fixed sum of money on demand or at a specified time.[1] Promissory notes are most common in the extension of bank credit.

A *certificate of deposit* is similar to a promissory note. It contains an unconditional promise to pay the amount of the certificate on demand to bearer or to the order of the holder. The purpose of a certificate of deposit, unlike that of a promissory note, is to permit a depositor of a certain sum of money in a bank to dispose of his right to the sum by mere transfer of the certificate.

Bonds, like promissory notes, contain a promise for the payment of a certain sum of money. There are many kinds of bonds, among them government and municipal bonds and corporate, industrial, and commercial bonds. *Corporate bonds*, which represent simply the obligation to pay a sum of money and which are not secured by mortgages, are commonly known as "debentures."

Municipal warrants, which counties and municipalities issue in anticipation of revenue to be derived from taxation usually contain promises to pay money and, therefore, are negotiable instruments and have the characteristics of promissory notes.

Drafts

A draft is an order in writing addressed by one person to another requiring the addressee to pay on demand or at a specified time a certain sum of money to the order of the person named or to bearer. Because checks are the most common type of draft, they are discussed separately on page 145.

A *trade acceptance* is a draft or bill of exchange drawn by the seller of goods on the purchaser for a fixed sum of money that represents the purchase price of the goods.

A *bank acceptance* is a draft drawn on and accepted by a bank as drawee.

An *accommodation paper* is a draft or note to which the drawer, maker, or other party has put his name without consideration for the purpose of lending his credit to the paper.

CHECKS

Besides currency (paper money), bank checks are the type of negotiable instruments most often used. As defined by the Uniform Commercial Code, a check is "a draft drawn on a bank and payable on demand." Thus, the provisions of law relating to a draft apply equally to check.

Types of Checks

A bank draft is a check drawn by a bank on another bank. And, of course, a garden variety check is a bill of exchange drawn by an individual on a bank and payable on demand.

A *certified check* is issued by a bank, which guarantees that the drawer's signature is genuine and that the amount for which the check is drawn has been set aside for payment from the drawer's account. When a bank's authorized representative puts the bank's stamp, "certified," on a check and signs it, the bank becomes liable for its payment. The maker of a check can stop payment on it any time before it is cashed. Once the check is certified, however, the maker can no longer stop payment.

Danger of Delay in Cashing Checks

The Negotiable Instruments Law provides that drafts payable on demand (uncertified checks) must be presented for payment within a reasonable time, in order to invoke the liability of the drawer and of any endorsers. In those states which have adopted the Uniform Commercial Code, a reasonable time is presumed to be thirty days with respect to the liability of the drawer and seven days after his indorsement with respect to the liability of an indorser.[2] From this reference to time it follows that it is unwise to delay cashing checks.

Delay in presenting a check for payment will discharge the maker of the check from liability only if he is injured by the delay.

$1050.00

Seattle, Washington
april 6, 1993

On demand I promise to pay to the order
of Saturday Diner, Inc., one thousand and
fifty dollars (value received)

Samuel S. Depler

Promissory Note

$ 600.00   Philadelphia, PA July 1 19 93

One month after sight pay to the order of Charles Janski

the sum of six hundred 00/100 Dollars (value received)

and charge to the account of

To Hartley Jones
New Orleans, La

Seldan Braun

Draft

No. 61   Chicago Ill. 19 93 ,   August 31 , 19 93

Sixty------------ after date pay to the order of /Ourselves

Three hundred and no/100 --------------- Dollars ($300.00)

the obligation of the acceptance hereof arises out of the

purchase of goods from drawer.

To   Jack Presidente
    (name of drawer)   Reginald Co., Inc.

    105 Fifth Avenue

Due   October 30, 1993   By Richard Depler, V.P.

TRADE ACCEPTANCE

ACCEPTED AT
PAYABLE AT
LOCATION Chicago Ill.
SIGNATURE Jack Presidente
DATE September 1, 1993
(citation of adduptor)
Jack Presidente
Chicago Ill.

Trade Acceptance

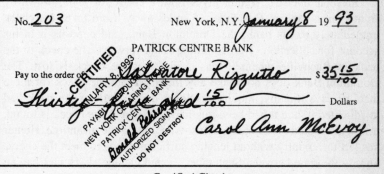

INDIAN STAR NATIONAL TULSA BANK

Park North at 117th Street, Tulsa, N.Y.

307

0 - 8
906

February 10 19 *93*

Pay to the order of *Table Top Linen Laundry Service* $ *6 07/100*

Six and 07/100 Dollars

Priscilla Brechau

Check

No. *203*

New York, N.Y. *January 8* 19 *93*

PATRICK CENTRE BANK

Pay to the order of *Salvatore Rizzuto* $ *35 15/100*

Thirty-five and 15/100 Dollars

CERTIFIED
JANUARY 8, 1993
PAYABLE THROUGH THE
NEW YORK CLEARING HOUSE
PATRICK CENTRE BANK
Donald Behrend
AUTHORIZED SIGNATURE
DO NOT DESTROY

Carol Ann McEvoy

Certified Check

No. 731

Denver, Colorado *July 3,* 19 *93*

CENTRAL COUNTY STATE BANK

Pay to the order of *R.C. Wilkins, State Treasurer* $ *1,000.00*

one thousand and no/100 Dollars

CASHIER'S CHECK

Jonas Rightone

Cashier

Cashier's Check

Greely has on deposit in the Excelsior Bank the sum of $525. He gives Kasker a check for $500, which Kasker puts in his desk drawer and fails to present for payment until two months later. In the meantime the bank fails.

Kasker then goes to Greely and asks him to make good on the check. Greely is not responsible for the check because he has been injured by Kasker's delay in not presenting the check for payment. (If Kasker had promptly presented the check for payment, instead of waiting two months, the check would have been paid, and Greely would have been $500 better off. But Kasker's failure to promptly present the check relieved Greely from liability for the check.)

Unavoidable delay in presenting a check for payment will discharge an indorser from liability for a check, whether or not the indorser is injured by the delay.

On September 21, Hunter gives Lord a check for $300, drawn by Hunter on a bank in Rushville, 15 miles away. Lord takes the check immediately to his bank, the Dominion Bank, and deposits it in his account for collection. The Dominion Bank forwards the check to the bank in Rushville where it was drawn, but the check is lost. The Dominion Bank does not make any inquiry about the check for more than 10 days. Finally, inquiry discloses that a clerk of the bank had misdirected it, and it had been misfiled. As soon as the check is found, it is again routed to the bank in Rushville, but, in the meantime, Hunter has left the country without leaving sufficient funds to meet the check. During the time between September 21 and October 1, Hunter had an adequate balance in the Rushville bank, and the check could have been paid. The court holds that the Dominion Bank did not use the diligence required by law, and Lord is discharged from his liability as an indorser on the check.

Stale Checks

Over the years, there have been various court decisions that a check presented to a bank five to twelve months after the date written on the check need not be paid by the bank without further inquiry. These checks are called "stale checks."

Now, the Uniform Commercial Code has established a definite rule. A bank is under no obligation to a customer (having a checking account) to pay an uncertified check presented more than six months after its date without consulting the depositor (its customer).

RIGHTS OF HOLDERS OF COMMERCIAL PAPER

The major characteristic of a negotiable instrument is that it circulates freely, that it may be taken or be held for what it appears to be.

A "holder" is anyone legally in possession of commercial paper. A holder in due course is a bona fide holder, for value, of commercial paper without notice of any legal defects. In order for one to be a holder in due course, he must receive the instrument (1) in good faith, (2) for valuable consideration, (3) without notice that the instrument is due and payable, and (4) without notice of any defect in title of the person who transfers the instrument and without notice of any defects in the instrument itself. A holder in due course holds an instrument free from any defenses which would exist between the original parties to the instrument, such as illegal consideration or fraud or mistake connected with the note.

Good Faith

It is necessary that a holder in due course take the commercial paper in good faith; that is, he should have no knowledge that there is something wrong with the instrument.

A promissory note is given by A to B, who loses it. C finds it, forges B's signature, and sells the instrument to D, who buys the instrument without knowledge of the forgery. D acts innocently and in good faith.

Transfer for Valuable Consideration

In order to make one a holder in due course, the transfer of the instrument must be for consideration sufficient to support a simple contract. It is not necessary that one give money for the instrument. He may give merchandise or credit or perform a service in return for the commercial paper.

Transfer before Maturity

In order for a holder in due course to acquire good title, he must obtain the instrument without notice that it has matured. The reason for this rule is the suspicion that something is wrong with commercial paper that remains unpaid after it has become due.

Calhoun gives Langhorne a promissory note for $500 due and payable December 1, 1988. On February 1, 1989, Langhorne transfers the note to Baker. Because the note had already matured, Baker is not a holder in due course; if there is something wrong with the note, Calhoun has a good defense when Baker demands payment.

Before buying an instrument that has reached maturity, the person should ask, "Isn't there something wrong with this instrument? Why was it not paid when it came due?"

Notice of Defenses or Defects in the Instrument

In order for a transferee of a draft or note to be a holder in due course, he must have no notice of any defect of title, of illegality, or of fraud or other defects in the instrument. The instrument must be complete and regular on its face and must have no blank spaces.

If the instrument says it is due "___ after date," there is something missing, and the incompleteness of the instrument prevents the transferee from being a holder in good faith. Even leaving blank the name of the person to whom the instrument is payable casts some doubt on the instrument.

In addition, in order to be a holder in due course, it is necessary that at the time the holder gets the instrument he have no notice of any infirmity in the instrument or of any defect in the title of the transferor. Written notice is not necessary, but actual knowledge of the claimed defenses to a note or knowledge of circumstances to put the transferee on notice may be sufficient to prevent the transferee from becoming a holder in due course.

Barlow borrows $5000 from Landers. Ingraham, who is in the habit of buying promissory notes, has heard some talk that Barlow claims that Landers exacted an exorbitant discount before entering into the transaction. Hearing this talk has put Ingraham on notice to look into the matter further, but he purchases the note without investigation. He does not become a holder in due course.

Barnes, treasurer of the River Lumber Company, makes out a promissory note on this company, payable to himself. He takes the note to a bank that discounts it and becomes the owner. Stockholders of the company protest that the note was issued without proper corporate authority and that the treasurer had no right to make the note payable to himself; they can successfully claim that the bank is not a holder in due course.

TRANSFER OF COMMERCIAL PAPER

If negotiable paper is payable to bearer, it may be transferred simply by delivery. If negotiable paper is payable to the order of a designated person, it may be transferred only by the indorsement of that person, completed by delivery.

Indorsement of Commercial Paper

An indorsement is a written signature on the back of a piece of commercial paper. Generally, it is the signature of the payee of a note or bill of exchange or of a third person, evidencing the transfer of the note. Indorsement is to be distinguished from assignment, which is generally made by a separate instrument. An indorsement is (1) a transfer of title to the instrument indorsed and (2) a conditional promise to pay the same.

The indorsement must be written on the instrument itself or on a paper attached to it. The signature of the indorser, without additional words, is sufficient indorsement. An indorsement may be special or in blank, restrictive or qualified, or conditional.

A *special indorsement* specifies the person to whom the instrument is payable, and the indorsement of that person, the indorsee, is necessary to further the negotiation of the instrument. This is usually done by saying "pay to the order of" and inserting the indorsee's name.

An *indorsement in blank* does not specify an indorsee, and an instrument so indorsed is payable to bearer and may be transferred by delivery. The last indorsee simply signs his name to the back of the instrument.

A *restrictive indorsement* (1) prohibits the further negotiation of the instrument, (2) establishes the indorsee as the agent of the indorser, or (3) vests title in the indorsee in trust for the use of another person. The effect of a restrictive indorsement is to allow the instrument to be used by the indorser without the indorsee parting with title to it.

A *qualified indorsement* establishes the indorser as a mere link in the chain of title without attaching any liability to the indorsement. The indorser has no liability for nonpayment of the paper, but he guarantees its validity and his title to it. An indorser may make a qualified indorsement by adding to his signature the words "without recourse."

A *conditional indorsement*, as the term implies, is an indorsement of a note to become payable on the completion of a condition, providing a specified event happens. Conditional indorsements are not favored in the commercial world and, thus, are rare.

Liability of Indorsers

When a person writes his name on the back of commercial paper, he becomes known as an "indorser." Some indorsers assume that they are responsible only for payment of the instrument (such as a check, promissory note, or bill of exchange). Others assume that they are simply transferring title. Neither assumption is wholly correct.

The liabilities and responsibilities of indorsers are considerable and are based on technical rules which have been codified in the Uniform Commercial Code. These rules are so strictly interpreted that if those seeking to impose liability on indorsers do not follow them explicitly, the indorsers are sometimes excused from legal liability. On the other hand, indorsers also have rights and privileges which are protected if the other parties to commercial papers do not live up to their obligations.

Liability to Holder of Commercial Paper

When he indorses commercial paper, an indorser creates a new and independent contract—one separate from the original contract of the maker or the signer of the original paper. By signing his name and transferring the commercial paper to the new owner, the indorser warrants the following:

1) He has good title to it or is authorized to receive payment from one who has good title.
2) The transfer is rightful.
3) All signatures are genuine.
4) The instrument has not been materially altered.
5) No defense of any party is good against him.
6) He has no knowledge of any insolvency proceedings instituted with respect to the maker or acceptor or drawer of an unaccepted instrument.

Indorsers are liable in the order in which they indorse an instrument. For example:

A gives his promissory note to B, payable in six months. One month after the note is given, B needs the money and indorses and sells the note to C. C indorses and sells the note to D, and D indorses and sells the note to E, who is the owner and holder of the note when it becomes due. At that time A, the maker of the note, is bankrupt. Then E may collect from D, D may collect from C, and C may collect from B, making B the ultimate loser.

Presentment for Payment

In order to hold an indorser liable, the commercial paper must be presented for payment. Presentment for payment is not necessary in order to charge the person primarily liable on the instrument, but it is necessary in order to make the indorser liable.

Presentment for payment must be made on the day when the commercial paper falls due (1) by the holder or by a person authorized to receive payment in his behalf, (2) at a reasonable hour on a business day, (3) at the place of payment specified in the instrument or, if no place of payment is specified, at the address or usual place of business or residence of the person required to make payment, and (4) to the person primarily liable on the instrument. In making presentment for payment, the instrument must be exhibited to the person from whom payment is demanded; when it is paid, it must be delivered to the person paying it.

Montgomery signs a promissory note payable to Smith. Smith sells and indorses the promissory note to Jones. Jones sells and indorses the promissory note to Brown. Brown goes to Montgomery and makes a formal presentment and demand for payment of the note. Montgomery says, "I am sorry, but I do not have the money." Brown sends a written notice to Jones that the note has not been paid. Brown has sufficiently complied with the Uniform Commercial Code in making the presentment for payment and giving notice of dishonor, and Jones thereupon becomes obligated to pay the note.

Long signs a promissory note stating, "I promise to pay to the order of Meco on September 1, 1989, the sum of $1,000." If payment is not made on the date the note is due, Meco may sue for payment. (No presentment for payment was necessary between the two parties to the note.)

An exception to this rule arises, however, in the case of a forged prior indorsement. The reason for this exception is that the indorser has warranted the instrument to be genuine and the holder of the note may rely on such warranty.

If in the example above facts were changed so that, in the first instance, someone had forged Montgomery's name, it would not be necessary for Brown to present the note for payment or give Jones notice of the nonpayment and dishonor of the note. After all, Jones had warranted that the note was genuine, and Brown is entitled to rely on that fact.

NOTES

[1] A promissory note may also be drawn for a specific date: two months after date; on the 16th day of May 1978 or on or before the 123d day of 1978. It may be made out to a person, firm, or bearer. It may also be drawn to person or order or to the person or bearer.

[2] However, the drawer, who has himself issued the check and normally expects to have it paid and charged to his account, is reasonably required to stand behind it for a longer period, especially in view of the protection now provided by Federal Deposit Insurance.

The indorser, on the other hand, who has normally merely received the check and passed it on and does not expect to have to pay it, is entitled to know more promptly whether it is to be dishonored, in order that he may have recourse against the person with whom he has dealt.

12

LABOR AND MANAGEMENT

Labor and management have frequently appealed to the government to assist in the settlement of their disputes. In the beginning of the industrial era, representatives of industry were able to obtain injunctions from the courts to halt strikes, picketing and boycotts. Later in the era, legislation was enacted to regulate the use of injunctions and the various activities of labor and management.

LABOR LEGISLATION

The most important federal laws dealing with employer-employee relations during the last fifty years are the Norris-La Guardia Act, the National Labor Relations Act, the Taft-Hartley Law (Labor-Management Relations Act), and the Labor Reform Act.

Norris-La Guardia Act

Many years ago Congress enacted the Norris-La Guardia Act, which prohibited federal courts from granting injunctions in so many types of disputes that in practice it did away with the use of injunctions in about 99 percent of the cases. This act also prevented the enforcement of "yellow dog" contracts (under which an employee binds himself not to join a union).

National Labor Relations Act

The National Labor Relations Act of 1935 (popularly known as the Wagner Act) might be said to be the real beginning of government intervention in labor relations. This act gave employees the right to form labor organizations and to bargain collectively through representatives of their own choosing. It declared that interferences by employers with the employees' right of self-organization constituted unfair labor practices, and it provided stiff penalties for such violations. The National Labor Relations Act also created the National Labor Relations Board with power to enforce the provisions of the act, including the curtailing of employer influence through a company-dominated union and the prevention of employer discrimination against employees for union activities.

Taft-Hartley Law

The wave of strikes that followed World War II prompted Congress to curb the power of the labor unions. The Taft-Hartley Law (Labor-Management Relations Act) enacted in 1947 was the result. Management described its enactment as an attempt to control the extreme power that was vested in the National Labor Relations Board. Unions, on the other hand, called it a "slave-labor law" and an attempt to undermine collective bargaining.

The provisions of the Taft-Hartley Law were many. The most important concerned (1) the establishment of a general counsel (which has authority to issue complaints); (2) the banning of the closed shop (through which only union members could be hired) but the sanctioning of the union shop (which requires an employee to join the union within a certain period of time after he is hired); (3) the prohibition of unfair labor practices by both labor and management (outlawing coercion, discrimination, and refusal to bargain by either one and illegal strikes or boycotts by labor); (4) the guarantee of free speech to employers in carrying their views to employees; (5) the institution of a sixty-day cooling-off period before work stoppage at the end of a collective bargaining contract; and (6) the creation of special procedures for dealing with strikes that threaten the safety of the nation. Other provisions barred Communists from holding union offices, forced unions to file financial reports, and placed unions for supervisory personnel outside the protection of the act.

Labor Reform Act

In September 1959 Congress enacted the Labor Reform Act, which made certain changes in the control of labor and management and set up a system to protect union members from the alleged corrupt influences of union leaders. The law established a bill of rights for union members, assuring them equal rights in the union. It attempted to help union members bring unscrupulous practices of union officials to light and established stringent restrictions on secondary boycotts and organizational picketing.

LEGAL CASES ARISING OUT OF LABOR-MANAGEMENT DISPUTES

Labor legislation has for the most part sought to soften the effects of the unrestricted interplay of labor-management pressures. The National Labor Relations Act had accomplished much of this; later legislation has sought mainly to clarify and improve the provisions of this act. Following are discussions of the types of legal cases which evolve most frequently out of the National Labor Relations Act, the Taft-Hartley Act, the Labor Reform Act, and from labor-management controversies.

Employers Subject to National Labor Relations Act

The so-called commerce clause of the U.S. Constitution, which gives Congress the power to "regulate commerce of foreign nations and among the several states," is broad enough to permit Congress to pass labor legislation governing more than 80 percent of the businesses in the United States. If a business is engaged in *interstate commerce* (trade, traffic, commerce, transportation or communication among states, the District of Columbia or foreign countries), it is subject to the National Labor Relations Act. The test of whether a business flows through interstate commerce is not what percentage of business flows through interstate channels, but whether any does. For example:

A department store pointed out to an appeals court that its out-of-state mail-order sales of $20,000 represented only .0024 percent of its total annual sales. The appeals court said that the "application of the Act does not depend upon the magnitude of the business nor the comparative amount of interstate sales." The department store was held to be engaged in interstate commerce and subject to the National Labor Relations Act.

The activities of transportation and communication companies, (including truckers and railroads, telephone companies, radio stations, magazines, newspapers, the motion picture industry), and building and construction, production, manufacturing, warehousing, storage, public utilities, banking and insurance concerns are all regulated by the National Labor Relations Act.

The National Labor Relations Board has declined to take jurisdiction in labor disputes involving a few classifications that it views as "local business." These disputes are handled by the state labor relations boards. In 1989, yardsticks of jurisdiction applied by the National Labor Relations Board to determine its regulation of business were amended by Congress.

The new regulations will assert jurisdiction of an "enterprise" (defined as a common or related activity under a unified or common control, e.g., a chain of stores) whose gross annual volume of business done or sales made is not less than $500,000, or which is a hospital, school or public utility.

Employees Subject to National Labor Relations Act

Under the National Labor Relations Act the term "employees" includes all those earning wages or salaries or commissions, except agricultural laborers, domestic servants, individuals employed by parents or spouses, independent contractors, and railroad employees. Supervisors, foremen, and executives are also excluded from the protection of the act.

This question often arises: Who is an "independent contractor"? If an employer has the right to control the manner or method by which the work is done, the workman on the job is regarded as an employee. If the workman can do the work whenever he pleases and is accountable only for the final result, he is quite likely to be held an independent contractor. For example:

The Kelly brothers formed a partnership, bought two trucks and worked out a deal with a cinderblock company to haul blocks at one-half-cent a mile within a given area. They bought their own vehicles, tires, gas, and paid all the vehicle maintenance bills. They were not on the cinderblock company's payroll, and the company did not pay any social security or unemployment taxes for them. The Kelly brothers were held to be independent contractors, not employees subject to the National Labor Relations Act.

The method by which he is compensated is not a deciding factor in determining whether or not a person is an employee. A person may be paid a commission or even a percentage of the profits instead of a salary and may still be held to be an employee. So broad has been the coverage of the National Labor Relations Act that insurance agents, newsboys, seasonal and part-time workers, and persons laid off have been held to be employees under the act.

Company Unions

Labor legislation prohibits an employer from installing or promoting a company-dominated union, known as a "company union," in his organization.

An employer calls in a few "trusted" employees and suggests to them it would be nice if they would form their own union; if they would do so, he would have a room in the plant set aside for the offices of the union and have the company lawyer show the employees how to draw up a set of bylaws for the organization. The union which is subsequently formed becomes an illegal, company-dominated union.

Sometimes an effort is made to convert employees' social organizations into company unions. Sometimes bona fide unions charge that social organizations such as employees' clubs are "company unions" in disguise. The true test in such cases is whether the employees' club is a purely social organization, without the purpose or power to deal with management in questions relating to wages and working conditions, or whether it is a disguised movement to keep out an external union.

Company unions are often formed to combat nationally affiliated unions. The National Labor Relations Board orders such unions disbanded and orders the employer to stop interfering with the rights of employees in the selection of their own bargaining representative.

There are, however, unions which are not affiliated with national labor organizations and which should not be confused with the prohibited company union. These organizations are truly independent of employer influence and faithfully represent employee-members in their dealings with management.

Discrimination in Regard to Employment

The National Labor Relations Act protects the employees' right to "engage in concerted activities for the purpose of collective bargaining or for their mutual aid or protection." Employees may form a union, they may strike, they may petition for a change in working conditions, they may engage in many concerted activities, which are protected under the law.

An employer may not refuse to hire an employee because he is a union member, nor may he discharge an employee for his union activities or because he is related to a union member. If he does either of these things, he is guilty of unfair labor practice.

Howard Rufkin, an employee, posted a notice on the bulletin board of the Solid Bookend Company, stating, "All employees interested in joining the Amalgamated Bookenders' Union will meet at Union Hall, Thursday at 7 o'clock." The next day he was dismissed by the company.

The National Labor Relations Board brought a proceeding against the Solid Bookend Company charging it with unfair labor practice. The company defended the dismissal, claiming that Rufkin had refused to obey orders and that the quality of his work was poor, and that was why he had been fired. The National Labor Relations Board held that the real reason for Rufkin's dismissal was his union activity and ordered him reinstated with back pay.

The law labels as unfair labor practice an employer's discharge of or other type of discrimination against an employee because he has filed charges or given testimony under the National Labor Relations Act.

Joe Thompson filed charges with the National Labor Relations Board claiming that his employer, the Viking Company, was guilty of an unfair labor practice. He was discharged by his employer. Subsequently, the National Labor Relations Board ordered him reinstated with back pay.

The National Labor Relations Board has held countless employers' practices to be discriminatory, and its contentions have been upheld by court decisions. Among those activities that have been found to be antiunion or discriminatory are the following: (1) refusal to hire, (2) failure to recall seasonal employees, (3) discharge of employees, (4) demotion, (5) layoff, (6) transfer to less desirable positions, and (7) reduction to part-time employment.

Many of these types of "discriminatory activities" also are prohibited by other federal laws. For example, refer to the discussion in Chapter 25 entitled "Civil Rights," beginning on page 362.

Strikes

Strikes may be classified for the purpose of this discussion into four groups: economic strikes, unfair labor practice strikes, wildcat strikes, and illegal strikes.

Economic Strikes Employees who strike as a result of a stalemate in negotiations for a contract are on an economic strike. They are protected by the National Labor Relations Act against unfair labor practices and retain their status as employees during the strike. An employer may not refuse to reinstate an employee solely on the ground that he participated in the strike, but the employer has a right to replace economic strikers. If they are replaced, the striking employees are not entitled to reinstatement. (Although they may not be entitled to reinstatement, under the Labor Reform Act, economic strikers may now vote in elections conducted by the National Labor Relations Board at any time within twelve months after the beginning of the strike.)

Employees represented by a union at the ABC Chemical Company plant during contract negotiations demanded a wage increase of 40 cents an hour. The company offered to grant an increase of 10 cents, but the union would not yield and called an economic strike. After it had been going on for five months, the union employees decided to call off the strike and go back to work.

In the meantime, about 60 percent of the striking employees had been replaced by other workers. The company refused to fire the replacements and take back all the strikers. The strikers took the matter to the National Labor Relations Board, which held that because it was an economic strike the company was justified in refusing to dismiss the replacements and was also justified in refusing to reinstate strikers whose jobs had been filled by others.

Unfair Labor Practice Strike Employees who strike because of an employer's unfair labor practices remain employees within the meaning of the National Labor Relations Act, and once the employer's acts are determined to be unfair labor practices by the National Labor Relations Board, they may have their jobs back. This is true even though the employer has in the meantime hired replacements.

In the course of the negotiations of the Plymouthe Company with the union representing its employees, the company dismissed several union leaders, who the company said were guilty of insubordination, and refused to continue contract negotiations because of what the company termed the union's hostile negotiations and unfair tactics. The union charged the company with unfair labor practice in discharging the employees and in refusing to bargain; then the employees went on strike to protest the company's unfair action. The National Labor Relations Board held with the union.

Meanwhile, the company had filled the positions left vacant by the strikers. The striking employees asked that their jobs be returned to them. The company refused. The National Labor Relations Board held that if the striking employees unconditionally applied for reinstatement, they had to be reinstated and the replacements had to be dismissed. (The N.L.R.B. decision held that the employees were engaged in an unfair labor practice strike and they could not be permanently replaced.)

Wildcat Strikes A wildcat strike is caused by a group of employees' unauthorized action that does not have the sanction of the law; an illegal strike (discussed in the next section) is absolutely prohibited by the law. *Wildcat strikers* are those who go out on a strike not authorized by the union that represents a majority of the employees. Such strikers are not entitled to the protection of the National Labor Relations Act and may be discharged.

On October 14 union representatives journeyed to Spartanburg, South Carolina, to attend contract negotiations with the D Corporation. Upon arrival the union leaders were told that the D Company's bargaining representative (and its secretary) was ill in Massachusetts and was unable to attend the conference. The secretary was in fact ill, but some of the employees were angry and resentful because they thought his illness was an excuse for delay. The next morning forty-one of the employees (about 25 percent of the total number) gathered in a corner of the factory and failed to go to work. They said they were carrying on a wildcat strike because they believed that the company was stalling; they demanded action. The workers were ordered by the superintendent to go to work or to get out of the plant. They refused to go to work or leave the plant and remained on company property. The next day the 41 workers were paid in full and were discharged for engaging in a sit-down strike.

On October 20, as a result of the efforts of the Federal Mediation and Conciliation Service, the company and the union arrived at a contract settlement. The forty-one striking employees presented themselves for work, but the company refused to hire them. The matter was taken to the National Labor Relations Board, which ordered the company to rehire the strikers and pay them back wages. An appeal was taken to the U.S. Court of Appeals (Fourth Circuit), which held that the wildcat strike did not fall within the protection of the strike provisions of the National Labor Relations Act; that the conduct of the workers amounted to insubordination; and that the company was justified in discharging them. It also held that the wildcat strike is a particularly harmful and demoralizing form of industrial strife and is destructive of collective bargaining, which it is the purpose of the law to promote.

Illegal Strikes The following strikes were made unlawful by the Taft-Hartley Law: (1) strikes to force an employer or self-employed person to join a union; (2) strikes to force an employer to stop doing business with another person; (3) strikes to force an employer to bargain with a minority union after the National Labor Relations Board has certified a majority union; and (4) strikes beginning within sixty days preceding the expiration of a labor contract. Employees who participate in an illegal strike lose their status as employees.

The National Labor Relations Board held an election to determine whether the AFL union or the CIO affiliate would represent the employees of the Bacon Company. The AFL group won the election 210 to 160. The CIO affiliate, contrary to instructions from its national headquarters, had its members go on strike and picket the Bacon plant. The National Labor Relations Board held the strike to be illegal and ordered the union to cease and desist from striking and picketing.

Employer's Rights and Obligations During Union Organizational Drive

The Taft-Hartley Law modified the Wagner Act by giving employers more freedom of speech in the following ways during a union organizational campaign:

The expressing of any views, arguments, or opinions, or the dissemination thereof, whether in written, printed, graphic, or visual forms shall not constitute or be evidence of unfair labor practice under any of the provisions of this Act, if such expression contains no threat of reprisal or promise of benefit.

This provision of the Taft-Hartley Law gives an employer the right to express his views on unionism generally, his views on a particular union, and his preference for one union over another. However, it is very dangerous for the average employer to criticize a union or its officers without guidance from another skilled in labor relations. For example:

When the Amalgamated Union sent representatives to his plant to convince the employees that they should join the union, Mr. Butterman (president of Butterman Manufacturing Company) said, in a speech to his employees, "The union is made up of a bunch of racketeers, and if the plant is unionized we will be put out of business." The union lost an election and filed unfair labor practice charges against the company. The N.L.R.B. held that the remarks of Mr. Butterman constituted an implied threat, which in turn constituted coercion and interference with the right of the employees to self-organization. It directed that the employer recognize and bargain with the union.

During an organizational campaign an employer should not make wage adjustments, threaten economic reprisals or discriminatory treatment, promise raises or increased benefits, bargain with individual employees, induce employees to sign individual employment contracts, question employees about their union business, or spy on their union activities.

After the organizational campaign, an employer can challenge a union's assertion that it represents the majority of employees if he does so in good faith. The election machinery of the National Labor Relations Board comes into play on petition of an employer or on petition of a union to hold an election to determine who is the representative of the employees for collective bargaining purposes. Such an election is conducted under the supervision of a representative of the National Labor Relations Board after the board determines a unit for bargaining purposes. On the basis of the election results, the N.L.R.B. certifies the appropriate bargaining unit, and this certification is final. For example:

Mr. Cleon, representative of the Amalgamated Union, comes to the office of Mr. Robert, president of Robert's Manufacturing Company, and says, "We represent the employees in your Utica plant and would like to enter into a contract governing wages and working conditions." Mr. Robert says, "That's news to me. How do I know you represent my employees?" Mr. Cleon says, "If you won't take my word for it, we'll go to the National Labor Relations Board." Mr. Robert says, "OK by me." Later a representative of the Board calls on Mr. Robert and says, "Will you agree to an election?" Robert says, "Sure." A meeting is held with the board representative, Cleon, and Robert. They enter into an agreement for a consent election. A bargaining unit is decided as "all production employees in the Utica plant excluding office and clerical employees, supervisors, executives, and so on." Ten days later the election is held; the union wins by a vote of 54 to 53 and is certified by the National Labor Relations Board as the bargaining representative of the Utica plant production employees of the Robert's Manufacturing Company.

Collective Bargaining

Collective bargaining is defined by law as the performance of the mutual obligation of the employer and representatives of the employees (1) to meet at reasonable times, (2) to confer in good faith with respect to wages, hours, and other terms and conditions of employment, and (3) to incorporate any agreement reached into a written contract. This obligation does not compel either party to agree to a proposal or require either party to make concessions.

Once the employees' bargaining representative (the union) has been certified by the National Labor Relations Board, the employer is duty bound to agree to discuss wages and employment only with it. Usually in collective bargaining proceedings the union submits a contract and the employer makes counterproposals.

Boycotts and Picketing

Under the Labor Reform Act of 1959 it is an unfair practice for the union to engage in a strike or to refuse to work or to threaten an employer when the purpose of these activities is (1) to force an employer not to handle the goods of another, (2) to stop a person from using, selling, handling, or transporting the products of another employer, (3) to make another employer recognize or bargain with a union unless it has been certified by the National Labor Relations Board, or (4) to force an employer to bargain with a particular union when another union has already been certified by the Board.

This law bans *secondary boycotts* in a more strict manner than the Taft-Hartley Law. The Taft-Hartley Law prohibited unions from putting pressure on employees of secondary employers, but the Labor Reform Act of 1959 makes it unlawful for a union to put this direct pressure on a secondary employer himself.

Many union contracts formerly contained "hot cargo" clauses, which provided that union employees were not required to handle the goods of a concern whose employees were on strike. Under the current law it is unfair labor practice for a union to engage in concerted activities in order to force an employer to sign an agreement refusing to handle the goods of another. Before passage of the Labor Reform Act, unions sometimes resorted to picketing and other activities to force an employer to sign a union contract when none of his employees belonged or wanted to belong to the union. Under the 1959 law it is unfair for a union to picket or threaten to picket an employer for recognition or to force employees to join the union if (1) a valid National Labor Relations Board election has been held within the preceding twelve months, (2) if such picketing has been conducted before a petition for an election has been filed with the National Labor Relations Board, or (3) if the employer has lawfully recognized another union.

LABOR RELATIONS INVOLVING PUBLIC EMPLOYEES

Until the early 1960s employees of federal, state, and local governments lived in a world of undefined rights. They did not have the same privileges to bargain collectively through representatives of their own choosing or other guarantees which nongovernment employees had.

Government employees and their unions waged and won a battle. First, the courts recognized the right of government employees to form associations (unions) and to speak freely regarding conditions of their employment. Then President Kennedy and later President Nixon issued Executive Orders granting bargaining and other rights to federal employees. Now, Congress has included most U.S. government employees subject to its Labor Relations Act.

More than twenty-two states that give all government employees, state and local, the right to be represented by unions and to bargain collectively. Those states include: California, Connecticut, Delaware, Hawaii, Kansas, Maine, Michigan, Minnesota, Missouri, Nebraska, Nevada, New Hampshire, New Jersey, New York, Oregon, Pennsylvania, Rhode Island, South Dakota, Vermont, Washington, Wisconsin, and Wyoming.

Eight states (Alaska, Florida, Georgia, Idaho, Maryland, Montana, North Dakota, and Oklahoma) give limited rights to government employees in special groups such as teachers and fire fighters. Labor relations involving government employees differ from labor problems in the field of private employment principally in that government employees for the most part are denied the right to strike.

OSHA

Congress passed the Occupational Safety and Health Act (known as OSHA). The purpose of this law is to guarantee to employees a safe and healthy working environment. OSHA gives the secretary of labor authority to promulgate standards regulating workers' exposure to unsafe or unhealthy conditions in the work place.

Many states have their own OSHA law. The federal OSHA Administration often attempts to have the state OSHA inspectors monitor the various work places.

Industry often regards OSHA's acts to be an intrusion and an ineffective way of enforcing health and safety regulations. For example, one of the complaints of the industry and mine owners under the OSHA statute and other similar statutes relating to mines is that too often inspections are made without notice and without a court order calling for the inspections. Such inspections are called warrantless inspections; however, OSHA continues to act without a court order and many courts have upheld their procedure.

13

CORPORATIONS

A corporation is a legal "person" composed of one or more natural persons and is an entirely separate and distinct entity from the individuals who compose it.

CHARACTERISTICS OF A CORPORATION

The powers of a corporation are fixed by its charter, which is granted to it by the state in which it is incorporated. A corporation may have perpetual existence, notwithstanding the death, withdrawal or disability of its members. It can sue or be sued; it can purchase and hold lands or other property, enter into contracts, or commit legal wrongs like a private individual. The corporation's ability to do these things depends upon the terms of the charter granted to it by the state; its activities are governed or limited by the state's statutes.

When two or more persons form a partnership, each business partner retains his identity as an individual. A partnership is not a legal entity separate and distinct from the individual members, but a corporation is, and its individual members legally lose their identity in the corporation. The members of the partnership are individually liable for partnership debts, whereas the stockholders are not usually liable for corporation debts. The death of a partner generally results in the dissolution of the partnership, but the death of a stockholder does not affect a corporation. (See Chapter 14 for more information on partnerships.)

In unincorporated societies and clubs, the individual members may be liable for actions taken by a majority of the members or for actions of its officers. This is not so in the case of a corporation. The corporation is liable for the acts of its officers, but the individual stockholders usually are immune. Thus, the modern trend is to incorporate most societies and clubs.

Although many states have in recent years revised their corporation laws and have patterned them after the Model Business Corporation Act of the American Bar Association (called the "Model Act"), the corporation laws still vary greatly among the states. For example, the duration of a corporation according to the laws in one state is twenty-five years; in another state, ninety-nine years; in still another, perpetual. In some states, the name of the corporation must include the word *Corporation* or *Incorporated* or *Limited* (or the abbreviations *Inc.* or *Ltd.*) to avoid confusion with individuals doing business under assumed names or partnership forms. Other states permit simply the word *Company* or the abbreviation *Co.*

ADVANTAGES OF INCORPORATION

The advantages to businessmen of incorporation over other forms of business organization are limited liability, permanency, and flexibility. Once a stockholder has paid for his stock in the corporation, he usually is not liable to creditors of the corporation. Thus, businessmen can put money into a corporate venture and not run the risk of personal liability if the venture fails. The corporation may continue indefinitely no matter what happens to its original stockholders.

Shares of stock represent fractional ownership interest in a corporation. They may be sold, given away, or pledged as security for loans by the stockholder without affecting the basic corporate organization.

KINDS OF CORPORATIONS

There are many different kinds of corporations, among them public, municipal, and private corporations; stock and membership corporations (sometimes known as not-for-profit corporations); and foreign and domestic corporations. Different legal rules determine the powers, liabilities, and privileges of each classification of corporation.

Public, Municipal and Private Corporations

Public or municipal corporations are instrumentalities of government, such as the federal government, cities, villages, towns, counties, school districts, school boards, and so on. They are to be contrasted with private corporations, which are owned by individuals.

Stock and Membership Corporations

A stock corporation is one in which the capital stock is divided into shares held by the owners of the corporation and which is authorized by law to pay its profits to shareholders in the form of dividends. Private business corporations are generally stock corporations. All corporations listed and traded on stock exchanges are stock corporations.

Stock corporations not so listed or traded on one of the stock markets often are referred to as "closely held" or "privately owned" corporations; that is, owned by a limited group of stockholders. Although they usually come within one of the exemptions to the Securities Laws (page 189), sometimes these state and federal laws nevertheless can be applied to redress a wrong. Of course, all corporations listed on any stock exchange (or whose stock is actively traded) are subject to the Securities Laws.

Membership corporations are nonprofit, nonstock corporations created for various purposes; examples are organizations or groups to promote or further political, religious, temperance, missionary, educational, scientific, musical, charitable, social, or other nonbusiness activities.

Members are those who have a vested interest in a corporation that has no capital stock. *Stockholders* are the owners of shares in a corporation which has capital stock.

Foreign and Domestic Corporations

A domestic corporation is one doing business in the state in which it is incorporated. It becomes a foreign corporation when it does business in another state. It is similar to the concept that a citizen of this country becomes a foreigner when he moves to another country.

Other Classifications

Corporations are also classified according to particular statutes as a cooperative, joint stock, religious, cemetery, library, agricultural, transportation, railroad, insurance, and so on.

ORGANIZING A CORPORATION

The Model Business Corporation Act of the American Bar Association provides that three or more natural persons[1] (at least two-thirds of whom are citizens of the United States or of its territories) may form a corporation. The Model Act provides, too, that the articles of incorporation shall specify: (1) the purpose of the corporation; (2) its duration; (3) its location and the post office address of its registered office; (4) the total number of shares of par value and the total number of shares of no-par value; (5) the relative rights, voting powers, preferences, and restrictions of each class of shares; (6) the amount of paid-in-capital with which the corporation will begin business; (7) the first directors and their post office addresses; and (8) the name and post office address of each of the incorporators and a statement of the number of shares for which each has subscribed.

According to the Model Act procedure, the proposed certificate of incorporation is first delivered to the state secretary of state. When he has approved it and when all taxes, fees, and charges as required by law have been paid, he approves and certifies the incorporation. At this point corporate existence begins.

Corporate Names

Before the articles of incorporation are approved by the secretary of state, the *corporate name* must be approved. It must not be the same as nor deceptively similar to the name of any other domestic corporation or any foreign corporation authorized to do business in the state. The following names have been contested and held to be too similar for duplicate filing of articles of incorporation:

J.S. Dodge Stationery Company

J.S. Dodge Company

Mount Hope Cemetery Association

New Mount Hope Cemetery Association

International Loan and Trust Company

International Trust Company

Glucose Sugar Refining Company

American Glucose Sugar Refining Company

Backus Oil Company

Backus Oil and Car Grease Company

Manchester Brewery Company

The North Shore and Manchester Brewery Company

The following names have been held to be not so similar as to come within the rule prohibiting the use of both names:

Los Angeles Trust Savings Bank

Los Angeles Savings Bank

Elgin Creamery Company

Elgin Butter Company

Industrial Mutual Deposit Company

Central Mutual Deposit Company

Corning Glass Works

Corning Cut Glass Company

Buffalo Commercial Bank

Bank of Commerce in Buffalo

In addition, the secretary of state may not approve a proposed corporate name of any ordinary business corporation if it contains prohibited words, such as "insurance," "bank," "fidelity," "state police," "doctor," or "lawyer."

Organization Meetings

When the articles of incorporation are filed, the incorporators hold a meeting, adopt bylaws, and approve the initial steps to be taken by the corporation. The directors, who in some states are named in the certificate of incorporation, hold their first meeting, elect officers, and decide what assets are to be acquired, what stock should be issued, and so on.

The incorporators adopt the bylaws, usually with the approval of the directors. Bylaws are rules and regulations established by a corporation for the government and guidance of its officers and stockholders in the management of corporation affairs. Generally, the bylaws contain a restatement of the state's laws governing the conduct of corporations and also contain provisions governing the day-to-day affairs of that corporation.

Powers of a Corporation

An individual has the legal power to do anything or to engage in any kind of business not prohibited by law. A corporation on the other hand may do only those things and engage only in those businesses permitted by law or set forth in its certificate of incorporation.

The corporation laws of each state specify the purposes for which corporation may be organized. Under the old rule corporations were organized for a single business, such as to sell real estate, manufacture automobiles, operate a store, or to conduct a specified business enterprise. If the corporation attempted to operate another type of business, its efforts would be considered illegal and it would have to organize a new company to operate the new type of business.

As the various states began to realize the importance of having corporations in their states, the rule was changed. Over the last forty years, the powers stated in certificates of incorporation were broadened so that a corporation could engage in many different enterprises. Most current certificates of incorporation contain an absurd enumeration of endless powers and purposes; incorporators seem to like to include in the corporate charter almost every conceivable kind of legal business. Modern draftsmen of corporate charters have attempted to end the enumeration of countless types of businesses by general statements of comprehensive scope.

The trend to simplify statements of corporate powers is illustrated by the following provision in the Model Business Corporation Act: "It shall not be necessary to set forth in the articles of incorporation any of the corporate powers enumerated in this Act."

The broadening of corporate powers is exemplified by the New

York Business Corporation Law, enacted in 1961, which states that every corporation has the power:

1) To have perpetual duration

2) To sue and be sued in all courts and to participate in actions and proceedings, whether judicial, administrative, arbitrative or otherwise, in like cases as natural persons

3) To have a corporate seal and to alter such seal at pleasure and to use it by causing it or a facsimile to be affixed or impressed or reproduced in any other manner

4) To purchase, receive, take by grant, gift, devise, bequest or otherwise, lease, or otherwise acquire, own, hold, improve, employ, use and otherwise deal in and with real or personal property, or any interest therein, wherever situated

5) To sell, convey, lease, exchange, transfer or otherwise dispose of, or mortgage or pledge, all or any of its property, or any interest therein, wherever situated

6) To purchase, take, receive, subscribe for or otherwise acquire, own, hold, vote, employ, sell, lend, lease, exchange, transfer or otherwise dispose of, mortgage, pledge, use and otherwise deal in and with bonds and other obligations, shares, or other securities or interests issued by others, whether engaged in similar or different business, governmental, or other activities

7) To make contracts, give guarantees and incur liabilities, borrow money at such rates of interest as the corporation may determine, issue its notes, bonds and other obligations, and secure any of its obligations by mortgage or pledge of all or any of its property or any interest therein, wherever situated

8) To lend money, invest and reinvest its funds, and take and hold real and personal property as security for the payment of funds so loaned or invested

9) To do business, carry on its operations, and have offices and exercise the powers granted by this chapter in any jurisdiction within or without the United States

10) To elect or appoint officers, employees, and other agents of the corporation, define their duties, and fix their compensation and the compensation of directors

11) To adopt, amend, or repeal bylaws relating to the business of the

corporation, the conduct of its affairs, its rights or powers, or the rights or powers of its shareholders, directors, or officers

12) To make donations, irrespective of corporate benefit, for the public welfare or for community fund, hospital, charitable, educational, scientific, civic, or similar purposes and in time of war or other national emergency in aid thereof

13) To pay pensions, establish and carry out pension, profit sharing, share bonus, share purchase, share option, savings, thrift and other retirement, incentive, and benefit plans, trusts, and provisions for any or all of its directors, officers, and employees

14) To purchase, receive, take, or otherwise acquire, own, hold, sell, lend, exchange, transfer or otherwise dispose of, pledge, use, and otherwise deal in and with its own shares

15) To be a promoter, partner, member, associate, or manager of other business enterprises or ventures or to the extent permitted in any other jurisdiction to be an incorporator of other corporations of any type or kind

16) To have and exercise all powers necessary or convenient to affect any or all of the purposes for which the corporation is formed.

The all-inclusive statements of powers in the New York statute give New York corporations the power to perform almost every conceivable business act that an individual could perform.

BOARD OF DIRECTORS OR TRUSTEES

The fundamental responsibility for the management of a corporation actually lies with its directors, who have full discretionary power. Ordinarily that power is delegated to the officers of the corporation, who actually make the day-to-day decisions. The board of directors or trustees is the corporation's governing body. In most states it must consist of at least three persons, although in some states where there is only one stockholder, there need be only one director.

Directors or trustees (these terms are often synonymous) usually are elected by the majority vote of the stockholders; the modern trend is to provide either by statute or in the bylaws or certificate of incorporation of the corporation that a director need not be a stockholder of the corporation. The directors may (and in many cases do if they so desire) consult the stockholders regarding their wishes.

Generally, directors have authority to act only at regularly called meetings, and they must act as a board; that is to say, individual or separate action of one of the directors does not bind the board or the corporation. Meetings of the board of directors may be held at any time and place within the state of incorporation or elsewhere.

Directors stand in a fiduciary relation to the corporation and are required to discharge their duties in good faith with diligence, care, and skill. A director of the corporation should not deal with himself when he is acting in behalf of the corporation, and he may not directly or indirectly derive personal benefit, by reason of his position as a director, that is not enjoyed by all the stockholders.

Mr. Garber was a director of the Union Manufacturing Company. While attending a directors' meeting, he learned that the corporation was contemplating the purchase of land on which to build a new factory. Mr. Garber had his real estate agent go out and buy land in the vicinity and subsequently offered to sell the land to the corporation at a profit. A minority stockholder, learning of Mr. Garber's double dealing, brought a court action against him and succeeded in recovering damages in behalf of the corporation for Mr. Garber's breach of trust.

Lawyers might label Mr. Garber's action as an "abuse of corporate opportunity." When a director assumes his or her office, that corporate director commits allegiance to the enterprise and acknowledges that the best interests of the corporation and its shareholders must prevail over any individual interest of his own. The basic principle to be observed is that the director should not use his corporate position to make a personal profit or to gain other personal advantage.

In other words, the first duty of a corporate director is a "duty of loyalty." The director should not have conflicts of interest; should observe a duty of fairness; should avoid abusing corporate opportunities; and should deal in confidence with all matters involving the corporation until such time as there has been general public disclosure of the matters. Abuse of the duty of "confidentiality" is often referred to as improper use of so-called "inside information."

Mr. Smith, a director of Acme Foundry Corporation, knows that the corporation is going "public"; that is, the corporation is about to list and sell its shares of stock on a stock exchange. Mr. Smith thereupon buys the stock of several minority stockholders (who do not know about the corporation's intentions to go public).

After the stock is "listed," it increases tenfold in value. Mr. Smith sells his stock at a great profit.

The minority stockholders (and the corporation) can successfully sue Mr. Smith to recover his ill-gotten profits.

As discussed beginning on page 189, the courts have expanded the rule against abuse of inside information to include not only persons who have a fiduciary duty to the corporation (its lawyers, its officers, and their families), but also to include anyone who might be in a position to misuse this information (e.g., newspaper reporters, printers, and so on).

The second duty of a director is a "duty of care"; that is, to act carefully in fulfilling the important duties of monitoring and directing the activities of corporate management. The duty of care involves acting in good faith and doing what he or she believes is in the best interests of the corporation.

The directors' performance should not be in hindsight. In this respect, there is in corporation law an expression known as the "business judgment rule," which holds that decisions made by the board of directors of a corporation, in good faith and honest judgment, should not be set aside by a court on the ground that a better judgment might have resulted in a different corporate decision.

In addition to the "business judgment rule," directors are entitled to rely on information, opinions, and financial statements prepared and presented to them by counsel, public accountants, or other persons whom the director reasonably believes to be reliable and competent and where he or she has no knowledge to the contrary which would cause the reliance to be unwarranted.

Perhaps one of the most important duties of a director is the "duty of attention." A corporate director, both of a business corporation and a not-for-profit corporation, has a responsibility to actively participate in the oversight of the enterprise's activities; such participation includes: attending meetings, reviewing adequate information and documentation, and monitoring delegated activities.

A corporate director (particularly an "outside director," one who is not an officer or employee of the corporation) can make a valuable contribution through inquiry and discussion of management's proposals.

A vacancy in the board of directors usually can be filled by the remaining board members. A director who obtains his status in this way remains until his successor is elected by the stockholders at their next annual meeting.

Although directors are chargeable with and have the authority to run the corporation and do not need to get stockholder approval of important business decisions, there are certain actions which require stockholder approval. For example, the Model Business Corporation Act provides that a sale, lease, exchange, mortgage, pledge, or other disposition of all or substantially all the property and assets of a corporation, if not made in the usual and regular course of business, must have the approval of the holders of two-thirds of the outstanding stock. Also, a merger, consolidation, or voluntary dissolution of a corporation, according to the Model Act, requires two-thirds stockholder approval. (Many states' statutes require the approval of only a majority—one more than one-half—of the stockholders.)

OFFICERS (AGENTS) OF THE CORPORATION

The Model Act provides that the board of directors of a corporation shall elect a president, a secretary, a treasurer, and one or more vice-presidents, and shall appoint such officers and directors as may be necessary for the business of the corporation. The states' laws vary; for example, the New York Business Corporation Law provides that: "Any two or more offices may be held by the same person, except the offices of president and secretary. When all of the issued and outstanding stock of the corporation is owned by the same person, such person may hold all or any combination of offices."

The officers and agents have authority to perform duties in the management and affairs of the corporation subject to such control of the board of directors as may be prescribed in the bylaws or as determined by the board. Officers of the corporation also occupy a fiduciary relationship to the corporation and are accountable for the same high degree of fidelity as are the directors. An officer or agent may be removed by the board of directors whenever in its judgment his removal is in the best interest of the corporation.

RIGHTS OF STOCKHOLDERS

Right to Information

The stockholders are the owners of the corporation and as such have the right to information about the business affairs of the company; they are privileged to visit and inspect the corporation's property and to inspect and examine the books and records of the corporation at a proper time and place and for a proper purpose.

The Model Act provides that every corporation shall keep at its registered office (1) appropriate books of account, (2) a record of the proceedings of the stockholders and of the directors, and (3) a register giving the names and addresses of the stockholders of the corporation, the number of shares owned by each, and the dates acquired. The Model Act also provides that every shareholder shall have the right to examine the corporation's books in person or by proxy (through an agent or an attorney) at all reasonable times and for any reasonable purpose. The act provides further that a corporation shall be liable to the state for a fine of $50 for each day that it neglects to keep these books or records.

Mr. Townsend, holding 15 percent of the stock of the Brewster Corporation, goes to the main office of the corporation and requests that he be permitted to examine its books and records. His request is denied. Mr. Townsend obtains a court order permitting him to examine the records. Mr. Townsend later learns that the corporation does not keep a record of stockholders as required by law. He reports this to the attorney general of the state, who brings a proceeding to collect fines from the Brewster Corporation.

Stockholders' Meetings

The Model Act provides that stockholders' meetings may be held within or without the state of incorporation and that at least one stockholders' meeting must be held within each calendar year. Stockholders' meetings may be regular or special. Special meetings of stockholders may be called at any time by the officers of the corporation or by the board of directors or by an individual director or under certain conditions even by an individual stockholder. The Model Act also provides that stockholders are entitled to written notice at least ten days prior to a stockholders' meeting.

A corporation organized in a handful of states may take certain action *without a meeting*, which would ordinarily require a meeting of stockholders, if the action is approved by a majority of the stockholders. This "privilege" also must be specifically spelled out either in the certificate of incorporation of the corporation or in the bylaws of the corporation.

Voting Rights

In a stock corporation, each shareholder is entitled to one vote for each share he owns. The Model Act provides that in the election of directors, each shareholder shall have the right of "cumulative voting"; that is, he has the right to determine the number of votes he has by multiplying the number of his shares by the number of directors to be elected. He may cast all his votes for one candidate, or he may distribute his votes among two or more candidates. For example, if five directors are to be chosen, a holder of five shares may have twenty-five votes.

However, in many states "cumulative voting" must be authorized specifically in the certificate of incorporation or bylaws.

At stockholders' meetings (unlike a director at a director's meeting, who must be present), a shareholder may cast his vote either in person or by proxy. A *proxy* is a person who has been duly authorized to vote for the stockholder by a written instrument (also called a proxy), filed with the secretary of the corporation. The Model Act provides that the validity of a written proxy shall cease eleven months after the date of its execution unless another definite period shall be specified; even when a definite time is specified in the proxy instrument, the instrument is generally not good beyond three years from the date of issue.

Voting Trusts

A voting trust is an agreement whereby several stockholders, in order to control the business and affairs of a corporation, turn over their shares to one or more persons as trustees to vote the stock. The Model Act, in referring to voting trusts, states that two or more shareholders may transfer their shares to any person or corporation to act as trustee for the purpose of vesting in such person or corporation all the voting rights pertaining to such shares for a period not exceeding ten years. It provides that a duplicate copy of the voting trust agreement shall be filed in the registered office of the corporation and shall be open to inspection by any shareholder. Any other shareholder may transfer his shares to the same trustee on the terms and conditions stated in the agreement. The voting trustee must then execute and deliver to the shareholder voting trust certificates, which are transferable in the same manner as stock certificates.

The Snell Company encountered financial difficulties. Realizing that the bank was about to foreclose the mortgage on the factory and that the creditors of the corporation were seeking bankruptcy, a group of stockholders went to a man who was reputed to be an "industrial doctor" and persuaded him to act as voting trustee with full power to vote stock of the majority of the stockholders and to throw out the management of the corporation. The voting trust agreement was valid and enforceable, and as a result of hard-boiled but prudent business tactics this person saved the company from bankruptcy.

Liability of Stockholders

Since a corporation is a legal entity entirely separate from its stockholders, the latter, except under very rare circumstances, are neither liable for the debts of the corporation nor for the acts or misdeeds of the officers or agents of the corporation. This is a fundamental principle governing corporations—the law of limited liability.

The stockholder who does not pay the corporation for his stock is liable to creditors of the corporation for the amount of the capital he had agreed to pay. As far as the relation of the stockholders to the creditors is concerned, only the capital of the corporation can be used for payment of debts. In the absence of fraud or the creation of a fictitious corporation, the stockholders have no further responsibility once they have paid in the capital. In determining whether stock is fully paid and whether actual or true value has been paid for the stock, the courts say that if the directors have acted in good faith (that is, without actual fraud or intentional overvaluation), stock is deemed to be fully paid up. This is so even though (against creditors) it may afterwards appear that through mistake or error in judgment there was an overvaluation of property received by the corporation in exchange for stock.

It must be borne in mind that the concept of a corporation as a legal entity, or "person" apart from its members, is a mere fiction of the law conceived for convenience in conducting business. In rare cases, the courts have disregarded this corporate fiction and, as the expression goes, have "pierced the corporate veil" in order to place the legal and moral responsibility for fraud on those persons who have attempted to hide behind a corporate entity. This has happened when several corporations have been owned by the same parties. In these cases, the courts have disregarded the legal fiction of distinct corporate entities because the corporations were so organized and controlled that one corporation was merely an instrument or an adjunct of another.

The Sword Steamship Brokerage Company organized the Sword Stevedore Company with identical officers for each company. The brokerage company furnished the facilities and offices of the stevedore company, kept its accounts, handled its funds, paid its losses, and retained its profits as a charge for handling its business. In a negligence action the court held that concerning third persons the two corporations were identical and both were liable for damages caused by the negligence of any employee of either company.

CAPITAL, SHARES, PROFITS, DIVIDENDS

A knowledge of the meanings of the terms capital, capital stock, capitalization, profits and dividends is essential to an understanding of corporation law. Here we will differentiate among these several topics.

Distinction between Capital Stock and Shares

The *capital stock* of a corporation is the amount fixed by the articles of incorporation (or in the case of no-par stock, by the directors) as the amount paid in or to be paid in by the stockholders as capital with which the corporation is to do business. In accounting terminology, the single word "capital" is also used to denote the amount of the capital stock.

Shares of stock represent the proportionate interest of the stockholders in the corporate property. The terms shares of stock and stock and shares are used interchangeably, as are the terms stockholders and shareholders. This distinction is made between capital stock and shares of stock: The capital belongs to the corporation, and the shares are the property of the individual shareholders.

The legal capital of a corporation and the number of shares into which the capital stock is divided and the amount or par value of each share are fixed by the articles of incorporation. However, in the case of no-par stock, the amount of the capital is fixed by the directors.

Each stockholder is entitled to a certificate of stock, signed and sealed by the president or vice president and the secretary or treasurer; this is the manner in which stock is issued. The stock certificate states (1) the name of the corporation; (2) the name of the registered holder of the shares of stock; (3) the number and class of shares which the particular certificate represents (that is, preferred or common stock, par stock or no-par stock); (4) the par value of each share or a statement that the shares have no-par value; and (5) the total number of par shares and the total number of no-par shares. A certificate of stock is not issued until the shares represented by the certificate have been paid for in full. To determine whether the shares have been fully paid and to fix the obligation of a shareholder to the corporation, the valuation placed by the incorporators or by the directors is final.

Different Kinds of Stock

There are many types of stock shares. The following are the major ones:

Common stock is the ordinary stock of the corporation that entitles the owner to a pro rata share of the profits of the corporation. No profits may be paid to common stockholders until dividends are declared by the directors.

Preferred stock gives the holder preference either in the distribution of earnings of the corporation or in the dissolution of the corporation over the holders of common stock or another class of stock. Holders of guaranteed stock, a form of preferred stock, are guaranteed dividends by the corporation.

Where the dividends on preferred stock are guaranteed, the preferred stock issue is often referred to as "cumulative preferred stock"; where the dividends are not guaranteed, the preferred stock issue may be referred to as "noncumulative preferred stock."

Preferred stock also sometimes may be *"convertible"* into common stock, at a conversion ratio set forth in the preferred stock certificate, but only if the certificate of incorporation so authorizes such conversion.

Nonassessable stock is that which has been legally issued by the corporation and is fully paid and on which no assessment against the stockholder can be made.

Treasury stock is stock that has been sold to stockholders and reacquired and held by the corporation.

Unissued stock is that which is authorized but which has never been issued.

Par stock is given a "price ticket" that indicates the nominal value of each share of stock.

No-par stock is stock without any named par value but which simply represents a fractional interest in the assets of the corporation.

Profits and Dividends

The dividends and the profits of a corporation are not the same thing. *Profits* become dividends when they are declared or set apart by the directors as such. Dividends become the property of the stockholders; they are distributed to the stockholders on the basis of their ownership interest in the corporation.

Dividends can be declared and paid only out of net profits or surplus funds of the corporation, except when a corporation is liquidated. The reason for this is obvious: distribution of capital as dividends depletes the capital of the corporation. In many states it is a criminal offense for directors to declare dividends out of capital, for it perpetrates fraud on the firm's creditors (who have extended credit to the corporation on the faith of its capital).

The Model Act strictly prohibits the payment of dividends except from the surplus profits of the corporation; if the directors knowingly vote in favor of illegal dividends, they are individually liable to the corporation for the amount of the dividend so paid.

MERGER AND CONSOLIDATION

The terms merger and consolidation are often confused and inaccurately used. A true consolidation is brought about when a new corporation comes into existence to take over the assets and liabilities of two or more former corporations, which are then dissolved. A merger, on the other hand, is brought about when one existing corporation is continued and one or more others are merged into it without the formation of a new corporation. For example:

The South American Steamship Company and the African Coastal Lines decide to put their assets together and form a new company to be called the Trans-African Transportation Company. A consolidation results.

The directors of the Johnstown National Bank vote to acquire the First National Bank of Meredith. After the acquisition, both banks will be known as The Johnstown National Bank, which will have a branch in the village of Meredith. The First National Bank of Meredith loses its identity. The Johnstown National Bank continues its corporate existence as before. The result is a merger of the Meredith Bank with The Johnstown National Bank.

Neither consolidation nor merger does away with the rights of creditors without their consent, and the surviving corporation (in a merger) or the new corporation (in a consolidation) is liable for the debts of the merged or consolidated companies.

Mechanics of Merger or Consolidation

Merger or consolidation may be limited by statutes or by antitrust laws. The Model Act (in Sections 65–71) provides that a merger or consolidation can be effected only as the result of a joint agreement entered into and filed as follows:

1) The board of directors of each such corporation enters into a joint agreement signed by the directors, describing the terms and conditions of merger or consolidation and the methods of effecting it.

2) The agreement is submitted for consideration to the stockholders of each merging or consolidating corporation at a meeting. If at this meeting the holder of two-thirds[2] of the voting power of all the stockholders of each corporation votes for the adoption of the agreement, then that fact is certified by the secretary of each corporation; the agreement so adopted and certified is then signed by the president and secretary of each corporation.

3) The agreement is delivered to the state secretary of state, who, if he finds the agreement lawful, files and records it in his office, whereupon the merger or consolidation becomes a fact.

Rights of Dissenting Stockholders

When a corporation plans to merge or to consolidate, a stockholder of either corporation who did not vote in favor of the move may (according to the Model Act), within twenty days after authorization to merge or consolidate, reject the proposal in writing and demand payment for his shares. If the corporation and the stockholder cannot agree on the value of his shares, it will be determined by three disinterested persons—one named by the stockholder, one by the corporation, the third by the two other appraisers. The finding of the appraisers is final. If their award is not paid by the corporation within thirty days after it is made, it may be recovered in a suit against the corporation.

DISSOLUTION

A corporation is dissolved when its existence is terminated, its affairs wound up, and its assets distributed among creditors and stockholders. Dissolution does not take place with the suspension of business, nor with the abandonment of a corporate franchise, nor with the sale of a corporation's entire assets or by the appointment of a receiver. Dissolution may be voluntary or involuntary. The proceedings may be conducted out of court (voluntary dissolution) or subject to the supervision of a court (involuntary dissolution).

Voluntary Dissolution

Voluntary dissolution may be achieved by the corporation stockholders. The Model Act provides that proceedings for voluntary dissolution may be instituted whenever a resolution therefore is adopted by the holders of at least two-thirds of the voting power of all the stockholders at a special meeting called for that purpose. Instead of having a stockholders' meeting to dissolve a corporation, there may be a voluntary dissolution on the written consent of all the stockholders. Also, there may be a voluntary dissolution by all the incorporators of a corporation within two years after the date of the issuance of its certificate of incorporation, provided (1) that the corporation has not commenced business, (2) that no debts of the corporation remain unpaid, and (3) that the majority of the incorporators desire that the corporation be dissolved.

The resolution for voluntary dissolution may provide that the affairs of the corporation shall be wound up out of court by a trustee or trustees. The appointment of the trustees cannot be made until duplicate copies of the resolution have been signed by a majority of the directors or by the stockholders holding a majority of the voting power and until one of these copies has been filed in the office of the state secretary of state.

Although it has been said that voluntary dissolution results from the expiration of a corporate charter, from merger, from consolidation, or from other proceedings which result in the corporation going out of existence, these are not true voluntary dissolutions. In order for there to be a voluntary dissolution (1) the stockholders must act, (2) a certificate of dissolution must be obtained from the proper state official (obtainable only after all state corporate taxes have been paid), and (3) a notice of dissolution to creditors must be published. Then steps are taken to terminate the affairs of the corporation by selling the assets and distributing the proceeds to creditors and stockholders.

In a few states voluntary dissolution, after approval by the stockholders, is carried out by application of the corporation to the court for supervision of the dissolution. In other states a voluntary dissolution may be effected only by a proper application to the court, and dissolution does not take place until a hearing has been held for the creditors and all interested parties, and the court has entered its decree.

Involuntary Dissolution

Involuntary dissolution may take place as a result of (1) the expiration of the corporate charter; (2) an equity suit by a stockholder or creditor asking the court to appoint a receiver and terminate the affairs of the corporation by reason of fraud on the part of the majority stockholders, mismanagement on the part of the officers or directors, or dissension among stockholders which renders impossible a continuation of the business; or (3) of the forfeiture of the charter by the state as a result of fraud practiced on the state by the corporation or failure to pay franchise taxes or failure to exercise corporate powers. The general rules and principles concerning involuntary dissolution have been codified in the Model Act, which sets forth three types of involuntary dissolutions:

1) In an action filed by the attorney general when it is established that:

The corporation has failed to file its annual report within the time required by this act or has failed to pay its franchise tax on or before the first day of August of the year in which such franchise tax becomes due and payable; or

the corporation procured its articles of incorporation through fraud; or

the corporation has continued to exceed or abuse the authority conferred upon it by law; or

the corporation has failed for thirty days to appoint or maintain a registered agent in this state; or

the corporation has failed for thirty days after change of its registered office or registered agent to file in the office of the state secretary a statement of such change.

2)   In an action by a shareholder when it is established that:

The directors are deadlocked in the management affairs and the shareholders are unable to break the deadlock, and that irreparable injury to the corporation is being suffered or is threatened by reason thereof; or

the acts of the directors or those in control of the corporation are illegal, oppressive, or fraudulent; or

the shareholders are deadlocked in voting power and have failed for a period that includes at least two consecutive annual meeting dates to elect successors to directors whose terms have expired or would have expired upon the election of their successors; or

the corporate assets are being misapplied or wasted.

3)   In an action by a creditor:

When the claim of the creditor has been reduced to judgment and an execution thereon returned unsatisfied and it is established that the corporation is insolvent; or

when the corporation has admitted in writing that the claim of the admitted in writing creditor is due and owing and it is established that the corporation is insolvent.

Professional Corporations or Associations

A professional corporation or association (commonly referred to as "PC" or "PA") is a corporation organized by members (or even one member) of a profession (such as medicine, architecture, dentistry, law, accountancy, or engineering) to enable them to practice their professions as a corporation. Until the 1960s, professional people were forbidden by state laws from practicing their professions as corporations. The prohibition against their incorporating was thought to work hardships on them. Advocates of professional corporations claimed that the law unfairly discriminated in favor of business executives and employees who received many fringe benefits, such as pension or profit-sharing plans, which professional people were barred from using. The subject was controversial and was debated for many years. Finally the fifty states now have laws which allow members of professions to incorporate.

Although professional corporations partake of many of the features of a private corporation, and have limited liability in some respects, the professional or professionals who have charge of a client or patient are still personally liable for their acts. In other words, the "corporate veil" may be pierced to that extent.

SECURITIES LAW

History In 1933 and 1934 Congress passed two laws, one called the Securities Act of 1933 and the other called the Exchange Act of 1934. These laws were designed to protect the public in securities transactions.

The federal government has, in recent years, become increasingly active in regulating disclosure practices and securities transactions of corporations and their directors, officers and employees. Today, under the 1933 act and the 1934 act, the federal government has a strong impact upon the day-to-day operations of most, but not all, corporations. Compliance with these two federal regulatory statutes, as well as other statutes administered by the Securities and Exchange Commission (the S.E.C.), is essential in order to avoid penalties provided by these laws. Violation of the Federal Securities Law may result in imposition of criminal penalties or civil injunctions against the corporation, with similar penalties, possibly including jail sentences for its directors, officers and employees. In addition, each state has laws regulating securities, which may be more or less strict than the federal laws. These state laws are known as "blue sky" laws.

Securities Transactions The question whether a transaction involves a security or whether it is a mere commercial transaction often arises. Securities should have investment rather than commercial attributes. The Supreme Court has laid down some tests to determine whether a transaction is a securities transaction or not. These tests are (1) the presence of an investment, (2) in a common venture, (3) premised on a reasonable exchange of profits, (4) to be derived from the managerial efforts of others.

Many if not most corporations and business enterprises are not covered by the 1933 and 1934 acts. Most of them are relatively small and do not involve "public officers"; that is, the stock or the securities is never offered to the general public. Therefore, they are only subject to the jurisdiction of the law of the state of incorporation or the laws of the states where they do business.

Some states have more stringent corporate laws and securities laws than other states. Hence, it is often advantageous to incorporate in one state rather than in another state; the relatively lax regulatory requirements of the state of incorporation may be better suited.

Victims of Security Fraud

Investors who are victims of securities fraud either may file suit under the Federal Securities Laws or under the law of the state of incorporation of the corporation.

Often the S.E.C. investigates the alleged securities fraud for many years, and these investigations are confidential. As a result, potential plaintiffs often find that the time limitations within which to file suit have expired.

Recently the U.S. Supreme Court ruled the plaintiffs in a securities fraud must sue within one year of discovering that they were bilked and within three years of the commission of the fraud. (At least one senator feels that considerably more time should have been given, and has introduced legislation to lengthen the one year, three year, limitation. The proposed legislation is being vigorously fought.)

State laws on the topic are a hodgepodge, and for years various federal courts have held that the limit set in the plaintiff's home state of incorporation applied to private claims charging investment fraud under federal statutes.

This is a complex area, professional help should be sought, and the following are a few definitions frequently used in securities law:

Churning is an illegal practice of a broker frequently putting a client in and out of securities not for the purpose of the client's best interests but to generate commissions for the broker.

Fraud: The acts of Congress are aimed at preventing fraud against the public. The acts are said to contain anti-fraud provisions.

The Sale of Business Doctrine: Some courts have held that the sale of 100 percent of a business does not involve a securities transaction but is simply a commercial transaction.

Shelf Registration Rule: The S.E.C. adopted on a trial basis the shelf rule, which allows companies to register all the securities they plan to sell during the following two years and then gives the company the right to sell any of those securities whenever they choose. The reason for the rule is to allow companies to more freely move on the sale of securities. Normally, a group of brokers gets together and forms a syndicate to sell and market securities. The shelf rule makes it unnecessary for them to have a syndicate. (This rule has come under criticism because of abuses.)

ANTI-TRUST LAWS

Although the common law against restraints of trade and state statutes on trade regulation were able to control competitive abuses during the last century after the Civil War when businesses began to leap state boundaries, it became clear that nationwide laws were required. The Sherman Anti-Trust Law was, therefore, enacted in 1890. It was eventually followed by the Clayton Act, the Federal Trade Commission and the Robinson-Patman Act (which dealt with resale price maintenance). The Sherman Act prohibits in general terms both monopolies and unreasonable restraints of trade.

The Clayton Act is more specific. It prohibits tying clauses, exclusive dealing arrangements and total requirements obligations if they involve commodities not services. It also prohibits such practices where either they may substantially lessen competition or tend to create a monopoly. As amended in 1950 (by another law), the Clayton Act also prohibits corporate mergers and acquisitions where the effect of such acquisition would be to substantially decrease competition or to tend to create a monopoly.

Although ordinarily the federal government enforces these laws, the acts also authorize private citizens to enforce them; if a private plaintiff succeeds in such an action, his damages award then is trebled.

The Federal Trade Commission Act, enacted in 1914 and amended in 1936, 1980 and again in 1985, supplement judicial enforcement of the anti-trust laws through an administrative commission, known as the Federal Trade Commission (F.T.C.). The act declares that "unfair methods of competition. . .and unfair or deceptive acts or practices in commerce. . . " are unlawful. The F.T.C. has broad powers, among other matters, to prohibit incipient restraints of trade, price fixing, and boycotts.

The original sponsors of the Sherman Act apparently only intended for Congress to enact federal legislation that codified the then-common law of the states. However, Congress and the federal courts have proceeded step by step to deal with competition as it has become more sophisticated.

Most states also have statutes regulating monopolies and other acts which may tend to lessen competition.

NOTES

[1]Many states have adopted much more simple procedures to encourage incorporation in that state. For example, the New York State Business Corporation Law provides that one or more persons may act as an incorporator or incorporators of a corporation.

[2]Some states have reduced the necessary approval percentage to one-half.

14

PARTNERSHIPS[1]

In about 1840, Chancellor James Kent, an eminent scholar and an appellate judge from New York State, gave one of the earliest and most concise and comprehensive definitions of a partnership, a definition that is still quoted today. Kent stated that a partnership is "a contract of two or more competent persons to place their money, effects, labor and skill, or some or all of them, in lawful commerce or business, and to divide the profit and bear the loss in certain proportions."

A partnership is an association of two or more persons formed to carry on a business for mutual profit. The partners (1) are co-owners of the enterprise, (2) intend through the partnership to make a profit, (3) are agents for and have a fiduciary relationship with each other,[2] and (4) consequently, each partner is responsible for the acts of the others.

Although there are many advantages to the corporate form of business, many businessmen prefer the partnership form of organization. This sentiment prevails when persons consider important equality of action and freedom from public supervision, corporation taxes, and corporation routine. A partnership, however, is not to be entered into lightly; its freedoms are balanced by equal responsibilities which in certain circumstances may become liabilities. The major disadvantage of the partnership form of doing business is the unlimited personal liability of each partner for all obligations of the business, including liabilities which result from wrongful acts of another partner.

KINDS OF ORGANIZATION AND PARTNERS

Partnerships may be general or limited (special). Over 90 percent of partnerships in this country are *general partnerships*, those in which all the partners share the liabilities of the partnership debts and in which each partner is an agent for the firm. In a general partnership partners may have the same or different investments of capital and may share the profits and losses in the same or different proportions.

A *limited partnership* is composed of one or more general partners and one or more special partners. A special partner may limit his liabilities in the partnership to the amount of his investment by inserting modifying articles in the partnership agreement.

Limited partnerships were never part of the English common law. In 1822, however, New York became the first common-law state to introduce limited partnership laws. Eventually, the Uniform Limited Partnership Act (1916) was approved by the National Conference of Commissioners on Uniform Laws, and it has been adopted with slight modifications by all states except Alabama, Connecticut, Kansas, Kentucky, Louisiana, Maine, Mississippi, Oregon, and Wyoming. This act, which was borrowed from the French Code, provides for the filing of a limited partnership certificate stating information about each partner, the amount of cash or other property contributed by each limited partner, and the share of profits each limited partner is to receive. The limited partnership certificate must not only be filed but must also be published once a week for six successive weeks in two newspapers of the county in which the original certificate is filed.

The Uniform Limited Partnership Act delineates the rights and liabilities of general and limited partners between themselves and in respect to other persons. Among other things, the act provides (1) that a limited partner shall not become liable as a general partner unless he takes part in the control of the business, (2) that a limited partner shall have the right to full information about all things affecting the partnership, and (3) that a limited partner shall receive his share of the profits or other compensation by way of income.

A partnership may exist where parties do not intend partnership or where the agreement between them even states otherwise. This happens when persons conduct themselves in such a manner that it may be reasonably inferred that they are partners. This is known as *partnership by estoppel*. For example, if a third party, assuming that two business-men are partners, extends credit to them, they may be held to be part-ners by the third party.

Partners have been divided into various classes such as dormant, silent, incoming, retiring, nominal, ostensible, and secret partners. These terms have no well-defined meaning in law. A silent partner is said to be the same as a sleeping partner: one who is neither an active partner nor generally known to the public as a partner; his connection with the firm is concealed in some way. A nominal partner is one who allows his name to appear as a member of the firm in which he has no real interest. This arrangement is similar to that of an ostensible part-ner, who may appear to be a partner but who has no actual interest in the firm.

FORMATION OF A PARTNERSHIP

No particular form of contract is necessary for the formation of a partnership. The contract may be oral or written or may be implied from the conduct of the parties. An oral contract is as binding on the individual partners as a written agreement between them. Nevertheless, it is preferable to establish a partnership by a contract in writing.

A partnership agreement is sometimes called "articles of copartner-ship" and usually contains in detail all things agreed to by the prospec-tive partners. The rules of law applicable to contracts generally, such as those relating to consideration, consent, and capacity of the parties to enter into a contract apply to partnership contracts, but the contract of partnership, as distinguished from other types, must be a contract to conduct a business for the *mutual profit of the partners*. The purpose to make money is the essential feature of a partnership.

People do sometimes enter into business arrangements for purposes other than to share a profit; for example, local merchants may form an association for the purpose of sharing losses in the breakage of plate glass, or several persons may agree to share the expense of paying rewards for the capture of thieves, or businessmen may band together for mutual protection or advancement. None of these cooperative ven-tures is a partnership. A mere community of interest, such as the joint ownership of property, does not make the owners partners. On the other hand, when co-owners of real estate agree to combine their efforts in the business of buying, improving, selling, or leasing it, they may be held to be partners.

Mason, Young, and McCee decide to build houses under an arrangement whereby Mason agrees to furnish the cash and the real estate, Young is to act as architect, and McCee agrees to do all clerical and mortgage work. It is further decided that each one is to receive a fair share of the profit on the sale of the houses. Such an arrangement constitutes a partnership.

Money may be loaned or advanced to the owner of a business with the understanding that the loan is to be repaid from profits of the business and that the profits shall take the place of interest on the loan. This arrangement does not constitute a partnership.

Sometimes a store is leased under an agreement that a percentage of the profits of the business of the store is to be paid as rent, but this arrangement does not make the landlord a partner in the business.

When people band together for other than business purposes, for example, for political, religious, or charitable reasons, no partnership exists.

PARTNERSHIP NAME

A partnership may choose to do business under a firm name consisting of all the names of the persons forming the partnership. However, practically all states have assumed-name laws, which require that any person (or persons) conducting business under any other title than his real name file in a public office a certificate stating his (or their) full real name and his residence. Some states prohibit the use of the name of a person and the phrase "and company" when the latter phrase does not represent an actual partner.

Messrs. Moon and Stellick operated a plumbing business in New York under the name of Empire Plumbing Company. Under the New York assumed-name law, they were required to file a certificate in the county clerk's office showing the name and address of the business and their individual names and residences, but they neglected to do this. One of their competitors brought the matter to the attention of the district attorney, who instituted a criminal proceeding against Moon and Stellick for failing to file an assumed-name certificate. Moon and Stellick claimed that they were the victims of needless persecution and pleaded innocent to the charge, saying that no creditor or other interested person was hurt. The court found Messrs.

Moon and Stellick guilty of a misdemeanor and they were subjected to unpleasant publicity.

Almost all other states have a law requiring that persons may not transact business as partners under a partnership name other than their own names unless they file in the county clerk's office in the county in which the firm operates a certificate showing the name under which the business is transacted and the name and address of each partner.

For example, three public accountants operate a partnership firm under the name, "Tax and Audit Co."; they must still file a partnership certificate giving their full names and addresses.

Some states also require that certain partnerships (and persons using an assumed name) publish a "legal notice" in a local newspaper.

RIGHTS AND DUTIES OF PARTNERS TO EACH OTHER

Although no formal contract is necessary to form a partnership, to have a written contract allows those individuals involved to specify the rights and the duties of the partners. It includes such items as place, name, term of partnership; amount of capital to be invested by each partner; types of partners to be included; distribution of profits; and so on.

Short and Long Agreements

A partnership, agreement may be a long or short document. Here is an example of points covered by a short partnership agreement:

Weaver and Levelle decide to open a stationery store. Their short partnership contract provides:

1) The name of the partnership shall be "Weaver and Levelle."

2) The term of the partnership shall be 10 years.

3) The place of the partnership shall be 214 Main Street.

4) The partnership shall open, manage and operate a stationery store.

5) The capital of the partnership shall be $10,000; each partner's contri-

bution is $5,000 cash. Neither party's contribution to the capital shall bear interest.

6) If either party, with the consent of the other, lends money to the partnership, such loans shall bear interest at the rate of 6 percent per annum.

7) Each partner shall devote all his time to the business and shall not engage in any other business.

8) Partnership profits or losses shall be divided equally.

The following is an example of the subject matter of a long partnership agreement:

Messrs. Kead, Bailey, Holden, and Ferber, about to engage in the business of wholesale distribution of food products, decide they would be better off if they did not incorporate. They tell their lawyer that they want to cover in detail in the partnership agreement all the points of their arrangement. Read is to contribute $25,000, Bailey $10,000, Holden $7,000, and Ferber $5,000.

The agreement drawn by the lawyer specifies the capital of the partnership; that additional contributions to capital may be made by the parties from time to time; how loans may be made by the partners and how they shall be repaid; how the bank account is to be maintained and what signatures are to be required on checks; the fact that Read will not be required to render active services to the business beyond weekly consultation services, but that Bailey, Holden, and Ferber will devote all their time to it; that Bailey is to be the managing partner, charged with the responsibility of making decisions concerning operational details; that for the first six months of the operation none of the partners is to receive a salary or drawing account but thereafter Bailey is to receive a salary of $600 each week, Holden $300 each week, Ferber $250 each week, and Read no weekly salary; that the first $25,000 of net profits should be divided equally between the partners, but that all profits after the $25,000 should be divided in proportion to the capital contributions; that no partner can withdraw more than 50 percent of his share of the profits in any one year without the consent of the other partners; that full and accurate account of transactions shall be kept in books of account; that the lives of Bailey and Holden shall be insured for $500,000 each and the lives of Ferber and Read insured for $200,000 each, payable to the partnership.

Also, that each partner should satisfy his own personal debts; that no partner shall assign, mortgage, or sell his interest in the partnership; that no partner shall make any assignment for the benefit of creditors or mortgage his personal real estate without the consent of the other partners, nor borrow, lend money, or indorse commercial paper except for the purpose of the partnership; that each year a complete statement and accounting shall be made of all assets and profits of the partnership; that if any party should elect to retire from the partnership, he should give the other partners notice in writing, and that the amount of his capital contribution shall be paid to him by the other partners; and other detailed machinery about the method of retiring from the partnership; provisions regarding the payment of a small percentage of the partner's share in the profits on the physical or mental disability of any partner; provisions as to how a partner can be expelled for misconduct; that death shall not terminate the partnership, but that the estate of the deceased partner shall be paid the amount of his contributions to the capital in equal annual installments extending over a period of ten years; and a provision for arbitration in the event of a dispute between the partners.

RESTRICTIONS ON INDIVIDUAL TRANSACTIONS OF PARTNERS

As do partners in a marriage, business partners also owe to each other the utmost good faith in all their mutual dealings, including abiding by the limitations placed on the outside activities of partners.

All profits made by a general partner in conducting the business of the partnership belong to the partnership. Thus, a partner may not derive a secret personal profit from any transaction of the firm or use partnership property for his individual profit or benefit. He must always disclose his personal interest in the matter.

Todd and Murdock were partners who owned several tobacco plantations and sold to many concerns. On one occasion they sold tobacco at a ridiculously low price to the Lost Continent Tobacco Company, of which Murdock was the principal stockholder. The transaction, unknown to Todd, resulted in considerable profit to Murdock. Upon discovery Todd sued. The court required Murdock to account to the partnership for his personal profit.

A partner cannot engage in the same kind of business as that of the partnership without the consent of his partners. However, there is nothing to prevent a partner from engaging in a trade or business different from that in which the firm is engaged. If his business is entirely different, he does not have to account to his partners for the profits.

The Kingsley Chalmers Company was engaged in the real estate brokerage business. Chalmers bought a tract of land with his own money, subdivided it, and sold lots. Kingsley Chalmers Company had never been in the business of buying or developing real estate subdivisions, but had limited itself to brokerage business. Therefore, Chalmers was not accountable to the firm for the profit he made in buying and selling lots for his own profit.

When a partner withdraws from the partnership, notice of his withdrawal should be given to all persons with whom the partnership has dealings so the withdrawing individual cannot be held liable for debts contracted after he has severed his connection with the business. Unless the other partners consent, a partner cannot sell his interest in the firm in order to give the transferee the right to become a member of the firm.

LIABILITY OF PARTNERS TO OTHER PERSONS

In the United States each partner may usually be held liable for the total amount of the partnership debt. If the partnership assets are depleted, the creditors may look to the individual partners for payment. This is true not only regarding contractual obligations but also concerning wrongs committed in behalf of the partnership that result in injuries and damages to others. The partnership firm as well as each member thereof is answerable for the acts of its agents and employees provided their acts are performed in the course of their employment.

Kress and Kaplan were partners engaged in the contracting business. They hired Dyer as their general superintendent. In supervising the construction of a building, Dyer did not follow the architect's plans, and, as a result of weak and defective supports negligently constructed, the building collapsed causing considerable destruction to the property. The partnership assets were subject to the claims of those who had been damaged, and Kress and Kaplan were individually responsible for the acts of Dyer.

DISSOLUTION OF PARTNERSHIP

A dissolution of a partnership is the cancellation or breaking up of the relationship of the partners. On dissolution the partnership is not terminated but is continued until the settlement of the partnership affairs. Dissolution does, however, terminate all the remaining partners' authority, except that which is necessary to wind up partnership affairs.

There is no such thing as an undissolvable partnership, because the courts have held that the right of a partner to dissolve a partnership is an inherent right. Any partner to a partnership may at any time take legal steps to dissolve the partnership.

According to the provisions of the Uniform Partnership Act, dissolution is caused:

1) Without violation of the agreement between the partners:
   a. By the termination of the definite term or particular undertaking specified in the agreement; or
   b. By the express will of any partner when no definite term or particular undertaking is specified; or
   c. By the express will of all the partners who have not assigned their interests or suffered them to be charged for their separate debts either before or after the termination of any specified term or particular undertaking;
2) By any event that makes it unlawful for the business of the partnership to be carried on or for the members to carry it on in partnership;
3) By the death of any partner; or
4) By the bankruptcy of any partner or partnership; or
5) By decree of a court.

A court of competent jurisdiction may decree a partnership dissolution:

1) When a partner has been declared a lunatic or has been shown to be of unsound mind;
2) When a partner in any way becomes incapable of performing his part of the partnership contract;
3) When a partner has been guilty of such conduct as tends to prejudice the partnership business;
4) When a partner has willfully committed a breach of the partnership agreement or so conducts himself in matters relating to the partnership business that it is not practical to carry on the partnership business with him;
5) When the business of the partnership can only be carried on at a loss; or
6) When other circumstances render a dissolution equitable.

In addition to court decree and the other causes listed in the Uniform Partnership Act, dissolution may be brought about by mutual consent of the partners, on the termination of the partnership, by war between belligerent countries of which the partners are respectively citizens, by an abandonment of the business enterprise, or by a partner's sale of his interest.

EFFECT OF DEATH OF A PARTNER

In the forty-seven states where the Uniform Partnership Act has been adopted, the death of a partner operates as a dissolution of the partnership unless there is a provision in the partnership agreement for the continuance of the partnership notwithstanding the death of a partner. The very nature of a partnership is the reason for its dissolution by the death of a partner; it is largely founded on the personal qualities of its members.

In the absence of a special agreement to the contrary, the surviving partner or partners become the legal owners of the assets of the partnership for the purpose of adjusting and terminating its affairs. The surviving partners hold the partnership property as trustees for the purpose of liquidation. New contracts or obligations should not be entered into by the surviving partners except as an incident to settling the business.

A partnership agreement may provide that the death of a partner shall not dissolve the firm and that the business may be continued by the surviving partner or partners. The agreement may provide that the capital of the deceased partner shall remain in the business and that the surviving partners shall pay interest on and ultimately return the investment of the deceased partner in the business, or pay to the representative of the deceased partner, a share of the profits of the business.

A partner also may in his will provide that the partnership shall continue after his death, may direct that his capital remain in the firm, or may give to the surviving partners the right to continue to carry on the business of the partnership and to enter into an agreement with his executor for eventual repayment of his share.

Settlement of Partnership Affairs

On dissolution, the partnership affairs must be settled before the rights of the various partners can be determined and property can be distributed among them. The most desirable way to terminate the affairs is for partners to enter into an agreement about the valuation and distribution of the firm's assets. If a partner insists, partnership assets may be sold and converted into cash. Otherwise they may be distributed in kind.

Ordinarily a partner is not entitled to compensation for his services in settling the firm's affairs. He is, however, entitled to the expenses which he incurs in accomplishing the dissolution.

The Uniform Partnership Act provides the procedure by which a retiring partner or the estate of a deceased partner may be compensated when there is no definite settlement agreement between a retiring partner or the estate of a deceased partner and the person (or persons) who continues the business. When there is no such settlement, the retiring partner or the estate of the deceased partner may have the value of his interest ascertained at the date of dissolution. He or his estate is entitled to receive as an ordinary creditor an amount equal to the value of his interest in the dissolved partnership plus either legal interest or the profits attributable to the firm property used in the partnership after retirement or death.

NOTES

[1]The rules and principles stated in this chapter are based on the Uniform Partnership Act, adopted by forty-seven states. Alabama, Louisiana, and Maine either follow common-law principles of partnership law or have adopted their own statutory provisions to govern the rights and duties of partners.

[2]The "fiduciary obligation" of one partner to another is a critical part of every partnership. This is discussed at length beginning on page 199.

15

MARHIAGE

In thinking of marriage or getting married, the average person usually thinks of a religious rite or a civil ceremony. But when a lawyer thinks of marriage, he thinks of its legal nature, in the form of a marriage contract. Marriage is a civil contract entered into by both parties. The marriage contract differs from ordinary contracts in that it cannot be dissolved by the parties but only by the sovereign power of the state.

It is the law in all Western countries that the marriage relation can exist only between one man and one woman at one time; hence, only a monogamous marriage is legal.

VALID AND INVALID MARRIAGE

The validity of a marriage is determined by the laws of the place where the marriage is contracted and validated.[1] If the marriage is valid by the law of the place where it occurred, it will be held valid wherever the question arises.

Bertha Jones and Harvey Jones, first cousins, lived in New Hampshire, where the marriage of first cousins is prohibited. But Bertha and Harvey wanted to be married so they went to the neighboring state of Maine, where first cousins may marry. Since they were married in Maine, their marriage is valid everywhere.

In order for there to be a valid marriage, there must be the legal, mental and physical capacity to enter into the marriage contract and the consent of the parties.

Legal Impediments to Marriage

Legal impediments to the marriage contract may result from (1) one or both of the parties being underage, (2) a marriage between relatives within the prohibited degrees of relationship, and (3) a previous marriage (of one of the persons) undissolved by death or divorce.

Where legal impediments exist there is a distinction between marriages which are *voidable* (recognized until set aside in court) and those which are *void* (never existed legally). For example, marriages where one or both of the persons are under the age required by law are voidable and may be set aside only at the election of one of the parties to the marriage.

Mental Incapacity to Marry

Mental incapacity means that a person may be of unsound mind or mentally incompetent; this may include insanity, imbecility, intoxication or other state of mind that deprives a person of the use of reason. A marriage contracted during the mental incapacity of one of the parties is *voidable*, but it may later be ratified by this person should he or she subsequently become competent.

Physical Incapacity to Marry

Physical incapacity (or impotence) to perform the marriage act may render the marriage *voidable*. As a general rule, sexual impotence must result from malformation, defect, or disease in order to preclude the possibility of sexual intercourse. (Impotence should not be confused with sterility, the inability to procreate.)

Consent of Parties to Marriage

It seems unnecessary to say that consent of the parties to the marriage is necessary for a valid marriage; yet there have been many court cases in which the question of consent has been seriously disputed. The law says that there is no valid consent to the marriage if there has been a mistake on the part of one of the parties concerning whether there was really a marriage.

A New Jersey court has held that a woman of another faith who went through a Jewish marriage ceremony on the supposition that it was merely a betrothal is entitled to have the marriage declared *void*.

LEGAL RELATIONSHIP OF HUSBAND AND WIFE

Years ago there was a fiction under common law that the husband and wife were one person. Today, all state legislatures have at least modified, if not destroyed, the common-law unity of the husband and wife.

Previously, the wife had no property rights, but modern laws give her rights in property, the right to make contracts, and the right to sue.

Husband: Head and Support of the Family

In the eyes of the law the husband is normally the head of the family. This is true despite the many laws which have attempted to put the wife on the same legal basis as her husband. Despite growing trends, in the majority of the states, the husband as head of the family still has the legal right to choose the family domicile; when the husband changes his place of residence, the wife is duty bound to follow him to his new address.

The legal idea that the husband is the head of the family carries with it the duty that the husband support and maintain his wife and family. The fact that the wife has property and means of her own does not relieve the husband of his duty to support her. The obligation of a husband to support his wife exists only while they are living together as husband and wife. If they are separated because of her fault, the husband is not bound to support his wife; if, however, the husband is responsible for the separation, he is bound to support her. Furthermore, if the separation resulted from the joint fault of the husband and wife, the husband must continue to support her.

Mr. Plymouth of New York had disagreements with his wife. He went to Nevada to sue for divorce, but she followed him to Nevada, retained a lawyer, and contested the divorce. She lost the case in Nevada, returned to New York, and brought suit against the doctor for support, claiming that he had abandoned her. The New York court held that the issue of whether the doctor was justified in leaving his wife had been properly tried in Nevada, where the court found in his favor; hence, the New York court held that she could no longer hold him responsible for her support.

Services and Earnings of the Wife

The common-law fiction still remains that it is the duty of the wife to render service to her husband. These "services" traditionally include the performance of household and other similar chores. Theoretically, the wife is supposed to render these services to her husband free. For this reason, a husband may sue for damages for loss of his wife's services when she is injured by another's negligence.

Mrs. Falkner is disabled as a result of an automobile accident, supposedly caused by the negligence of Mr. Preston. Not only does Mrs. Falkner sue Mr. Preston for damages, but her husband sues Mr. Preston for the value of the loss of his wife's services while she is disabled.

However, as discussed in the chapters on torts (pp. 57, 81) a growing number of the states allow a wife to sue for loss of her husband's services ("loss of consortium"). This trend is a result of an erosion of the common-law doctrine that only a husband has a duty to support his wife, as well as the "right" to her services.

GENERAL PROPERTY RIGHTS

Under the common law and also the civil code, what belonged to a husband was his and what belonged to his wife was also his. But practically all state legislatures have changed their laws to allow husbands and wives to own property separately and to have rights in each other's property.

Ownership of Household Goods and Wedding Gifts

This question often arises: Who owns the household goods? The answer is: *In the absence of a special intent to the contrary*, the household goods belong to the husband. It is commonly believed that the wife owns the wedding gifts, but this is not necessarily true. If the husband's relatives give him a present that is particularly suitable to his use, the gift may be presumed to belong to him. If the wife's relatives do likewise, then the item belongs to her. Otherwise, wedding gifts belong to both husband and wife.

Ownership of Property by Husband and Wife

Ordinarily, when husband and wife both acquire a piece of real estate, they are said to own it as "tenants by the entirety." This is a survival of the old common-law theory of unity. Tenancy by the entirety does not mean that the husband owns half and the wife owns half, but that they both own the whole property and that neither one can convey away his half. On the death of one of the two tenants by the entirety, the entire property goes to the survivor.

Mary and Frank Baker, husband and wife, buy a home. The deed reads "Mary Baker and Frank Baker, husband and wife." Though they are not specified as "tenants by the entirety," the law says that is the way they have acquired the property. If Frank dies, Mary becomes sole owner of the home.

Property owned by husband and wife as tenants by the entirety is not good security for a creditor who has a claim against the husband alone or against the wife alone, for when the creditor's claim is reduced to judgment, it attaches only against the survivorship interest of the husband or wife, as the case may be. If the creditor's claim is against the husband, and the husband and wife own the property as tenants by the entirety, the creditor cannot attach the property during the lifetime of the wife and may levy against the property only if the husband survives the wife. If the wife survives the husband, the creditor has no interest in the property to attach. (However, a trustee in federal bankruptcy may have power to sell the interests of the nondebtor spouse.)

Bill and Mary Strater own property as tenants by the entirety. Bill goes into debt and one of his creditors gets a judgment against him. The sheriff sells Bill's interest at public auction. At the sheriff's sale the creditor purchases Bill's interest in the property. Bill dies, Mary survives. The creditor gets nothing.

Obviously, a husband or wife cannot sell his or her interest in property that is owned in tenancy by the entirety without the other spouse's consent.

Husband's Liability for Wife's Debts

A husband is required to supply his wife with all the necessities of life. If he fails to do so, his wife can go out and pledge his credit. To that extent, the wife is the husband's agent.

Mr. Smyley is very stingy. He will not supply his wife with adequate money for groceries. Mrs. Smyley goes to the grocery store and buys on credit. Mr. Smyley is liable to the grocery store for the bill.

There is a limit, however, to the agency of the wife. Her purchases or bills must be in keeping with her husband's income or financial standing and appropriate to his level and manner of living.

Mr. Kedly is a hard-working hardware store clerk who is embarrassed to find that his wife has been making excessive and extravagant charges at the millinery store. Mr. Kedly has adequately clothed his family and provided all the necessities. He is not responsible for the unreasonable, extravagant purchases made by his wife.

Generally, the remedy of a husband whose wife overspends is to notify merchants that he will not be responsible for what she buys. He may do this with a public published notice or by writing to local merchants or both. But, if his published notice disclaiming responsibility for his wife's purchases does not reach the attention of a merchant who furnishes his wife with goods, the merchant will still be able to recover the money for the purchases from the husband. Thus, written notice mailed to the merchants his wife patronizes is an additional advisable remedy. *Necessaries* are those things necessary for one to live in the manner appropriate to one's ability and station in life. The following have been considered in law as necessaries: food, shelter, household furniture and supplies, decorations, clothing, medical and dental services, and certain legal services.

Marriage Settlements

In the absence of fraud, mistake, or a failure of consideration, marriage settlements relating to the property of the husband and wife are recognized by the courts as proper. Marriage settlements may be made either before or after marriage and must relate solely to property. The very nature of marriage prevents the settlement from altering the obligations of the marital state. This statement does not summarize the duties of the marital state.

A provision in an *antenuptial* contract (a contract entered into before the marriage, sometimes called a "premarital settlement") by which a husband attempted to bind himself to pay $5,000 to his wife annually for her clothing and incidentals was held by the court to be contrary to public policy and void, because the husband had the duty to support his wife according to his ability and station in life—regardless of whether her clothing and incidentals cost $5,000 or more or less.

Generally, marriage settlements are entered into by persons who have property rights which would be affected by marriage. Such settlements must be fair and reasonable, and both parties must have knowledge of all the facts; any concealment might invalidate the agreement. As long as the prospective wife has full knowledge of her prospective husband's means and wealth, she may make any settlement agreement she wants.

Mr. Ranken, 80, decides to marry his housekeeper, Mrs. Gouch, 55. Mr. Ranken tells Mrs. Gouch, honestly, that he is worth $200,000. Mrs. Gouch enters into a *premarital* settlement agreeing that on the death of Mr. Ranken, she will accept $50,000 as her share of his property. The agreement is valid because she knew all the facts.

Community-Property System

In the eight states (Arizona, California, Idaho, Louisiana, Nevada, New Mexico, Texas, and Washington) which have adopted the community property system, all property acquired during the marriage, as a result of the work and efforts of either the husband or wife or both the husband and wife, belongs to both the husband and wife. The only property that a husband or wife can hold separately under the community property system is that owned by the individual before marriage or acquired by gift or inheritance during the marriage.

Although there are many advantages to this system, it is often difficult to determine the source of community property. The courts of the community property states are constantly required to interpret the rules and rights and liabilities of parties involved in community property disputes.

This problem also arises when a couple who lived in a community property state moves to a common-law state and then becomes divorced. As discussed in Chapter 16, (beginning on p. 216), the "character" of the personal property, whether acquired in a community property state or in a common-law state, is often in question. The law of the common-law state usually is applied, although the fact that the couple moved (to a common-law state) should not change its character.

LAWSUITS ARISING OUT OF BREACH OF PROMISE TO MARRY

A few decades ago, newspapers and magazines contained lurid stories of suits for breach of promise arising out of promises to marry and of suits for alienation of affection evolving out of betrayal of marital fidelity. Nowadays, such suits are a rarity.

Critics of these "heart-balm" suits felt that the actions for damages offered too many opportunities for abuse. Finally, most state legislatures eliminated actions for breach of contract to marry as well as suits for "alienation of affections," "criminal conversation," and seduction. The state legislature of New York said:

Remedies for the enforcement of actions based upon alleged alienation of affections, criminal conversation, seduction and breach of contract to marry having been subjected to great abuses, causing extreme annoyance, embarrassment, humiliation and pecuniary damage to many persons wholly innocent and free of any wrongdoing who were merely the victims of circumstances, and such remedies having been exercised by unscrupulous persons for their unjust enrichment and such remedies having furnished vehicles for the commission or the attempted commission of crime and in many cases having resulted in the perpetration of frauds, it is hereby declared as the public policy of the state that the best interests of the people of the state will be served by the abolition of such remedies.

Breach of Promise

Allowable recovery in breach-of-promise and similar suits came under such unmeasurable headings as mental suffering, injury to affections, wounded pride, loss of social standing, "loss of market," and expenses incurred in the preparation for marriage. Breach-of-promise suits are predicated on the idea that an engagement is a contract or a promise to marry. Before the state legislature disallowed such suits, the New York Court of Appeals said:

We can conceive of no more suitable ground . . . for compensation than that of a violated promise to enter into a contract on the faithful performance of which the interests of all civilized countries so essentially depend. When two parties of suitable age to contract, agree to pledge their faith to each other . . . and one of the parties wantonly and capriciously refuses to execute the contract which is thus commenced, the injury may be serious, and the circumstances may often justify a claim of pecuniary indemnification.

Alienation of Affection

Although not as popular as they once were, there still are actions brought for alienation of affections. It is often done when a married person can show that someone else has alienated with malice and intent the affections of his or her spouse; in such a case the interferer may be liable for damages. In these suits it is not actually necessary to show that a divorce or a physical separation of the husband and wife resulted, but the wronged person must be able to show that the wrong-doer directly interfered with the married lives of the couple and caused a loss of companionship to the wronged. The entire basis or theory of the rights of actions for alienation is the loss of the companionship and relationship of the husband and wife.

Mere adultery of one spouse does not give the other a right of action for alienation. If it can be shown that adultery was the sole cause of the alienation or separation, there is no basis for the action. Undoubtedly, that is the reason why in so many cases it is difficult to prove alienation of affection.

It is not only an interloper who can be sued for alienation, but also a parent if he or she wrongfully and maliciously alienates his or her married child. Ordinarily, a parent would not be sued for alienating the affection of his child; if he acts in good faith, even if it results in the breakup of a marriage, the parent is not liable.

Criminal Conversation

When somebody invades the marital rights of a couple and has adulterous relations with one of the parties, the interferer conceivably may be sued for what is known as "criminal conversation." These suits are so rare as to be almost obsolete.

Damages in an action for criminal conversation are for the loss of the love and the society of the plaintiff's spouse, the destruction of home and happiness, the suffering endured, and the distress of mind resulting from the defendant's adulterous acts.

NOTE

[1]See the end of this chapter for the marriage requirements in each state.

Marriage Requirements by State

	MINIMUM AGE WITH PARENTS' CONSENT		MINIMUM AGE WITHOUT PARENTS' CONSENT		BLOOD TEST REQUIRED	WAITING PERIOD	MARRIAGES BETWEEN FIRST COUSINS PROHIBITED	COMMON-LAW MARRIAGES RECOGNIZED
	Men	Women	Men	Women				
Alabama	14	14	18	18	yes	no	no	yes
Alaska	16	16	18	18	no	3 days	no	no
Arizona	16	16	18	18	no	no	yes	no
Arkansas	17	16	18	18	no	no	yes	no
California	no	no	18	18	yes	no	no	yes
Colorado	16	16	18	18	no	no	no	no
Connecticut	16	16	18	18	yes	4 days	yes	no
Delaware	18	16	18	18	no	24–96 hrs.	yes	no
Florida	16	16	18	18	no	3 days	no	no
Georgia	16 & under	16 & under	16	16	yes	3 days	no	yes
Hawaii	16	16	18	18	no*	3 days	yes	no
Idaho	16	16	18	18	no*	no	yes	yes
Illinois	16	16	18	18	yes	24 hrs.	yes	no
Indiana	17	17	18	18	no*	3 days	yes	no
Iowa	under 18	under 18	18	18	no	3 days	yes	yes
Kansas	18	18	18	18	no	3 days	yes	yes
Kentucky	under 18	under 18	18	18	no	no	yes	no
Louisiana	under 18	under 16	18	18	yes	3 days	yes	no
Maine	16	16	18	18	no	3 days	yes	no
Maryland	16	16	18	18	no	48 hrs.	no	no
Massachusetts	18	18	18	18	yes	3 days	yes	no
Michigan	16	16	18	18	yes	3 days	yes	no
Minnesota	16	16	18	18	no	5 days	yes	no

State						
Mississippi	17	15	15	yes	3 days	yes	no
Missouri	18	15	15	no	no	yes	no
Montana	18	16	16	yes**	no	yes	yes
Nebraska	18	17	17	no*	no	yes	no
Nevada	18	16	16	no	no	yes	no
New Hampshire	18	18	18	no	3 days	yes	no
New Jersey	18	16	16	yes	3 days	no	no
New Mexico	18	16	16	yes	24 hrs.	no	no
New York	18	16	16	no	no	no	no
North Carolina	18	16	16	yes	no	no	no
North Dakota	18	16	16	no	no	yes	no
Ohio	18	18	18	yes	5 days	yes	yes
Oklahoma	18	16	16	yes	no	yes	yes
Oregon	18	17	17	no	3 days	yes	no
Pennsylvania	18	16	16	yes	3 days	yes	yes
Rhode Island	18	18	16	yes	24 hrs.	no	yes
South Carolina	18	16	14	no	24 hrs.	no	yes
South Dakota	18	16	16	no	no	yes	no
Tennessee	18	16	16	no	3 days	no	yes
Texas	18	14	14	no	no	no	yes
Utah	18	14	14	no	no	no	yes
Vermont	18	16	16	yes	24 hrs.	no	yes
Virginia	18	16	16	no	no	no	no
Washington	18	17	17	no	3 days	yes	no
West Virginia	18	18	18	yes	3 days	yes	no
Wisconsin	18	16	16	no	5 days	yes	no
Wyoming	16	16	16	yes**	no	yes	no

* States which do not require a blood test but require either medical examination or medical statements stating immunity to Rubella for females only.

** States which require blood tests for females only.

16

DIVORCE, SEPARATION AND ANNULMENT

Marriage is a social institution protected by the state and, therefore, traditionally was difficult to terminate. The difficulty of termination was further complicated by the great diversity of state laws governing the marriage relationship.

TERMINATING THE MARRIAGE RELATIONSHIP

The marriage relationship may be terminated or set aside by divorce, separation (voluntary or judicial) or annulment. Divorce is a judicial act by which the marriage relationship is dissolved. Unlike ordinary contracts, marriage contracts may be legally dissolved only by *divorce* or by death. There is a technical distinction between divorce, which completely breaks the bonds of marriage, and *judicial* or *legal separation* ("divorce from bed-and-board"), which suspends the marriage relation and provides for the separate maintenance of the wife by the husband. A separation agreement arises out of a *voluntary separation* (as distinguished from a judicial separation), whereby a husband and wife agree to live apart with an arrangement for the support of the wife and the custody and support of any children of the marriage. *Annulment* is a court decree holding that a marriage is a nullity from the beginning; that is, no valid marriage ever existed. It differs from a divorce in that it must be founded on a cause that existed at the time of the marriage. In a divorce, the court dissolves the marriage; in an annulment, the court holds that the marriage was invalid from the beginning.

DIVORCE

Serious questions often arise about the residence of the parties to divorces, the jurisdiction of the court, and the consequent validity of divorces. Does the husband or wife who moves to another state for the purpose of getting a divorce truly become a resident of that state? Are Nevada (or any of the other state's or country's) divorces valid? When is a decree of divorce rendered by a foreign state (a state or country other than the state of residence) binding on the courts of other states in accordance with the "full faith and credit" clause of the U.S. Constitution? When is a divorce decree rendered by one state a bar to a subsequent suit brought by the defendant in another state?

Formerly, the U.S. Supreme Court resolved the conflict between the courts of the various states by establishing the general rule that only the courts of the state where the parties had their last "matrimonial domicile" (where they last lived together as husband and wife) had jurisdiction to grant divorces.

In the famous *Atherton* case (1901), the matrimonial domicile was in Kentucky. The wife left her husband there and returned to her mother's home in New York. The husband began suit for a divorce in Kentucky because the laws of Kentucky accepted her abandonment as cause for divorce. He gave her notice of his suit through the mails, and she did not respond or contest it. The Kentucky court granted the husband an absolute decree of divorce, and the U.S. Supreme Court upheld the decree, reasoning that Kentucky had been the last matrimonial domicile of the Athertons and was entitled to "full faith and credit" under the constitution.

In the equally famous *Haddock* case (1906), the husband and wife were domiciled in New York, from which state the husband abandoned the wife. He acquired a domicile in Connecticut, where he obtained a divorce. The wife did not contest this, but she later sued for divorce in New York (where she had continued to maintain a residence). The New York court refused to accredit the Connecticut decree, reasoning that at no time had there been a Haddock matrimonial domicile in that state. The Supreme Court upheld the New York court and held that full faith and credit need not be given to the Connecticut decree.

Justice Oliver Wendell Holmes dissented in the *Haddock* case, saying that the rule was "poor fiction and fiction always is a poor ground for judging substantial rights." Thirty-six years later (1942), the U.S. Supreme Court accepted Justice Holmes's view and stated that when one state grants a divorce decree, other states must give the decree full faith and credit. In 1944, the Supreme Court also explained that even though the divorce decree of a state was presumed to be good, there was nothing to prevent a foreign state from inquiring whether the domicile was acquired in good faith in the state granting the divorce or whether it was merely a sham. The Court said in effect that it was no longer necessary to have a divorce granted in the state of the last matrimonial domicile, but that it was necessary for a person to establish a residence in another state "in good faith" to obtain a valid divorce there. The Supreme Court decisions have been known as Williams I and Williams II:

Williams I, a case decided in 1942, involved two married couples who lived in North Carolina. The husband in couple number one and the wife in couple number two went to Nevada and obtained divorces against the wife of couple number one and the husband of couple number two. The husband and wife who had obtained divorces in Nevada were thereafter married in Nevada; they returned to North Carolina where they lived as husband and wife. They were subsequently tried and convicted of bigamy in the courts of North Carolina. The case was appealed to the U.S. Supreme Court, which held that the courts of North Carolina had to give full faith and credit to the Nevada divorce decree because Nevada's finding of a bona fide residence had not been questioned.

Williams II involves the appeal from the second trial. The big issue was whether the husband of couple number one and the wife of couple number two had established *bona fide* domiciles in Nevada and, hence, whether or not the Nevada courts had jurisdiction. The jury was told that if the two people went to Nevada "simply and solely for the purpose of obtaining divorces" and intended to return to North Carolina on obtaining them, they never lost their North Carolina domiciles and did not acquire new domiciles in Nevada. The jury convicted the defendants of bigamy, and the Supreme Court upheld the conviction.

Despite the efforts of the Supreme Court to clarify the rules of law governing foreign divorces, much confusion ensued. In *Cook v. Cook*, decided in 1951, the United States Supreme Court reversed the decision of the Vermont Supreme Court for a marriage annulment. The ground for annulment was that the woman at the time of the marriage was the lawful wife of a third person, although she had prior to the marriage obtained a Florida divorce decree against the third person. The Vermont court held the Florida decree invalid. The Supreme Court, in reversing the Vermont Supreme Court, held that the Vermont court had no right to invalidate the Florida decree.

In the case of *Vanderbilt v. Vanderbilt*, decided in 1957, the U.S. Supreme Court held that a husband could not be relieved from his financial obligations by a state that had no jurisdiction over his wife.

The Vanderbilts, who lived in California, separated in 1952. In 1953 the wife established residence in New York. In March 1953 the husband filed suit for divorce in Nevada. The wife was not served with process in Nevada and did not appear before the court. Later in 1953 the Nevada court granted a final divorce decree. Subsequently, the wife instituted an action in the New York Supreme Court for separation and alimony. While the New York court found the Nevada decree valid and held that it had effectively dissolved the marriage, it nevertheless entered an order directing the husband to make designated support payments to the wife. The U.S. Supreme Court upheld the New York court; a majority of the Supreme Court justices held that the Nevada court had no personal jurisdiction over the wife and no power to extinguish her personal rights under New York law to financial support from her husband.

Thus, a decree of divorce contains two essential elements: first the decree dissolving the civil contract of marriage, and second, a ruling on the ownership of property rights and alimony obligations of the couple.

The *Vanderbilt* appeal in effect said that although a court could dissolve the marriage, it could not rule on the issue of property rights unless it had personal jurisdiction over the parties to the lawsuit.

NO-FAULT DIVORCE

No-fault divorces are valid in all but two states (Illinois and South Dakota). The "irretrievable breakdown" of the marriage or similar grounds is sufficient reason for a divorce. So long as both parties agree that the marriage is beyond repair, most states grant divorces without further inquiry. Of course, if one of the parties denies that the marriage is irretrievably broken, facts may have to be proved in court.

Statistics show that the laws facilitating divorces have brought a dramatic increase in the number of divorces and a considerable decrease in the number of annulment cases. This may be happening because under the old divorce laws in some states it was difficult to get evidence for divorce, so annulment was an easier way to dissolve the marriage. Now when it is easier to get a divorce, resort to an annulment is no longer necessary.

Grounds for Divorce

Although the courts of 48 states grant divorces based on "no fault" or "quasi no fault" grounds, it is important to enumerate the traditional grounds for divorce. (These reasons for divorce are still recognized by courts, and these may be good reasons, e.g., increased leverage in property settlements, for their use today.)

There are at least fifteen major grounds (or causes) for divorce, but these grounds are not uniformly recognized among the fifty states. The problem is left to the individual state legislatures, each of which has a different basic policy. The principal grounds for divorce are as follow:

Adultery

For years adultery was considered to be the principal cause of divorce in most states. That is no longer true, although it still is one of the causes for divorce (see discussion of no-fault divorce, page 219).

Conviction of a Crime or Felony

The laws of about forty states provide that conviction of a felony or an infamous crime or imprisonment for a certain number of years in a state prison or penitentiary is grounds for divorce.

Extreme Cruelty

Cruelty in one form or another is a ground for divorce in most states. The language of the various statutes differ. Some refer to it as "cruel and inhuman treatment," others as "cruel and barbarous treatment," and so on. The courts of some states have become quite liberal in interpreting the word "cruelty." It may include acts of violence; conduct which causes fear of personal harm or mental suffering, such as offensive language; false charges of adultery; conduct imposing hardship, such as failure to provide necessities; conduct directly injuring health; communication of disease; habitual intemperance; refusal to cohabit; and so on.

Desertion

Over forty states list desertion as a ground for divorce. The courts have defined desertion as a voluntary separation of one spouse from the other without consent, without justification, or with the intention of not returning. Whether a continued refusal of one spouse without cause or justification to have marital relations with the other constitutes desertion, although the parties still live under the same roof, is a question on which the courts of the various states differ. Some hold that refusal to have relations amounts to desertion and constitutes grounds for divorce; other states disagree.

Fraud

Seven states list fraud as a ground for divorce, if it involves the concealment of something that was, in those states, essential to the validity of the marriage itself. The following examples of fraud and concealment could be grounds for divorce: (1) nondisclosure by the husband that he was an escaped convict; (2) nondisclosure by the wife that she was pregnant by another man at the time of the marriage; (3) nondisclosure that one party to the marriage is intermittently insane, although sane at the time of the marriage; or (4) concealment of unchastity or a false representation concerning fortune, social standing, or previous marriage.

Habitual Drunkenness or Habitual Use of Drugs

In over thirty states, habitual drunkenness is a ground for divorce; in fourteen states the habitual use of drugs is a ground.

Duress

Duress is the legal word for force. Four states provide that divorces may be granted when the marriage was contracted by force or by threat of bodily harm.

Insanity

Over twenty states list insanity or idiocy as grounds for divorce, and a few states include mental incapacity at the time of the marriage.

Impotence

Twenty-six states consider impotence a ground for divorce, but if the condition is present at the beginning of the marriage, it may be a cause of action for annulment. Generally, impotence refers to physical incapacity that prevents either copulation or (in some places) procreation.

Personal Indignities

"Indignities" are a form of mental cruelty and must consist of rudeness, vulgarity, abusive language, malicious ridicule, or other forms of hateful action. Divorces are granted on the ground of indignities in nine states. Examples of personal indignities are false charges of infidelity or crime; habitual intemperance; excessive use of opiates; lewd conduct; sexual excesses; refusal of marital relations; nonsupport; or abuse and personal insults, name calling, and public defamation.

Nonsupport of Wife

Nonsupport is allowed by twenty-two states as a ground for divorce. It consists of a husband's willful refusal and neglect to provide suitable maintenance for his wife, generally for at least one year. What constitutes maintenance and support required of the husband depends upon the condition and standing of the parties in the community and is generally determined by the circumstances peculiar to each case. The courts have held that the failure of a husband to give his wife money is not of itself failure to support, nor is stinginess necessarily nonsupport.

Fuller at the time of his marriage had accumulated considerable property by a lifetime of thrift. He was regarded as wealthy; yet he failed to give his wife the niceties that she felt her station in life justified. A Michigan court held that Fuller's stinginess did not constitute failure to provide, even though his means would have justified much larger expenditures.

Pregnancy at Time of Marriage

Eleven states list pregnancy existing at the time of marriage as a ground for divorce, provided the pregnancy is proved to have been caused by a man other than the husband.

Disappearance (Enoch Arden Laws)

In four states, disappearance for specified periods, varying from two to seven years, constitutes grounds for a divorce when the absence of a spouse might indicate that he or she is dead.

Other Grounds for Divorce

A few states have unique grounds for divorce. Among them are: joining a religious sect believing cohabitation unlawful; loathsome diseases; malformation preventing sexual intercourse; unnatural behavior; vagrancy; and venereal disease.

Residence Requirements

In forty-one states there is a minimum period (varying from six months to two years) during which a person must have been a continuous resident before he or she may begin a divorce proceeding. Most states try to discourage the residents of other states from shopping around for easy divorces, but Arizona, Arkansas, Colorado, Illinois, Kansas, Missouri, Montana, Nevada, Utah, and Wyoming allow "quickie divorces," those which may be obtained after residence periods of from forty-two to ninety days.

DEFENSES TO DIVORCE ACTIONS

Although there are fifteen major causes of divorce in the United States, a divorce is not always granted when an appropriate cause for a divorce appears to be probable. Often there are extenuating or aggravating circumstances that cause a court to deny a divorce. These circumstances are known as "defenses" and include cases in which the person seeking the relief has either deliberately brought on the grounds for divorce, has forgiven the offending party, or where there has been some justification or excuse for the offense; condonation, provocation and justification, and collusion are typical defenses.

Condonation

Condonation is the legal word for forgiving a matrimonial offense, which would otherwise constitute a ground for divorce. The idea behind condonation as a defense is that the offender is forgiven with the understanding that the offense will not be repeated. Although condonation applies to all charges of matrimonial misconduct, it most frequently arises in the case of adultery.

When one spouse learns that the other has been guilty of adultery and thereafter cohabits with him or her, the law says that the adultery has been forgiven and is no longer a ground for divorce.

Provocation and Justification

When a divorce is sought on the ground of cruelty, desertion, nonsupport, or similar grounds, the defendant may very often reveal misconduct on the part of the one seeking the divorce and thus defeat the action for divorce. The misconduct may amount to provocation and justification.

Collusion

Sometimes a husband and a wife agree that one of them will commit a matrimonial offense for the purpose of permitting the other to obtain a divorce. Such collusion is a fraud on the court and is one of the chief vices in our divorce system. When one of the parties changes his mind and discloses to the court that the ground for divorce was set up by collusion, the court may deny the divorce.

SEPARATION

The law cannot compel husband and wife to live together. Therefore, they may separate with or without judicial decree. However, neither party is free to remarry.

Voluntary Separation

Where marriage has become intolerable for either or both parties, they often separate voluntarily. Although many men and women walk out on a marriage, they may be prejudicing their future legal rights by so doing. If the husband on the one hand gets fed up with the wife's faults and leaves her, he immediately leaves himself open to court action by the wife wherein she will claim alimony, counsel fees, and so on. The wife who can no longer tolerate a husband's faults should, instead of leaving his bed and board, consult her lawyer. If, after living separately for a period of time, the husband and wife are unable to settle their differences, they usually begin to think in terms of a separation agreement.

Separation Agreement

Separation agreements (sometimes called "postnuptial contracts" or "agreements in contemplation of divorce"), which are the result of voluntary separations, state that the parties are living separate and apart and shall continue to live separate and apart, provide settlement of property rights, and state that the parties shall not molest nor interfere with each other.

Specifically, a separation agreement may settle the household goods and the property to be retained by each. It may likewise provide that one party have possession of the family home or apartment, and, unless there is a lump-sum property settlement, provide for the payment of a weekly or monthly amount of money to the wife by the husband. An important feature of a separation agreement is a provision for the custody, control, and upbringing of the children, if any. Sometimes separation agreements provide that the husband shall keep in force insurance on his life for the benefit of wife and children. Depending on the property settlement, the wife may be entitled to certain benefits in the event of the husband's death or she may waive her right to receive any benefits under her husband's.

Judicial Separation

In order to maintain an action for judicial or legal separation, there must be the ground prescribed by the laws of the particular state.

Grounds for judicial separation in most states include desertion and cruel and inhuman treatment. Other grounds for separation may be adultery, habitual drunkenness, idiocy or insanity, impotence, violent temper, conviction of felony, incompatibility, willful neglect to provide, indignities rendering life intolerable, conduct calculated to make living together unsafe or improper, habitual use of drugs, attempt on life of other party, refusal to cohabit, absence without tidings for three to seven years, or loathsome disease. In certain states a judicial separation may be decreed for any cause for which a divorce may be granted.

. ANNULMENT

Annulment is a judgment of a court (of competent jurisdiction) declaring a marriage void.

The legal distinction between a voidable marriage and a void marriage is tenuous and fine-spun. As discussed in the previous chapter, a voidable marriage is one that a competent court rules to have been invalid from the beginning, such as a marriage that one party claims to have been induced by misrepresentation or fraud. But the courts will not grant an annulment when an originally voidable marriage has been sanctioned by the couple's living together with full knowledge of the facts. A void marriage is one that the courts arbitrarily say never existed legally because it was invalid from the beginning (such as bigamous or incestuous marriages). When such a marriage has been contracted in good faith, the parties to the marriage should not rely on their own interpretation of the law and decide for themselves that their marriage is void; they should apply for a court decree stating so.

Grounds for Annulment

An action for annulment may be brought for any of the reasons which would render the marriage invalid. In some states, however, cohabitation after knowledge of the facts on which annulment could have been granted removes the right to annulment.

Twelve states do not list specific grounds for an annulment, but leave it up to a court of equity to decide whether the marriage is valid under law. A few states, such as Maine, Massachusetts, New Hampshire, South Carolina, Utah, Washington, and Wyoming, have laws providing that either party may petition the court in equity to "avoid" a marriage when "doubt is felt about the validity of the marriage." In a few states, it is left to the discretion of the courts to grant an annulment when "any impediment" renders the marriage contract void. Grounds for annulment may include underage, want of understanding (insanity), physical incapacity (impotence existing from the beginning of the marriage), prohibited degree of blood relationship, fraud, duress (force), previous undissolved marriage, or communicable, loathsome disease.

CUSTODY AND SUPPORT OF CHILDREN

In matrimonial proceedings, the question often arises as to which of the parents should have custody of the children. Generally, courts give primary consideration of the welfare and best interests of the children.

At least five factors are considered in determining custody:

1) The age and sex of the child;
2) The wishes of the child regarding who should be his or her custodian;
3) The interaction and interrelationship of the child with parent or parents, siblings, and any other person who may significantly affect the child's best interests;
4) The child's adjustment to home, school, and the community; and
5) The mental and physical health of all parties involved.

Appellate courts are loathe to disturb the findings of trial courts in custody cases unless a particular trial court has not considered all relevant factors.

Parents have a natural right to custody, but in some cases where death or remarriage has resulted in children's being reared by grandparents, courts, after studying all factors involved, sometimes have held that the interest of the child requires awarding custody to persons other than parents.

Congress recently enacted an *Aid to Families with Dependent Children* program. This gives the individual states the right to qualify for federal funding to help poor families, particularly those not headed by a father. Every state has chosen to take part in the program. The state must provide benefits to any person who qualifies as a dependent child under the Social Security Act.

Congress also has authorized the Internal Revenue Service (and other federal agencies) to withhold paying income tax refunds (and other payments) to fathers of children who are delinquent in payment of court-ordered support payments to their children.

VISITATION RIGHTS

It is the right of the parent who does not have custody of the minor children to visit those children (or to have them visit him or her) while the children are in the custody of the other spouse. The matter of the frequency of the visitation rights, their duration, their policing, etc., is ordinarily a matter of negotiation. Where the matter cannot be negotiated, it is a matter for a court decree. Visitation rights are not necessarily a part of any decree of divorce or separation, but can be so incorporated.

Recently the courts have expanded the concept of visitation rights to include the rights of grandparents to visit their minor grandchildren while the child is in the custody of their parents. The courts have reasoned that the best interests of the minor child would be served by allowing visitation rights to their grandparents, even over the objection of their custodial parent.

ALIMONY

The idea of alimony comes from the common-law obligation of the husband to support his wife. At the beginning of matrimonial court proceedings, the court will award *temporary* support to a spouse during the *pendency* of the case. The courts usually realize that the wife, if she has no independent income, has to have some means of support, so they generally give her the benefit of the doubt about the probable outcome of the case and make an allowance for her temporary alimony at the beginning of the lawsuit. *Permanent alimony* is the allowance that the court compels the other spouse to pay for support and maintenance after judicial separation or divorce.

Some states limit alimony to a certain percentage of a husband's income. Other states may award a wife a definite amount to be paid either at once or in installments. In some community property states, the courts have the power to make a division of community property and to fix a lien on separate property of the husband in order to insure the support and maintenance of the wife and children.

In those states where alimony is not controlled by statute, the amount is left entirely to the discretion of the court. Some courts have said that alimony should never exceed one-half of the husband's estate, others that one-third of a husband's income is a proper portion. Basically the courts take into consideration all the circumstances, including the size of the husband's estate, his earnings and capacity to earn, other obligations (such as supporting aged relatives), his age and health, and his conduct in the particular circumstances. The courts also take into consideration the actual needs and obligations of the wife, her age and health, her personal wealth, her earnings or capacity to earn, and her conduct in connection with the subject matter of the litigation.

(In Delaware and Texas permanent alimony is not granted to the wife. In a few states, such as Illinois, West Virginia, and California, husbands sometimes are granted alimony.)

In most states, the usual method of enforcing an order for alimony is to hold the husband in contempt of court if he fails to pay the alimony. If the husband has the ability to pay the alimony awarded by the court and refuses to do so, he may be imprisoned. When a husband breaches a separation agreement by failing to supply to the wife the amount of money to be paid to her periodically under the agreement, the same legal steps may be taken to enforce his compliance as in any breached contract.

Generally, a court order for alimony provides that it should cease upon remarriage of the wife. In some states, it is specifically provided by law that alimony terminates upon the divorced wife's remarriage.

Courts, in granting no-fault divorces, usually do not take the culpable conduct of either spouse into consideration when determining the alimony (or property settlement) issues. Hence, it may be advantageous for an aggrieved wife of an adulterous husband to sue under the traditional ground for divorce when the husband's culpable conduct is in issue.

However, contemporary alimony awards in most states are based primarily on the needs and abilities of both parties to divorce; specifically, courts take into account such factors as age, health, physical condition, earning capacity, and present income.

The courts of some states are inclined to put some obligation on the non-earning wife to earn money within her qualifications. Some courts encourage the wife to re-educate herself, and within a reasonable period become self-supporting; therefore, the court may allow alimony only for a temporary transitional period.

There is a growing trend among courts today to consider alimony to be "rehabilitative,"that is, to be for the primary purpose of helping an ex-spouse to "get on her feet," after which time payments may cease.

Sometimes the court orders that if the circumstances of the parties change or if inflation becomes too high, the recipient spouse may apply to the court to increase alimony and child support payments. The converse also is true. If the circumstances of the payer-spouse change, so that *through no fault of his or her own*, he or she is no longer able to meet the court-ordered alimony and support payments, the court may decrease the amount of these payments.

COUNSEL FEES

Except when a wife is a plaintiff in an annulment action, the husband is often required to make payment for expenses incurred by her, including the fees of her lawyer. The court orders the payment to be made at the beginning of the lawsuit; this is because it may be a considerable length of time before the case is brought to trial and the wife's lawyer should be paid for preparing the case. Generally, the opening round in a divorce or separation action is the determination of the amount of counsel fees to be paid, along with temporary alimony. Before making the award of counsel fees, the court looks superficially into the merits of the case to determine whether the wife has some chance of success. If it appears to the court that there is merit in the wife's case, it will award her an amount for lawyer's fees on the theory that it is one of the necessaries for which the husband is responsible. The court determines from its experience in similar cases the amount of the lawyer's fees.

New Rules for Alimony

The U.S. Supreme Court has recently held that state statutes providing for the payment of alimony to wives only and not husbands are unconstitutional. Some states have modified their statutes on alimony to comply with this decision. Pennsylvania was the first state to take the initiative in amending its divorce law to provide that alimony may be payable to either party thus eliminating sex discrimination.

UNMARRIED PARTNERS LIVING TOGETHER

According to the U.S. Census Bureau, there are over 4.9 million unmarried-partner households in this country. These households may consist either of a heterosexual couple living together without benefit of clergy or a homosexual couple.

Although no state recognizes homosexual marriages, about twenty-five cities, counties and states allow unmarried couples (either homosexual or heterosexual) to register as domestic partners. (This gives only limited benefits, e.g., continued occupancy of apartment, health benefits and so on.)

Despite assumptions to the contrary, that a heterosexual couple living together for a long time has a common-law marriage usually is not true. Only thirteen states (most of which are in the South or the Southeast) recognize common-law marriages.

Living-Together Agreements

Couples who are living together should have a written agreement that might cover such mundane things as who does the dishes, but which certainly should also specify, for example, who gets which assets in the event of a split or death. Otherwise, where there is no will, the unmarried partner has very few rights. It is best to consult a lawyer.

Palimony

Several high-profile legal cases have been brought for *palimony*. When a court awards payments to an unmarried former partner, the payments are often called palimony. The circumstances under which such awards can be made are strictly circumscribed. Some examples follow:

Mary lives with Joe, a TV star, for a number of years, without benefit of clergy. Mary and Joe break up. Mary sues Joe for palimony. The court dismisses the lawsuit on the grounds that it is based on an illegal, meritricious union. If, however, Mary and Joe had had a child, Mary (assuming she was awarded custody) would be entitled to support payments.

Sarah and Sam, a bandleader, live together for ten years, again without benefit of clergy. Sarah and Sam part company. Sarah sues Sam for palimony, alleging that she did all of his laundry and made all of his bookings and plane reservations. Courts have held that she is entitled to recover the value of those services.

17

REAL PROPERTY LAW

Real property has been defined by the courts as "land, and whatever is erected or growing thereon, and all things connected with it which are permanently fixed and immovable."

PURCHASE OF REAL ESTATE

Some people buy and sell real estate without seriously considering the legal problems connected with their transactions. They claim to have bought and sold parcels of land for years without title searches or representation by lawyers. Real estate title complications, however, lie dormant often for years and when uncovered may cost the persons involved in the transactions thousands of dollars and unnecessary litigation. For this reason, sound legal advice should be obtained at the outset of the negotiations.

Purchase Contract

Although real estate brokers sometimes advise an individual to sign a contract as a "memorandum agreement" or a "binder," neither these nor any other contract for the purchase or sale of real estate should be entered into by anyone without benefit of legal counsel. A buyer or seller should also beware of printed forms, for each purchase or sale has its own problems that cannot be fitted to the provisions of a stereotyped printed contract. The purchase contract is the blueprint for the entire purchase and sale transaction. It must be in writing, and it should be prepared by an attorney.

Identity of Seller

Particularly in large cities where persons who are strangers to each other buy and sell real estate, the identity of the alleged owner of real estate is important. The problem of identification in small communities is not so great because lawyers and real estate brokers frequently know the persons involved in real estate transactions.

A man representing himself as James Brown, the owner of a house and lot which he wishes to sell for $20,000, accepts a deposit of $2,000 from a purchaser. The man who represents himself to be James Brown takes the $2,000 and disappears. An even more serious (but fortunately rare) loss takes place when the purchaser has the title searched and finds that James Brown owns the house and pays over the balance of the purchase price of $20,000 to a man who is not James Brown. When the real James Brown (who may be out of the area when the transaction was closed) shows up, the purchaser finds that he has purchased a forged deed.

In the case immediately above, if the purchaser had bought title insurance at the time of the transaction, the title insurance company would reimburse him (or his lender, the mortgagee) because he did not get good title. Insurance companies are very careful about establishing the correct identity of sellers of properties.

Marketable Title

No deed or mortgage should ever be accepted unless the title to the property has been properly examined and the purchaser has been advised by his attorney that when he gets the deed he will have good and marketable title to the property. The title should also be examined for restrictions which might limit the uses to which the property might be put.

In some communities lawyers or abstract companies make title searches which indicate the validity or invalidity of titles to real property. In other communities the purchaser of real estate buys a title insurance policy to protect himself against loss in the case of faulty title.

Title Search

In many small communities throughout the United States, real estate buyers do not purchase title insurance. They rely on an abstract of title made by an abstract company, a lawyer or by the clerk of the court. Whether the search is made by a lawyer or by an abstract company or the clerk of the court depends on the area where the property is located and the local custom.

An *abstract of title* is a summary of deeds and other instruments, which have been recorded in the county clerk's office or other public office, arranged in chronological order, and containing a statement of all liens and encumbrances against the real estate covered by the abstract. The existence of an abstract, which is a summary and digest of the public records relating to the land, does not prove anything about the title. What the abstract shows is important.

The examiner of the abstract must consider the history of the ownership of the property and all facts relating to the title to the property as shown by the abstract of title, and then he must determine whether or not the owner of the property has *marketable title*. The title examiner must check the abstract description throughout the years and see that every link in the chain is present. If a link is missing, title may be defective.

Where title insurance policies are not frequently used, the seller usually agrees to furnish to the buyer an abstract of title showing good and marketable title, free of all liens and encumbrances, to the property. In such a case, the attorney for the buyer examines the abstract to determine whether the abstract of title shows that the seller has good title to the property.

Title Insurance

Title insurance premiums and rates vary from place to place. A title insurance policy specifies an amount of money, which is usually the amount that is usually the amount that the purchaser has paid for the property, and guarantees the owner or the mortgagee, or both, against all the loss and the damage that he shall sustain by reason of defects in the title to the real estate described in the policy or by reason of liens or encumbrances affecting the title at the date of the policy, except liens and encumbrances and other matters specified in the policy. Thus, if the purchaser pays $200,000 for his property, his title insurance policy must be taken in that amount. And, if the purchaser's property is subject to an existing $50,000 mortgage, this amount would be specifically excepted from the responsibility of the title guaranty company.

In those cases where title insurance has been obtained, the seller does not pass along to the buyer his title insurance policy; the buyer buys his own policy. Before the transaction is closed, the buyer makes an application to the title guaranty company for a title policy. Sometime before the closing of title, the title guaranty company furnishes the buyer a preliminary report, and if that report indicates that the title company will not guarantee the title, the buyer knows that the seller cannot give him good title. Questions or objections frequently considered in connection with the marketability of title are the following:

1) *Afterborn or posthumous children:* (These phrases refer to children born after the making of a will and children born after the death of their father.) When title is derived through a will, the question may arise concerning whether there is a posthumous child or afterborn child. If there is, he or she inherits the property in the same manner as though there had been no will. In such a case, the will might be a bad link in the chain of title.

2) *Adverse possession*: Titles acquired through adverse possession are difficult to prove, and ordinarily lawyers and title companies do not honor them.

3) *Covenants and restrictions in a deed*: Often prior deeds in a chain of title contain restrictions concerning the use of property. Violation of covenants or of restrictions generally renders the title unmarketable.

4) *Debts of a decedent*: Debts may be a charge on real estate and may make title unmarketable.

5) *Insufficient or defective descriptions in prior deeds*: Unless correction deeds can be obtained, the defective descriptions may render title unmarketable.

6) *Release of dower rights*: Some states give the wife a right of dower in real estate. A wife must execute a release of dower before marketable title can be given. In certain states, a dower question may arise when a previous owner of property conveyed the property and failed to set forth in the deed his marital status. There is always the risk that the owner may have been married at

the time of the conveyance and that his wife may have a dower interest in the property.

7) *Encroachments*: Often a slight encroachment by the wall of a structure on adjoining property may render the title unmarketable. The only way the question can be settled is by a survey. A caveat to be watched for in connection with contracts or the purchase of real estate is a clause "subject to any state of facts which an accurate survey may show." A survey might show that a building is not entirely within lot lines or that the building of a neighbor may encroach on the property being sold.

8) *Easements*: Easements held by others may render title unmarketable. One of the most common easements is a right-of-way that someone else may have on the property in question. A survey should show the exact location of the easement.

9) *Federal or state estate or inheritance taxes*: Federal estate taxes are a lien on real estate generally for a ten-year period from the date of an owner's death. Unless the tax is paid the title is unmarketable. The laws of most states provide that the state inheritance tax is a lien on real estate for a specified period of time and may prevent the property from being marketable. Certain federal income tax assessments may be a lien on real property even though not filed in the county clerk's office with jurisdiction over where the property is located. Therefore, a tax search always should be done.

10) *State corporation taxes*: Taxes unpaid by the corporations which are or have been owners of the property may be liens on the property.

11) *Judgments*: A judgment obtained against the owner or a former owner of the property may be a lien against the property.

12) *Mechanic's liens*: A lien filed by a laborer or one who has furnished material in connection with the improvement of real estate is a lien against the property.

13) *Petitions in bankruptcy*: Bankruptcy or assignment for the benefit of creditors would render the title unmarketable if the bankrupt person were the owner of the property or had been the owner at the time of the filing of the petition. Often the problem of identification arises when a petition in bankruptcy is filed by a person with a name identical or very similar to the property owner.

14) *Land taxes and assessments*: Real estate taxes must be paid before the seller can give good title.

15) *Tax sales*: Sometimes, although a person is currently paying his taxes on schedule, a search of the records may show that a prior owner had not paid his real estate taxes and that the property had been sold for taxes by the city, village, or town. This may mean that a stranger is holding a tax deed that renders the title defective.

16) *Mortgage foreclosure*: If someone has started a foreclosure action, the owner cannot give good title. Likewise, if the property had previously been sold on a mortgage foreclosure, the question arises whether proper steps were taken in that foreclosure action so that the purchaser on the foreclosure action acquired good title.

17) *Leases or other tenancies*: In either event, a purchaser is required to investigate carefully and verify the nature of the lease or tenancy of any person in possession of all or part of the property.

18) *Legacies under a will*: Unpaid legacies under a will may constitute a prior charge on real estate.

19) *Mortgages (ancient or modern)*: A recent mortgage release must be obtained before good title can be given. An ancient mortgage may be disregarded after the lapse of many years, but generally it is considered advisable to institute a court proceeding to cause the ancient mortgage to be discharged from the record. Careful examination must be made

20) *Proceedings in decedent's estate*: Careful examination of the records in a probate court must be made to determine whether the court had jurisdiction of the estate and whether proper steps have been taken and all interested parties have received notice.

Most banks (or mortgagees) today require a title insurance policy as a condition for the loan. Unless stated, a policy that insures the lender *does not* insure the owner.

Environmental Considerations

Diligent research should be had regarding the existence of environmental hazards. If, in the chain of title to the property, there appears an owner that might have been a factory, a gas station, etc., both a physical examination of the premises as well as a search of the Department of Environmental Conservation and Environmental Protection Agency records to determine the existence of any toxic waste or leaching should be made.

In addition, municipal approval of the septic system should be secured. A title insurance company also would require "satisfactory flow tests" of the water supply.

If the property is near water, then the federal and state flood-plan maps should be perused, to make sure that any proposed construction is not prohibited, and if the property is near salt water then the federal (as well as state) setback maps should be studied.

The whole subject of environmental liability is a new and evolving area of the law. For example, in a recent court case in New York, a developer innocently purchased and filled in several acres of wetlands, which had been so designated on maps of the New York State Department of Environmental Conservation. As a result, the developer was ordered by the D.E.C. to purchase comparable acreage nearby, and to develop it into wetlands. This order was upheld by the court.

Title Restrictions

Before accepting a deed to property, a purchaser should also determine whether there are restrictions in the title that would prohibit the use of the property intended by him. The courts have held that a contract to sell property free and clear from encumbrances is broken if there are restrictive covenants on the property to be conveyed.

The courts permit property owners to put in deeds almost any reasonable restriction on the use of the property. For example, if an owner sells a piece of property and puts a restriction in the deed that the property may not be used for the sale of alcoholic beverages, the courts will uphold the restriction. If a provision in the deed specifies that the property may be used only for residential, not business, purposes, again the courts will enforce the restriction.

There are many kinds of restrictive covenants contained in deeds including those which prevent the use of the property by any business that is "dangerous, obnoxious, or offensive." There are also title restrictions against boardinghouses, hotels, barns, garages, gasoline stations, apartment houses, funeral establishments, public markets, chicken houses, theaters, restaurants, and the like. The Supreme Court, however, has held that racially restrictive covenants are unenforceable in the courts.

A common form of restrictive covenant is the "set-back restriction," that is, a restriction which provides that buildings must be set back a certain distance from the street. In connection with this restriction, questions arise whether the construction of bay windows, fire escapes, permanent awnings, verandas, porches, steps, sun parlors, and so on, which are built within the setback line constitute violations. In most cases such structures are held to be violations of the setback restriction.

How are the restrictive covenants enforced? A neighbor or other interested person asks the court to issue an injunction against violation of the restrictive covenants and, in some cases, to remove the building or objectionable structure. The courts, however, are practical in their enforcement of restrictive covenants. When an ancient restrictive covenant exists in a neighborhood whose character has meanwhile changed, the court often takes into consideration the changed conditions and refuses to enforce the restrictive covenant.

ZONING RESTRICTIONS

The particular zoning of a property, even though it may prevent the present contemplated use of the property, can be amended. For this reason, the courts have held zoning restrictions not to be an encumbrance which would justify the purchaser in rejecting title to a piece of real estate. It is important that zoning ordinances be thoroughly investigated before one contracts to purchase real estate. Many a purchaser has contracted validly to buy property that he later discovers is not "zoned" to his purposes.

Delivery of Deed and Closing of Title

There are various kinds of deeds. Their use varies even within states. The popular type of deed in New York City and its vicinity is the bargain-and-sale deed, which contains no guarantee of title but simply the owner's covenant that since he has owned it he has done nothing to encumber the property. In other parts of New York State, this type of deed is not accepted, but warranty deeds, whereby the seller warrants and guarantees the title, are. A quit-claim deed is a third kind of deed, through which the owner releases all title and interest he may have to the property.

The contract of purchase and sale "cuts the die"; it controls the closing.

A well-drawn contract simplifies the closing of a real estate transaction. If no unforeseen or difficult problems arise, and the procedure is relatively simple, the following matters are taken care of by the closing of title:

1) Disposition of objections to title found in examining the abstract of title or in examining the title guaranty company's preliminary report. Sometimes unpaid taxes or an old unsatisfied mortgage of record is a lien on the property, and sometimes all the heirs of an estate have not signed off their interests. Often the title objections are mere irregularities that can be straightened out at the closing.

2) Adjustment of financial matters, such as proration of taxes, rents, and insurance premiums.

3) Final checking and execution of deeds, mortgages, and other legal documents.

4) Payment of the purchase price.

5) Delivery and recording in the public office of the deeds, mortgages, and other closing instruments.

Title companies and lawyers who frequently handle real estate transactions usually make their own checklists of matters to be handled at the closing. The following is an example of a typical checklist:

1) Complete execution of deed from seller to purchaser.

2) Obtain old deeds and other title papers in the possession of the seller.

3) Examine instruments, including leases, which are not recorded in public offices and which affect title.

4) Affidavits regarding death of prior owners, occupancy of premises, and so forth.

5) If seller is a corporation, obtain proof of the officer's authority to execute deed, e.g., resolution or certificate of incorporation.

6) Get bill of sale of personal property on the land.

7) Obtain copies of leases.

8) Obtain list of tenants, rents, and estoppel certificate from holder of mortgage showing amount due and date to which interest has been paid.
9) Examine tax and water bills and proration computation.
10) Prepare closing statement showing all debits and credits and net amount of purchase price.
11) Deliver instruments and pay purchase price.
12) Pay or adjust transfer, recording and mortgage taxes.
13) Notify all insurance companies of ownership change and see that necessary mortgagee clauses are effective.
14) Notify utilities and other interested parties of change of ownership.

MORTGAGES

A mortgage is a conveyance of land as security for a debt, and in most states it is accompanied by a note or bond as the evidence of the indebtedness. The *mortgagor* is the owner of the land and giver of the mortgage. The *mortgagee* is the person who loans the money and who takes the mortgage as security.

Mortgages are one of the oldest forms of investment. Under English common law, a mortgage was an absolute conveyance and not merely security for a debt. Through this interpretation land was commonly forfeited at much less than its true value; the mortgagee was legally entitled to possession at any time.

Despite later rulings protecting debtors, the courts in England and in some of our states still view a mortgage as an absolute conveyance of land to which the mortgagee has legal title until the debtor has paid the entire debt. Connecticut, Maine, New Hampshire, North Carolina, Rhode Island, and Vermont still hold to this archaic theory in part. The majority of the states, however, accept the "lien theory": The mortgage is merely a lien for the security of the debt. Many authorities believe the old common-law interpretation will eventually disappear from our jurisprudence.

Mortgage Loans

A mortgage is given to secure a loan or a debt evidenced by a promissory note and mortgage; hence, the phrases "bond and mortgage" and "note and mortgage." The mortgage is not the written evidence of the debt; the debt is evidenced by the bond or the note.

A mortgage may be a first mortgage, second mortgage, third mortgage, and so on. Obviously, the first mortgage is the one which has a preferred lien against the property. Subsequent mortgages are subordinate and secondary in lien to a first mortgage.

Before the prudent lender will lend money on the strength of mortgage security, he will have the property appraised by an expert and make a careful study of the physical condition and the marketability of the property. Then he will have the title carefully searched. Ordinarily the lender will investigate the financial status of the borrowers, too. He wants to know that the mortgaged property is good security for the debt, and that the mortgagor (the one who borrows the money) has the financial ability to pay the debt.

Existing Mortgages

Sometimes a property is sold *subject to* or *by assuming* an existing mortgage. For example:

Mr. Hendrick agrees to buy Blackacre from Mr. Smythe for the amount of $750,000 by paying $250,000 cash and assuming the existing mortgage in the amount of $500,000. Mr. Hendrick, in assuming the existing mortgage, becomes personally liable to pay it; as an alternative, he could buy Blackacre subject to the existing mortgage, in which case he is not personally liable thereon. (In either case, Mr. Smythe remains personally liable on the mortgage.)

Establishing Identity in Mortgage Transactions

Establishing the identity of the property owner is even more important in a mortgage transaction than in an ordinary real estate transaction, because more losses have occurred through false claims of ownership in mortgage transactions than in the sale of property. The following is an example of a loss that resulted from failure to establish the identity of the property owner:

A man who said his name was Joe Hoffman went to the office of a real estate broker specializing in mortgage loans and asked for a $250,000 mortgage loan on choice building lots in the metropolitan area. The mortgage broker at the end of a few weeks' time notified Mr. Hoffman that he had found a man who was willing to lend $250,000 on the lots. He told Mr. Hoffman to obtain a search and other title data. The title search disclosed that the title was vested in Joe Hoffman free and clear of all encumbrances. The attorney for the lender was satisfied that Joe Hoffman owned the property and he prepared the necessary bond and mortgage, which was properly executed and delivered by Joe Hoffman. The lender gave a certified check to Joe Hoffman for $250,000, and Hoffman paid the real estate broker. Seven months later, the lender, who had not received interest on the bond and mortgage, contacted his lawyer; an investigation disclosed that Joe Hoffman, the owner of the property, lived in Denver, Colorado. Upon communicating with Joe Hoffman, it was discovered that the bond and mortgage were forgeries. The phony Joe Hoffman had taken the $250,000 less a 6 percent brokerage fee and vanished. Failure to identify correctly the fake Joe Hoffman who got the money resulted in a loss to the lender.

KINDS OF MORTGAGES

Mortgages may be divided into three general classes: mortgages for monies loaned, purchase-money mortgages, and building-loan mortgages.

Mortgages for Moneys Loaned

Mortgages for moneys loaned are sometimes referred to as straight bond and mortgage loans. (The person who borrows the money gives a mortgage on his property as security for the repayment of the loan.)

Purchase-Money Mortgages

Purchase-money mortgages are those given by purchasers to sellers in part payment of the purchase price. In some cases a purchase-money mortgage has superiority over other liens on the property.

Building-Loan Mortgages

Building-loan mortgages are those by which the total amounts of the mortgage loans are advanced in installments as the work progresses on improvements to real estate. A building-loan mortgage may be used for a new house or for the renovation of an old house. A building-loan agreement is executed and filed with a mortgage; it provides that advances are to be made according to a schedule, and that on the completion of the building the lender will lend to the borrower the full amount of the mortgage loan, which will be repaid at the end of a specified period in the same way as any other mortgage. A building-loan agreement may provide, for example, that in the case of a $100,000 mortgage loan, $20,000 is to be advanced when the roof is on, an additional $10,000 when the exterior trim is completed, another $20,000 when the rough plumbing and heating is in and the rough plaster completed, another $10,000 is to be advanced when the white plaster is finished, and the balance of the mortgage loan is to be advanced when the premises have been completely graded, landscaped, and all interior trim and fixtures have been installed and the building finished according to plans and specifications.

Trust Deeds

In Alaska, Arizona, California, Colorado, Georgia, Idaho, Illinois, Mississippi, Missouri, Montana, North Carolina, Texas, Virginia, and West Virginia, it is popular to use "deeds to secure debt," "trust deeds", or "loan deeds" instead of mortgages. A trust deed or loan deed secures a debt to a trustee subject to the condition that the deed shall be void upon payment of the debt. Trust deeds usually give the trustee power to sell the property in case of default.

Foreclosure

In ancient times, English courts of chancery or equity relieved the hardship resulting from mortgages (absolute conveyances of land) with the doctrine known as the debtor's "equity of redemption"; that is, the debtor could recover the ownership of the land by paying the debt even long after it became due. This doctrine in turn led to evils, for unless it was restricted, the creditor might never know whether or not the land was rightfully his. The courts, therefore, set up a procedure known as "foreclosure," whereby the equity of redemption was cut off (foreclosed). Foreclosure actions in the United States today are the usual remedies for nonpayment of mortgages, although there are other remedies which a creditor may exercise instead of going through a court action for foreclosure of the mortgage.

In states where trust deeds are used, the trustee is frequently given a power of sale so that if the debt is not paid, the trustee can sell the property for the benefit of the creditor. In order for the creditor to sell the mortgaged property in some states, there must be a foreclosure action. In other states, foreclosure of a mortgage may be obtained by means of an "advertisement procedure," that is, by publishing notice of the sale of the property to satisfy the debt. A number of states give the debtor the right of redemption—the right to reclaim the property even after foreclosure. The right of redemption in at least ten states is preserved for periods varying from six months to three years.

Legal Documents in Mortgage Transactions

In addition to *mortgage indenture* and a *bond* or *note*, some of the most common of the many types of legal documents used in connection with mortgages are discussed below.

An *assignment of mortgage* is an instrument through which the owner of the mortgage transfers ownership of the mortgage to another person.

In an *estoppel certificate*, the *mortgagor* (the one owing money on a bond and mortgage) specifies the amount of principal and interest due on the mortgage and also that there are no offsets or defenses to the mortgage. An estoppel certificate protects the purchaser of a mortgage and prevents the debtor from claiming that he has already paid all or a large part of the mortgage.

A *release of part of the mortgaged premises* is an instrument often used when the owner of property wishes to sell part of the mortgaged premises, before he can give good title to the section of the mortgaged premises, the owner must obtain such a release from the holder of the mortgage; this instrument should quit-claim and transfer all interest in the part of the mortgaged premises to be released.

An *extension agreement* extends the time of payment of the mortgage.

A *consolidation agreement* has the effect of combining several mortgages into one.

Spreader agreement extends an existing mortgage to cover property other than the original mortgaged property for the better security of the debt.

A *subordination agreement* is an instrument whereby the holders of several mortgages or other liens agree among themselves which liens are to be superior and which are to be subordinate.

A *satisfaction of mortgage* (sometimes called a discharge of mortgage) is an instrument executed by the owner of the mortgage acknowledging that the mortgage has been paid in full and may be discharged of record.

OTHER LIENS ON REAL PROPERTY

Several other types of liens besides mortgages may be made against real property. Among them are mechanic's, judgment, attachment, and tax liens.

Mechanic's Liens

A mechanic's lien is a legal (statutory) claim against land (or the buildings and the improvements thereon) for priority of payment to one who performs labor or furnishes material for improvement on the land. Sometimes the state statutes name the classes of persons entitled to mechanic's liens—laborers, mechanics, materialmen, and so on. In some states, such as New York, a material man, laborer, or subcontractor, may not claim a lien for a sum greater than that which is due the contractor at the time the notice of lien is filed. In other states, such persons have a direct lien on the property regardless of the amount owing to the general contractor; in such cases the owner acts at his peril if he makes payments to the contractor without first being sure that claims of subcontractors, material men, and laborers have been paid.

The statutes generally provide that one who has a mechanic's lien must file a notice of the lien in a public office where deeds or mortgages are filed and also serve a notice of the lien on the owner of the land. The lienor (the person who asserts the lien) is required to file a sworn statement about the contract he made with the owner or contractor, the work he has done, the materials he has furnished, the property on which the lien is claimed, and certain other details. Once the lien is filed, the lienor may eventually sell the property (at a foreclosure sale) to satisfy the lien.

Judgment Liens

By statute in the various states, a judgment creditor has a lien for his judgment against his debtor's land within the jurisdiction of the court rendering the judgment. Generally, this is restricted to the limits of a particular county, but the statutes provide that a transcript of the judgment may be filed in other counties; thus, the lien of the judgment may be extended to real estate in other counties.

A creditor gets a judgment against his debtor for $5,250. The judgment is entered in Ontario County. The debtor owns no real property in Ontario County; hence, the lien of the judgment extends to no real property. But, the debtor owns real property in Erie County, and the creditor files a transcript of the judgment in that county. Thereupon the real estate in Erie County becomes subject to the lien of the judgment obtained in Ontario County.

Attachment Liens

For good reasons—such as when fraud has been committed or when a debtor plans to leave the state in order to defraud his creditors—many states will grant a writ of attachment before judgment is entered. As soon as the attachment is filed, a lien becomes effective against the property attached.

Tax Liens

Many state statutes provide that taxes on land-corporation taxes, inheritance taxes, and others become a lien on real property of the person or corporation against whom the tax is assessed. Also, United States Internal Revenue taxes may be made a lien on the real estate of one liable for the taxes, by the filing of a written notice called a tax lien.

LEASES

A lease is a contract transferring the right to possession and enjoyment of real estate for a definite period of time. A lease is a binding contract whether it is for a short term or a long term. Many leases, especially for business property or for a long term, should not be entered into by owner or tenant without legal advice. The lessor is the owner, the one who leases the property; the lessee is the tenant.

Verbal Leases

Tenancies from month-to-month and week-to-week are verbal in most cases, and some year-to-year tenancies are verbal. Such leases are called periodic tenancies. They are terminable at the end of one of the periods by means of a previous notice from the landlord to the tenant or from the tenant to the landlord. (At common law, a six months' notice was necessary to terminate a year-to-year tenancy.)

Today, most states require one month's notice to terminate a month-to-month tenancy.

L rents an apartment to T on a month-to-month basis. T moves in and starts paying rent on the fifteenth of the month. One spring T decides that he would like to move out on May 15. On April 20 he gives notice to L of his intention to move on May 15. The notice is insufficient; it should have been given by April 14 at the latest. Because of the insufficient notice, T is liable for rent for the period from May 15 through June 14.

Written Leases

In forty states a lease for more than one year must be in writing. In Indiana, Maryland, New Jersey, New Mexico, North Carolina, Ohio, and Pennsylvania, a lease for more than three years should be in writing. In Maine a lease for more than two years must be in writing. In Maryland, Massachusetts, and New Hampshire, a lease for more than seven years may be invalid unless recorded in the Registry of Deeds. In Louisiana leases may be either oral or written. Leases may be very simple documents, printed or typed on one page, or they may be complicated business arrangements consisting of several hundred pages. Sometimes important business leases run for ninety-nine years. Generally, a printed lease is a "landlord's lease," for it contains clauses which favor the landlord. For this and other reasons it is advisable to have legal advice before signing such a lease.

Sublease and Assignment

In the absence of a provision in the lease to the contrary, a tenant may assign or sublet the lease.

An assignment is different from a sublease: In an assignment, the tenant transfers his entire interest in the lease; in a sublease, the tenant retains some interest or control in the lease.

Holding Over

A tenant who continues in possession of leased premises after the expiration of the term of his lease is said to "hold over." Holding over is usually regarded as wrong, and the landlord may take steps to oust the tenant. In general practice, a tenant for a year or more who wrongfully holds over may be compelled by the landlord to leave or be treated as a holdover tenant for another period of one year.

The A & B Holding Corporation owns store property and leases it to the Haberdashery Corporation for a period of three years, expiring March 1. The Haberdashery Corporation, instead of moving out on March 1, continues to occupy the property until June 1, and then tells the holding company that it is moving out of the property. The officials of the holding company say to the Haberdashery Corporation people, "Nothing doing, we elect to treat you as a holdover tenant for an additional period of one year, and we will treat you as a tenant for one year commencing April 1."

Dispossess Proceedings

At common law when the tenant did not pay his rent or when he held over after the expiration of the term of the lease, the landlord had to bring an action for ejectment (a slow and cumbersome proceeding) in order to get the tenant out. To speed up the procedure, most states today provide that the landlord may bring dispossess proceedings (commonly known as "summary proceedings") to force the tenant out on short notice.

Landlord's Lien for Rent

In the absence of a state statute covering the subject, the landlord has no lien on the personal property of his tenant for unpaid rent. That means the landlord has no right to hold the tenant's property for payment of the rent. In some states, a *hotelier's lien* has been successfully asserted against a tenant in a boarding house. On the other hand, sometimes leases contain special provisions whereby the tenant agrees that the landlord can hold his property for payment of the rent.

In some states the legislature has given the landlord a lien against the tenant's personal property on the leased premises, except property exempt by law from execution. The following states have adopted laws giving landlords liens against property such as crops of the tenant: Alabama, Arizona, Arkansas, Florida, Georgia, Illinois, Iowa, Kansas, Kentucky, Louisiana, Missouri, New Jersey, New Mexico, North Carolina, Oklahoma, Oregon, South Carolina, Tennessee, Texas, Utah, Virginia, and Washington.

Types of Leases and Lease Arrangements

There are no clear definitions of short-term and long-term leases. Arbitrarily speaking, a lease for a period of ten years or less is a short-term lease. Obviously a long-term lease (for example, one for ninety-nine years) must be drawn with the greatest care because it may be reviewed later by persons who were not alive at the time the original agreement was drawn; therefore, nothing should be left to the imagination. All provisions of the lease should be spelled out. Even in short-term leases printed forms should be avoided, unless inspected and found acceptable to the situation by an attorney. A layman should never attempt to draft a lease agreement himself.

A *percentage lease* is one in which the tenant pays as rent a stipulated percentage of either (1) the gross volume of sales of merchandise or services or (2) a percentage of the net profit of the tenant's business. Generally under a percentage lease, the landlord is paid a minimum rental; thus, if the tenant's sales are low or he makes no profit the landlord still receives an income from his property.

In a *sale-and-leaseback transaction*, which is a relatively new development, property is sold and immediately leased by the buyer to the seller for a long term at a stipulated annual rental.

NEW TRENDS FAVORING TENANTS

Until recent years the law governing landlords and tenants was that, unless otherwise expressly provided in the lease, a tenant took the leased premises "as is," and assumed all risk as to their condition. Today, legal scholars and some courts are coming around to the view that a lease is a contract that contains an implied warranty of fitness for use by the tenant.

In Hawaii, Mr. Lem rented an apartment for his family. They took possession and found the building infested with rats. After three harrowing nights and after attempts to exterminate the rats failed, Mr. Lem and his family moved out. Mr. Lem sued for the return of the advance rent he had paid. The courts ruled in Mr. Lem's favor.

In New Jersey, Mr. H rented an apartment under a lease which contained no specific agreement on the part of the landlord to make repairs. After repeated attempts by Mr. H to get his landlord to repair a cracked toilet, he hired a plumber and deducted the plumber's bill from the rent. The New Jersey court held that the lease contained an implied warranty to keep the premises in repair, and that the tenant was right in deducting the plumber's bill from the rent.

If the property is not habitable, a tenant may decline to pay rent. There is an implied warranty of habitability, the breach of which warranty may give the tenant some rights. No express warranty is needed.

CONDOMINIUMS

The term "condominium" is relatively new in law in some parts of the country. It means co-ownership or joint ownership of real property. Generally, it involves dwelling units which are owned separately but have a common area or some space that is owned by all of the owners of the dwelling units. Or the common area may be leased back to the owners, sometimes for 99 years.

A condominium is not necessarily limited to dwelling units. It may include business units. Each of the 50 states has its own condominium law. The condominium may be a new high-rise structure, a garden-type apartment with appropriate surroundings, or an old rental structure that has been modernized. The developer or the original owner of a condominium regime prepares a brochure to give the prospective buyers an overall picture of the condominium development that will be sold to the purchaser.

Generally, the common areas are owned by the owners of the dwelling units and are managed and supervised by a board of directors elected by the owners of the dwelling units. The owner or the developer of the condominium complex usually pays for liability insurance coverage on the common areas. Taxes and special assessments are assessed against the individual units separately and not against the condominium as a whole.

There is a general document that describes the condominium. It is known by different names, such as *master deed, declaration of conditions, covenants, restrictions, or plan of condominium ownership*. The general document is called the declaration. The managing corporation usually provides bylaws covering the administration of the condominium, the owner's responsibilities, the responsibilities of board officers and directors, the use and maintenance of common areas, the establishment of budgets and reserves, the collection of monthly charges and assessments, provision for management, and use of recreational facilities, fire and other insurance, general liability insurance, use of the dwelling units, compliance with state and local laws, and so on.

LANDMARK PRESERVATION LAWS

Throughout the United States landmark laws authorize landmark commissions to restrict the change or modification of designated historic or cultural landmarks. The U.S. Supreme Court upheld the constitutionality of these laws in the *Penn Central* case (1978), which involved the Grand Central Terminal in New York City. The court also said that the designated landmark is not an eminent domain "taking," requiring compensation under the Fifth Amendment of the U.S. Constitution.

Although the impact of this landmark designation did not rise to the level of a "Fifth Amendment taking," the dispute rages on. However, the Supreme Court's decision in *Penn Central* did strengthen landmark preservation laws and the power given to landmark commissions throughout the United States.

DUE ON SALE CLAUSE

Some mortgages have a clause stating if the owner of the property sells it, the mortgage becomes due and payable. These provisions in mortgages are known as "due on sale" clauses.

A case recently reached the U.S. Supreme Court that considered the validity of due on sale clauses. The Court held that where a federal agency (the equivalent of the federal government) puts a due on sale clause in the mortgage, that clause would be governed by federal law and was valid. Some states question the validity of due on sale clauses and, hence, federal banks are in a more advantageous position in investing in mortgages than state banks.

18

DEBTORS AND CREDITORS

Broadly defined, a judgment is a decision given by a court as a result of legal proceedings instituted therein; it may direct that certain acts be performed, that property be transferred, or that one person recover a certain sum of money from another person. Although there are many different kinds of judgments, this chapter is concerned only with money judgments.

MONEY JUDGMENTS

A money judgment adjudges that one person is entitled to a certain sum of money from another person. The form of a money judgment is as follows:

Adjudged that John Jones, the plaintiff, recover of Tom Brown, the defendant the sum of thirty thousand dollars ($30,000) damages, with one hundred and forty-seven dollars ($147) costs and disbursements, amounting in all to thirty thousand and one hundred and forty-seven dollars ($30,147), and that the plaintiff have execution therefore.

William Smith
Judge of the District Court

Money judgments bear interest at the legal rate from the date that the judgment is entered in the court.

Before judgment is entered, the person seeking the judgment is known as the *plaintiff*, and the person against whom the judgment is sought is called the *defendant*. After the judgment is entered, however, the person who has obtained the judgment is known as the *judgment creditor*, and the person against whom the judgment is rendered is called the *judgment debtor*.

THE LAW OF CONTRIBUTION

The definition of contribution as used in a legal sense is the right of a person who is jointly liable with others for some wrongdoing to compel the other person to reimburse him for any overpayment he has made.

Contribution applies where two or more persons participate in a monetary injury to a third person, and the plaintiff has paid more than his share to the third party.

Mr. X, Mr. Y, and Mr. Z purchased an old building to be used as a garage. One wall of the building had a crack in it, and a city inspector notified Messrs. X, Y, and Z that the wall must be repaired. A storm and high winds knocked the wall down, causing damage to several expensive automobiles. The automobile owners sued Mr. X and received a judgment of $60,000. At the time the lawsuit was tried, Messrs. Y and Z were in Europe and were not present at the trial. Mr. X sued Mr. Y and Mr. Z for a contribution, which would equalize payment between the three owners of the building. In the suit he said, in effect, "I have paid $60,000 plus court costs. You men should pay me $30,000, plus court costs, so as to equalize the amount we have to pay." The contribution suit was successful.

ENFORCEMENT OF MONEY JUDGMENTS

Money judgments are not self-enforcing. When a money judgment is rendered, it is simply a final and binding statement by the court that one person owes money to another. After the judgment is entered, the judgment creditor has to take steps to enforce or collect it. Although most of the states have gradually abolished the common-law writs in enforcing judgments, the states of Georgia, Delaware, Kentucky,

Maryland, New Hampshire (writ of scire facias), Virginia, and West Virginia (writ of fieri facias) still sometimes (as an alternative) use them. The other states use a straight form of execution. The result is the same by either method: the sheriff is directed to levy upon the personal property (or goods and chattels) of the debtor and sell the same and pay the judgment from the proceeds.

There are various auxiliary proceedings to assist creditors in enforcing judgments; among these are receiverships, garnishee proceedings (to levy on wages or earnings of a judgment debtor), and proceedings supplementary to execution; but there is great lack of uniformity and countless discrepancies and contradictory provisions in the proceedings to collect money judgments in the United States.

Moreover, although creditors have a vast number of remedies, the procedures are often cumbersome, clumsy, inequitable, and technical.

Executions against Property

After the judgment is entered in most states, an execution is issued. An execution or writ of execution is a mandate or official order by the court to the sheriff, marshal, or constable, or other officer of the court directing him to take into possession property of the judgment debtor, to sell it, and to satisfy the judgment out of the proceeds of the sale.

As discussed in the preceding chapter on real estate, a judgment is a lien on real property; however, it is not a lien on personal property. A judgment only becomes a lien on personal property when an execution has been issued (and filed) against that particular piece of personal property.

Certain property is exempt from execution; generally, only personal property is subject to an execution. Real estate can be sold to satisfy a judgment, but the procedure is more complicated; an ordinary execution does not usually extend to real estate. When the execution is delivered to the sheriff, he makes a levy, the act by which he takes the property into his possession. Property under levy may be redeemed by payment of the judgment before the sale.

Sale of Property

When the sheriff intends to conduct a public sale, the judgment creditor has to take steps to enforce or collect it. Although most of the states have gradually abolished the common-law writs in enforcing judgments, the states of Georgia, Delaware, Kentucky, Maryland, New Hampshire (writ of scire facias), Virginia, and West Virginia (writ of fieri facias) still use them. The other states use a straight form of execution. The result is the same by either method: the sheriff is directed to levy upon the personal property (or goods and chattels) of the debtor and sell the same and pay the judgment from the proceeds.

There are various auxiliary proceedings to assist creditors in enforcing judgments; among these are receiverships, garnishee proceedings (to levy on wages or earnings of a judgment debtor), restraining orders and proceedings supplementary to execution, but there is great lack of uniformity and countless discrepancies and contradictory provisions in the proceedings to collect money judgments in the United States.

Warrant of Attachment

An execution should not be confused with an attachment. A writ of attachment is a special proceeding authorizing the sheriff or other court officer to seize the property at the beginning of an action and hold it pending the outcome of the action. An attachment is granted in certain types of cases when it can be proved that the debtor intends to defraud his creditors by leaving (or having left) the state; removing property from the state; or that he has been guilty of other gross wrongdoing (such as fraud or obtaining property under false pretenses). Before a writ of attachment is granted the plaintiff, he must show the court a probability of success, and he also must post with the court a bond that will cover losses to the defendant as the result of an unjustified attachment.

After the plaintiff obtains judgment, he may proceed in the usual manner to obtain satisfaction of judgment. Having obtained the attachment, he is then in the advantageous position of selling the very property that has been held for him by the sheriff while he was obtaining a judgment.

PROCEEDINGS SUPPLEMENTARY
TO EXECUTION ("SUP-PRO")

It is one thing to issue an execution against property and another to find property that can be sold to satisfy the execution. In nine executions out of ten, the sheriff cannot find any property on which to make a levy. Thus, the judgment creditor usually has to institute supplementary proceedings, commonly known as "sup-pro."

The purpose of supplementary proceedings (authorized in most states) is to give the judgment creditor an opportunity to establish under oath the status of the property of a dishonest debtor or of an honest debtor whose property cannot be reached by execution. The testimony given by the judgment debtor or others in support determines the steps the judgment creditor then takes to collect the judgment. Most often, the judgment creditor just tells the sheriff what property he can seize and sell. Sometimes the judgment creditor has to have a receiver appointed to handle the judgment debtor's property. At other times the judgment creditor may get an order directing the payment or delivery of the property to the sheriff or an order for the payment of money, in one sum or in periodic installments, to satisfy the debt.

Executions against Persons (Body Executions)

Debtors may be sent to jail for nonpayment of obligations that originated in moral wrongs. Most state constitutions prohibit imprisonment for debt, but many courts hold that this prohibition applies only to ordinary debts and that there are certain obligations which are not ordinary debts. The theory is that if the debtor has been guilty of wrongdoing that is the equivalent of a crime and if he has no property to satisfy the debt, he himself should pay a penalty by being put in jail. In the case of an execution against the person or body execution, the sheriff arrests the judgment debtor and imprisons him until he satisfies the judgment or is otherwise discharged by law.

Among the debts for which it may be permissible (in a handful of states) to imprison a debtor are those cases where judgments have been entered in actions for fraud or deceit; in actions for official or professional misconduct; in actions for libel or slander; seduction; malicious prosecution; conversion of personal property; misappropriation of public funds; and similar actions. Many students of the law believe that body executions should be abolished entirely and that the punishment for these crimes should rest with the criminal courts.

Executions against Wages or Other Income

Many state laws provide that a judgment may be collected by regular deductions from wages or other income of the judgment debtor. Executions against income due the judgment debtor have been variously designated as "garnishee execution," "suggested execution," "installment execution," and so on. In some states the execution against wages or income of a judgment debtor, may not be issued until the judgment creditor has first tried unsuccessfully to recover under a general execution. By law a special execution requires the sheriff to collect a fixed percentage of wages, debts, earnings, profits, or income due from trust funds owing to the judgment debtor, provided that such income exceeds a certain designated sum per week. The sum designated varies from state to state.

The Federal Wage Garnishment Law (passed in 1970) restricts the amount payable under a state garnishee execution to the lesser of 25 percent of the weekly earnings of an employee (after deductions) or thirty times the federal minimum hourly rate. This law also forbids employers firing employees when their wages are garnisheed.

Property Exempt from Execution

All fifty state legislatures have enacted laws exempting certain kinds of property from execution. When property is exempt from execution, neither sheriff nor marshal nor constable can seize the property and sell it to satisfy a judgment. Furthermore, federal bankruptcy laws recognize the exemptions created by the state in which the bankrupt person lives. Thus, when a debtor goes into bankruptcy, he may retain the exempt property as his own.

Most states allow a homestead exemption of real estate. In some states there is a flat homestead exemption of a specified amount, which varies from $1,000 to $20,000. In other states there is a specified amount of land that may be claimed as a homestead for a farm and a lesser amount for a home in the city. The legislatures of most states seem loath to modernize property exemptions (though in many cases the lists are a carry over from colonial or pioneer days and have little application to modern living). Many states also establish unrealistic monetary limits for exemptions. Some states put an overall limit of

$500 for the furniture, wearing apparel, and so on for a whole family and $200 for an unmarried person's.

The following property is typical of that exempted by the various states from the claims of creditors:

Ohio exempts these six items of personal property: (1) wearing apparel and certain household and kitchen furniture; (2) livestock or household furnishings not exceeding $600 in value; (3) books used in the family and all family pictures; (4) $150 worth of provisions; (5) tools and implements of the debtor for earning or carrying on business or trade not exceeding $600 in value; (6) all articles, specimens, and cabinets of natural history or science, except such as are kept for exhibition for gain.

In most states life insurance is not totally exempt; in other states it is exempt up to $10,000; in still other states it is exempt if the annual premiums do not exceed $500.

Pensions, veterans' and old-age benefits, worker's compensation payments and so forth, family Bibles, and burial lots are exempt (in almost all states).

Variety in the exemption laws among the states is endless.

TRUTH IN LENDING

Truth in lending is a key portion of the Consumer Credit Protection Act, which was passed by Congress in May 1968. Congress assigned to the Federal Reserve System the job of writing regulations that would serve as guidelines for the interpretation and enforcement of the truth in lending law. The board of governors of the Federal Reserve System released what has become known as Regulation Z, covering truth in lending, effective July 1, 1969. Regulation Z applies to banks, savings and loan associations, department stores, credit card issuers, credit unions, automobile dealers, consumer finance companies, and other organizations that extend or arrange credit for which a finance charge is payable. When personal property is sold on credit, the seller is required to set forth (1) the cash price; (2) the downpayment itemized as to cash and trade-in; (3) the unpaid balance of the purchase price; (4) other charges; (5) any prepaid finance charges or required deposit balances; (6) the amount financed; (7) the total finance charge; (8) the time sales price; and (9) the annual percentage rate of finance charges, and so on.

The purpose of Regulation Z is to let the consumer know the costs of his credit so that he can compare the credit plan offered him with those of other credit sources and avoid the uninformed use of credit. Regulation Z does not fix maximum, minimum, or other charges for credit. The finance charge and the annual percentage rate are the two most important disclosures that it requires. Many states have credit laws which require that the interest and credit service charge be disclosed. Few define the disclosures required in the same detail in which the federal Truth in Lending Act does. As a result, an effort is being made to get the states to adopt a uniform consumers credit code that will be consistent with the federal law.

CREDITORS ENTITLED TO FAVORED TREATMENT

In order to collect his money, the ordinary creditor has to look to a debtor's general financial responsibility, earning capacity, and general assets.

However, the class of creditors called "lienors" are given favored treatment against those who owe them money. A lienor is one who holds a lien, that is, a preferred claim against particular property. For example, when a garageman repairs an automobile, or a livery stable boards a horse, or a jeweler repairs a watch, the garageman, the proprietor of the livery stable, or the jeweler may hold onto the automobile or the horse or the watch until the bill is paid. Certain liens have always been recognized by traditional law. But today, most liens are created by statute. In analyzing the special statutory liens created in the states, it becomes obvious that each state made those workmen and suppliers on which the state's economy depends special classes of creditors. For example, maritime states have special laws giving liens on boats or vessels to those who repair boats or furnish fuel or provisions for them. States with large mineral deposits recognize miners as a special class of creditors. Inland states give special protection to threshermen, corn shellers, wood choppers, and the like. The following are the general classifications of persons for whom liens are given by statute in most states: repairmen; keepers of inns, hotels, and lodging houses; artisans; owners of stallions or bulls (on their progeny); garagemen; those furnishing seeds for crops; blacksmiths; lumbermen; boatmen; owners of laundries and dry cleaning establishments; warehousemen; and so on.

Many states give hospitals or other institutions of similar function liens on the proceeds of the injured person's damages awarded in actions for the injuries. It would seem that the interests of the hospitals are better represented in the legislatures than those of medical personnel, for only a very few states protect physicians, nurses, and dentists in the same way.

In New York, for example, when an injured person has a claim for $100,000 arising out of an automobile accident, the hospital where the injured person was treated may file a lien against the proceeds of the settlement, and the insurance company, before paying the claimant, must make sure that the hospital gets the money. Doctors and nurses, on the other hand, may receive nothing from the proceeds of the insurance settlement.

ASSIGNMENT FOR THE BENEFIT OF CREDITORS

An assignment for the benefit of creditors is a voluntary transfer of property by a debtor to someone in trust. Generally, the assignment is made pursuant to state statutory law where the debtor resides and for the purpose of discharging the debtor's obligations to those creditors who file claims and consent to the (assignment) proceedings. The statutes in forty-two states permit debtors to make assignments for the benefit of creditors. (Alaska, Illinois, Maine, Maryland, Nebraska, Oregon, Washington, and Wyoming lack special statutes for this purpose.)

According to these statutes, a debtor may transfer (assign) all his property to another, an assignee. The assignee must file a bond, and debtor and assignee each must file an inventory of the debtor's property. The assignee then gives notice of the assignment (usually by publication) to the creditors; after this, the creditors present their claims, and the assignee liquidates the debtor's property to pay the creditors.

Some regard assignment for the benefit of creditors as bankruptcy under state law, but these proceedings are not as effective as bankruptcy under the federal law. Under the assignment plan, the debtor's debts are discharged only to the extent of the money received by the creditors. For this reason the law of assignment for the benefit of creditors is seldom used; indeed, the federal law suspends these proceedings and makes them an act of bankruptcy.

An assignment for the benefit of creditors should be distinguished from a composition with creditors, which is a contract between a debtor and his creditors discharging debts on the payment of less than the full amount owing them. An assignment does not contain any agreement on the part of creditors to discharge their claims on the payment of less than the full amount of indebtedness. Sometimes a composition plan can be worked out with creditors as part of an assignment for the benefit of creditors. The federal Bankruptcy Code even encourages a composition with creditors in order to accomplish a settlement whereby the debtor secures his discharge in bankruptcy in return for the payment of a specified sum to be distributed among the creditors.

BANKRUPTCY

The adoption of the U.S. Constitution placed bankruptcy legislation in the Congress under the power "to establish uniform laws on the subject of bankruptcies throughout the United States." In this jurisdiction, Congress has enacted many laws. Bankruptcy law classifies different kinds of bankruptcy, such as liquidation bankruptcy (standard bankruptcy), a municipal bankruptcy, a debt adjustment (for the relief of a political subdivision of a state or a public agency or municipality of a state that desires to effect a plan to adjust its debts), and a reorganization, of which there are several types.

Periodically, Congress has made major changes in the bankruptcy laws. (These changes were made in 1800, 1841, 1867, 1898, 1938, and the latest, in 1978.) Our current Bankruptcy Law is called the Bankruptcy Reform Act of 1978. It became law on November 6, 1978, but certain provisions took effect in October 1979, and it became completely effective in April 1984. It is now known as the Bankruptcy Code. Although the Bankruptcy Code supersedes state legislation in the debtor and creditor field, it does so only to the extent that it conflicts with federal legislation on the subject.

CHANGES IN THE 1978 LAW

Among the more important changes in the 1978 law are the following:

1) Bankruptcy courts and judges become more important, more independent, and less dependent on Federal District Courts. Beginning in 1984, bankruptcy judges will be appointed by the

president, subject to approval by the Senate, and will serve a fourteen-year term at an annual salary of equal to 92 percent of the then-salary of U.S. District Court Judges.

2) There was a program that ended in 1984, whereby so-called United States Trustees will handle administrative matters formerly handled by bankruptcy judges.

3) There is a uniform federal exemption exempting certain debtors' property from claims of creditors, subject to certain exemptions that may exist under state law.

4) Debtors who get a discharge in bankruptcy are protected from post-bankruptcy harassment by creditors.

5) Secured creditors are given special relief, and their collateral is protected.

6) The new law retains the old "garden variety" of liquidation whereby assets of debtors are sold in order to pay administration expenses and claims of creditors. However, in order to avoid a complete liquidation in bankruptcy, a plan was enacted by the 1978 law whereby a corporation or other business entity unable to meet its debts can ask the protection of the bankruptcy court pending a plan of reorganization. During reorganization proceedings, the business of the debtor can be continued without interruption, lawsuits against the debtor can be stayed by the court, and the rights of secured and general creditors, stockholders, and bondholders can be protected and revised pursuant to a plan of reorganization.

The Excelsior Hotel Corporation was helplessly in debt. Creditors had obtained judgments and were threatening the sale and liquidation of the hotel. The Excelsior Hotel Corporation filed a plan of reorganization whereby a new corporation would be organized and the hotel conveyed to the new corporation for the sum of $1,000,000,000 cash, furnished by the Jones Corporation. The Jones Corporation would be issued a thousand shares of A stock of the new corporation. Creditors of the Excelsior Hotel Corporation having claims of less than $50 and employees of the Excelsior Hotel Corporation having wage claims would be paid cash in full. Other creditors of the Excelsior Hotel Corporation (having claims in excess of $50) would receive a subordinate B stock in the amount of their claims. Seventy-five percent of the large creditors of the Hotel Corporation approved the plan, as did the federal judge, and the plan became effective.

7) The old bankruptcy law (the 1938 Chandler Act) permitted a debtor to seek reorganization under four different chapters, and reorganizations were governed by three chapters. Sometimes there was needless expense and litigation in determining which chapters governed a particular reorganization. The new law contains only one chapter dealing with reorganizations and does away with litigation to decide which chapter should apply. Now all partnerships, individuals, and corporations are subject to one reorganization chapter. There are many technical requirements for a reorganization.

8) A special provision of the 1978 law stipulates that wage earners or other individuals with regular income (including Social Security, pensions, and alimony) can avoid or postpone liquidation of their assets.

   The mere filing of a petition by an individual with such income operates as a stay against a suit or liquidation proceeding against a debtor by a creditor. This is sometimes referred to as an *automatic stay*.

9) The so-called four-months rule has been changed. This rule applied to what were called preferential transfers: transfers to creditors or others made within four months of the filing of a petition in bankruptcy. Formerly, the rule was that a creditor must have reasonable knowledge of the debtor's insolvency. This has been eliminated under the new bankruptcy law. Now the debtor's insolvency is presumed; also the four-month period has been reduced to ninety days. There are some other time-related changes; for example, payment of a debt incurred in the ordinary course of business or financial affairs of the debtor made within forty-five days after the debt was incurred in the ordinary course of business is a valid payment.

   Furthermore, there is a new provision that makes it possible for a failing debtor to obtain financial help without a lender running the risk of having its security called invalid.

10) Under the new bankruptcy law, creditors may force a debtor into bankruptcy (called involuntary liquidation) only if the petitioning creditors are at least three in number with unsecured claims totaling at least $5,000.

   If the debtor has fewer than twelve creditors, then only one creditor may file the petition. Under the former law, petitioning creditors had to show that the debtor had been guilty of an "act of bankruptcy." Under the new law, proof of an act of bankruptcy is no longer necessary. All that the petitioning creditors have to show is that the debtor is not paying debts as they mature or that a custodian of the debtor's property has been appointed within the preceding ten days.

Creditors may file an involuntary petition against any debtor except farmers, charitable corporations, railroads, insurance companies, banks, savings and loan associations, and credit unions. This exempted group of debtors was deemed by Congress to be essential to the ongoing economy of the country.

Creditors' Meetings and Appointment of Trustees

Creditors' meetings are held soon after the filing of a petition. The debtor must attend and submit to an examination under oath.

Under former bankruptcy law, a referee in bankruptcy or judge in bankruptcy presided at meetings of creditors, but that is no longer true. Now United States Trustees or other trustees preside.

In the garden-variety of bankruptcy cases, where the object is liquidation of assets for distribution to creditors, the bankruptcy judge may appoint an interim trustee, whose services are terminated if the creditors elect a trustee. Certain individuals called "insiders" (persons having family or business connections with the debtor) are always disqualified from acting as trustees.

Creditors may elect a "creditors' committee" (not less than three or more than eleven), which has an important advisory function.

If a debtor files for a reorganization, a trustee may or may not be appointed. If a trustee is not appointed, the debtor is left "in possession" of the bankrupt estate and will continue to operate the business.

In a reorganization, a creditors' committee is not elected by the creditors but is appointed by the bankruptcy judge. This committee has a say in formulating a plan for the reorganization. In both voluntary and involuntary cases, the petition must be accompanied by a filing fee. (In certain cases the filing fee may be paid in installments.) The filing fee for an individual bankruptcy is $120 and $600 for a corporate reorganization. Creditors must file proofs of their claims where the debtor lists those claims in his or its schedules. The primary duties of a trustee in a liquidation case are to convert the debtor's assets into cash, to account for all cash and expenditures, to report to the court, and then, after paying all administration expenses, to distribute the balance pro rata to the creditors.

Approval of the Plan

If a plan of reorganization is partially accepted by certain creditors and is approved by the court, the plan may be "crammed down"—that is, confirmed by the court as against and over the objections of non-consenting creditors, as long as the court finds that the plan is fair and equitable as far as objecting creditors are concerned.

In the case of a voluntary petition in bankruptcy, the debtor must file a list of all creditors with a description of their claims, a list of the debtor's property, and so on. These lists are sometimes called schedules.

Priority Claims

Some claims must be paid before claims of general creditors are paid. These claims are known as "priority claims." They are (1) administrative expenses and filing and court fees; (2) claims incurred after the filing of an involuntary petition; (3) wage claims up to $2,000 earned within 90 days (formerly $600); (4) claims based on employee benefit plans; (5) consumer deposit claims; and (6) taxes and customs duties.

Discharge

A debtor in a liquidation case may be discharged or released from all debts unless guilty of misconduct (fraud, false financial statement, embezzlement, breach of fiduciary duties, false pretenses, etc.). Reaffirmation of debts discharged in bankruptcy requires the bankruptcy court to pass on the reaffirmation. It must be shown to the court that the reaffirmation will not place an undue hardship on the debtor and that it is in the best interests of the debtor. The effect of this change is to reinforce the opportunity to make a "fresh start."

19

AGENCY

Agency is the relationship between two or more persons by which one (the principal) consents that the other (the agent) or others shall act on his behalf. The law distinguishes between kinds of agents and kinds of principals.

A *general agent* is a person authorized to conduct a series of transactions with continuity of service; a *special agent* is one authorized to conduct a single transaction; an *apparent agent* is a person who, although not really authorized to act as an agent for another, seems to third persons to have that authority; a *subagent* is a person employed by an agent to assist him in conducting the affairs of his principal.

A *principal* may be disclosed, partially disclosed or undisclosed. A *disclosed principal* exists in a transaction when the third party is notified of the identity of the principal for whom the agent is acting; a *partially disclosed principal* exists when the third party is notified that an agent may be acting for a principal but without identifying the principal; an *undisclosed principal* exists when the third party is not informed that the agent is acting for a principal.

The law also distinguishes between agents and servants and agents and independent contractors, as well as trustees. A *servant* is a person employed to perform services for another, a master, who himself controls the conduct of these services. An *independent contractor* is a person who contracts with another to perform work but who is not controlled by the *principal* in the methods of performing it.

CREATION OF AN AGENCY

There is no particular way in which an agency must be created; on the one hand, an agency may be created by an express formal contract, such as in conferring a power of attorney. It may be spelled out from the dealings of the principal and agent over a period of time. An agency also may be formed when the principal appoints the agent and the agent accepts the appointment. Although no writing is necessary to establish an agency, and verbal authorizations to an agent are generally good, the Statute of Frauds requires written authorizations to sell real estate or to enter into certain other types of contracts.[1]

Actual and Apparent Authority of Agents

The principal is responsible for the acts of his agent when he has given actual authority to the agent to act. Sometimes it is difficult to determine whether or not the principal has actually given an agent this authority. Many circumstances are taken into consideration in this determination. Authority to conduct a transaction generally includes authority to perform acts which are incidental to it or which usually accompany it.

Cable employs Enright to obtain photographs illustrating life in central Africa. Enright finds it necessary to employ an interpreter to make small goodwill gifts to the natives. Enright's authority includes the authority to spend money for an interpreter and gifts.

Stillwell directs Baker to sell goods at auction in a community where an ordinance forbids anybody but a licensed auctioneer to conduct sales by auction. Baker's authority includes authority to employ a licensed auctioneer.

The extent to which an agent can bind his principal often depends on whether a third person would normally believe that the agent is empowered to go as far as he does in handling a transaction. If the principal entrusts an agent with all evidence of authority, the principal may be responsible (and liable) if the agent misleads third persons.

Bowler turns over his automobile to Garber to sell, telling Garber he is authorized to take any reasonable price but that he is not to guarantee the performance of the motor or the speed of the car. Garber sells the car with the warranty that it can be driven at 80 mph. Garber had apparent authority to give the warranty, and if the automobile can only do 60 mph, Bowler may be liable for breach of warranty.

Types of Apparent Authority

Authority to make a contract may be inferred from authority to conduct a transaction. This should not be confused with authority to solicit business.

Pembrow employs Austin Estate Brokers to find a purchaser for his farm at a stated price. This employment, however, does not give Austin authority to contract for the sale of the property.

When an agent has been given broad powers to handle certain property or to carry out a transaction, is he authorized to sell a portion of the property involved in the transaction? An agent who is empowered to handle a particular transaction has apparent authority to handle all customary things incidental to the transaction.

Birdman sends Apell down the Mississippi River in charge of a flatboat loaded with produce, which Apell is to sell in the market at New Orleans. Nothing is said about what Apell shall do with the boat after the produce is sold. It would cost more than the boat is worth to send it back, and also it is the usual practice on the river in such cases to sell such flatboats in New Orleans. Apell is authorized to sell the boat.

Ordinarily, authority to manage a business does not include authorization to sell items of property necessary in its operation.

Putnam, a farmer, goes on an extended trip and gives his neighbor a general power of attorney to manage all his business affairs "as fully as if Putnam were personally present." In Putnam's absence, the neighbor gets an opportunity to sell a portion of Putnam's farm at a handsome price. The sale is not valid. The neighbor is not authorized to sell any part of the farm.

An agent has implied or apparent authority to act in an emergency.

Eggleston, a fruit grower, ships fruit to Megler, his agent in the city. Twenty-four hours before the fruit is due to arrive, Megler learns that in this city, owing to excessive shipments, fruits will not bring enough to satisfy freight charges, but if it is sent to another city, it will. Megler cannot communicate with Eggleston in time to make the change. Megler is authorized to reroute the fruit, and the fact that it is unexpectedly destroyed in a train wreck in another city does not subject Megler to liability to Eggleston.

Apparent Authority

When a principal has taken such actions as would indicate to third parties that someone is his agent, he is held to have given apparent authority to the "agent" and will be liable for his acts.

Many times the principal raises the question of whether the agent has gone beyond his bare authority to buy and sell. Following are some examples of implied authority of the agent stemming from his authority to buy and sell:

Howard telegraphs Paul, "Sell my cotton F.O.B. Memphis at 106." Paul, although not specifically authorized to do so, sells the cotton at a cash 1 percent discount in accordance with local custom. Paul had the authority to give the discount.

Buckels gives to Barnes a power of attorney to sell and convey land, but does not actually authorize him to receive the purchase price. Barnes negotiates the sale, gives a deed, and receives the purchase price in cash. Barnes had implied authority to receive this.

Lorillard employs Palmer to sell farmland 1,000 miles away from Lorillard's home. To prospective buyers, Palmer represents the farmland as fertile and the countryside prosperous. Neither statement is true. Lorillard is bound by Palmer's misrepresentations.

Thurston authorizes Fritz to sell gas furnaces. Fritz tells a purchaser that a certain size gas furnace is large enough to heat his house adequately. The gas furnace is much too small to heat the house. The purchaser may sue Thurston.

Generally, authority to sell includes only the authority to sell for cash.

Torbitt authorizes Jordan to sell his house and lot for $300,000. Jordan finds a buyer and conveys the house for $150,000 and takes back a mortgage for $150,000. Torbitt can disaffirm the deal because Jordan was not authorized to accept the mortgage.

The H & H Railroad employs Steadfast as its station agent at Podunk. Occasionally, when Steadfast leaves the station, he permits Herbert, the town ne'er-do-well, to take charge of the station and wear a railroad cap, a custom known to the railroad superintendent. During one of Steadfast's absences, a customer, thinking Herbert is the station agent, checks his trunk with Herbert, who rifles the trunk of valuables. The customer has a valid claim against the H & H Railroad.

Ratification of Authority by Principal

Despite the fact that he did not give his agent authority, or the fact that the agent exceeded his authority, the principal may later be bound by his agent's actions if he has ratified or approved them. There are many ways in which a principal may ratify or confirm an agent's acts; two examples follow:

McNeil, pretending to represent Gregory, contracts with Harris to take care of his horse for a year. McNeil places the horse in Gregory's stable. Gregory learns of the facts and does nothing about it for a week. Normally, his behavior would be considered an affirmation or ratification of the contract.

Durst authorizes Ross to sell a refrigerator at a specified price and without a warranty. Ross, pretending to have the authority to do so, sells the refrigerator with a two-year guarantee. Durst, knowing all the facts, receives the purchase price. He is bound by his silence to the two-year guarantee, although originally Ross had no authority to make the warranty.

Once a principal acquiesces in the acts and conduct of an agent, such acquiescence indicates authorization to perform similar acts in the future.

Lyman appoints Bernette as purchasing agent for his plant. During the first six months, Bernette purchases a grade of material not previously used in the plant. Lyman pays the bills, knowing that the grade of merchandise has been changed, but later claims that he gave no express authority to Bernette to make the purchases. However, Lyman is responsible for Bernette's acts; Bernette had apparent authority since his previous purchases had been approved.

Delegation of Authority by Agent

Ordinarily, an agent is not clothed with authority to delegate his responsibility to someone else.

Snyder employs Calkins, an auctioneer, to sell his cattle. Calkins sends the cattle to another auctioneer, requesting him to put the cattle up at public sale. Calkins had no authority to do this, and Snyder can repudiate the sale.

An agent has apparent authority to appoint subagents if it is in accordance with the established custom or when the very nature of the business indicates that subagents are required.

Butler is appointed general manager of a store. He is authorized from the very nature of the business to employ clerks, who thereby become subagents.

An insurance company employs King as state manager. A reasonable interpretation of this appointment is that King has authority to appoint selling agents throughout the state.

It is a general rule that a person who holds a fiduciary position cannot delegate his responsibility to someone else. Therefore, a trustee, executor, administrator, or guardian cannot delegate those of his responsibilities which involve elements of discretion.

DUTIES AND LIABILITIES OF AN AGENT

The law seems to impose many more duties on an agent to his principal than on a principal to his agent. In most circumstances, the duties and liabilities of an agent are governed by the terms of the agreement between the principal and the agent, but there are certain rules which apply to most agencies.

Agent's Obligations to Principal

In general, an agent has the following duties: (1) to use care and skill; (2) to act with such propriety as not to bring disrepute on his principal; (3) to give his principal all pertinent information; (4) to keep and render accounts if the nature of the work requires them; (5) to stay within the limits of his authority; (6) to obey his principal and carry out all reasonable instructions; (7) to act with utmost good faith and loyalty in advancing the interests of his principal; and (8) above all, to act solely for the principal's benefit in all matters connected with his agency.

The last duty is commonly misunderstood; it is simply a duty of loyalty—first, last, and always—during the period of agency. The relationship between agent and principal should be one of trust and confidence. However, an agent will sometimes err, and when he does, the courts may penalize him.

VanNess gives to Martin, his selling agent, a broad power of attorney to sell his real estate. Acting under this power, Martin sells the property to himself. This is self-dealing by an agent, and if he desires, VanNess can have the conveyance set aside.

If an agent makes a profit in transactions he handles on behalf of his principal, he is obliged by his duty of loyalty to offer the profit to the principal.

Pike, acting for Hun, sells a parcel of land to Bridgeman for $500,000. As an inducement to sell the property to him rather than to other persons who are interested, Bridgeman pays Pike a bonus of $10,000. This money really belongs to Hun, and Pike must disclose the bonus payment and also pay it to Hun on demand.

An agent is further obligated not to act on behalf of an adverse party in a transaction connected with his agency and moreover not to receive any compensation directly or indirectly from the adverse party.

Springman employs Connelly to sell his house at the best price and agrees to pay Connelly a commission of 5 percent. Unknown to Springman, Connelly has been employed by Franklin to obtain a house for him at a low price. Connelly introduces Springman to Franklin and, without disclosing his relationship with Franklin, urges Springman to sell the house at the price offered by Franklin. This breach of duty on Connelly's part could be Springman's defense if Connelly sues him for his 5 percent commission.

An agent must not act during the period of the agency for persons whose interests would conflict with the interests of his principal.

Delafield is employed by Potts as manager of Potts's business. He decides to go into business himself, and he secretly contracts with Potts's employees to work for him. Delafield has committed a breach of loyalty to Potts.

Burrmann, a real estate agent, has been asked by the Bankers Bank whether they should renew their lease on a building or buy it. Burrmann secretly visits the owner of the building and obtains a lease on his own account. Owing to his breach of duty, Burrmann may be required to hold this lease for the bank's benefit (as "constructive trustee" or "trustee ex maleficio").

The principal who is the victim of a disloyal agent has various legal remedies at his disposal. He may bring actions for (1) damages for breach of contract; (2) damages for wrongful breach of duty (tort action); (3) impressing a trust on the property acquired by an agent; (4) an accounting; and (5) an injunction. The injured principal may also discharge the agent, refuse to pay him compensation and/or rescind the contract of employment.

Agent's Liabilities to Third Parties

The liability of the agent himself to third parties involves the important question of whether the principal is disclosed, partially disclosed, or undisclosed.

An agent who makes a contract for a disclosed (identified) principal is not personally bound by the contract.

Finley, known by Stone to be the agent for Hawkins, writes to Stone, "I will sell you 100,000 broiler chicks at 10 cents each." Stone accepts. Hawkins defaults on the contract. Finley, having disclosed the fact that he was acting as agent for Hawkins, is not personally liable.

An agent acting for a partially disclosed principal (he discloses his agency but not the principal's name) becomes a party to the contract.

Clifton writes Felix offering to sell goods and states that he represents a manufacturer who would prefer at this time that his name not be disclosed. Felix accepts. Clifton becomes a party to the contract.

An agent who does not disclose to a third person the fact that he is acting for another is a party to the contract. If the third party later finds out the identity of the principal, he has the option of holding either the agent or the principal responsible.

Forster agrees to sell Hadley's lumber to York without revealing Hadley's identity. When York discovers Hadley's identity, he tells Forster that he will sue Hadley. Later, York changes his mind and sues both principal and agent. Hadley and Forster are liable for their obligations under the contract.

DUTIES AND LIABILITIES OF THE PRINCIPAL

A principal's duties are not so numerous nor on such a high plane as those of an agent to his principal. The principal's duties are mainly contractual.

Principal's Obligations to Agent

The principal owes his agent just compensation. The basic right of an agent to recover compensation rests on contract, express or implied, and on custom or usage in the particular field. But when an agent has been guilty of such gross negligence as to render his services of no value, the agent can recover no compensation.

A principal is liable to his agent for damages if he breaches his contract by prematurely terminating the agency. In such a case of wrongful discharge, the agent, in addition to damages, may recover from the principal all monies advanced and expenditures made in behalf of the principal. When the agent has in his possession money or property of the principal, he is entitled to retain them to satisfy his lien (for compensation or monies advanced or expended for the principal).

Principal's Obligations to Third Parties for Agent's Acts

A principal is liable to third parties for contracts made by the agent within his authority, whether actual or apparent. When the agent violates his secret instructions, the principal may be liable on the contract.

Bowers instructs Green to purchase a house for him and gives Green a letter indicating that he represents Bowers. Bowers advises Green that he should pay $200,000 for the house, $100,000 in cash and a $100,000 mortgage. Green buys the property for Bowers, but in violation of his instructions he agrees to pay $200,000 in cash. The transaction binds Bowers, and he must complete the purchase of the house in cash or respond to a suit for damages.

In order for a principal to be considered liable for a wrongful act of his agent, the law must presume that the principal intended the wrongdoing. Intent on the principal's part may spring from specific instructions to complete the act complained of, or it may result from wrongful instructions on the principal's part.

Sims, fearing intruders, directs Coe to shoot any person entering Sims's premises. Coe shoots a business visitor rightfully entering the premises. Sims is liable for Coe's wrongful act.

Prentice directs Stamply to wash his windows three stories above the street and not to use safety catches. Stamply carries out instructions, slips and falls to the ground injuring a passerby. Prentice is subject to liability to the injured persons.

Generally, the principal is not liable for physical harm resulting from the conduct of an agent who is not an employee and who is not under his control for the completion of his activities. Examples of such agents would be attorneys, brokers, real estate agents, or the like.

Ebers employs Brush as his real estate agent to convey land for him. While Brush (who has made a sale) is signing a deed, he negligently knocks over an ink stand and ruins a valuable rug. Under such circumstances, Ebers would not be liable for the damage to the rug.

However, when an agent who is not an employee performs wrongful acts which do not involve physical damage, the principal may be subject to liability. The principal may be liable to another for loss occasioned by deceitful representation by his agent if the agent was actually authorized to make such a statement or if it was within his general or apparent power to make such representations.

Schopp, as the agent of Carpenter, sells a farm to Winthrop, misrepresenting that the well and the spring on the farm have never run dry. Winthrop purchases land relying on the statement. Carpenter is liable to Winthrop in a lawsuit for deceit just as though he himself had made the statement.

The principal, however, would not be liable for his agent's deceit if the person dealing with the agent had reason to believe that the misrepresentations were not authorized by the principal or reason to seriously doubt the misrepresentation.

Vergason, employed by Marshall to sell lots in a residential area, misrepresents to Ryan that oil has been discovered on an adjoining tract of land. Ryan buys a lot. Ryan, knowing Vergason's reputation for falsehood, does not believe that Vergason's statements were authorized by Marshall, so Marshall is not liable for deceit.

LIABILITY OF MASTER FOR SERVANT'S ACTS

Related to the status of principal and agent is the relationship of master and servant. A *master* is usually liable for injuries caused by the wrongful conduct of *servants* acting within the scope of their employment.

When is a person a servant (or an employee), and when is he an independent contractor? A person working for another is a servant or employee when the master or employer has control of the method and means by which the work is done. If the person doing the work, however, retains control over the manner or method of doing the work, he would be held to be an independent contractor, and under most circumstances the person for whom the work is being done would not be responsible for negligence or other wrongful acts.

Bear in mind that the master (employer) is liable only for injuries caused by the wrongful acts of his servant (employee) when committed "within the scope of his employment," that is, when they are of the same general nature as that authorized by the employer or are incidental to such employment.

Sam, a millhand, develops considerable skill in one particular operation and is assigned to that operation. Another employee in the mill has some difficulty operating the machine and calls on Sam for assistance. Sam has not been directed to assist the other employee; yet his doing so is within the scope of his employment.

Nye, proprietor of a pharmaceutical concern, requires all his employees to wash their hands in his washroom before beginning work. Although hand washing is not part of the specific work covered by the employment, it is incidental to it and within its scope. One of the employees turns on the water to wash his hands and fails to turn it off and flooding results. Although employees may perform irresponsible acts, they may sometimes be held to be within the "scope of employment" and the responsibility of the employer. Such was the conclusion here.

A professional ball club requires its ballplayers to eat what the manager directs under his supervision at a training table. Any act of a ballplayer during mealtime while the players are under the manager's control is "within the scope of employment."

A proprietor of a sporting goods store directs his salesmen never to insert a shell while exhibiting a gun to a customer. However, Dexter, a salesman, does so, and a customer is injured. The act is within the scope of Dexter's employment, and the proprietor may be held liable, despite his instructions to his salesmen.

Even deliberate criminal acts may sometimes be within the scope of employment.

A chauffeur, on an errand for his boss, driving on the left-hand side of a double line and greatly exceeding the speed limit, is still acting within the scope of employment and his employer may be responsible for the consequences of a serious accident.[2]

Acts of an employee are held to be within the scope of employment only within the particular locality of employment or in a locality not unreasonably distant. If an employee leaves the area of employment or deviates from his regular route for his own personal benefit, he may be acting beyond the scope of his employment.

McChesney directs Preble, his chauffeur, to drive to the railroad station to meet an incoming guest. Preble, hearing that the train will be late, leaves early and drives to a village ten miles distant to call on his girlfriend and en route has an accident. In those states which limit liability in accident cases to agents or employees acting within the scope of employment, McChesney would not be liable. However, if Preble had seen his girlfriend and had had the accident on his way back on his regular route, McChesney would be liable.

The common law held that the employer (master) was not liable to an employee (servant), acting within the scope of his employment, who was injured solely by the negligence of a fellow servant. This harsh *fellow servant rule* has been partially displaced by the states' adoption of worker's compensation laws, but it still applies to employees, such as farm laborers or domestic servants, who generally are not covered by these laws.

Employees engaged in the same enterprise and by the same employer are not fellow servants unless their work is so related that they are likely to come in close contact with one another or unless there is a special risk of harm to one by the negligence of the other.

Duff is employed by Bergdorf in a meat-processing plant. While he is carrying meat from one floor to another in Bergdorf's plant, Duff is injured by the negligent operation of the plant elevator. The elevator operator is regarded as a fellow employee in daily working contact with Duff; hence, Bergdorf is not liable to Duff.

Archibald employs McGillis as a maintenance man whose duties take him to all departments in his machine shop. McGillis is injured by the negligence of the packing-room foreman who throws a crate in the passageway just as McGillis approaches. Archibald is not liable to McGillis because of the fellow servant rule.

Fortunately, the almost universality of workers' compensation limits the application of the *fellow servant rule*.

TERMINATION OF AGENCY

An agency is usually terminated by mutual consent. It may also be terminated if the principal revokes the agent's authority or if the agent renounces his agency. Such revocation or renunciation may constitute a breach of contract between the principal and agent and may be the basis for a lawsuit for damages. Nevertheless, as far as third persons are concerned, the agency itself is terminated.

Jackson writes Mobey, "I authorize you to sell my house on Front Street any time within six months." Mobey writes back and says, "I agree to try and sell your house." Two months later Jackson writes to Mobey, "I've changed my mind; I do not want to sell now." Mobey's authority as an agent is terminated.

An agency may be terminated even though the parties themselves agreed that it was to be irrevocable for an indefinite period. This is the very nature of an agency: It can be terminated at any time.

Jenners gives Winans a power of attorney to sell Jenners's property at a stated price and agrees to pay a commission of 20 percent. The power of attorney ends with the statement, "I agree that this power shall be irrevocable for a period of one year." At the end of four months Jenners says to Winans, "I revoke the power of attorney." Under those circumstances the agency is terminated. Winans may have a claim for damages against Jenners for breaking his agreement, but the authority for his agency is terminated.

Agency may also be terminated by the death of either the principal or the agent or when it becomes impossible to carry out the agent's authority, as in the destruction of the subject matter or in the bankruptcy of the principal.

If the principal authorized his agent (by power of attorney or otherwise) to do certain acts, it is prudent for the principal to terminate that agency relationship by document of termination. Such writing can be quite simple and straightforward or else it can sound very "legal." It is advisable to have it executed in the same way the original document was executed. If the grant was recorded and filed in any office of the public records, then most likely the document of termination also should be filed.

NOTES

[1]In this connection, see the earlier discussion of the Statute of Frauds.

[2]This rule is important in a majority of states that do not follow the rule that every owner of an automobile is liable for the negligence of the person driving the car with the consent or permission of the owner.

20

CRIMINAL LAW

A crime is a wrong that affects the public welfare, a wrong for which the state has prescribed a punishment or penalty (see Glossary for explanations of particular crimes). It is an act or omission prohibited by law because it is injurious to the public (as distinct from a private wrong).

POWER TO DEFINE AND PUNISH CRIME

The individual states have broad powers to prohibit and punish crimes. The state legislature has inherent power to define crimes and to enact laws punishing them. It does so, first, by a definite description of the act or acts constituting a crime and, second, by prescribing a penalty for the particular crime.

Unlike the state legislatures, the United States Congress has no inherent power to punish crimes. All its power derives from the U.S. Constitution; thus, Congress may define and punish crimes in the District of Columbia and the territories and may punish crimes relating to postal matters, interstate commerce, securities and United States coinage, federal elections, and other matters expressly referred to in the constitution.

CLASSIFICATION OF CRIMES

Crimes may be classified as treason, felonies and misdemeanors. *Treason* is the offense of a citizen in attempting to overthrow the

U.S. government or in betraying a state into the hands of a foreign power. *Felonies* are those crimes punishable by death or by imprisonment in a state prison, although a lesser punishment may be imposed by the court. Crimes not so serious in nature as felonies are *misdemeanors*.

Sometimes crimes are labeled as *mala in se* (crimes inherently or morally wrong) or *mala prohibita* (crimes not inherently wrong, but crimes because they are prohibited by statute). Examples of crimes which are *mala in se* are murder, rape, arson, burglary, larceny, forgery, and the like. Examples of crimes which are *mala prohibita* are crimes that violate government requirements for licensing, failure of corporate directors or officers to follow requirements of the corporation law, failure to comply with government regulations or government requirements for the labeling of products, printing or publishing copyrighted musical compositions without the consent of the owner, bookmaking and the use of gambling apparatus, violations of the labor law, and so on.

PUNISHMENT AND PREVENTION OF CRIME

It is generally agreed that the purpose of punishment for a crime is to deter the criminal and others from committing similar crimes. When a court imposes punishment for a breach of the law, the object is not vengeance but rather is to discourage the person who has broken the law from repeating his act.

A legislature may impose more than one penalty for the same offense; thus, a statute may provide for imprisonment in the state prison for a term of years and also for a fine that may be double the amount of money stolen or embezzled or double the value of the goods involved in the crime. The U.S. Constitution and most state constitutions prohibit cruel and unusual punishments.

Although the legislature may fix the limits of punishment, the trial court has the power to fix the actual punishment within statutory limits. In those states where the jury makes a recommendation for mercy in connection with its verdict, the recommendation is no part of the verdict; in fixing the punishment in the exercise of its discretion, the court may disregard the recommendation of the jury.

It is normally the function of police officers to prevent the commission of crime. But a private individual who sees another person actually perpetrating or about to perpetrate a felony may interfere and employ such force as is necessary to prevent the commission of the crime.

DEATH PENALTY

While the high courts of the various states were upholding the constitutionality of death penalties, the number of executions in the United States dropped from forty-seven in 1962 to none in the years 1968 to 1971.

Finally in 1972 the long-awaited death penalty decision was made by the U.S. Supreme Court in the case of *Furman v. Georgia.* By a vote of five to four, the highest court in the land held that discretionary death penalties are unconstitutional because laws that give unlimited discretion to judges and juries to impose the penalty are "pregnant with discrimination." Only two of the nine justices, however, voted to hold mandatory death penalties invalid, and some states have moved to reinstate the death penalty as mandatory for specific crimes.

Then, in 1976, the Court ruled that the death penalty is not necessarily cruel and unusual punishment so long as it is not mandatory for specific crimes and the jury has sufficient information and guidelines to determine its appropriateness in a particular case.

The Supreme Court has also held that other serious crimes such as rape and robbery do not call for the death penalty. There are over 1,000 prisoners throughout the country who are on death rows of various states.

Since 1976, when the U.S. Supreme Court permitted the resumption of the death penalty, there have been over 200 persons executed.

SENTENCING GUIDELINES

Nearly all states have in recent years enacted stringent anti-crime laws and mandatory minimum sentences. However, as costs have climbed and particularly when ordered by federal courts to relieve overcrowding (either by building more facilities or by early release of inmates), many states have begun to review their criminal sentencing policies.

The legislatures of North Carolina, Arkansas, Minnesota and Kansas have begun the process of remodeling their sentencing procedures and punishment programs. (Under the proposed North Carolina program, a criminal sentence could be reduced by 80% while supervised community programs would be substituted.)

Criminal justice experts say that other states, including Pennsylvania, Delaware, Florida, Tennessee, Louisiana, Texas and Ohio, may slowly be moving in a similar direction.

CLASSIFICATION OF PARTIES TO CRIME

Persons involved in felonies may be classified as principals in the first or second degrees and as accessories before or after the facts. Parties to treason or misdemeanors, if guilty in any degree, are all classified as principals.

The principal in the first degree is the person who actually perpetrates the crime. He need not actually be present when the harm is done (for example, if he mixes a poison potion for another who takes it in his absence). A person who causes a crime to be committed through the instrumentality of an agent is the principal in the crime and is punished as such.

The principal in the second degree is one who aids and abets in the commission of the crime, one who advises, encourages or helps in the actual perpetration of the crime. A common example of a principal in the second degree is one who stays a distance from the scene of a felony but who keeps watch in order to warn of the approach of danger.

The *accessory before the fact* is one who is not present at the time the crime is committed but who counsels, urges, or commands the crime to be committed or in some way aids the principal in the commission of the crime. The *accessory after the fact* is one who knows that a felony has been committed and who receives, comforts, and assists the principal criminal or criminals. In this situation, the accessory after the fact is not connected with the commission of the crime; his offense occurs afterwards and is, therefore, distinct from the principal crime.

CRIMINAL CAPACITY, INTENT, ATTEMPT

If a person lacks the mental or other capacity to commit a particular crime, his acts, no matter how forbidden by law or how damaging to the public, are not criminal. Want of capacity is a complete defense and not merely an extenuating circumstance.

In law, intent is considered the purpose to use a particular means to cause a particular result. In nine out of ten cases, a felony crime must be accompanied by such intent, or criminal intent. The crime must be accompanied by intent to commit the crime or such negligence or indifference to duty or consequences that the law regards it as equivalent to intent.

An attempt to commit a crime has been defined by the courts as an act performed in partial execution of a criminal design, amounting to more than mere preparation but falling short of actual completion of the crime. Ordinarily, an attempt to commit a crime is a misdemeanor, although at times legislatures have classified attempts to commit particular crimes as felonies.

In order to be convicted of an attempted crime, the accused must take at least one step beyond preparation. The step must be in the direction of the completion of the crime but obviously not the last act of completion.

Webb and Johnson decide to break into a house. They meet at a saloon and talk over their plans. Webb has a revolver, and Johnson goes into a drugstore to buy some chloroform. Johnson is arrested when he comes out of the drugstore. Neither Webb nor Johnson has committed an attempted crime; they are simply in the preparation state.

The courts have pointed out that there is a wide difference between preparation for the commission of the crime and the actual attempt. The step that may constitute an attempted crime need not be an act that is ordinarily a criminal act but one that may lead up to it.

Quince decides to set fire to a building in order to collect the insurance. He buys kerosene, spreads it around the property, and makes a deal with another person to set fire to the property. His accomplice decides he wants no part of the crime of arson. Quince, however, has made an attempt to commit the claim of arson and can be convicted.

DEFENSES FOR COMMISSION OF CRIMES

When a person is charged with committing a crime, he may plead guilty or not guilty. If he pleads not guilty, he must be prepared to overcome whatever proof the prosecutor offers to establish that he committed the crime; the facts he presents to do this and to maintain his innocence constitute a defense.

A general defense may be that the accused person did not commit the crime. There are other defenses that may admit for the moment that the accused did certain acts but claim that there are special circumstances or reasons why the accused person should not be found guilty of the crime of which he is accused.

Under our system of law, every accused person is entitled to avail himself of all legal defenses no matter how technical they may be.

Ignorance of the Law

The courts in the United States have supported the principle that every person is presumed to know the law of his country and that ignorance of the law is no defense to criminal prosecution. For example:

The agents of the California, Oregon & Santa Fe Railroad Company, did not know that the law prohibited the solicitation of alien contract laborers for work in this country and prohibited the prepayment of transportation of alien laborers. When confronted with a criminal prosecution, the railroad agents, who had sought Italian immigrant laborers in Canada to work in Oregon for the railroad and had paid the immigrants cash and had issued railroad passes to them, pleaded that they did not know of the existence of the law. The court held that their ignorance was no defense.

Although ignorance of the law is no defense in a criminal prosecution, it may sometimes be a matter considered by the judge in determining punishment for a crime.

This rule rests on public necessity, for the welfare of society and the safety of individuals depend on the enforcement of criminal laws. If persons accused of crime could shield themselves behind a defense of ignorance of the law, criminal laws would be practically impossible to enforce.

Ignorance of the Facts

On the other hand, if a person technically commits a crime but is ignorant of a fact essential to the crime or makes a mistake regarding the facts, he may have a good defense. In the following instances the accused person may actually have a good defense: (1) if one takes another's property in the honest belief that it is his own; (2) if stolen goods are received by one who does not know that they have been stolen; (3) if one has possession of forged instruments or counterfeit coins in ignorance of their character; or (4) if one marries believing that a legal spouse is dead.

Sometimes, however, the legislature specifically provides punishment for a crime regardless of whether the party committing the crime had the necessary actual knowledge. For example, the legislatures of many states prescribe penalties for those who sell intoxicating liquors to minors and specify that it makes no difference whether the persons who sell the liquor are unaware that the purchasers are under age.

Custom or Usage

The practice of law enforcement officers in some situations to overlook certain crimes does not establish a legal precedent or a legal defense. Even though the failure to enforce a law or erroneous interpretation of a law may have permitted violators to escape punishment, no right to violate the law is created; furthermore, it does not provide a defense against criminal prosecution for a person committing a crime heretofore considered lightly in the community. For instance, ship officers have been convicted of the crime of appropriating small portions of the ship's cargo, even though it had been a custom to overlook such offenses. Others have been subject to criminal action for indecent exposure for indulging in the seemingly accepted practice of exposing themselves while bathing in public places.

Direction or Duress

A person is considered guilty of his illegal acts even when he commits them under the direction of his superior. For instance, an employee who on orders of his employer pays money to a public official to induce him to neglect his official duty is guilty of bribery.

Occasionally, though rarely, a crime may be excused on the ground that it was committed under *duress* or *compulsion*. The compulsion that will excuse a criminal act must be grounded on fear of death or serious bodily harm. A threat of future injury is not sufficient defense.

For example:

Adams and Decker are buddies. Adams plans to rob a store on February 1 and threatens to kill Decker if he does not help him complete the crime. On February 4, both Adams and Decker rob the store and are caught. The mere fact that three days before the crime Adams has threatened Decker with death is no defense for Decker. They are both convicted.

Entrapment

The courts of the United States are not in complete accord as to when a defendant in a criminal case can successfully assert the defense of entrapment. The general rule is that entrapment is a valid defense only when the crime is the product of "creative activity" on the part of the government (police).

Pedro was suspected of importing heroin into the United States from Mexico. He was promised $5,000 by a man working for the United States government if he would bring heroin to Mexicali, a town across the border in California. The narcotics agent sent word to Pedro at Mexicali that he would have to bring the heroin to Calexico, California, to get his money. Pedro did so, got his money, and was arrested for bringing heroin into the United States. The federal court dismissed the case against Pedro, holding that the government induced Pedro to bring the heroin into the United States and therefore Pedro was entrapped.

Mr. K. was charged with using the mails for delivery of obscene, lewd, and lascivious films. The Post Office Department had placed an advertisement in a magazine known for its obscenity. Mr. K. responded to the ad, corresponded with the Post Office Department, which used an alias, and delivered the film to a government agent. The court held that the government induced the offense and failed to show that Mr. K. was predisposed to commit the offense without government encouragement. The court said that the Post Office Department's action was typical of "creative activity" on the part of the government necessary to constitute the defense of entrapment.

Mr. M., a reputed Mafia boss, was charged with assaulting an officer of the FBI. Mr. M., when arriving at an airport, angrily confronted a group of news photographers, asking if they had taken enough pictures. Collins, an FBI agent who was in the crowd, answered, "No." Mr. M. asked, "Are you looking for trouble?" Collins answered, "I can handle trouble." Mr. M. assaulted Collins and was later arrested. The court held that Collins's refusal to back down in the face of Mr. M.'s threats did not constitute entrapment.

Instigation amounts to encouraging or soliciting a person into the commission of crime, as distinguished from entrapment, the final act of springing the trap to catch the criminal.

Whether the defense is called entrapment or instigation, it must be shown that the officers of the law or their agents instigated and incited the accused into committing an offense that he otherwise had no intention of committing; such entrapment is a valid defense.

Most courts today also will determine whether the accused was predisposed to commit the crime. If he was predisposed in any event (without government help), then the defense of entrapment or instigation cannot prevail.

Consent, Forgiveness or Settlement

Crimes are public wrongs which a private individual has the power neither to condone nor to absolve. The crime is determined by the act of the person in committing the crime. Therefore, the fact that the victim of the crime subsequently forgives his wrongdoer is usually no defense in a criminal prosecution.

Nick Bonn, desperate for money, breaks into Cromwell's home and steals some heirlooms. Nick is apprehended by the police, but Cromwell is so glad to get his heirlooms back and so sympathetic with Nick's plight that he forgives Nick and so informs the police. The district attorney, however, says Nick must be prosecuted. The court agrees, for a crime of burglary was committed, and the homeowner has no power to nullify the law. (However, Cromwell, although he cannot refuse to testify against Nick, can be a "reluctant witness.")

There is no requirement that a complainant in a criminal case follow through with the prosecution but, in the case of a felony, there may be the temptation to accept money offered in return for an agreement not to prosecute the felony. Such an act may constitute the new crime of *compounding a felony* or a crime of *obstructing justice*.

Alibi

An alibi has been called a perfect defense. It is proof that at the time the crime was committed the defendant was not at the scene of the crime and could not have participated in it. In order to constitute a complete alibi, it must be proved that it was impossible for the defendant to have been at the place where the crime was committed.

Religious Doctrine or Belief

As a general rule, religious beliefs cannot be recognized as justifications for committing crimes. Usually neither the law nor the government interferes with religious beliefs, but they may interfere if religious practices constitute crimes. For example, the court's of Utah have in the past century forced Mormon residents of the state to stop practicing their belief in polygamy. Religious practices are subject to the rules of government.

Turning State's Evidence

When an accomplice in the commission of a crime becomes a witness for the prosecution and discloses his guilt and that of his associates, the law says there is an implied promise that he will not be prosecuted and that at least a pardon will be granted to him. This right to freedom from prosecution, to a reduced sentence or to a pardon is based on fair dealing and is considered a pledge of faith by the public. It is within the discretion of the public prosecutor to determine whether to use an accomplice as *state's evidence*. Once an accomplice has testified for the prosecution, the court is honor-bound to pardon him or to reduce the charges against him. This rule has many refinements in the various states. The federal courts have held flatly that, although the United States district attorney has no power to guarantee an accomplice that he will not be prosecuted, an accomplice who gives testimony essential to the conviction should not be prosecuted.

However, more often than not, this "implied promise" of the prosecution to "go easy" on an accomplice who is willing to turn state's evidence becomes a matter of hard bargaining between the prosecutor and the defendant's lawyer. (See page 296 for a more complete discussion of plea bargaining.)

Insanity

One who is so mentally deranged that he is incapable of having a criminal intent cannot be guilty of a crime or be held criminally responsible for his acts. In order for insanity to be a solid defense, it must appear that the accused was insane at the time of the commission of the crime and not merely before or after the crime. Mere mental weakness is not an excuse for criminal acts. When the defendant has a low order of intelligence but sufficient mental capacity to know that his act was wrong, he has no defense on this ground.

The test used in most jurisdictions is whether the defendant was so unsound mentally at the time he committed the offense that he did not know the difference between right and wrong. In some jurisdictions the courts have held that a person is not responsible for criminal acts if the jury finds that by reason of mental disease or defect he had lost the power to know right from wrong or had insane delusions or irresistible impulses to do wrongful acts. On the other hand, the courts of some states refuse to accept the "irresistible impulse" theory.

In one leading case, the New York Court of Appeals said:

Whatever medical or scientific authority there may be for this view, it has not been accepted by courts of law. The vagueness and uncertainty of the inquiry which would be opened and the manifest danger of introducing the limitation claimed into the rule of responsibility, in cases of crime, may well cause courts to pause before assenting to it. Indulgence in evil passions weakens the restraining power of the will and conscience; and the rule suggested would be the cover for the commission of crime and its justification.

Alcohol and Drug Intoxication

Voluntary drunkenness is no defense for commission of a crime. If a person voluntarily becomes intoxicated, and while in that condition commits a crime, he is responsible for his acts. However, in certain crimes, a specific *intent* is an essential part of the crime; and if the defendant was stupefied by the consumption of alcoholic beverages, he may not have had the specific intent necessary for commission of the crime or he may not have had the mental capacity to form a deliberate intent. This situation should not be confused with one in which a person voluntarily becomes intoxicated for the purpose of committing the crime.

A person broods upon his unhappiness and gets drunk; in this condition he kills his wife. He is indicted for murder, a felony. He probably would be acquitted by a jury if it feels he did not have the ability to plan a premeditated murder. However, he also probably would be convicted of a lesser degree of murder, such as manslaughter.

Another man first makes up his mind to kill his wife and then becomes drunk and commits the crime. He is likely to be found guilty of murder.

The use of drugs has resulted in court rulings similar to those involving alcoholic intoxication. Temporary insanity resulting from the voluntary use of drugs constitutes no defense to a criminal charge. On the other hand, mental incapacity caused by medicinal use of drugs may excuse the commission of what otherwise would constitute a criminal act.

CRIMINAL JURISDICTION, EXTRADITION AND PLACE OF TRIAL

There are two kinds of criminal jurisdiction: first, the *jurisdiction of the subject matter of the crime*, that is, the power of the court to hear and determine the particular case; second, the *jurisdiction over the person accused of the crime*. Jurisdiction is necessary to a valid prosecution and conviction; if the court has no jurisdiction the conviction is a nullity. Thus, the question of prime importance to a criminal lawyer is whether or not a particular court has jurisdiction in his case.

Jurisdiction of Subject Matter

No state or sovereignty can enforce the penal laws of another country or punish offenses committed in another country. (For that reason, many members of the legal profession have been shocked at the attempt of certain courts to punish international criminals for acts committed outside the jurisdiction of those courts.) The jurisdiction of particular courts to hear and determine crimes is determined by the constitution of each state. The statutes of the various states say that certain crimes shall be heard and determined in each level of courts. The particular offense, therefore, must be heard and determined by the court designated by the legislature.

State courts have exclusive jurisdiction in state offenses, and federal courts have exclusive jurisdiction in federal offenses. Sometimes the same act can constitute a violation of both state and federal laws, and state and federal courts have concurring jurisdiction.

Prosecution under federal and state laws for the same conduct is well established. As long ago as 1847, the U.S. Supreme Court held that dual prosecutions were constitutional because of the dual sovereignty of the federal government and the states, and the allegiance a citizen owes to both. It has been said that each has a different agenda. However, the debate continues whether the subsequent federal prosecution (if there is an acquittal in the state court) constitutes double jeopardy. (See the discussion on page 299.)

Jurisdiction of Accused

Before a court can have personal jurisdiction of the accused, he must be in the custody of the court. The presence of the accused is essential to jurisdiction. The court has no jurisdiction to hear and determine the charge of crime unless the accused (1) is in its custody, (2) has been admitted to bail, or (3) has consented to the jurisdiction. In other words, the jurisdiction of a court to try and punish one accused of a crime cannot be acquired by mere assertion or the filing of a complaint or indictment. There is no excuse for failure to bring the prisoner before the court so that the court may have custody of him. It has been held that when the accused is a prisoner in a state penitentiary, the mere filing of an indictment against him does not give the court jurisdiction of the new offense.

Extradition

Extradition is the surrender by one state or nation to another of an individual accused of a criminal offense. The average case of extradition in the United States arises between various states. The right of a foreign power to demand extradition exists only when that right is given by treaty. In the absence of a treaty, the United States will not surrender a fugitive criminal to a foreign government. The right of extradition between states is controlled by article IV, section 2, of the U.S. Constitution, which provides "that a person charged in any state with treason, felony, or other crime, who shall flee from justice, and be found in another state, shall on demand of the executive authority of the state from which he fled be delivered up, to be removed to the state having jurisdiction of the crime." The responsibility for demanding extradition of a person charged with a crime and the duty to deliver up such a person on proper command are vested in the governors of the states involved.

Generally, a person may be extradited only when he is a "fugitive from justice," who has been charged with a crime in one state and has left that state and is found in another state. Many court decisions have involved the question of whether a person was knowingly running away from a crime. The courts have held that when a person leaves the state where he is charged with a crime, it is immaterial what his purpose or motive is for leaving the state; he will usually be considered a fugitive and will be returned to the state where he is charged with the crime.

In seeking the return of a fugitive from justice, the governor of the prosecuting state sends a requisition to the governor of the asylum state requesting that the fugitive be delivered up. The requisition must be accompanied by a copy of papers charging the person with a crime. For example, when the alleged fugitive has been indicted, there must be a copy of the grand jury's indictment or a copy of the magistrate's warrant seeking the arrest of the alleged criminal. Proceedings are held before the governor of the state to which the alleged criminal has fled. Before sending the accused person back to the state seeking his extradition, the governor must first determine that the person demanded has been legally charged with a crime and is a fugitive from justice.

Place of Trial (Venue)

Venue has been defined as the locality where the offense is triable; in criminal matters, it means the locality (ordinarily the county) where the criminal act is alleged to have occurred. When the offense consists of the omission of an act, venue is usually the locality where the act should have been performed.

There is a certain amount of flexibility in the rules of venue for the prosecution of crimes; some of this is indicated in the following examples of particular crimes.

The venue of a prosecution for abandonment or nonsupport of a wife or child is the place where the abandonment occurred or where the duty to support should have been performed.

The crime of kidnapping is properly laid in the county where the victim is seized even though he is carried into another county.

The crime of bigamy is triable in the county where the bigamous marriage took place, although some statutes provide that the bigamist may be tried in the county where he or she resides or where the parties afterward reside.

Bribery may be triable in the county where the offer is made or accepted.

Burglary must be prosecuted in the county where the breaking and entering took place, not in the county where the property was carried.

The crime of robbery is triable in the county where the property was originally taken.

When one steals property, he may be prosecuted for larceny in the county where he stole the property or where he brought it.

The crime of receiving stolen goods may be prosecuted in the county where the property was received.

Venues for the crimes of conspiracy and monopolies may be tried either in the county where the conspiracy was entered into or where the further acts of the conspirators took place.

Embezzlement may be tried in the county where the property was taken or in the county where the accused was supposed to have accounted for the embezzled property.

The crime of escape from imprisonment must generally be prosecuted in the county where the escape occurred, although in some states the convict may be tried in any county or the state.

The venue of a prosecution for extortion is the county where the offense was committed.

The trial of the crime of obtaining money or property under false pretenses should be tried in the county where the money or property was obtained.

Forgery must be prosecuted in the county where the forgery was committed.

The general rule is that the crime of homicide is prosecuted in the county where the crime was committed, but in some states it is prosecuted at the place where death occurred.

The venue in a criminal prosecution may be changed only on the application of the accused. Changing the place of trial is within the sound discretion of the court.

Most state laws permit a court to grant the accused a change of venue when it seems necessary in order to secure an impartial and fair trial for him. Disqualification or prejudice on the part of the judge is ground for a change. Other grounds include local prejudice and inability to obtain a fair jury. In order to justify a change of venue, the prejudice must be against the accused and exist throughout the entire locality; for instance, newspaper articles and other means of public communication may have so aroused public hostility as to preclude a fair trial for the accused.

PLEA BARGAINING

Most criminal cases are never tried. They are disposed of before trial because either the defendant pleads guilty or the case is dismissed. Plea bargaining plays a large role in the disposition of criminal cases. In 1970, for example, it occurred in 90 percent of all criminal cases disposed of in New York City. In plea bargaining, the accused defendant, on the advice of his lawyer and the consent of the prosecuting attorney, pleads guilty to a lesser crime than that with which he was originally charged.

A person is charged with a crime of burglary for which he might expect a sentence of five to ten years in jail. After discussion with his attorney, the defendant pleads guilty to the lesser crime of larceny, for which the likely sentence would be two years.

Many people object to plea bargaining. The subject is debated regularly by lawyers, professors, criminologists, and others, but there is little dispute as to the importance of plea bargaining in our criminal justice system. Our courts are understaffed and simply cannot resort to trials to dispose of all the indictments that are handed out by grand juries.

For example, in a recent year there were 20,231 felony indictments in New York City alone. At best only 4,000 of these felony charges could be tried. The rest had to be handled by dismissal or guilty pleas. Former Chief Justice of the U.S. Supreme Court Earl Warren said, "Plea discussions leading to disposition of cases are indispensable to any rational administration of criminal cases."

CONSTITUTIONAL AND COMMON-LAW PROTECTION OF ALLEGED CRIMINALS

Unthinking persons today claim that there are too many safeguards for the protection of criminals. They overlook the fact that such safeguards also protect the innocent. The safeguards have come down to us through the English common law (some were wrested from King John at Runnymede and were included in the Magna Carta for the protection of Englishmen), and several of them are explicitly stated in the Constitution of the United States.

Presumption of Innocence

It is a fundamental principle of American criminal law that a person charged with the commission of crime is presumed to be innocent until proven guilty.

The presumption of innocence cannot be changed into a presumption of guilt even if the accused fails to testify or call witnesses to the stand. An accused person does not have to take the stand in his own behalf, and the prosecution may not comment to the jury on his failure to do so.

Necessity for Arraignment and Plea

Depending upon the class of crime[1] (whether a felony or a misdemeanor), the accused is entitled to certain preliminary hearings before the court before the accused can be held for trial to determine whether there is probable cause. In most states, these are called *grand jury* proceedings, or *arraignments.*

A person accused of a crime is arraigned by being called to the bar of the court to answer the accusations contained in an indictment or other form of criminal charge. The accused must be called by name and definitely identified. The indictment or charge must be read to him, he must be advised of his rights, and he must make a plea of guilty or not guilty.

In some jurisdictions, the person accused of a crime may make a plea of *nolo contendere*, which means that he will not dispute the prosecuting authority. Nolo contendere is considered an implied confession of guilt for the purpose of the case only and is accepted as equivalent to a plea of guilty.

Personal Presence of the Accused

It is essential to a valid trial and the conviction of a defendant for a felony that he be personally present, not only when he is arraigned but

also at every subsequent stage of the trial. The same is true in misdemeanor cases when the punishment may be imprisonment. In some
states, when the punishment is by fine only, the trial may be held in the
defendant's absence.

Speedy Trial

A speedy trial is another fundamental constitutional right guaranteed to all persons accused of crime. The right to a speedy trial is
intended to avoid oppression and to prevent delays, to relieve the
accused of the hardship of being held in jail indefinitely, the anxiety of
a pending prosecution, and the resulting public suspicion. A speedy
trial is one which can be had as soon as the prosecution with reasonable diligence can prepare for trial.

The courts have never been able to devise a single test to determine
what amounts to undue delay. In certain cases a trial held within six
months has been held to be a speedy one, while in other cases the same
period of time has been held to be excessive and in violation of the
accused's rights and sufficient justification to grant a discharge of the
accused on denial of his right for a speedy trial. It all depends on how
complicated the case is.

Time Limits for Commencing Criminal Proceedings

There is no time limit within which prosecution for murder must
be commenced. It may be begun at any time after the murder. The
same situation exists in various states for kidnapping and other
crimes.

Time limits for beginning other criminal actions vary in the fifty
states. In some states prosecution for any misdemeanor must be commenced within two years after its commission and within five years
for more serious crimes (felonies). In some places, when the accused
has been absent from the state of jurisdiction, the time limit for prosecution becomes operable only after his return to the state. If the
defendant departs from the state or remains within the state under a
false name after the crime is committed, the time of his absence or of
such residence within a state under a false name is not part of the
time limit for the commencement of the prosecution. To determine
whether it has been commenced within the proper time limit, the

prosecution is said to have begun when information, charging the commission of the crime, is laid before a magistrate and a warrant is issued by him or when an indictment is duly presented by a grand jury in open court.

Double Jeopardy

The word *jeopardy* means the danger of conviction and punishment that an accused in a criminal action incurs when he is charged with a crime. The prohibition against double jeopardy is a sacred principle of criminal law. It was incorporated into the Fifth Amendment to the Constitution of the United States, which states that no person "shall be subject for the same offense to be twice put in jeopardy of life or limb." The constitutions of nearly all the states contain similar provisions. Simply applied, the rule is that once a person is acquitted or has paid the penalty for his crime, he may not thereafter be arrested for the same crime. The rule has no application to civil proceedings, such as deportation, contempt of court, prosecutions for abandonment or failure to support children, proceedings under motor vehicle laws to revoke or suspend licenses, and other proceedings for forfeiture, penalties, and damages.

When a number of offenses grow out of the same criminal act or the act seems to be comprised of a sequence of criminal acts, it is a highly technical matter to determine whether the accused is being tried for several crimes or being tried for one several times; nevertheless, being put in double jeopardy is a violation of his constitutional rights.

However, the U.S. Supreme Court has in a limited number of cases held that dual prosecutions (in a federal court after an acquittal in a state court) do not offend the Fifth Amendment prohibition against double jeopardy. In those cases—involving counterfeiting, harboring fugitive slaves, violations of prohibition laws, dynamiting of a communications facility in a labor dispute—the court held that the federal government had a unique interest in the alleged crime, which—in light of our dual sovereignty—gave it the constitutional right of a dual prosecution.

Miranda Rules

The U.S. Supreme Court has established rules for custody interrogation by the police of those suspected of crime. The suspect must be advised before interrogation (1) that he has a right to remain silent; (2) that anything he says may be used against him; (3) that he has a right to have present an attorney during the questioning; and (4) that if he has no money to pay for a lawyer, he has a right to a lawyer without charge.

These warnings to be given by the police to a person suspected of a crime have become known as "Miranda warnings" because they were promulgated by the U.S. Supreme Court in the case of *Miranda v. Arizona* (1966). If the fourfold warnings are not given, then no evidence may be given in court of any admissions or confession made by the prisoner as a result of police interrogation.

The U.S. Supreme Court under the leadership of Chief Justice Earl Warren became known as a court that protected the constitutional rights of those accused of crime. The Miranda Rule grew out of the protection by the court of the constitutional rights of the accused. When the makeup of the court changed, however, and Warren Berger became chief justice, the new court narrowed the scope of the Miranda rule and defined interrogation of prisoners so as to permit disclosure of facts, not the result of interrogation.

In recent years, although the Supreme Court has even further narrowed the Miranda Rule, the court has relied on technicalities of the rules of impeachment of witnesses in a trial to allow confessions secured without following the Miranda rules, but one cannot predict a position that might be taken by the Supreme Court on the subject of constitutional safeguards for the protection of those accused of crime.

CRIMINAL LAWS VOID FOR VAGUENESS

Some courts hold that state laws which are vague and indefinite invite arbitrary police action and are unconstitutional.

In New York, Pennsylvania and Colorado, laws making vagrancy a crime were struck down by the courts of those states because the legislatures did not sufficiently define what constituted vagrancy.

In Philadelphia, after a series of mass arrests in Rittenhouse Park, a gathering place for hippies and others considered undesirable, a United States district court held that the obvious motive for the arrests had been to clear hippies from the area and that mass arrests, directed at the status of the arrestees rather than at criminal actions, were illegal.

When rioters were arrested in Washington, D.C., one of the defendants appealed claiming that such statutory terms as "public disturbance," "tumultuous and violent conduct," and "grave danger of damage or injury" did not provide an "ascertainable standard" by which to judge conduct and that the statute should be held void for vagueness. By a two-to-one decision the court held that the statute was not ambiguous and that few people would not recognize a riot if they saw one. One of the federal judges dissented, holding that a person might be reluctant to exercise his constitutional right of peaceful assembly for fear of being charged with aiding a riot if the demonstration became violent.

An Oregon court held that a law making it a crime to encourage, cause, or contribute to the delinquency of a minor was unconstitutionally vague since the causes of delinquency are broad and uncertain.

By a five-to-four decision the U.S. Supreme Court in *Coats v. Cincinnati* held a loitering ordinance unconstitutional for vagueness. The ordinance made it criminal for "three or more persons" to assemble on any sidewalk and "conduct themselves in a manner annoying to persons passing by."

POLICE INVESTIGATION AND ACTIVITIES

The courts continue to restrict police activities that are claimed to infringe on the constitutional rights of those charged with crime.

Electronic Surveillance (Bugging)

A man was convicted of narcotics violations largely on the basis of conversations transmitted to law enforcement agents by a device concealed on the person of an informer. The U.S. Court of Appeals for the Seventh Circuit reversed the conviction on the ground that the defendant's "reasonable expectations of privacy" were violated.

In 1993, a federal district court in Texas held that the *Privacy Protection Act of 1980*, which mandates subpoenas in many cases, applies to electronically stored information (computer bulletin boards, electronic mail, etc.) and that a federal government raid and seizure without a warrant was unconstitutional and illegal.

Search and Seizure

Mr. Chimel was arrested at his home, under an arrest warrant. Despite Chimel's objections, police conducted a one-hour search of his home and found various items that were used against him as evidence on his trial. The

U.S. Supreme Court reversed his conviction. holding that the mere arrest of an individual at his home does not give police the right to search the entire house. A valid search warrant is necessary.

Ordinarily there must be a court warrant to justify an arrest in the suspect's home. In their words, the police may not arrest an alleged criminal in his home unless they first obtain a warrant for his arrest.

In recent years, the U.S. Supreme Court has addressed questions of criminal procedure and has modified previous court precedents. For example, a criminal conviction now will be upheld on appeal even though some of the evidence was unlawfully seized by the police, if there was other lawfully seized evidence submitted to the jury and if that lawfully seized evidence alone would have been sufficient to convict.

TRIAL PROCEDURES

Six-Member Jury

For years civil cases have been tried before six members, but criminal cases have not. In 1970, however, the U.S. Supreme Court overruled an 1898 decision and held that twelve jury members were not required under the Constitution. All that is required is that the number of jurors "be large enough to promote group cooperation and a fair possibility for obtaining a representative cross-section of the community."

Unanimous Jury Verdict

In landmark cases in 1972, the Supreme Court held in two 5-to-4 decisions that unanimous verdicts are not required for conviction in state criminal courts.

Disruptive Tactics in Court

Under the United States Constitution, one accused of a crime has the right to confront and cross-examine his accusers and the witnesses against him. This is often referred to as the "right of confrontation." For a time there was much confusion and doubt as to what trial judges should do with defendants who threatened and abused judges and tried to break up court proceedings. Some feared that if they were bound and gagged or put behind jail bars they might be deprived of their right to be present at the trial at all times (the right of confrontation).

The U.S. Supreme Court in deciding an Illinois case in 1970 gave courts the tools to maintain order and decorum in the courtroom. The Court outlined three methods of handling obstreperous defendants:

1) They could be bound and gagged and remain present at the trial. (This remedy to be used only as a last resort because it would be an affront to the dignity of the court.)

2) The trial court could cite an unruly defendant for criminal contempt and imprison him, discontinuing the trial until such time as the defendant promised to behave. (This method has its disadvantages because it may cause the very delay that an unruly defendant is seeking.)

3) The disruptive defendant may be excluded from the courtroom while the trial continues. (Before his removal he must be warned that his continued misconduct will result in his waiving his right to be present in the courtroom.)

Right to Counsel

The Sixth Amendment of the U.S. Constitution gives an accused person the right to counsel. The right to representation by counsel has been held by the U.S. Supreme Court to apply in juvenile cases and in post-indictment identification lineups. However, although the Court has also held that the accused has the right to dispense with counsel and to represent himself, the Court has never wavered from its decision in *Gideon v. Wainwright*, that an accused is guaranteed under the Sixth Amendment to the U.S. Constitution of the right to counsel at every stage of a criminal proceeding.

However, the court's ruling has its exceptions. In 1983, a defendant who had been convicted of a felony after a trial argued on his appeal to the Supreme Court that his counsel was "ineffective." The court rejected his appeal, over the vigourous dissent of Justice Marshall. He said " every defendant is [constitutionally] entitled to a trial in which his interests are vigorously and conscientiously advocated by an able lawyer."

Justice Marshall, like Justice Holmes, has become known as the "great dissenter." His most powerful voice was in dissent, as a political prophet.

In Camera Hearings

An *in camera* hearing is defined as a hearing in the judge's office, outside the hearing of the jury that will decide the case. The U.S. Supreme Court, however, does not favor *in camera* hearings but favors complete instruction of the jury by the court as to the legality or the sufficiency of the evidence in question. *In camera* hearings are sometimes held in cases involving trade secrets, where disclosure in a public courtroom might jeopardize one of the litigant's competitive advantage.

NOTE

[1]Crimes include felonies and misdemeanors. They do not include violations, e.g., a parking ticket is a violation, not a crime.

21

SALES

A sale is a contract by which one party (the seller) transfers property for a valuable consideration to another (the buyer). Since a sale is a contract, the general rules of the law of contracts apply to sale transactions except where modified by the Uniform Commercial Code, which has been adopted in every state except Louisiana.

In an *executed sale* (a complete sale, one in which nothing remains to be done by either party to complete the transfer of title to the property) or an *executory sale* (an incomplete sale, one in which something remains to be done by either party to complete the transfer of title), there must be (1) parties capable of entering into the contract of sale; (2) consideration; (3) valid subject matter (existing goods or goods likely to exist); and (4) mutual assent (with intent to pass title).

Contracts to sell goods valued at more than a specified amount must be in writing. This is a part of the *Statute of Frauds*. The written contract may be a formal agreement or just a written memorandum embodying the terms and signed by the party to be charged. When a written contract does not exist, the contract to sell may still be enforceable if the buyer accepts part of the goods or pays a deposit on the purchase price.

In addition to the law of contracts, the Uniform Commercial Code plays an important part in everyday commercial transactions. Questions of interpretation of sales transactions are among those covered by these laws: Who owns goods while they are in shipment? If the goods are destroyed in shipment, who stands the loss? If a person in New

York makes a contract to buy goods in California, when does the title pass? When does the buyer become the owner? What responsibility does the seller take when he sells goods? What does he warrant, if he says nothing about the warranty? What are the remedies of an unpaid seller? May he stop goods in transit? May he take back the goods? When may he rescind the contract? What are the remedies of the buyer, if the goods are not as represented or are not delivered?

The Uniform Commercial Code covers not only the law of sales but also negotiable instruments and nearly all other phases of commercial transactions. Louisiana, because of its French heritage, follows the civil law in sales contracts. Because the Uniform Commercial Code is in effect in all other states and the District of Columbia, the information in this chapter (unless otherwise noted) is based on that law and is applicable only to the sale of personal property.

TRANSFER OF TITLE TO GOODS

A *bill of sale* is a written instrument evidencing the transfer of title to property. A *document of title to goods* (chattels and property other than intangibles or money) is any bill of lading, dock warrant, warehouse receipt or order for the delivery (voluntary transfer of possession from one person to another) of goods. There are two kinds of goods: *Specific goods* are those identified and agreed on at the time of sale or when the contract to sell is made. Any specimen or part of *fungible goods* may be used as the equivalent of another specimen or part in the satisfaction of an obligation; for example, a storage bin of oats may be referred to as fungible goods, because every bushel of oats is the same as every other bushel of oats in the same bin.

WHEN TITLE PASSES

Under the Uniform Sales Act, which was the predecessor to that portion of the Uniform Commercial Code dealing with sales, title to specific goods passed to the buyer at such time as the parties intended. Under the Uniform Commercial Code, passage of title does not depend entirely upon the intention of the parties; in the code, title to goods cannot pass before the goods are identified as being part of the contract.

Goods may be identified to a contract at any time and in any manner explicitly agreed to by the parties. In the absence of an explicit agreement, identification occurs: (a) when the contract is made if it is for the sale of goods already existing and described, or (b) if the contract is for the sale of future goods, then when the goods are shipped, marked, or otherwise designated by the seller as goods to which the contract refers.

Fox visits the Proctor Lumber Company, selects the quality of lumber he wishes to buy, and places an order for it. As the goods are already existing and described at the time the contract is made, title passes to Fox at that time.

The Simplified Vacuum Company agrees to sell 100 vacuum cleaners to the Bradley Distributing Co., and agrees to hold the cleaners in its warehouse for 60 days. As soon as Simplified ships the cleaners or otherwise designates the specific cleaners as the ones covered by the contract, title to the cleaners passes to Bradley.

The parties are free to agree when title transfers to existing goods. In the absence of an explicit agreement, title passes at the time and place at which the seller completes physical delivery of the goods. Of course, the acts of the seller which complete physical delivery will vary according to the contract involved in the transaction. Where the contract requires the seller to ship goods but does not require him to deliver them at a destination, title passes to the buyer at the time and place of shipment. On the other hand, if the contract requires delivery at a destination, title passes on tender of the goods there.

The Smith Importing Company purchases 100 tons of hemp from the Peru Exporting Company with the understanding that the exporting company would ship the hemp by boat. Since the contract did not require the exporting company to deliver the goods at a particular destination, title passes to the Smith Importing Company on shipment.

The Bargain Department Store ordered ten gross of toy trucks to be shipped for the Christmas trade, instructing the manufacturer to have the trucks delivered to its store in Albany, New York. Title to the trucks passes to the department store when the manufacturer tenders delivery of them in Albany.

Risk of Loss

Under the former Uniform Sales Act, the problem of determining whether the buyer or seller was required to bear the loss of goods that were lost or destroyed in transit was usually solved by determining which party had title to the goods. The Uniform Commercial Code has updated the former rules by taking into consideration the actual practices of modern merchants and their more sophisticated contracts.

The five main rules are:

1) Where the contract requires or authorizes the seller to ship goods by carrier, but does not provide for delivery of the goods at a particular destination, the risk of loss passes to the buyer on the delivery of the goods to the carrier.

(The Dexter Card Company contracted to buy 1,000 rolls of paper from the English Paper Company to be used in several of Dexter's plants. The contract required English to ship the paper by carrier but was silent as to the particular destination. A truck load of paper was destroyed by fire en route to one of Dexter's plants. Dexter would have to bear the loss because the goods had been delivered to the carrier.)

2) Where the contract requires the seller to deliver the goods at a particular destination, the risk of loss passes to the buyer when the goods reach that destination.

(Mr. Wilson purchased a boat from the Hydro Boat Co. with the understanding that Hydro would have to ship the boat to his cottage at Silver Lake, New York. The boat was destroyed in an accident en route. Hydro would bear the loss because the boat had not yet reached its destination.)

3) When goods are held by a bailee to be delivered without being moved, the risk of loss passes to the buyer upon his receipt of a negotiable instrument of title or upon an acknowledgment on the part of the bailee of the buyer's right to possession.

(Samuels owned 1,000 boxes of bookends that were stored in the Ajax Warehouse. Edwards entered into an agreement with Samuels to purchase the bookends, but Edwards wanted them to remain stored. Samuels, who had a warehouse receipt, endorsed it and gave it to Edwards. A few days later the warehouse was destroyed by fire. The risk of loss would be on Edwards because he had received a negotiable instrument of title, the warehouse receipt.)

4) When the seller is a merchant (defined in the statute as a person who in his business normally deals with the type of goods sold) and is in possession of the goods, and the contract does not require or authorize shipment by a carrier, the risk of loss passes to the buyer when the buyer takes physical possession of the goods.

(Kearse owns an appliance store specializing in household items, such as stoves, refrigerators, and freezers. Bullock decides to buy a stove and negotiates a deal. It is agreed that Bullock will return in three days to pick up the stove and take it home. Later that day there is an explosion in the store that destroys the stove. Bullock will not have to bear the loss because Kearse is a merchant who still had possession of the stove at the time of the loss.)

5) When the seller is not a merchant (as described above) and is in possession of the goods, and the contract does not require or authorize shipment by a carrier, the risk of loss passes to the buyer when the seller tenders delivery of the goods to the buyer.

(Everett, a policeman, agrees to sell his used refrigerator to his neighbor Bertram. They agree that Bertram, as part of the deal, must move the refrigerator, which is located in Everett's garage. Everett offers to let Bertram have the refrigerator at the time of the deal, but Bertram wanted to wait a few days. Before Bertram got around to hauling the refrigerator home, it was destroyed by fire. The buyer would have to bear the risk of loss because the seller was not a merchant and had tendered delivery of the goods.)

Ineffectual Transfer

When goods are sold by a person not the owner, the buyer ordinarily acquires no better title to the goods than the seller had. Title, like a stream, cannot rise higher than its source.

Professional auto thieves steal an automobile from Preston, install a new motor and substitute the model numbers, and sell the automobile to Miller. Ownership of the automobile remains with Preston, and Miller does not get good title to it.

The question often arises: How does a bona fide purchaser who has no notice of any defect in title acquire ownership of the property? The answer is: When he can prove the owner led him to believe that he was getting good title. The mere fact that the owner turns possession of goods over to a third person does not mean that he has clothed that third person with authority to sell.

For instance, when goods are stored with a warehouseman and the warehouseman wrongfully sells them to a bona fide purchaser, the bona fide purchaser does not acquire good title.

On the other hand, when the owner clothes an agent or other third person with the apparent right to sell, the owner is precluded from asserting his claim against a bona fide purchaser.

Hamilton, residing in California, employed Carmichael as his agent to enter into a contract for and superintend the building of an expensive power boat in New York City and furnished him with funds for that purpose. Hamilton advised Carmichael that he wanted the ownership of the boat kept a secret and suggested to Carmichael that if anyone asked him who was the real owner of the boat that he, Carmichael, could say that he was. Hamilton said to Carmichael, "In any event, don't let people know that I am the owner of this boat." Carmichael got into a squabble with Hamilton and claimed Hamilton owed him money. Hamilton denied this. Carmichael sold the boat to Forrest, representing himself as the true owner. Under such circumstances, even though Carmichael had no real title to transfer, Forrest as a bona fide purchaser became the owner because Hamilton had clothed Carmichael with apparent title to the boat.

WARRANTIES

A *warranty* grows out of a contract of sale; there can be no warranty without a sale. A warranty is a statement or representation made by the seller (of personal property), promising that certain facts are or shall be as he represents them. There are two kinds of warranties, *express* and *implied*.

A warranty should not be confused with other independent agreements between sellers and buyers, such as a seller's agreement to do certain things with respect to the goods sold. If the statements or representations which make up the warranty are false and the buyer is harmed by reason of such falsity, the seller is said to be guilty of a breach of warranty, or breach of contract. The buyer then may sue the seller for his damages. There is a distinction between claims for breach of warranty and claims arising out of misrepresentation, deceit, and fraud. The seller may be innocently liable for a breach of warranty. The goods may not measure up to what he thought they were. However, in the case of misrepresentation or fraud or deceit, there is an element of wrongdoing that does not necessarily exist in the case of a breach of warranty.

Warranty of Title

The Uniform Commercial Code provides that there is in every contract for the sale of goods a warranty by the seller that the title conveyed shall be good, and its transfer rightful, and that the goods shall be free from liens or encumbrances held by other people.

The following examples illustrate warranties of title:

Penny buys an automobile from Crocker, who had purchased the car in good faith from a dealer and did not know that the registration transfer had been forged and that the car was a stolen vehicle. The rightful owner of the car proves it was stolen from him and takes possession from Penny. Penny then sues and recovers judgment against Crocker because, even though Crocker had acted in good faith, he had warranted to Penny that he was the owner and had a right to sell when, in fact, he did not have such right.

Sanborn buys "distress" merchandise consisting of new stoves, refrigerators, and washing machines from a merchant "going out of business." He resells the refrigerators to the McClure Furniture Company. It develops that the original owner had given a chattel Mortgage on the refrigerators to the Faithful Trust Company to secure a bank loan. The Faithful Trust Company repossesses the refrigerators from McClure Furniture Company. Sanborn, having warranted that the refrigerators were free from any lien or encumbrance, becomes liable to the McClure Furniture Company for the value of the refrigerators.

Express Warranty

An express warranty is a statement of fact or a promise by the seller phrased to induce the buyer to purchase the goods. Examples of express warranties follow:

A claim that a radio could pick up any station in Europe

A statement that seed peas would "pick four or five days earlier than other seed on the market"

A claim that a derrick would require a load of 250 tons to break it

A statement that a horse was not lame

The law also says that a seller expressly warrants that the bulk of goods shall correspond to any description of the goods given by the seller or to the quality of any sample or model that was used in arriving at the contract. For example:

The Henry Printing Company submitted a sample of printing and by accident used alkali-proof ink, which the purchaser, the Stone Manufacturing Co., required. The alkali-proof ink was used in the first order but not in the second and third orders. The Henry Printing Company was bound by the sample submitted and was liable to the Stone Manufacturing Co., for its failure to print the remaining orders in the same ink.

Mere "puffing," or dealer's talk, may be just opinion and does not constitute an express warranty. Such puffing includes:

Claims that an article was "unsurpassed and unsurpassable"

A claim that a suit of clothes "will wear like iron"

A statement that certain books "were very fine reading literature, fit for anybody to read"

A statement that certain roses came from "very fine stock"

A claim that a horse was "well-broken and will fill the bill"

The old rule of *caveat emptor* ("let the buyer beware") has been largely replaced, first, by the Uniform Commercial Code, and second, by the tendency of the courts to enlarge the responsibilities of the seller.

Implied Warranty

In the average case, warranty does not have to be spelled out because, even though silent on the subject of warranties, a seller is deemed to have made a statement or promise amounting to an implied warranty. According to the Uniform Commercial Code, there are two kinds of implied warranties: of merchantability and of fitness for particular purpose.

Implied Warranty of Merchantability

Where the seller is a merchant (a person who normally deals with the type of goods sold), there is implied a warranty that the goods shall be merchantable. In order to be merchantable, such goods must meet the following tests:

1) pass without "objection in the trade" under the contract description;
2) be of fair average quality within the description in the case of fungible goods;
3) be fit for the ordinary purposes for which such goods are purchased;
4) run of even kind, quality, and quantity when goods are purchased in units;
5) be adequately contained, packaged, and labeled as the agreement may require; and
6) conform to any promises which may be on the container or label.

The sale of food or drink to be consumed either on the premises or elsewhere gives rise to an implied warranty of merchantability.

Alexander buys a can of crab meat from the Singer Delicatessen Company. He brings the can home and makes a crab meat salad, which makes him sick. An analysis discloses that the crab meat was contaminated and unfit for human consumption. Alexander presents to the Singer Delicatessen Company his hospital and doctor bills and claims for lost wages because of his illness. The delicatessen company says, "Sorry, we bought it from one of the country's leading distributors, and we shouldn't be liable." Alexander sues. The court holds that the Singer Delicatessen Company was responsible under its implied warranty that the food was fit for human consumption and must pay Alexander. The delicatessen company has a remedy: It can file a claim against the distributor that sold it the canned goods. In such case, the distributor could in turn bring a cross-suit against the manufacturer.

Miss Howard was made sick when she ate dessert served to her by the Excelsior Restaurant. The restaurant claimed that it had taken all necessary precautions and disclaimed negligence. Miss Howard, however, was able to prove that there was ground glass in the food and that it made her ill. The court held that negligence is not the test in implied warranty cases and that when foreign objects get in the food, the food is not fit for human consumption. The court ruled in Miss Howard's favor.

Of course, in these examples, both Alexander and Miss Howard would in all likelihood name the manufacturers, the distributors and the stores as defendants in their lawsuits. (However, in some cases, a defense could be raised if what was sold was in a sealed package. In a number of states, the defense of a "sealed package" has been successfully used by an innocent middleman, usually the distributor.)

Implied Warranty of Fitness for Particular Purpose

Where the seller of goods at the time of making the contract has reason to know any particular purpose for which the goods are required and also has reason to know that the buyer is relying on the seller's skill to select or furnish suitable goods, there arises an implied warranty that the goods shall be fit for such purpose.

Madigan is in the process of refinishing an antique maple table. He goes to the Acme Paint Store and explains to the owner that he needs a sealer, but doesn't know what kind to buy. The owner picks out a can of sealer and sells it to Madigan. If the sealer doesn't work, there would be a breach of an implied warranty of fitness for a particular purpose because the seller knew the particular purpose for which the sealer was to be used and also knew that Madigan was relying on his skill to select the proper sealer.

In order to disclaim or negate either express or implied warranties, the seller must make clear to the buyer, either through language or through a course of dealing or through usage in the trade, that there are no warranties or that the warranty is limited.

The courts of most states have construed the Uniform Commercial Code by applying the following test: Are the warranty disclaimers unconscionable or reasonable? Practically every sale involves some type of warranty.

A statement relating to the value of goods or a statement purporting to be only the seller's opinion or recommendation of the goods does not create an express warranty. For example:

"Chevrolet cars are better" creates no warranty. However, a number of courts have held that statements such as "This tractor is in A-1 condition" does create an express warranty.

One of the most common ways of disclaiming implied warranties is to say that an automobile is being sold "as is." However, the seller's description of an "automobile" creates an express warranty, and the disclaimer does not negate the basic obligation of delivering an automobile.

In 1975 Congress passed the Federal Consumer Product Warranties Law, known as the "Magnuson-Moss Law." Under this act, if a consumer products manufacturer or marketer issues any written warranties, they must comply with several requirements. If there is a full written warranty, then implied warranties cannot be disclaimed. If the written warranty is described as a limited warranty, then implied warranties cannot be modified, but they may be limited to the duration of the written warranty. Congress, in passing the Magnuson-Moss Law, sought to protect consumers from an unscrupulous manufacturer's "fine print."

REMEDIES IN SALES CONTRACTS

The buyer and the seller are parties to a contract and hence have certain contractual obligations toward each other. If either the buyer or the seller fails to live up to the contract of sale, the other party has the ordinary legal remedies which every party to a contract has and, in addition, has certain special remedies which are tailored especially to sales.

Remedies of the Seller

The seller may protect himself in a number of ways. He may (1) part with title and retain possession of goods until paid; (2) part with possession and retain title; or (3) he may part with both title and possession before payment.

In any event, once a seller has elected to pursue one remedy, he may not thereafter resort to another inconsistent remedy. For example, it would be inconsistent for a seller to bring an action for a recision of the contract of sale and at the same time act as if there had been no recision and bring an action for the full purchase price.

Seller's Lien

Unless there is a specific contract to extend credit to the buyer, the seller who retains possession of goods has a lien for the purchase price. This simply means that the seller can hold onto the goods until the purchase price is paid.

Stoppage in Transit

If the buyer becomes insolvent and the seller has turned the goods over to a *common carrier* for transportation to the buyer, the seller may stop the goods in transit. As long as the goods are in transit he may retake possession and may retain them until the purchase price is paid.

Resale

If without just cause the original buyer refuses to receive and pay for the goods, the seller who is in possession of the goods may, as one of his remedies, resell them. When the seller resells on the default of the buyer, he is also entitled to recover his damages for breach of contract, that is, the difference between the contract price and the price realized at the resale.

Action for the Purchase Price

When goods have been delivered to the buyer and title has passed to him, the remedy of the unpaid seller is generally limited to bringing an action for the price or value of the goods.

Action for Damages

The seller generally has a right of action for damages when the buyer has failed to live up to his obligation under the contract. In order to be entitled to maintain an action for damages for the buyer's breach of contract, the seller must show his performance of the contract or his offer or readiness to perform. Unless it can be shown that the buyer notified the seller in advance that he would not take the goods or similarly indicated that he was going to breach the contract, the seller either must have delivered the goods or tendered an offer of delivery in order to recover damages. The purpose of the law in awarding damages to a seller for the buyer's breach of contract is to put the seller in the same position as he would have been in had the buyer performed his contract.

Broadly speaking, the measure of damage is the loss that the seller sustains by reason of the breach when the buyer refuses to accept and pay for goods which are offered to him. Generally, the seller's legal damages, when there is an available market for the goods, is the difference between the contract price and the current market price at the time when the goods were to be delivered and paid for. Obviously, under such circumstances, the seller is not entitled to recover the full contract price. For example:

The ABC Company agrees to buy wool and yarn from the Triple Z Yarn Company at a price of thirty cents a pound and then refuses to accept the goods. The Triple Z Yarn Company, in suing for damages for the ABC Company's breach of contract, may, if the market price has dropped to twenty-five cents a pound, recover the difference between the contract price of thirty cents and the market price of twenty-five cents, namely, five cents a pound.

Rescission

When the goods have not been delivered to the buyer and the buyer has repudiated the sale, or has indicated or demonstrated his inability to perform his obligations under the sale, or has otherwise breached the contract of sale, the seller may totally rescind the contract of sale by giving notice to the buyer. In addition, when there is fraud on the part of the buyer, the seller has the option of rescinding and disaffirming the contract of sale and recovering the property or affirming the contract of sale and suing for the price or for damages.

Remedies of the Buyer

In the breach of an ordinary contract, the buyer, as well as the seller, is given special remedies (in addition to those afforded by law). Under certain circumstances, the buyer may keep the goods and sue for damages arising out of the seller's breach of the contract; under other circumstances he may rescind the contract; and in other cases he may recover the purchase price.

Suit for Damages

When the seller neglects or refuses to deliver goods, the buyer may maintain an action against the seller for damages. Damages usually amount to approximately the loss naturally resulting from the seller's breach of contract. When there is an available market for the goods in question, damages are ordinarily the difference between the contract price and the market or current price of the goods at the time when the goods should have been delivered.

The April Department Store entered into a contract with the Georgia Mills to purchase 5,000 yards of cotton goods at forty cents a yard, to be delivered at the department store on June 1. Because the Georgia Mills defaults in the delivery of the cotton, the April Department Store is forced to buy the cotton goods in the open market at eighty cents a yard. The April Department Store may sue the Georgia Mills for breach of contract and recover the difference between the contract price of forty cents a yard and the market price of eighty cents a yard, or $2,000 damages.

Under the Uniform Commercial Code, a buyer is afforded the option to fix the market value by purchasing substitute goods. His monetary damages will then be measured as the difference between the contract price and the cost of these substitute goods. This is known as "covering."

Specific Performance

The Uniform Commercial Code provides that when the seller breaks his contract by refusing to deliver the goods specified, a court of equity may, if it thinks fit, direct specific performance of the contract; that is, the court may require the seller to deliver the goods.

Under the previous Uniform Sales Act, this remedy was rarely granted; a court of equity only would require specific performance of a contract if the goods were so unique or unusual that the simple remedy for damages would be a gross injustice.

Manley, a collector of rare jewels, makes a contract with the R. Importing Company to purchase from them a collection of rare emerald stones for $600,000. The contract was formally signed, and Manley makes a payment of $50,000. R. Importing Company then discovers that it can sell the stones for $750,000 to another customer and declines to make the sale to Manley. Manley demonstrates to a court of equity that there is no other similar collection of emeralds available and that damages would not be adequate compensation. Thus, the court of equity requires the R. Importing Company to comply with its contract and deliver the jewels to Manley on his payment of the balance of the purchase price.

Rescission and Other Remedies

In the event of the seller's fraud or default, the buyer may elect to rescind the contract (refuse to accept the goods) and sue for damages. When title to the goods has passed to the buyer and the seller wrongfully neglects or refuses to deliver the goods, the buyer may maintain an action against the seller for wrongfully converting or withholding the goods and may even maintain an action for *replevin* (an action to recover possession of the goods).

Breach of Warranty

When the seller commits breach of warranty, the buyer may act in one of the following three ways:

1) He may accept or may keep the goods and maintain an action against the seller for damages for breach of warranty (or if the purchase price has not been paid, decline to pay it).
2) He may refuse to accept the goods if title therein has not passed and maintain an action against the seller for damages for breach of warranty.
3) He may rescind the contract of sale and may refuse to receive the goods or, if the goods have already been received, return them or offer to return them to the seller and sue to recover the price or any part of it that has been paid.

When the buyer elects to claim one of these remedies, he cannot thereafter change his mind and claim another remedy.

If the buyer knew of the breach of warranty when he accepted the goods, or if he failed to notify the seller of it within a reasonable time, he cannot rescind the sale. Furthermore, if he fails to return the goods to the seller in substantially as good condition as the property was in when transferred to the buyer, he cannot rescind the sale. On the other hand, if deterioration or injury to the goods is caused by the breach of warranty, deterioration or injury shall not prevent the buyer from returning or offering to return the goods to the seller and rescinding the sale.

When a buyer of carpeting knew at the time of purchase that carpet dyes were not color fast, he may not thereafter claim a breach of warranty and sue to recover the purchase price or rescind the contract.

In a similar case, when Easter hats were delivered in February and held for 36 days after delivery and thereafter were returned to the seller on the ground that the hats were defective, the court held that the retention of Easter hats for 36 days constituted a waiver of the right to rescind by reason of breach of warranty.

CONDITIONAL SALES CONTRACTS

A conditional sale is a contract for the sale of personal property; under this type of contract the goods are delivered to the buyer (he takes possession of them), but the title is retained by the seller until the payment of the purchase price. Installment sales of merchandise, whether it be clothing or household goods or automobiles, play an important part in our economy today. In an installment plan sale, the seller, by means of a conditional sales contract, receives only a small down payment, but he is protected until the entire balance of the purchase is paid. His property rights in the article sold are protected against others who have no actual personal knowledge of the transaction.

Under the Uniform Commercial Code, all agreements which create or provide for a security interest in personal property are called "security agreements." Where a seller retains a security interest to secure all or part of the purchase price of an article (such as in the case of a conditional sales contract or chattel mortgage), the code defines such interest as a "purchase-money security interest."

Filing the Conditional Sales Contract

Conditional sales contracts are used most frequently for the purchase of goods that may be classified as consumer goods. Under the Uniform Commercial Code, consumer goods are defined as those used or bought for use primarily for personal, family, or household purposes. Examples would be stoves, refrigerators, clothing, and automobiles. Except in the case of automobiles, purchase-money security interests in consumer goods do not have to be filed in order to be effective, except in the case of fixtures.

The Beauty Furniture Company sells a suite of living room furniture to Slitt on a conditional sales contract whereby Slitt pays $100 down and the balance in 40 installments of $100 a week. The Beauty Furniture Company does not file the contract. Six months thereafter, Slitt is in need of money and sells the furniture to Canyon, who moves it into his house. The Beauty Furniture Company goes to Canyon and says, "Sorry, this furniture is not paid for; it is ours." Canyon takes the matter to court, only to learn that the Beauty Furniture Company may repossess the furniture and sell it.

In those circumstances where filing is required, the failure to file the *security interest* will render it void when any purchaser or creditor acquires the property without notice of the seller's interest in the property.

Adam enters into a conditional sales contract with the Eddy Motor Company for the purchase of a used car. The motor company fails to file the contract or a security agreement (called a "UCC-1"). Later, Adam's creditors bear down and he gives the car to one of them in payment for his debt. When Adam defaults in his payments to the motor company, it will no longer have the ability to take back the car, because it failed to file the contract.

The place of filing will vary from state to state and will also depend upon the type of goods purchased and the nature of the parties, but generally it will be filed in the county clerk's office in the county where the individual buyer resides. It is important to note that the filing will be ineffective where improperly made and where a subsequent purchaser or creditor does not have knowledge of the existence of the security agreement.

DISTINCTION BETWEEN CHATTEL MORTGAGE AND CONDITIONAL SALES CONTRACT

In both conditional sales contracts and chattel mortgages, property is held as security for debt. In a conditional sales contract, the debtor is the buyer of the property, but he does not become the owner of the property until the debt (purchase price) is paid. In a chattel mortgage, the property is owned by the debtor, who gives the chattel mortgage.

Meaker buys a refrigerator from the Daily Ice Machine Company. He agrees to pay $35,000 for the refrigerator in 70 monthly installments of $500 each. The conditional sales contract provides that Meaker does not become the absolute owner of the refrigerator until the last payment is made.

Jennings borrows $5,000 from Colby. Colby asks for security for the debt. Jennings executes a chattel mortgage on his automobile, which will be discharged as soon as the debt is paid in full.

Repossession of Goods Conditionally Sold

When the buyer is in default in the payment of any sum due under the contract, the seller has the right to take possession of the goods, unless otherwise agreed in the security agreement. This may be done without resorting to the courts, if the seller can repossess his property without committing a breach of the peace. If it is provided in the security agreement, the seller may also require the buyer to assemble the property and make it available to him in a reasonably convenient place. The buyer has the right to redeem the goods at any time before disposition of them by the seller. This may be accomplished by paying in full all monetary obligations then due and performance in full of all other obligations then matured.

Resale or Retention by the Seller

If the seller repossesses the goods, he has one of two choices: He may resell the goods or keep them in satisfaction of the debt.

The Uniform Commercial Code provides that a seller may resell the goods at either a private or public sale at any time or place and on any terms, provided that it be done in a "commercially reasonable" manner. The buyer must be given notice of the time and place of the sale. Under the code, there is no set period during which the goods must be held by the seller before resale. Likewise, there is no set time within which the sale must be made, but it must be done within a commercially reasonable time.

As an alternative, the seller may keep the goods in satisfaction of the buyer's obligation if he proceeds as follows: (1) sends written notice to the buyer of his proposal to keep the goods; (2) sends notice to other persons who have a security interest in the goods (except where they are consumer goods); and (3) refrains from disposing of the goods for thirty days. If the seller does not receive an objection to his proposal within the thirty-day period, he may keep the goods. The buyer is then discharged of all obligations.

Proceeds of Resale

The proceeds of the resale shall be applied (1) to the payment of the reasonable expenses of retaking, holding, and disposing of the property, including restoring the property to its condition at the time of the original sale, and, where the security agreement permits, attorney's fees and other legal expenses permitted by law; (2) to reimbursing the seller for the balance due under the contract; and (3) to the satisfaction of any indebtedness secured by other security interests, provided such other parties submit a written notice before the proceeds are distributed. Any sum remaining shall be paid to the buyer. If the proceeds of the resale are not sufficient to defray the expenses of the sale, the expenses of retaking, keeping, and restoring, and the amount due on the purchase price, the seller may sue the buyer for the deficiency.

Liquidated Damages

Damages for breach by either party may be liquidated in the agreement, but only in an amount which is reasonable. The code provides that "unreasonably large" liquidated damages are void as a penalty.

22

PATENTS, COPYRIGHTS AND TRADEMARKS

Patents, copyrights, and trademarks seem to be related subjects but are actually separate and distinct entities. Although all three grant certain exclusive rights or privileges, it should be borne in mind that they are based on different principles of law. A *patent* rests on the principle of protecting original inventions. Originality is not necessary to a valid *trademark;* it is a question of distinctive identification of goods. A *copyright* possesses the same qualities of monopoly as a patent or trademark but differs from both of them in that it applies exclusively to works of art.

PATENTS

A *patent* is a contract between the federal government and an inventor whereby, in consideration of the disclosure of a new and useful device to the public, the inventor and, in certain instances, his heirs and assigns, is granted the exclusive right to manufacture, use, and sell the device for a fixed period (usually seventeen years).

Determining an Invention

Although admitting that the word *invention* is not susceptible to precise definition, the courts have said that an invention is a new, useful, and operative idea. A change merely in form or degree of a device or method ordinarily will not constitute an invention when it involves doing something substantially the same by a new means, nor will the substitution of one material for another constitute a patentable invention unless the substitution went beyond what was intended by the originators of the idea. An invention, however, may result from a substitution of materials when the substitution involves a new method of construction or operation or results in new functions of the art or machine.

A change in the location of parts of a machine without changing the functions performed is not an invention even though the new method brings about better results, but an invention does result when a problem is solved by reason of relocating parts, and new and useful results are obtained.

When old elements are combined in one or more inventions, the new combination must produce a new and useful result in order to be an invention.

Is a particular discovery an invention? Each case must be answered after considering its originality and the history of the product or the operation. Among the facts considered as good evidence of an invention are novelty, utility, commercial success, satisfaction of a long-felt want, others' unsuccessful efforts, attempted imitation of others' disclosed methods or apparatus, and the like.

Requirement for a Patent

In order to be *patentable* an idea must (1) relate to new arts, machines, manufactures, compositions of matter, plants or designs; (2) be useful and novel; and (3) result in an actual invention. By art is meant a process or method of producing a new and useful industrial result; by machine, an apparatus that will perform a function and produce a definite result; by manufacture, any article useful in trade and produced by hand, labor, or machinery; by composition of matter, chemical compounds or mixtures of ingredients and so on; by plant, a development of a new form of vegetable life; by design, only the appearance of an article, not its structure or utilitarian features.

Part of the second basic requirement of patentability is that an invention be new or novel. If the invention has been previously disclosed or is something identical with the art or instrument for which the patent is sought, the inventor is either not granted a patent or the patent which may have been erroneously granted is invalid. In addition, in order to be patentable, an invention must possess a basic utility or be useful. The courts have said that the term useful means that the art or machine must be capable of performing a beneficial function and not be just frivolous. Thus, a Rube Goldberg machine, which goes through a lot of motions without accomplishing anything in particular, would not be patentable.

Moreover, the mere existence of something new or something useful will not suffice. The third requirement is that an actual invention must result from the idea in order for the patent to be valid.

Types and Duration of Patents

The Constitution gives Congress the power to "promote the Progress of Science and the useful Arts, by securing for limited Times to Authors and Inventors the exclusive Right to their respective Writings and Discoveries." In keeping with this power, Congress has passed legislation which gives the commissioner of patents the right to grant to an inventor for a specified period the right to exclude others from making, using, or selling his invention.

Patents may be classified as patents for (1) an art or process, (2) a machine, (3) composition of matter, (4) an improvement on an existing patent, (5) a design, or (6) a plant.

A plant patent is granted to one who has invented or discovered and asexually reproduced any distinct and new variety of plant. (Asexually propagated plants are those that are reproduced by means other than from seeds, such as by the rooting of cuttings, by layering, budding, grafting, and so on.) Patents have been recently granted to certain genetically engineered plants.

Patents (except design patents) are granted for a term of seventeen years. Design patents may be granted for a term of fourteen years.

Admission to Practice before the Patent Office

Representation of an inventor before the Patent Office of the United States is permitted only to those registered to practice. Admission to practice before the patent office is by examination. Qualified persons are designated patent attorneys (if they are lawyers) or patent agents (if they are not lawyers).

Procedure for Obtaining a Patent

A valid patent can be secured only by the inventor himself or by his guardian or estate. If an inventor is dead, the administrator or executor of his estate may apply for the patent. If the inventor is insane, the application may be made by his guardian or committee.

An inventor should submit his invention to his attorney, who will have a drawing or model of the invention prepared to conform with the requirements of the United States Patent Office.

If an inventor is dead, the administrator or executor of his estate may apply for the patent. An inventor should have a drawing or model of the invention prepared to conform with the requirements of the United States Patent Office. If his attorney is satisfied that his idea may be patentable, he will make a preliminary patent search. Although an inventor may think that he is the pioneer in his discovery area, others may have filed patents or claims covering the same or substantially the same invention. A patent search must be made in Washington, D.C., because only the patent office there has a complete record of all American patents. The search will include a review of similar patents granted within the past seventeen years. The patent search may cost at least $600 and in some complex cases considerably more.

In applying for a patent, the inventor must file: (1) a petition requesting the commissioner of patents to grant letters patent; (2) a specification containing a description of the invention, the inventor's name, title of the invention, a brief summary of the invention, drawings, and also the respects in which the inventor claims that his invention is patentable; (3) an oath stating that the applicant believes that he is the first inventor; (4) a basic fee of $500 plus certain extras, depending on the classification and the period of time for which protection is sought. The specification for a plant patent should include a complete detailed description of the plant and the characteristics that distinguish it from related known varieties and its antecedents, expressed in botanical terms and in the general form followed in standard botanical textbooks or publications dealing with the varieties of the kind of plant involved. The application is turned over to an examiner, who searches for prior patents both in the United States and foreign countries and prior available literature to determine if the invention is new. As a result of his search, the claim then will be allowed or disallowed. If the examiner rejects some of the claims in the patent application, he must give the applicant the reasons why. If the inventor persists in his application, he may request that the patent office reexamine the application. If it is rejected a second time, he may appeal to the board of appeals in the patent office and, subsequently, to the courts.[1]

If there are two or more pending applications for the same invention, the patent office initiates a proceeding to determine who is the first inventor and, thus, entitled to the patent. This proceeding, known as an interference, occurs in only about 1 percent of patent applications.

Assignment and Licenses

A patent is a property right and may be assigned; that is, licenses to manufacture and sell patented articles with or without royalties may be granted to others by the inventor. In order to be valid against a future purchaser of the patent, the assignment must be recorded in the patent office within three months after the date of the assignment.

Effect of Registration (Letters Patent)

The issuance of a letters patent simply raises the presumption of validity; it does not mean that the patent is valid for all purposes. Anyone may attack the validity of a patent and have the question decided by a federal court.

Among the reasons for holding that a patent is invalid are (1) that there was prior use or knowledge of the alleged invention, that is, the patent was not novel, (2) that the subject matter of the patent was covered by a prior patent in this or a foreign country, or (3) that the patent was not issued to the inventor.

Infringement Suits

One who wrongfully manufactures or sells a patented article or makes any unauthorized use or sale of the invention is guilty of infringement. The owner of the infringed patent has two remedies: (1) he may apply to the court for an injunction to restrain the unlawful infringement of the patent or (2) he may bring an action for damages. The infringement suit may consist of either a claim for damages or an application for an injunction or both.

An infringement suit is generally a long, drawn-out affair, and the judge has the difficult task of weighing technical data regarding patents. It has been proposed that the determination of the validity of patents should not be entrusted to federal judges who have limited knowledge in highly technical scientific fields but that these suits should be referred to experts.

In 1982 the Court of Appeals for the Federal Circuit, was created; this specialized court in Washington decides almost all appeals involving patents and trademarks. It has brought some coherence to what had been conflicting legal standards in lower trial courts.

COPYRIGHTS

A copyright is the registration of the owner's exclusive right to print, to publish, and to sell literary, dramatic, musical, artistic, and similar works. The holder of the copyright is protected (by copyright) only in his form of expression; that is, his ideas, themes, emotions must be embodied in a form of expression (for example, a book, painting, composition, or letter) in order to be protected by a copyright.

Copyrightable Material

The copyright act classifies copyrightable material into thirteen groups: (1) books, (2) periodicals, (3) lectures, (4) dramatic and dramatico-musical compositions, (5) musical compositions, (6) maps, (7) works of art and models or designs for works of art, (8) reproductions of works of art, (9) drawings or plastic works of scientific or technical character, (10) photographs, (11) prints, pictorial illustrations, and commercial prints or labels, (12) motion picture photoplays, and (13) older motion pictures.

The following matters are excluded from copyright protection:

1) Words and short phrases such as names, titles, and slogans; familiar symbols or designs; mere variations of typographic ornamentation, lettering, or coloring; mere listing of ingredients or contents.

2) Works designed for recording information that do not in themselves convey information, such as time cards, graph paper, account books, diaries, and the like.

3) Works consisting entirely of information that is common property and containing no original authorship, such as standard calendars, height and weight charts, tape measures and rules, schedules of sporting events, and lists or tables taken from public documents or other common sources.

4) Sound recordings and the performances recorded on them.

5) Government publications. (Material contained in government publications may be gleaned, however, from copyrighted sources.)

6) Seditious, libelous, obscene, or fraudulent works

7) Ideas, plans, methods, systems, or devices as distinguished from the particular manner in which they are expressed or described in a writing.

For example, the federal courts recently held that the material in a telephone book was not subject to copyright protection.

Procedure in Securing a Statutory Copyright

The copyright law provides that the author may secure a copyright by *publication* of the work containing a *notice* of the copyright.

The notice, which is specifically prescribed by statute, shall be affixed to each copy published and offered for sale in the United States.

Form of the Notice

As a general rule, the copyright notice should consist of three elements:

1) The word "copyright," the abbreviation "copy.," or the symbol ©. Use of the symbol may result in securing copyright in countries which are members of the Universal Copyright Convention.

2) The name of the copyright owner

3) The year of publication. If the work has previously been registered as unpublished, the year of such registration should be given. These three elements should appear together on the copies in one of the following ways:

Copyright, John Doe, 1989
John Doe, 1989 ©
Copyright by John Doe, 1989
Copyright by HarperCollins Publishers, Inc., 1989

Optional Form of Notice

A special form of notice is permissible for works registrable in classes F through K, which include: maps, works of art, models or designs for works of art, reproductions of works of art, drawings or plastic works of a scientific or technical character, photographs, prints and pictorial illustrations, and prints or labels used for articles of merchandise. This may consist of the symbol accompanied by the initials, monogram, mark, or symbol of the copyright owner if the owner's name appears on an accessible portion of the work.

Position of the Notice

For a book or other publication printed in book form, the copyright notice should appear on the title page or page immediately following. The "page immediately following" is normally the reverse side of the page bearing the title; in books, the copyright notice appears much more frequently on this page than on the title page, so much so that this page is called the "copyright page."

In a periodical, the notice should appear on the title page, on the first page of text, or under the title heading.

In a musical work, the notice may appear either on the title page or on the first page of music.

On a painting or work of art, the notice should appear on a readily accessible part of the work of art.

Rights Granted by a Copyright

The statute gives the owner of a copyright certain exclusive rights as follows;

The right to print, copy, sell, or distribute. This restriction not only prevents someone from reprinting the copyrighted work, but also prevents the reproduction of the work by any other means of expression.

If a book or periodical is printed in English, it must be printed from type or plates made in the United States; if it is produced by another process, the process must be completely performed in the United States and the book or periodical must also be bound here.

The right to translate, transform, or revise the work by means of dramatization, translation, musical arrangement, or the like. The importance of preservation of the right to transform is illustrated frequently by the substantial amounts which are paid authors of stories or novels in return for the right to make motion pictures of stories.

The right to deliver, record, or perform. The right to deliver, record, or perform relates to lectures or sermons prepared primarily for delivery as well as dramatic works and musical compositions.

The right to transfer, mortgage, or bequeath. Copyrights may often be valuable. Thus, their owners may wish to sell them (transfer ownership), use them as collateral for a loan, or bequeath them by will.

Does an assignment or granting of permission to use a copyrighted work, such as a song, in a movie carry with it the right to use that song in a later videocassette format or in a subsequent TV creation? Federal courts have held both ways.

Fair Use

The courts have said that "fair use" may be made of every copyrighted production. Sometimes it is difficult to draw the line between fair and unlawful use of copyrighted works.

For example, teachers may copy portions of a textbook, copyrighted by another, for use in their own lectures. And, a book or dramatic review may actually quote portions of the copyrighted work.

But, if the teachers want to write their own textbooks and use in them the material they have copied from the first text, they must obtain the copyright holder's permission and also print notices of the source of the quoted material in their books.

Again, if another author wishes to quote a book or dramatic review in his book, he must obtain permission to do so from the newspaper or magazine which first printed the review, and he must cite the periodical and the reviewer (if the review is by-lined) as the source of the review.

One must obtain permission from the copyright holder to reproduce even one line of a poem in a book, but one may quote a small portion of a book in another work. This is fair use.

A person writing a biography of William Faulkner must obtain permission from the copyright holder to quote in his book a total of 9,500 words from Faulkner's works.

Another person writing a textbook on English composition may use an eight-line prose quotation from Faulkner, as an illustration of effective writing, without the copyright holder's permission; he must, however, cite the source of the quotation.

What is "fair use" is a continual source of interest and litigation in both the literary and legal worlds. In a 1992 case, a Federal District Judge said there are four factors to be considered in deciding fair use: the purpose and character of the use, including whether it is commercial; the nature of the work; the size of the portion used; and the effect of the use on the potential market.

The court ruled that the publication by a magazine of some 52 percent of the writer's 2,300-word otherwise unpublished letter to his students went beyond "fair use" and was copyright infringement.

Infringement of Copyrighted Works

Before a suit for infringement is brought in the courts, The holder of the copyright must deposit copies of the copyrighted work in the copyright office. In other words, the owner should "register" his or her mark before commencing legal action.

The requirement of the statute is that after the copyright has been secured by publication of the work containing a notice of the copyright, "there shall promptly be deposited in the copyright office or in the mail addressed to the registrar of copyrights, two complete copies of the best edition then published," accompanied by a claim of copyright and the fee. The courts have been liberal in interpretation of the word "promptly." In one case the U.S. Supreme Court held that the right of infringement was not lost even though the deposit in the copyright office was delayed for fourteen months.

In bringing an infringement suit, the owner of a copyright may seek an injunction to stop the reproduction of the infringing material against the person improperly using the copyrighted work, and he may also seek damages by reason of the infringement. In some cases, the court may require that the infringing material be delivered up for destruction. The statute also permits the successful party in an infringement suit, unlike most other legal proceedings, to recover a reasonable attorney's fee. The owner of the copyright may recover from the infringer the actual damages he has sustained plus the profits the infringer has made as a result of his wrongful use of the copyright. This is ordinarily done by an "accounting proceeding."

Sometimes it is not possible to prove the actual damages, or even if there were any. In that event, the statute sets up certain guidelines to assist the court in awarding penalties if the plaintiff elects to accept the statutory penalties in lieu of damages. These statutory penalites range from $500 to $20,000. However, an appeals court upheld a district court's judgment of $80,000 statutory damages for multiple infringments. These penalties (which are specified by statute) are popularly referred to as "in lieu" damages.

New Copyright Law

The copyright law, enacted in 1976, supersedes the copyright act of 1909. The provisions of the new copyright law became effective on January 1, 1978.

Here are the highlights of the new law:

- The old law protected the owner of a copyright for twenty-eight years from the date of first publication and may be renewed for a second period up to forty-seven years. For works created after January 1, 1978, the new law provides protection for the author's life plus an additional fifty years after the author's death.
- The law specifies the circumstances under which the marketing or distribution of single copies of works by libraries and archives for noncommercial purposes do not constitute a copyright infringement.
- The law creates a Copyright Royalty Tribunal whose purpose will be to determine whether copyright royalty rates in certain categories are fair.
- The law makes a number of changes in the system providing compulsory licensing for the recording of music. Among other things it raises the royalty rate per minute of playing time.

The law removes the previous general exemption of a public performance of nondramatic literature and musical works where the performance is not for profit. Under the law, noncommercial transmissions by public broadcasters of published musical and graphic works are subject to a compulsory license. When the copyright owners and the public broadcasters cannot reach an agreement, the subject will be submitted for determination by the Copyright Royalty Tribunal.

The law removes the previous exemption for performances of copyright in music by jukeboxes.

The law provides for the payment under a system of compulsory licensing of certain royalties for the early transmission of copyright works on cable television systems. (There are other provisions in the new law, but they are not discussed here in detail. For example, Congress recently enacted legislation regarding "syndication rights.")

The Copyright Office will prepare regulations in accordance with the new law and will revise its application forms, instructions, and other printed matter to conform to the new law.

Berne Copyright Convention

Traditionally, books and works of art that enjoyed copyright protection within the United States did not have the same protection in foreign countries. However, in 1988, the United States signed the Berne Copyright Convention. This gives protection to works of U.S. authors in those foreign countries which are signatories to the convention, and it also gives protection to the works of foreign origin within the United States.

Moral Rights Statutes

European countries traditionally have recognized that an author or an artist has certain rights in his or her work and can object to any distortion, mutilation, or other modification of the work. This protection has only been recognized very recently in the United States.

For example, moral rights have surfaced in the colorization controversy, as the charge that the adding of color to black and white motion pictures violates the creators' "right of respect"; that is, the right to have the motion pictures exhibited in the form in which they were originally released.

Today ten states have some form of protection (statutes) of moral rights: California, Connecticut, Louisiana, Maine, Massachusetts, New

Jersey, New Mexico, New York, Pennsylvania, and Rhode Island. In addition, Utah and Montana provide some statutory protection, but do not have comprehensive moral right statutes.

TRADEMARKS

A trademark is a distinctive mark or symbol or device that a manufacturer affixes to the goods he produces so that they may be identified in the market. It should not be confused with a *trade name*, which is a name used in the trade to designate as an entity the particular business of certain individuals or sometimes to designate a class of goods.

The registered trade name identifies both the goods and the persons selling or making them, whereas a registered trademark designates only the product.

For example, the product "Sunshine Cola Drink" could be the subject of a trademark, and the "Sunshine Soft Drink Company" could be a trade name.

Besides registration of marks and names of manufacture, service, certification, and collective marks may also be registered.

A *service mark* is a device used in the sale or advertising of services to distinguish the services of one from the services of others; service marks include without limitation the marks, names, symbols, titles, designations, slogans, character names, and distinctive features of radio or other advertising used in commerce. For example, a fire insurance agency might use as a service mark a fire engine rushing to the scene of a fire to indicate the type of service rendered by the agency.

A *certification mark* is a mark used in connection with the products or services of one or more persons other than the owner of the mark to certify regional or other origin, material, mode of manufacture, quality, accuracy, or other characteristics of such goods or services or to certify that the work or labor on the goods or services was performed by members of a union or other organization. For example, the I.L.G.W.U. label indicates that a garment was made by members of the International Ladies Garment Workers Union.

A *collective mark* is a trademark or service mark used by the members of a cooperative association or other collective group or organization. Marks used to indicate membership in a union, an association, or other organization may be registered as collective membership marks. For example, a group of textile manufacturers could join together under the name "Atlantic Ocean Textile Manufacturers Association," devise a trademark "Atlantic Ocean Products," and use the trademark on all products manufactured by members of the association.

Trademarks serve to indicate the manufacturer, producer, and origin of the product. They may also serve to insure uniformity of quality in the goods bearing the mark and, through advertising, to create and maintain a demand for the product. Registration of a trademark in the U.S. Patent Office does not in itself create or establish any exclusive right but rather indicates recognition by the federal government of the owner's right to use the mark in commerce to distinguish his goods from those of others.

Common-Law Rights in Trademarks

Although Congress and the various states have enacted laws authorizing the registration of trademarks, registration is not necessary for the legal protection of the marks.

Rights in a trademark are acquired only by use, and use must continue if the rights so acquired are to be preserved. Valid trademarks can be obtained by showing priority of adoption and use.

When the Federal Trademark Law was adopted in 1905, Congress said that nothing should change the rights or remedies which then existed, even if the trademark law had not been passed. Thus, Congress indicated that common-law rights in trademarks will prevail over registered trademarks provided the claimant of the trademark can show from business records that he was the first to adopt and use the trademark.

Registration under Federal Laws

Though trademark rights are acquired without registration, it is advisable to register a trademark and to register it under federal law. Registration under the federal law gives the owner the stamp of approval of the federal government and creates a presumption of ownership, which would have to be overcome in litigation by proof that someone else had previously used the mark. Also, registration in the U.S. Patent Office may make it easier to register the mark in foreign countries, and it would restrict certain imports which bear the registrant's mark. The registration of a mark gives the registered owner the right to sue in federal courts and to recover under the statutory provision for treble damages for unlawful use of the trademark. (When there are complicated problems in connection with the registration of the trademark, a patent attorney should be consulted.)

Marks Subject to Registration

For a trademark to be registered in the patent office, it must be a distinctive design, combination of letters, words, or figures, and must be shown to be first adopted and used by the applicant.

Marks Not Subject to Registration

A trademark cannot be registered if it (1) consists of or comprises immoral, deceptive, or scandalous matter or matter that may disparage or falsely suggest a connection with persons living or dead, institutions, beliefs, or national symbols or bring them into contempt or disrepute; (2) consists of or comprises the flag or coat of arms or other insignia of the United States or of any state or municipality or of any foreign nation or any simulation thereof; (3) consists of or comprises a name, portrait, or signature identifying a particular living individual except by his written consent or the name, signature, or portrait of a deceased president of the United States during the life of his widow, if any, except by the written consent of the widow; (4) consists of or comprises a mark that so resembles a mark registered in the Patent Office or a mark or trade name previously used in the United States by another and not abandoned as to be likely, when applied to the goods of the applicant, to cause confusion or mistake or to deceive purchasers.

Procedure for Registration of Trademarks

Under federal law the application for registration of trademarks must be filed in the name of the owner of the mark and must consist of (1) a written application on a form suggested by the U.S. Patent Office; (2) a drawing of the mark; and (3) five specimens or facsimiles and payment of the filing fee in the amount of $200.

The drawing of the trademark should be an exact representation of the mark as actually used in connection with goods or services. It must be made on pure white durable paper, the surface of which must be calendared and smooth. India ink alone must be used for pen drawings to secure perfectly solid black lines. The use of white pigment to cover lines is not acceptable. The sheet on which the drawing is made must be eight inches wide and eleven to thirteen inches long. The size of the mark must be such as to leave a margin of at least one inch on the sides and bottom of the paper and at least one inch between the mark and the heading. Across the top of the drawing, beginning one inch from the top edge and not exceeding one-quarter of the sheet, there should be a heading, listing on separate lines the applicant's name and post office address, the dates the mark was first used, and the goods or services recited in the application. All drawings must be made by a process that will give them satisfactory reproduction characteristics. Every line and letter, names included, must be blacked. This direction applies to all lines, however fine, and to shading. All lines must be clean, sharp, and solid, and they must not be too fine or crowded. If otherwise suitable, a photolithograph reproduction or printer's proof copy may be used.

If the Patent Office concludes that the mark is not entitled to registration, after examining the application, the applicant is advised of the reasons for rejection. The applicant has six months from the date of the Patent Office's notification to respond. If the applicant responds, the application may be reexamined and reconsidered. If after further examination and reconsideration the registration is still refused, an appeal may be made to the Trademark Trial and Appeal Board. If on examination it appears that an applicant is entitled to have his mark registered, the mark is published in the Patent Office's official gazette. The mark may then be opposed by any person who believes he would be damaged by registration of the mark. Opposition to the registration should be made within thirty days after publication. If conflict is found between two co-pending trademark applications, an interference will be instituted, in the same manner as in the case of a patent application, to decide which applicant is entitled to register.

Despite the fact that the statute governing trademarks seems straightforward, disputes still arise. For example:

Since the mid-1980s, the question whether a mere color—for example, beige—can be trademarked, and thus monopolized by a single company, has confounded companies.

In 1985, the U.S. Court of Appeals for the Federal Circuit, which hears only trademark and copyright cases, held that the color pink was subject to registration by Owens-Corning Fiberglass Corp. Since then, a few appellate judges have followed the lead of that decision; however, most have said mere color does not deserve trademark protection.

Trademark Registration under State Laws

Federal registration is restricted to marks of goods sold in interstate commerce. In instances where products are sold only within the boundaries of a particular state, it is advisable to register the mark with the state government.

Proof of Prior Use of Trademark

When a domestic corporation applies to the Patent and Trademark Office for the issuance of a trademark in the United States, the applicant must show that it has previously used the trademark commercially in the United States. When a foreign national applies for a federal trademark, the question of prior use is more complicated and requires a complete analysis and study of the facts.

Incontestability of Some Federal Trademarks

While state trademarks are said to be simpler to obtain than federal trademarks, there are some advantages to federal trademarks. For example, under federal law the right of a registrant to a trademark mark becomes incontestable after five years of continuous use subsequent to the original registration. The five-year use of the registered trademark is sufficient to establish such incontestability.

NOTE

[1]A more detailed outline of procedure may be found in the pamphlet, "General Information Concerning Patents," which may be obtained from the United States Government Printing Office, Washington, D.C., 20102.

23

CONSUMER PROTECTION

During the last several decades lawmakers have been actively concerned with the interests and rights of the consuming public. The consumer movement sought to put an end to the doctrine of *caveat emptor*. True, the law will enforce contracts. True, freedom of contracts is an American principle. But if the parties to the contract are in an unequal position, the weaker of the two parties must have the protection of the courts. Laws were passed to try to eliminate injustices and improve distribution methods and the quality of products.

Today, all states have passed laws to protect consumers. In addition, many large cities have established consumer affairs departments, which administer local laws affecting consumers' rights, because there are some laws which can be enforced only within the jurisdiction of the city, county or state. Provided that all agencies cooperate, the result is good and the consumer is the beneficiary.

FEDERAL LAWS

Early in the history of our country, the U.S. Supreme Court upheld the rule that in matters which were delegated by the U.S. Constitution to Congress, laws passed by Congress were supreme. This rule of federal supremacy applied to interstate commerce. In the 1870s Congress passed the first consumer protection law; it prohibited mail frauds. The Federal Trade Commission originally was not a consumer agency. Its duties were largely concerned with business practices.

In the 1960s Ralph Nader became a factor in persuading Congress to pass consumer laws. Nader is credited with being responsible for the passage of laws by Congress as follows: The National Safety Act, Wholesome Poultry Products Act, Wholesome Meat Act, Coal Mine Health and Safety Act, Radiation Control for Health and Safety Act, and the Comprehensive Occupational Safety and Health Act (often referred to as OSHA).

Many federal agencies are involved in the protection of the public and the consumer. Among them are (1) The Interstate Commerce Commission, which regulates the rates of interstate carriers such as railroads and buses; (2) the Department of Health, Education, and Welfare (HEW), which administers laws on the misbranding and adulteration of food products, devices, cosmetics, and hazardous household products; (3) the Federal Reserve Board, which regulates the flow of money and credit, examines banks to determine if they are financially sound, and is the authority on Truth in Lending; (4) the Commerce Department, which establishes flammable fabric standards; (5) the Civil Aeronautics Board, which licenses and regulates air carriers and handles consumer complaints of airlines; (6) the Department of Agriculture, which inspects poultry and meat products; (7) the Federal Trade Commission, which prohibits false advertising and other deceptive practices; (8) the Department of Housing and Urban Development (HUD), which regulates housing and house loans and approves building materials for houses; (9) the Securities and Exchange Commission, which administers laws to protect investors; (10) the Department of Transportation, which supervises the national transportation system; (11) the United States Postal Service, which attempts to prevent fraudulent use of the mails; and (12) the Office of Consumer Affairs in the President's office, which coordinates consumer protection activities.

There is no end to federal regulation of business and merchandising for the benefit of the public.

In 1975 Congress enacted the Magnuson-Moss Act (also called the Warranty Act), which established a major uniform minimum disclosure standard for written warranties and responsibility. The Federal Trade Commission was given broad power to define unfair and deceptive practices and received additional enforcement powers. The act authorized the Federal Trade Commission to promulgate rules for the disclosure of warranties by sellers.

The main effect of this provision is to inform the consumer about the"warranty." The law gives the Federal Trade Commission the right to require the seller to disclose product results; specify the duration of the warranty; and fully outline steps the warrantee may take if the product fails to meet the warranty criteria.

As stated previously, there are two kinds of warranties: *express warranties* and *implied warranties*. An express warranty specifies in writing what the product will do, what it will not do. An implied warranty accompanies all products and guarantees that the product is fit for the purpose for which it is intended. Federal law changed the old rule. Under the old rule, covering most state laws, the warrantor would say in effect, "We are not liable for any implied warranty." The new federal law says, "No, you cannot disclaim your liability under implied warranty." For example:

The ABC Company manufactures and sells fire extinguishers. The fire extinguisher contains no express warranty. Mr. Jones, a purchaser of a fire extinguisher, tried to put out a small kitchen fire with the fire extinguisher. He used the extinguisher and pushed a button in accordance with the directions on the outside of the fire extinguisher. But nothing happened except that the extinguisher seemed to fizzle. Mr. Jones sued the fire extinguisher company for breach of implied warranty. The implied warranty was that the fire extinguisher would put out fires. Mr. Jones was successful and recovered damages from the ABC Company for breach of an implied warranty.

The new law encourages informal mechanisms which take the place of legal proceedings in case of a dispute. The Federal Trade Commission is given the right to set out basic standards for such dispute mechanisms for the benefit of the consumer.

Formerly, the Federal Trade Commission didn't concern itself with unfair and deceptive trade practices unless they occurred in interstate commerce. The new law says the commission will concern itself with unfair practices wherever they occur. Congress acted under the supremacy clause of the Constitution to supersede some state laws, but many state laws continue; for example, the federal law does not affect state laws on the sale of consumer goods. Other recent federal laws include the Fair Credit Building Act, the Equal Credit Act, and a new amendment to the Truth in Lending Act (see p. 260), which creates a three-day cooling-off period during which any consumer has the right to rescind a sale where a security interest is taken other than a purchase mortgage on a home. The Consumer Product Safety Act created the Consumer Product Safety Commission.

Among other numerous federal laws to protect consumers are the Hazardous Substances Act and the Poison Prevention Packaging Act.

STATE LAWS

States have tried to prohibit all types of unfair sales practices. The machinery of state governments is often more educational than legal, teaching consumers how to be alert and protect their rights before they are "ripped off." For example:

Connecticut's Department of Consumer Protection issues and distributes to the public a pamphlet entitled "Help," which warns the public about high-pressure sales tactics, problems which arise from too hastily signed guarantees, credit contracts, purchasing of automobiles (new and used), apartment renting, and advising about assistance which the consumer may obtain from the state.

In Ohio, the consumer is encouraged to phone the Ohio Attorney General through a toll-free Public Action Line. A trained investigator talks with the consumer and encourages him to file a complaint if warranted. A complaint specialist will contact the business involved and attempt to negotiate some kind of settlement and perhaps initiate legal action.

The attorney general's office of North Dakota, as part of its educational program, puts out a booklet entitled "Consumer Survival Manual." The attorney general has adopted the slogan, "If something seems to be too good to be true, it probably is," and advises consumers to "look before you leap." The Consumer Survival Manual gives illustrations of "bait and switch" advertising; warns the public on home study courses that offer misleading inducements; warns about going to a person who will make repairs cheaper than anyone else; about weight-loss programs; about sewing-machine deals; about out-of-state (subdivided) land deals; about people who attempt to gain entrance to homes on suspicious pretexts; about vacuum cleaner gimmicks; about bankruptcy or fire sales; about buying a used car; etc.

"Unfair and Deceptive" Practices

The federal government has encouraged the enactment by the states of what are known as "mini-FTC acts." The following states have enacted laws that generally prohibit unfair and deceptive trade practices: Alabama, Alaska, Arizona, Arkansas, Colorado, Delaware, Florida, Georgia, Hawaii, Idaho, Illinois, Indiana, Kansas, Kentucky, Maine, Massachusetts, Michigan, Minnesota, Mississippi, Nebraska, Nevada, New Hampshire, New Mexico, North Carolina, Ohio, Oklahoma, Oregon, Pennsylvania, Rhode Island, South Carolina, South Dakota, Texas, Vermont, Virginia, Washington, West Virginia, and Wyoming.

The U.S. Postal Inspection Service gives the following examples of deceptive trade practices:

Chain-referral schemes. Consumers say, "Why shouldn't we get this $800 TV set free? It will hardly cost us anything because the commissions we earn as we get our friends to buy a set will cover the monthly payments." Getting an expensive appliance for almost nothing is the bait sometimes used in chain-referral selling. Each year thousands of families end up paying exorbitant prices for such appliances as a central vacuum system, color TV, intercom system, and burglar alarm unit system: they were lured into an unlimited market for this "wonderful new product" because "with all our friends we will have no trouble getting enough $50 commissions to reimburse us for our purchase." The victim may be lucky enough to earn even one or two commissions and the family is stuck with a product they couldn't afford to buy at half the price.

Fake contests. "You've won" is often the bait used in fake contests. A telephone solicitor excitedly announces that the Ludry family is the winner of a brand new sewing machine. "All you have to do is come to our office to select the cabinet you want." In order to receive the "free sewing machine," the contestant must buy a cabinet. The victim may end up paying more for the cabinet than the combined unit is worth.

Low-price trap. A ridiculously low offer, also known as the "low ball," is the bait used by those who do not intend to furnish the goods ordered through the mail.

Example: A coin dealer convicted of mail fraud in offering a 1913 V nickel for "only $10" in coin magazines. Hundreds of numismatists lured into thinking they could get a $50 coin for $10 were tricked before the promoter was stopped by the postal inspectors.

Home improvements. In one typical case the debt-ridden family was lured into signing a $6,100 second mortgage in exchange for $400 in cash and improvements which actually only cost the promoter $407. The monthly payments were $69.95 for five years. At the end of five years, the home owner paid off only $4,197, leaving $1,928 due on the sixty-first month. The promoter was brought to federal court by the postal inspectors.

Debt consolidation. Dishonest debt consolidators lead families to believe that their debt problems will be solved if they turn over all their payment books and debt records to them. "Just pay us blank dollars a week and forget your problems," they say. In these schemes, stopped by postal inspectors, the victim's trouble is just starting. For the first few weeks the checks are paying off the consolidator's basic fee instead of being paid to creditor merchants.

Automobile insurance fund. Poor-risk drivers, unable to purchase liability insurance from reputable companies, are likely targets of fraudulent insurance companies. Assets are dissipated before they are forced to pay claims. They use up reserves. Within two or three years the insurance company is declared bankrupt and hundreds of drivers will be unable to collect for claims, and thousands of other motorists will discover they are not receiving the liability insurance they thought they were buying,

Retirement homes. Those wishing to invest in a retirement homesite can be trapped by ads reading, "Buy a king-size Western estate, just $10 down and $10 a month." The price is so low a family thinks it cannot lose in buying land in the sunny Southwest or in Florida. But $10 a month is not cheap when the consumer buys desert land miles from the nearest habitation or Florida sites which are under water.

Missing heir schemes. Recently thousands of families named Kelly received legal-appearing documents offering to buy legal information which could aid them in establishing a claim to an estate left by a Mary Kelly. While the cost of this information was $10, thousands of persons thought it would be worth the gamble and thought there was a valid reason for the offer. Postal inspectors found that even with the odds of 1,000 to 5, it wasn't a good gamble. This is a typical missing heir scheme.

Door-to-Door Sales

The following thirty-six states have adopted laws regulating door-to-door or home solicitation sales: Alabama, Arizona, Arkansas, Colorado, Connecticut, Delaware, Florida, Hawaii, Illinois, Indiana, Kansas, Kentucky, Louisiana, Maine, Maryland, Minnesota, Mississippi, Missouri, Montana, Nebraska, Nevada, New Hampshire, New York, North Dakota, Ohio, Oklahoma, Oregon, Rhode Island, South

Carolina, South Dakota, Tennessee, Texas, Vermont, Virginia, West Virginia, and Wyoming.

Among the attempts at regulation by the states has been to provide that every home-to-home sale has written into it a "cooling-off-period," which allows the buyer three business days in which to think the matter over and decide whether or not he wants to go through with the purchase of the merchandise. (New Hampshire provides four days and Arizona two days for the cooling-off period.) The laws require the seller to return down payments and trade-ins and require the buyer to tender back goods without damage in the event the buyer changes his mind during the cooling-off period. The seller is obliged to give the buyer a form of notice of cancellation of the sale, so that the buyer does not have to scurry around to get a legal form of cancellation.

Certain transactions are excluded from these provisions by the state laws. Cash sales are not included; nor are sales pursuant to a preexisting account with a seller whose primary business is selling goods or services at fixed locations. Those engaged in the business of door-to-door sales claim that the solicitation acts are unconstitutional because they interfere with the freedom of contracts. The courts, however, have held that the acts are constitutional.

Packaging, Labeling, Unit Pricing

At least seven states (Arizona, California, Colorado, Maryland, Massachusetts, New York, and Rhode Island) have passed laws on packaging, labeling, and unit pricing. Most states look to the federal government for regulations governing packaging, labeling, and rules regarding unit pricing.

Unsolicited Merchandise

The following thirty-nine states have passed laws governing unsolicited merchandise sent to consumers: Alaska, Arizona, Arkansas, Colorado, Connecticut, Delaware, Florida, Georgia, Hawaii, Idaho, Illinois, Indiana, Kansas, Kentucky, Louisiana, Maine, Massachusetts, Michigan, Minnesota, Mississippi, Missouri, Montana, Nebraska, Nevada, New Hampshire, New Jersey, New York, North Carolina, Oklahoma, Pennsylvania, Rhode Island, South Carolina, South Dakota, Vermont, Virginia, Washington, West Virginia, Wisconsin, and

Wyoming. The gist of the laws is that if a consumer receives merchandise in the mail which he has not ordered, the consumer may regard the merchandise as a gift and ignore the billing for it.

Credit Codes

The following twenty states have passed laws seeking to protect debtors from overreaching creditors and abusing legal process to harass debtors: Colorado, Connecticut, Delaware, Idaho, Iowa, Kansas, Louisiana, Maine, Maryland, Massachusetts, Minnesota, Nevada, New Hampshire, New Mexico, North Carolina, Ohio, Oregon, South Carolina, West Virginia, and Wisconsin. The federal Truth in Lending Act, passed in 1968 (see p. 260), requires the disclosure of credit terms in almost every type of credit transaction. It prohibits extortionate credit transactions and limits the garnishee of wages. The National Conference of Commissioners on uniform state laws sponsored what is known as the Consumer Credit Code. This code not only provides for disclosure to consumers of finance and other charges on items purchased, but it also limits finance charges. Many states have adopted the Consumer Credit Code; other states have passed their own laws on the subject. For example, the Alabama law provides for licensing and investigating by the state; it sets up maximum credit charges for consumer loans for personal and family purposes, and it generally regulates consumer credit loans not exceeding $300.

False and Misleading Advertising

The following thirty-three states prohibit false and misleading advertising: Alaska, Arizona, Arkansas, California, Colorado, Delaware, Georgia, Hawaii, Idaho, Illinois, Indiana, Iowa, Kansas, Kentucky, Louisiana, Maryland, Michigan, Minnesota, Mississippi, Missouri, Nevada, New Jersey, New Mexico, North Carolina, North Dakota, Ohio, Oklahoma, South Dakota, Tennessee, Texas, Utah, West Virginia, and Wyoming. For example:

Objectionable advertising includes "bait and switch" advertising. In such advertisements the seller advertises a particular product at a very low price with the intention of getting the purchaser into the store. When the seller gets the customer into the store, he then sells him a much more expensive model of the same product. The seller does not sincerely want to sell the advertised product and deliberately avoids selling it. The seller's purpose is to get the customer into the store and then sell him something else instead. Those states which prohibit "bait and switch" advertisements say in effect, "No advertisement containing an offer to sell a product shall be published when the offer is not a bona fide advertisement to sell the product."

Referral Sales

Eighteen states prohibit what is known as referral sales and other similar types of promotional sales. They are Alabama, Alaska, Arizona, Connecticut, Illinois, Kentucky, Minnesota, Mississippi, Nebraska, New Hampshire, New Mexico, New York, North Carolina, Ohio, Pennsylvania, Tennessee, Washington, and West Virginia. A referral sale generally involves a promise by the seller to give the buyer a commission, rebate, or discount for the buyer's furnishing a list of prospective customers. In the case of a referral sale, the buyer may (1) elect to treat the contract as enforceable; (2) rescind and return all the past goods sold and recover either a partial or the full amount of the sale; or (3) return the goods or the benefit or the service without any further obligation to pay the contract.

Consumer Remedies

Nearly all the states have a Consumer Affairs Office. Most states have procedures for acting on consumer complaints and enforcing laws against unfair and deceptive practices. The following twenty-four states have given their attorney generals the right to take action in behalf of the consumer: Alaska, Arizona, Arkansas, Colorado, Delaware, Florida, Hawaii, Indiana, Iowa, Kentucky, Maryland, Massachusetts, Michigan, Minnesota, Mississippi, New Hampshire, New Jersey, New Mexico, New York, Ohio, Oklahoma, Texas, Virginia, and Wyoming. Some states, instead of turning consumer matters over to the state attorney general, have consumer fraud bureaus and consumer protection divisions. When the consumer office receives a complaint, most of the offices try to settle the matter rather than take legal action. Conciliation, rather than legal action, is the rule.

If the state office cannot settle the matter by negotiation, then there are plenty of remedies for consumers to take. The state office, whether it be the attorney general's office or the consumer fraud bureau, or some other office, may represent the consumer or the consumer may bring a "class action." A "class action" in most states requires a group of persons with a common interest in the matter in controversy. Sometimes there is an overlapping between the federal laws and the state laws, but most consumers and consumer agencies feel that in such cases the matter should be taken care of by state laws because the state is closer than a Washington bureau to the scene of action.

SAFETY OF CONSUMER PRODUCTS

Congress created the National Commission on Product Safety. The commission is authorized to investigate hazardous products and the risk of injury to consumers. A Consumer Product Safety Commission was also created with broad powers to regulate safety of consumer products. The commission was authorized to study the hazards and safety of consumer products and to recommend any needed changes. Under certain circumstances the commission may ban the public sale of products that may cause injury to consumers.

CONSUMER CONTRACTS

Most states apply more liberal rules to consumer contracts.

For example, New York, in 1988, adopted a law governing contracts for house remodeling and improving and for custom built homes, which proves in part that:

- The contract must be written, legible, and in plain English, if the cost of the job, including labor, material, and service to be furnished by the contractor amounts to more than $500.

- The contract must also contain a specific description of the work to be done (not just "repair upstairs"), with materials and services to be furnished, including make, model, and other identifying information. It must also include a specific hourly labor rate and specific prices for materials provided.

- A date when the work will be begun and when it will be substantially completed and a statement of any factors that could delay these dates will be stated. (If time is not a concern to the homeowner, it must be written into the contract as well.)

• The cancellation policy must be spelled out. *Consumers have three days after signing to cancel.*

Consumers must get a copy of the signed contract before the work begins. They must also get copies of any amendments or other documents connected with the contract.

24

BRANCHES OF THE LAW

ADMINISTRATIVE LAW

Administrative law is that branch of law relating to the powers and procedures of government branches and agencies other than courts or the legislature. It is largely procedural and does not involve substantive law of the particular government branch or agency. The problems of administrative law include: (1) the extent to which the legislature has delegated or may delegate power to the government agency; (2) the exercise by the agency of that power; (3) the power of a court to review the action of the agency.

Congress recently passed what has come to be known as the "Bumpers Amendment," named after Senator Dale Bumpers of Arkansas, to the effect that interpretations of law by administrative agencies are subject to independent judicial review and that a federal court may hold unlawful a finding not based on substantial evidence.

Most states also have a law known as an Administrative Procedure Act. Many states define an administrative agency as being a state board, bureau, commission, department or officer authorized to hear contested cases involving individual citizens or corporations.

It is a basic principle of administrative law that the government agency must provide for the adoption and publication of rules and make them available to the public for inspection. An important requirement in all states is the giving of reasonable notice of the taking of action by the agency and the holding of hearings after notice to all parties affected by such hearings.

John Jones is involved in an automobile accident. The state motor vehicle bureau decides that Jones was to blame for the accident and that his license should be suspended. Therefore, the agency suspends Jones' license.

The motor vehicle bureau, however, violates a fundamental rule of administrative law in that it took adverse action against Jones without holding a hearing regarding the accident in question, giving Jones an opportunity to be heard, or notifying Jones of the proposed action of the motor vehicle bureau.

The American government, state and federal, is divided into three branches: executive, legislative, and judicial. So complex and multifaceted is the government's operation that it cannot possibly perform all its functions without the help of what have become known as administrative agencies. These agencies have been called the "fourth branch" of United States government.

Records have to be kept of hearings and actions taken by the agency. The granting or denial of licenses must be preceded by hearings. Most states permit a judicial review by a court or courts of contested cases and detail the procedure to be followed.

The Federal Administrative Procedure Law, like many state laws, first defines the term agency and many other words and phrases involved in the administrative law. The federal law, like the state laws, prescribes procedures for rule making, the procedure for issuing subpoenas, and the imposition of sanctions and applications for extension, revocation, and tenure of licenses, the review and recision of administrative orders and the like, and how such review by courts may be obtained.

Congress created the *Administrative Conference of the United States*. The conference consists of not less than 75 or more than 91 members made up of heads of branches of government and boards, commissions, or agencies. The purpose of the conference is to assist federal agencies, outline mutual problems, and exchange information. The purpose of the federal law is also to protect private rights and regulate activities in the public interest. This statute specifies the powers and duties of the conference and how it shall be organized.

Since 1950 one of the most important developments in the field of administrative law has been the passage by Congress of the *Freedom of Information Act*. The law provides for the disclosure to the public of material heretofore held privileged and confidential. A government agency is required to furnish the requested information within ten days, though extensions of this time limit may be granted in some instances. There is certain information that the government will not furnish under the Freedom of Information Act. Such information includes acts regarding (1) national security; (2) agency personnel practices; (3) trade secrets; (4) interagency memoranda; (5) law enforcement; (6) financial institution data; and (7) gas and oil wells.

Each agency submitted to for information must make available to the public a description of the central and field organization from which the public may obtain information and of the methods whereby the public may obtain this information, and the methods by which information is channeled to the public.

The Freedom of Information Act gives federal courts the right to issue injunctions requiring federal agencies to furnish the information requested by the public.

After the passage of the Freedom of Information Act, government agencies at first were reluctant to disclose information that they previously had considered confidential, but when they saw that the courts would uphold requests for information, most government agencies decided to cooperate.

The Privacy Act

In 1947 Congress enacted the Privacy Act, which restricts Congress from disclosing to the public personnel information that is contained in government files.

Most states have "sunshine laws," which require meetings of public agencies to be open to the public. In 1976 Congress passed a sunshine law that required most meetings of federal agencies to be open to public observation. It is very difficult for any government agency to close a meeting to the public. The theory of the sunshine acts is that they give the public a better understanding of how government operates and dispel public distrust of official bodies that act in secret.

ADMIRALTY LAW

Admiralty is that branch of law relating to commerce on the high seas and navigable waters, navigation, ships, and maritime contracts and torts (wrongs). The U.S. Constitution confers upon the federal courts basic admiralty jurisdiction; Congress provided that district courts shall have exclusive jurisdiction of any civil case of admiralty or maritime jurisdiction saving to all the suitors' remedies to which they are otherwise entitled. This provision, known as the "saving face," gives federal and state courts concurrent jurisdiction over admiralty and maritime matters.

As a practical matter, most admiralty cases are heard in federal courts. The rule has developed that concurrent jurisdiction applies only in personal actions known as actions "in personam." Where the action is against the vessel itself rather than the owner, this is known as an action against property (an action "in rem"), and federal courts have jurisdiction over actions in rem. U.S. admiralty jurisdiction extends to any navigable water, including the Great Lakes and a number of canals and rivers, some of which are entirely within the boundaries of one state. For example:

In New York State, the Erie Canal, extending from the Great Lakes to the Hudson River, was at one time a main source of navigation. The Erie Canal was later supplanted by the Barge Canal. Any accident occurring on the Erie or the Barge Canal was subject to admiralty jurisdiction.

Admiralty courts also have jurisdiction to enforce a lien against a vessel. Such an action is called a "'libel action."

Sam Jones, a seaman employed on the steamship *Good Hope*, has wages due him for services on the steamship *Good Hope*. He brings a lawsuit in admiralty court for unpaid wages and may start a proceeding called a libel against the steamship *Good Hope*.

Admiralty has jurisdiction over all vessels privately owned and operated on navigable waters. Public vessels engaged in government service are not subject to suit, but the United States government has consented to be sued for damages caused by its vessels. Admiralty has jurisdiction over maritime contracts and concurrent jurisdiction over commercial maritime torts (wrongs).

Under maritime law, in the event of a personal injury (a tort) either to a passenger or to a seaman, and the ship is show to be "unseaworthy" in any respect, then the ship owner is liable for damages as a result of the personal injures.

This doctrine has been said to be akin to "strict liability." Seaman and ship employees purposely are not covered by Workers' Compensation; they retain the right to sue their employer for personal injury damages.

There is in the law of admiralty a doctrine known as *salvage,* which allows compensation to a person who voluntarily saves or assists in saving a vessel or its cargo or crew from the perils of the sea. The amount awarded to the person saving or recovering a vessel lost at sea is left to the discretion of the admiralty court. The law of salvage is so important that Congress has specified rules for vessels stranded on foreign coasts; rules about property wrecked on Florida coasts; special licenses to wreckers on Florida coasts; rules about Canadian vessels aiding vessels wrecked or disabled in United States waters; and rules establishing a two-year statute for suits for salvage.

Congress has authorized the president of the United States to make international treaties or agreements as to reporting and marking for removal dangerous wrecks or derelicts or the taking of other measures for the safety of navigation in the North Atlantic Ocean, and has also authorized international agreements as to ice patrols.

Congress created the Federal Maritime Commission, which was put in charge of shipping and freight rates.

So-called Merchant Marine acts were passed by Congress in 1928 and 1936 governing a multitude of marine subjects. The Merchant Marine Academy was created to train Merchant Marine personnel.

Laws under the heading of "Carriage of Goods by Sea" defined the rights, responsibilities, and accommodations of sea carriers.

In addition, Congress has periodically passed laws regulating the safety of boats in all United States waters.

A shipowner is not liable for property lost in a fire at sea unless the fire was caused by the shipowner's negligence. To recover for jewelry or other valuable property, the owner must have disclosed in writing to the owner of the vessel the value of the property before the loss. The liability of the owner of a vessel is limited by law to the value of the owner's interest in the vessel. (In some cases the owner's liability is limited to $60 a ton, but all that is technical material. A reader who has a case in point should consult an admiralty lawyer.)

There used to be a separate set of admiralty rules in federal court, but now admiralty and other federal rules have been unified in one set of federal rules.

In a purely federal admiralty court there is no jury. Many plaintiffs prefer to have the case decided in a state court where there is a jury.

In many respects admiralty law has a special jargon. For example, in the case of *salvage*, the person entitled to a reward as above indicated is called a *salvor*. A *charter party* is a contract to lease a vessel to another, called a *charterer*. Another example is the verb *libel*, which in admiralty law means to seize property at the beginning of a suit.

The shipment of merchandise in containers has become such an important and popular part of world trade that one recent incursion of Congress into the field of admiralty was the passage in 1977 of laws implementing an international convention held relating to safe containers. The legislation provided for government inspection, testing, and approval of containers and measures for development of economical, safe, and expeditious use in handling of container cargoes.

The U.S. Constitution gives Congress the power to regulate commerce "with foreign nations and among the several states." Congress realized that the whole field of commerce was within its domain, and as far back as the 1790s began to pass laws regulating commerce on land and on navigable waters.

Congress established a Bureau of Marine Inspection and Navigation. The commandant of the Coast Guard and the commissioner of customs were placed in charge of marine commerce and navigation, and United States merchant seamen were authorized to register and license vessels. The commandant and the commissioner are required to make a list of vessels and their home ports, and of their dates and places of building, and to establish penalties for violation of laws relating to vessels.

Congress also passed laws to establish and mark "load lines" on vessels and provided penalties for violation of such laws. Collectors of designated ports were granted the right to clear vessels for departure upon filing with the individual collectors of ports a manifest (list) of all the cargo on board the vessel. Crowded and unsafe or unhealthy conditions for steerage passengers on transatlantic liners at the end of the nineteenth and the beginning of the twentieth century caused an international scandal, which Congress rectified by passing laws for improvements in accommodations for immigrants coming into this country.

For many years Congress has defined the duties and obligations of officers and members of a merchant ship crew and has regulated the conduct of such officers and crew. In addition, Congress has prescribed rules for the investigation by the Coast Guard of marine casualties and also has the legal machinery for the control, inspection, and regulation of all private vessels, including fishing and whaling boats. Congress is very zealous in passing laws for fire prevention and for the safety of passengers on river, ocean, and lake steamers.

ARBITRATION LAW

Arbitration has been defined as the hearing and determination of a controversy by a person or persons chosen to decide or settle the controversy. Fundamentally, an arbitration hearing must be the result of a contract provision to arbitrate. The decision of the arbitrator or arbitrators, called an award, may be just as binding on the parties to the controversy as a judgment of a court of law.

Some states have what is known as a statutory arbitration, and this proceeding may be submitted in writing and is entered in the court minutes. Actually, the award of the arbitrator or arbitrators may be the equivalent of a judgment of the court. In parts of the country where commerce or business interests regularly use arbitration as a means of settling disputes, arbitration is popular because some business people feel that court procedure is too cumbersome.

Many states have enacted a so-called uniform arbitration act. A uniform arbitration act provides that the courts shall assist in enforcing arbitration agreements. Throughout the United States courts will enforce arbitration, provided the parties have actively consented to it.

The U.S. Supreme Court has held that arbitrators must not have any business relation with the parties or be subject to any valid charge of bias or favoritism. Arbitrators, like jurors and judges, should be impartial.

Arbitration is to be distinguished from *mediation*, in which a mediator (or panel of mediators) tries to bring the principals to an agreement.

Many automobile insurance policies provide for arbitrating claims involving uninsured motorists and hit-and-run drivers. This provision in insurance policies has resulted in expediting insurance claims. Often the "uninsured motorist clause" provides that if the insurance company and the insured cannot agree on the amount of damage caused by an uninsured motorist, the amount of damage is subject to arbitration.

The law favors and encourages arbitration. Whenever arbitration proceedings are reviewed by a court, there is a presumption that the award is valid.

BAILMENTS

A bailment is a delivery to another person of personal property for some specific purpose with the understanding that the property is to be returned or redelivered when the purpose is accomplished.

John Jones delivers a suit of clothes to a dry cleaning establishment to have the suit cleaned. When the suit is cleaned, it is redelivered to John Jones. The delivery of the suit to the cleaners is a bailment.

The person who delivers the property to another is called the *bailor*. The person who receives the property under a contract of bailment is the *bailee*. (In the preceding example, John Jones is the bailor and the dry cleaning establishment is the bailee.)

The following transactions are to be distinguished from bailments:

1) A sale is different because there is a transfer of ownership. In the case of a bailment, only the possession of the property is transferred.

2) A loan of property (for a definite or indefinite period) differs from a bailment in that it involves only the delivery of property and the purpose of the delivery is specified. In the case of a loan for an indefinite period, the loan is terminated by the death of the borrower or the death of the person to whom the property is lent. Death does not terminate a bailment. Only when the purpose is accomplished is the property returned.

3) A chattel mortgage differs because there is a transfer of title of property.

A bailee may be liable for injury or loss of the property bailed when the bailee is negligent.

The bailee is not an insurer. For example, the bailee placed a space heater near a suit of clothes that was to be repaired. The clothes caught fire and were burned. The bailee was responsible because he was negligent in placing the heater too near the clothes.

What constitutes negligence of the bailee may depend on the nature of the bailment. In any event, the bailee must use care and diligence in the handling of the property.

John Smith left his car in a parking lot. Employees sat in the automobile smoking cigarettes. The cigarettes caused a fire in the automobile upholstery. The bailee was negligent to allow the employees to smoke in the automobile.

A tailor received a suit to be altered. The tailor left the door of the tailor shop unlocked. As a result the suit was stolen. The tailor as a bailee was negligent in not protecting the property left with him.

If the bailee can show care and diligence, he is not liable for injury or loss to the property. However, sometimes liability is limited if the limitation of liability is part of the contract.

For example, if John Jones brings an old suitcase to a luggage shop for repair and tells the proprietor that the bag is only worth $20; if then the proprietor of the shop loses the bag, he is liable only for $20.

The question often arises: Is there a real bailment?

John Jones and his wife entered a restaurant about one o'clock in the morning and ordered some food. John Jones left an overcoat and some gloves on a hatrack in the restaurant. When Mr. and Mrs. Jones were through eating, John went for his coat and it was gone. He blamed the restaurant and sued. The court held that there was no bailment because he had not expressly turned his coat and gloves over to the restaurant for safekeeping.

The legal distinction and the degree of care between "gratuitous bailments" (where the bailee receives no compensation) and "bailments for hire" (where the bailor pays) are fast eroding in most states.

ELDER LAW

According to the Census Bureau, by the year 2010, over 25 million households will be headed by persons 65 years of age or older. This is a 38 percent shift from 1985 and more than double the population over 75 years of age and older. As a consequence, laws (and lawyers) are becoming much more sophisticated in *elder law*.

In New York City (and the environs), laws now protect the rights of elderly tenants in rent-controlled or rent-stabilized premises; elderly tenants of build-ings which became "cooperatives" cannot be forced to buy or face being evicted.

Estate planning now also may involve "Medicare Trusts" or "Sup-port Trusts."

INTERNATIONAL LAW

There are two types of international law: *public international law* (dealing principally with treaties, protocols and relations between nations) and *private international law* (dealing with two or more pri-vate individuals or corporations in different countries).

It has been said that private international law is the same as any other law, except that the parties do not reside in the same country. However, this is oversimplistic; the rules of international law are com-plex and ever-changing. Moreover, the arguments which became a part of "public international law" often have impact on the daily practice of private international law.

The United Nations has a treaty regarding sale and carriage of goods between countries. If the U.S. and India are parties to this protocol, then the treaty gov-erns the sale and purchase of Indian Madras cloth by a New York manufac-turer.

25

CIVIL RIGHTS

Civil rights are those rights guaranteed to citizens under the U.S. Constitution. In recent years, the term civil rights also has come to refer to those rights guaranteed to blacks and other minorities against segregation or discrimination in voting, education, public facilities, places of public accommodations or employment.

The original civil rights are guaranteed by the first ten amendments to the Constitution, familiarly known as the Bill of Rights. They include freedom of religion, speech, press, assembly, and petition for redress of grievances, the right to bear arms, freedom from having troops forcibly quartered, freedom from unreasonable search and seizure, trial by jury, the ancient writ of habeas corpus to protect one from unlawful detention, and speedy and impartial trial.

The Constitution also prohibits double jeopardy, self-incrimination, excessive bail, and cruel and unusual punishment. It guarantees the right not to be held for capital or other infamous crimes except on indictment by a grand jury, the right to due process of law, and compensation for the taking of property for public use.

Following the Civil War various federal laws as well as the Thirteenth, Fourteenth, and Fifteenth amendments to the Constitution were adopted. The Thirteenth amendment abolished slavery and "involuntary servitude" in the United States. The Fourteenth and Fifteenth amendments granted voting rights to all citizens, including blacks, and prohibited discrimination in various fields.

Congress in the 1860s and 1870s passed the so-called Civil Rights

Acts, but they were in many respects a dead letter until nearly a century later, when the U.S. Supreme Court under the leadership of Earl Warren put an end to discrimination in education in the famous case of *Brown v. The Board of Education of Topeka* (1954). Then in the 1950s and 1960s Congress passed new civil rights acts putting an end to segregation and discrimination in voting, in matters of public accomodation or transport, and providing for equal opportunities in employment. These recent laws have teeth in them and effectively prohibit discrimination if such discrimination in areas of housing, employment, or education is based on race, color, sex, age, or national origin. The Civil Rights Act of 1964 prohibited discrimination in employment on the basis of race, color, or national origin.

In 1967 Congress passed the Age Discrimination in Employment Act, which prohibited discrimination in employment of persons between the ages of forty and sixty-five if such discrimination was based on age. Under this law it is unlawful to advertise for a young person.

The Jones Manufacturing Company put an ad in the paper for a night watchman and stated that applicants forty-five and over need not apply. The general manager of the Jones Manufacturing Company was held guilty of violating the Age Discrimination in Employment Act.

In 1972 the Civil Rights Act of 1964 was amended to prohibit discrimination in employment on the basis of sex. This law is designed to guarantee women equal job opportunities, both in pay and in status. Employers are prohibited from indicating a sex preference in their advertising for employees. Advancement, transfer opportunities, and wages must be equal for men and women.

The Smith Clothing Company put an ad in the paper for piece workers to work on machine tools. The company hired 200 men and no women. A number of women were turned down for employment with no reason given. The personnel manager of the plant was found guilty of violating the Civil Rights Act.

Congress established a Civil Rights Commission to monitor voting rights and other rights of minority groups.

AMERICANS WITH DISABILITIES ACT

On July 26, 1990, the Americans with Disabilities Act (ADA) was signed into law. Viewed by many as the most significant civil rights legislation since the Civil Rights Act of 1964, the ADA prohibits discrimination on the basis of mental or physical disability in employment and access to public services. These prohibitions took effect July 26, 1992 for employers with 25 or more employees and will take effect July 26, 1994 for employers with 15 to 24 employees. The nation's state and federal courts are among those who must comply with the ADA.

The ADA applies to private-sector employers and to state and local governments, including courts. It prohibits discrimination in four broad areas:

1) Terms, conditions, and privileges of employment
2) Receipt of public services or participation in programs or activities provided by state or local governments
3) Enjoyment of goods, services, facilities and advantages of any place of public accommodation
4) Availability and use of telecommunication relay services.

Under the ADA, state and federal courts are required to make reasonable accommodations for people who have a disability, defined as a physical or mental impairment that substantially limits one or more major life activities, or being regarded as having such and impairment. Reasonable accommodation means making existing facilities readily accessible to and usable by people with disabilities.

Discrimination in Education

In *Brown v. The Board of Education of Topeka*, the Supreme Court held compulsory segregation in the public schools invalid, as a violation of the Fourteenth Amendment. For twenty-five or thirty years after *Brown*, the Supreme Court sent to the U.S. district courts various problems in desegregating public schools, and even after that the Supreme Court wrestled with various problems arising out of the interpretation of *Brown*. There were actually two *Brown* cases, known in legal terminology as *Brown I* and *Brown II*. In *Brown I* the Supreme Court struck down the dual system of education—one system for whites and one for blacks. The Court said that a "separate but equal" system for blacks was invalid.

In *Brown II* the Supreme Court gave the superhuman job of supervising school desegregation to the U.S. district courts. In this case the Court not only ordered the termination of the dual school system but ordered such termination to be done "with all deliberate speed." School districts in the South were slow to act on the Supreme Court decisions, and over thirty years after *Brown,* we still have segregated schools. Throughout the country, particularly in the South, the speed of the school districts was very deliberate. Separate but equal facilities were no longer legal.

Discrimination in Transportation

Discrimination in both intrastate and interstate transportation is prohibited, according to a Supreme Court decision of 1956.

Discrimination in Employment

Whenever an employer refuses to hire or discharges an employee by reason of racial discrimination, the employer is liable to the employee for back pay.

John Smith, a black, applied for the position of night watchman with the XYZ Company. The XYZ Company, instead of hiring Smith, hired two white men. The court held that the XYZ Company discriminated against Smith because of his race. Smith sued the XYZ Company, claiming that he lost $5,000 in wages before he was able to get another job. A court and jury found the XYZ Company was liable to Smith for $65,000.

The Civil Rights Act of 1964, which Congress later supplemented by the Equal Employment Act of 1972 and the American with Disabilities Act of 1992, prohibits discrimination in employment on the basis of race, color, sex, and other factors. Most large-scale employers have pre-employment tests. Some employers improperly use those tests to discriminate against blacks and other minority groups. To discourage such practice, Congress enacted Title VII of the Civil Rights Act of 1964 to provide as follows:

It shall not be an unlawful employment practice for an employer ... to give and to act upon the results of any professionally developed ability test, provided that such test, its administration, or action upon the results is not designed, intended, or used to discriminate because of race, color, religion, sex, or national origin.

If a person is discriminated against in employment, promotion, or transfer, Title VII gives that person the right to sue his or her employer for damages.

A black man applied for a skilled position with a leading airline. The black man showed that out of over 5,000 employees, the airline had only seven black employees. The airline countered by showing that it had logical and job-related tests and that the applicant didn't meet a sufficient standard in taking the test. Among other things, the airline said that the applicant in seeking a job as a flight officer failed to show that he had enough flight hours of experience as a pilot; also, that he was not a college graduate. The court refused to substitute its judgment for that of the airline and denied the suit.

Title VII of the Civil Rights Act of 1964 also provides that if a person is employed as the result of a preference being given to him or her by reason of sex, the person who is denied employment by reason of sex discrimination may sue the employer.

Mary Smith applied to the Brown Steel Company for a job as a watchman. The Brown Steel Company refused to employ her, and instead employed a man. Smith may sue the Brown Steel Company under Title VII for discrimination in employment.

The *Civil Rights Act of 1991* overturned eight Supreme Court decisions (most from 1989) that restricted the application of existing federal civil rights laws. The courts have wrestled with whether this law should apply retroactively.

For example, under Title VII of the Civil Rights act of 1964, the plaintiff in an employment discrimination suit is not entitled to a trial by jury and is provided back pay as the only remedy. The 1991 act guarantees a right of trial by jury and right of reinstatement plus damages.

The question for the U.S. Supreme Court is whether—in the absence of any expression of Congressional intent—the 1991 act should apply to pre-1991 acts.

Discrimination in Housing

The 1968 Fair Housing Act prohibits discrimination in the sale or rental of real estate and authorizes the attorney general to take court action to prohibit such discrimination.

The Jones Realty Company owns a series of apartment houses and refuses to accept blacks as tenants. The federal attorney general successfully institutes a court action for an injunction prohibiting the Jones Realty Company from refusing to accept blacks as tenants.

Discrimination in Public Accommodations

The 1964 Civil Rights Act also prohibits discrimination in public accommodations, including recreation parks, restaurants, commercial buildings, places of entertainment, and YMCAs.

VOTING RIGHTS ACTS

Congress has passed, and the commission has now implemented, laws intended to create an atmosphere where minorities have an equal voice in government. The voting rights acts give the commission authority to, for example, reject a proposed voting district that unfairly discriminates against minorities representation. The commission also investigates voters fraud or intimidation.

Discrimination on Account of Sex, Race, Color, Religion, National Origin, Age or Handicap

Each year Congress debates and usually adopts laws governing discriminatory treatment on account of persons' race, color, sex, religion, national origin, age or handicap, usually by an employer, labor union or an employment agency.

A victim of, for example, sexual harassment in the workplace, has a number of avenues of redress: a lawsuit for damages a complaint to the Equal Employment Opportunity Commission (EEOC) and/or a complaint to the state Human Rights Division. (Most states have adopted laws regarding discrimination.) Some states (and subdivisions thereof) have adopted laws prohibiting discrimination which are more strict (and also more all encompassing) than the federal laws on the subject.

The Rehabilitation Acts of 1973 (as amended)

Congress also has specifically prohibited discrimination against handicapped persons, not only in the workplace, but elsewhere. By law, any building that has received certain federal funding since 1969 is required to comply with federal accessibility standards for the handicapped. (These ensure wheelchair access to appropriate facilities.)

In addition, an educational institution receiving federal funds is prohibited from sexual (and other) discrimination.

Wrongful Discharge from Employment

Although it is developing slowly, there is a trend on the part of the courts to grant relief to employees who have been "wrongfully discharged." It used to be that unless an employee had a contract, he had no vested right to the job. Now, however, some courts find for the employee and grant him damages for wrongful discharge. Courts are apt to hold under certain circumstances that express contracts are not necessary, but when all of the facts of a case are carefully analyzed, it appears that the employee had an implied contract of employment. Under the old rule, an employer could discharge an employee at will and not be held responsible for arbitrary or capricious action on his part.

There are many facets to wrongful discharge, cases included implied contracts of employment, fairness, and justice between the parties. The courts of several states have differed on the treatment of these problems and time along will determine the rules of law which the courts should follow.

Voting Rights Act of 1965

In 1965, Congress enacted the Voting Rights Act. In 1982, it amended the act to incorporate some ethnic and racial proportional representation and to give minorities new grounds for challenging apportionment of voting districts.

Various minority groups have used the provisions of the act as a tool to maximize the power of their individual group—sometimes at the expense of another minority group.

In 1992, the U.S. Supreme Court heard an appeal concerning a Florida redistricting plan that gave Hispanics enhanced representation but which—it was contended—had adverse consequences for blacks and Jews in that county.

The Voting Rights Act has many parts to it, and sometimes even a municipality can run afoul of one of its provisions.

Since 1880, Dade County, Florida, has had an "English only" law. The law, which requires that English be the only language used in nonemergency material published by the county, has withstood all challenges. However, the Voting Rights Act requires that vital election information be distributed in any language used by at least 5 percent of the voting-age population. Half of Dade County's population is of Hispanic descent. In 1993, a federal district judge ruled that the county misinterpreted the "letter and spirit" of the act when election material was not printed in Spanish. Dade County promptly printed and distributed new election material written in Spanish.

Education of the Handicapped

The U.S. Supreme Court interpreted the Education of the Handicapped Law as requiring school authorities to provide special education to take care of the handicapped, even though the place of education be different than the regular school and to reimburse the parents of the handicapped for such special education.

AFFIRMATIVE ACTION PROGRAMS

To have an affirmative action program, there must be a history of past discrimination by the employment unit. There seems to be some problem as to whether the history of past discrimination must be found as a fact or whether such past history may simply be determined by the governmental unit involved or by the court.

In the mandatory hiring of minority races, required by affirmative action programs, there must be no discharge of qualified employees. The statute also provides federal remedies for racial discrimination in private or public employment.

STERILIZATION

In the past, courts quite frequently ordered sterilization of a retarded person. Many years ago, in a U.S. Supreme Court case involving the issue of whether or not a retarded person should be sterilized, Justice Oliver Wendell Holmes said, "Three generations are enough..." However, in recent years, the courts seem to pay more attention to the rights of the patient and will not order sterilization in the absence of special circumstances.

PATIENTS' RIGHTS

Today when one enters the hospital as a patient, one has far more rights than in years gone by. Many times, either on request or as a matter of routine, the hospital gives the patient a list of his or her rights. The hospital also may not discriminate against a patient on account of race, color, age, religion, national origin or medical condition.

PRISONERS' RIGHTS

In the early days of our country, the courts treated prisoners as slaves of the state, and they didn't have many rights. Then the Supreme Court said that prisoners have certain constitutional rights just the same as persons outside the prison.

Gradually the courts have taken a more enlightened view that prisoners, though they have been convicted of crimes, still have rights under the Constitution.

The courts now hold that procedural safeguards must be taken to ensure that arbitrary action may not be taken by the prison authorities relating to classification, restriction of liberty, and prison discipline. Due process requires that in certain cases that the prisoner must have advance notice of charges brought against him and that the right to a hearing before an impartial tribunal before which the prisoner may present evidence, swear witnesses, and cross examine adverse witnesses.

The Supreme Court says that prisoners are entitled to certain protective rights relating to their personal liberty or their property, although not their complete privacy from the authorities.

For example, the courts have recently held that it is "cruel and unusual treatment" to have more than a certain number of prisoners in the jail. This has resulted in, among other things, the release of prisoners, in order to accommodate the court maximum.

"What are the prisoner's rights when the state seeks to transfer the prisoner from a prison to a mental institution?" The Supreme Court has laid down certain rules for the transfer of a prisoner to a mental institution: (1) notice of the impending transfer of a prisoner to a mental institution must be given to the prisoner; (2) a hearing before an independent tribunal must be held at which the prisoner may produce and cross-examine witnesses; (3) a written notice to the prisoner of reasons for the decision by the court must be given to him; and (4) notice must be given to the prisoner of the above rights.

Wiretapping

It is against federal law to eavesdrop on a private phone conversation and then disclose the contents of the conversation.

This is equally applicable to both private individuals and to prisoners. Federal law prohibits interception of a prisoner's phone conversations by wiretapping devices. Prisoners in some cases may have the same rights as other citizens to prevent tapping of telephone conversations. However, a prisoner in, for example, Attica (a prison in New York State) has no right of privacy from prison officials (although he may have a right of privacy from the F.B.I.). As part of police or prison investigations, court orders may be obtained to monitor phone conversations.

Rules governing wire tapping apply not only to prisoners but also to institutions operated by the state.

Right of Parole

Courts give wide discretion to parole boards in granting prisoners' release from prison. Sometimes parole boards change their minds and deny the prisoner's rights to freedom. In such events, the courts generally uphold the parole body.

Access to Courts

Prisoners are guaranteed what is called meaningful access to the courts. That only means access to a law library and also in some cases access to persons trained in the law.

In recent cases, the U.S. Supreme Court in effect limited a prisoner's right of access to the Court. It held that the number of times that a prisoner could bring a writ of habeas corpus, whereby he or she demanded to know why he was being wrongfully held, could be limited, without violating the Constitution.

In the above case one McClesky was sentenced to death for killing an Atlanta policeman. His two appeals to the Supreme Court resulted in rulings that have dramatically narrowed the options for appeal open to death row inmates and their lawyers.

In 1987, in a five-to-four ruling, the Court ruled that the death penalty was constitutional, despite statistics showing that killers of white people were far more likely to be executed than killers of black people. Mr. McCleskey was black, and the police officer was white.

In 1990, in a six-to-three ruling, the Court on his second appeal sharply curtailed the ability of death row inmates and other state prisoners to file multiple appeals. The Supreme Court ruled that the failure to raise legal objections on an earlier appeal—in this case, that the prosecution's witness was a police informer—was fatal.

In 1992, the Supreme Court ruled that a state death row inmate who presents belated evidence of innocence is not ordinarily entitled to a new hearing in federal court before being executed.

In the court's six-to-three ruling, it left open the prospect of an exception for "truly persuasive" evidence. However, that did not benefit the Texas inmate, who had been convicted of murdering two police officers in 1982.

Minors

In 1993, the U.S. Supreme Court ruled that the question whether the Texas death penalty could constitutionally be applied to those who committed murder before the age of eighteen could not be brought through a *habeas corpus* petition.

CONFLICT OF LAWS

Conflict of laws is the branch of law that determines whether the law of the forum (the state where the lawsuit is brought) should be applied to the case or whether the law of a foreign state (generally the law of another state of the United States) should be applied.

The courts of Pennsylvania blazed a trail in the field of conflict of laws by disregarding the old rule in a torts case that the law of the place where the injury occurred should control. In this case the decedent, a resident of Pennsylvania, purchased in Pennsylvania an airline ticket for a flight from Pennsylvania to Arizona. The defendant airline was incorporated under the laws of Delaware. The decedent was killed in an accident that occurred in Colorado. The Pennsylvania court rejected the old rule that in a torts case the law of the place where the accident happened, Colorado, should apply. The high court of Pennsylvania held that the law of Pennsylvania should apply, because most of the essential facts were centered in Pennsylvania.

Jim Smith of Ohio is driving his car through the state of Indiana and has an auto accident with Bob Jones, also of Ohio. Subsequently, Smith and Jones take up residence in New York, where Smith sues Jones to recover damages resulting from the auto accident. Should the New York court apply New York law in determining liability for the accident, or apply the law of Indiana or Ohio? The New York court properly applied the law of New York because, of the three states involved, New York State had the greatest interest in the controversy.

However, some states still adhere to the old rule that the law of the place where the accident happened rather than the law of the state that has the most significant contacts should apply. The forum state (the state where the case is heard) may base its decision on the law of another state not because the laws of the other, foreign state have any extraterritorial effect, but because of rules of comity or courtesy—that is, the laws of a foreign state—may be applied as a matter of fairness or social expediency and convenience.

In making a choice of which law should be applied to the case, the forum judge has a number of choices. The old traditional rule that existed for centuries in Anglo-American law was that in the case of a contract dispute, the court should apply the law of the state where the contract was made to be performed, referred to by lawyers as the *lex loci contractus*. In tort cases the traditional view was to apply the law of the place where the wrong was committed (lawyers refer to it as the *lex loci delictus*).

THE GROUPING OF CONTACTS

In recent years judges of some states, legal writers, and some scholars have developed a new rule to replace the traditional rules. The new view is that courts in making a choice of foreign law to be applied should take into consideration all the facts and circumstances of the case and choose the law of the place that has most significant relationship to the parties. This new doctrine is known as the "grouping of contacts" or "center of gravity" doctrine.

Susan Jones of New York State was a guest of the Robert Smiths, also of New York State, on a weekend trip to Ontario. Jones was injured in an automobile accident involving the Smith car and sued Smith in New York State for negligence. According to the old rule, New York would have applied Ontario law, which has a so-called "guest statute," making it very difficult for a guest to recover damages by reason of the negligence of a host owner of the car. Bear in mind that all parties to the action were New York residents and the car was garaged in New York State. The New York court applied the New York law, which made it easier for Jones to recover damages against Smith. The old rule was to apply the law of the place where the accident happened—namely, Ontario. However, the court applied the more modern rule of significant contacts and center of gravity.

In the case of disputes involving real property, the traditional view is that the law of the state where the property is located governs. According to the traditional view, the validity of a marriage is governed by the law of the state where the marriage was performed. Traditionally, the law of the domicile of the married parties is generally applied in divorce action. In determining the legal effect of wills and testaments of deceased persons, the traditional rule is to apply the law of the place where the will was executed or the law of the place where the will was probated.

The advocates of the "grouping of contacts" or "center of gravity" rule say that it is more flexible than the rigid *lex loci contractus* or the *lex loci delictus* rule, and because of its flexibility may more often result in justice and the carrying out of the intention of the parties.

Some states in making a choice of law rely on the governmental interest theory, that is, the interest that a particular state has in the outcome of the litigation.

Probably the majority of the states of the United States still adhere to the traditional views in making a "choice of law" where there is a conflict of laws, but the more modern rule of determining the place of most significant contacts or center of gravity is supported by legal writers and law school professors.

The choice of law problem is illustrated by a California court case:

John Jones of California was driving his car in Missouri when it collided with a car owned by Robert Smith of Ohio. Occupants of the Smith car were killed.

Survivors of the deceased members of the Smith family subsequently moved to California and brought suit against John Jones in California for damages. The California court was faced with the problem of whether to apply the rule of damages as it existed in Missouri or to apply the rule of law of California or Ohio on the question of damages.

The rule of law in Missouri was more favorable to the defendant. The California court didn't apply the old rule, which was that the law of the place where the accident happened governs, but applied the rules of law as they existed in Ohio and California—namely, the "grouping of contacts" rule.

LONG-ARM STATUTES

A long-arm statute is a law whereby the courts of a forum state (the state where the suit is brought) may obtain jurisdiction of a person in another state if the action that is the basis of the lawsuit grew out of a transaction in which the defendant was in, or doing business in, or had an interest (such as land) in, the forum state. Before the days of long-arm statutes, ordinarily a court in a forum state had jurisdiction only over people within the confines of the forum state.

The XYZ Company (located in Illinois) sent one of its salesmen to Syracuse, New York, to sell tractors. One of the tractors sold by the salesman of the XYZ Company ran into an automobile because of a faulty transmission in the tractor. John Jones, the owner of the automobile, was injured in the accident and brought suit in the New York courts against the XYZ Company. Jones claimed damages for personal injuries and property damages caused by the faulty transmission of the tractor. To accomplish service on the XYZ Company, the lawyer for Jones sent a summons and complaint to Missouri to be served on an officer of the company. The XYZ Company contested the suit, claiming that New York courts didn't have jurisdiction over an Illinois corporation. The New York court rejected the claim of the XYZ Company and held that by reason of a long-arm statute a New York court had jurisdiction over the XYZ Company.

Some states hold that if a manufacturer puts goods into the stream of interstate commerce with the probability that some of those goods will eventually be sold in the forum state, long-arm jurisdiction should be granted. Other states hold that if the manufacturer could not have anticipated that his goods would reach the forum state, then long-arm jurisdiction should be denied.

CONSTITUTIONAL LAW

Because constitutional law concerns itself with constitutions, we may properly ask what is a constitution. It is the original law that sets up the framework for a system of government and to which the various branches of government must look for their power and authority.

The U.S. Constitution is the supreme law of the United States. Constitutions of the various states of the United States define and limit the powers of the different branches of state governments of the fifty states of the union.

A fundamental principle of American government is that it is divided into three branches: the executive, the legislative, and the judicial. Each of the three branches operates separately and independently of the others, though the powers are intermingled so that each branch serves as a check and balance on misuse of power by the other two branches.

Legislative power includes: the power to make laws and also the power to ascertain facts that would be the basis for legislation; the creation of municipal governments; the establishment of school districts; the control of public utilities; the promotion of public health and welfare; the supervision of professions and occupations; the levying and collection of taxes; the regulation of elections; the direction of public work or improvements; and the definition of crimes and public offenses and the setting of penalties for the commission of such crimes or offenses. In the United States, most of these powers are exercised by state legislatures.

The judiciary has the power to hear and determine those matters that affect life, liberty, and property and has the power to interpret, construe, and apply the law.

The executive department enforces the laws as interpreted by the courts.

The Bill of Rights

As every school boy or girl knows, a bill of rights (a statement of fundamental and guaranteed rights of persons) was not included in the original United States Constitution. Such a bill was omitted for a number of reasons, including the fact that it was thought unnecessary because most state constitutions had bills of rights.

Some of the original thirteen states refused to ratify the Constitution until a Bill of Rights was added. As strange as it sounds today, many of the Original Framers were opposed to amending the Constitution with any sort of a Bill of Rights. For example, Alexander Hamilton strongly defended the Constitution against the Bill of Rights arguing that the constitution itself was a bill of rights. As James Madison said, men are not angels. In the end, the original Constitution was amended by adding the first ten amendments, the Bill of Rights, to ensure that at least nine of the original thirteen states ratified the Constitution.

Most people believe today that the Bill of Rights is the sole limitation on the national government's powers. However, there are those that argue that this apparent misunderstanding of the significance of the Bill of Rights appears to be a modern phenomenon. The Bill of Rights actually embodies all of the constitution principles of popular sovereignty and limited government, and originally was meant to reinforce and not supplant the limitations contained in the United States Constitution.

First Amendment Rights

The rights set forth in the First Amendment to the United States Constitution read as follows: "Congress shall make no law respecting an establishment of religion, or prohibiting the free exercise thereof; or abridging the freedom of speech, or of the press; or the right of the people peaceably to assemble, and to petition the government for a redress of grievances."

Historically, this country was ambivalent about the scope of protection of the First Amendment. Though freedom to criticize the government is felt to be paramount, a scant seven years after adoption of the First Amendment, the Sedition Act of 1798 made it a crime to oppose the government or the president (then John Adams). A congressman was jailed after he wrote a letter to the editor criticizing the government's "foolish adulation and selfish avarice."

This may be difficult to believe today; yet, it is part of the evolution of the First Amendment. Today, the right of free speech involves erotic art, minorities vilified in verse, and so on. There are some limitations of free speech and of the press. Despite the current chaos, free speech is still restrained by libel. The extent to which First Amendment rights may be abridged is unclear with regard to a case of clear and present danger or to protect national security.

The Constitution nobly protects, in Justice Holmes's words, "not free thought for those who agree with us but freedom for the thought that we hate." Nevertheless, the Supreme Court's duty is to let federal and state governments know they can protect citizens from hate-motivated action.

As a matter of common sense, the right of free speech can be subject to abuse.

The best example of abuse is the example given by Justice Holmes, who cited the case of a person who shouts, "Fire!" in a crowded theater. That is an abuse of freedom of speech.

However, Judge Marshall, in a 1968 Supreme Court decision upholding the right of fair speech, said, "The mere fact that speech is accompanied by conduct does not mean that the speech can be suppressed under the guise of prohibiting the conduct."

There are, however, measures that regulate freedom of speech and of the press during wartime and in periods of insurrection and rebellion.

Religious Activity in Public Schools

The Supreme Court declared unconstitutional laws of Idaho and Colorado providing for compulsory reading in the public schools of verses from the Bible. It also held unconstitutional laws providing for prescribed public school prayer.

The public in general apparently does not like the Supreme Court decision banning school-ordered prayers. Some of the lower courts have permitted prayers in school so long as those prayers were not official and were voluntarily said by the children.

Despite the Court's disapproval of prayers in schools, in a recent case the Court held invalid a regulation of a university prohibiting the use of university buildings or grounds for religious purposes.

Symbolic Conduct

The Supreme Court disallowed the action of a school board in forbidding the use of black armbands by students as a protest against the Vietnam War.

Handbills

The Supreme Court disallowed the forbidding of handbill distribution on school premises unless the educational authorities could show that the activity tended to create a disorder or disrupted the school.

RIGHT TO ASSEMBLE

One of the fundamental rights guaranteed by the First Amendment to the Constitution is the right of people to assemble peaceably. Sometimes a law or ordinance gives public officials too much power to determine whether or not the proposed assembly will cause public disorder.

The City of Podunk had an ordinance that prohibited any picketing or assembly other than labor picketing within certain areas. The court held that such ordinances were unconstitutional because they denied the right to assemble.

Obscenity

Freedom of speech is protected by the First Amendment to the Constitution, and a person who exercises the right to speak freely may not be arrested or prosecuted. An exception to this principle is the freedom to write or speak obscenely.

Whether people disseminating obscene material, such as artistic or literary work, should be arrested and convicted or should be protected by the freedom-of-speech clause in the Constitution became the subject of many cases coming before the Supreme Court; but the members of the Supreme Court had so many different views on *what constituted obscenity* that the Court decisions furnish little guidance to the judges of the trial courts hearing obscenity cases.

Finally, the Supreme Court, as a guidance to law courts, defined obscenity as being:

1) Whether "the average person, applying contemporary community standards, would find that the work, taken as a whole, appeals to lewd interests."
2) Whether the artistic or literary work depicts or describes, in a patently offensive way, sexual conduct specifically defined by the applicable state law.

3)   Whether the artistic or literary work, taken as a whole, lacks serious literary, artistic, political, or scientific value.

Desecration of the Flag

All fifty states have some statute prohibiting desecration or destruction of the American flag. The states seek to preserve the integrity of the American flag, but perhaps some of the statutes should be revised in view of the Supreme Court's holding in flag-abuse cases.

In the state of Washington, soon after the American invasion of Cambodia and the shooting of students at Kent State by members of the National Guard, a college student was arrested for displaying in his window an American flag upside down with a removable black tape as a symbol of protest. The Supreme Court held that the state law forbidding the desecration or abuse of the American flag was too vague, and, therefore, it reversed the conviction of the student.

In a number of cases, however, the Supreme Court made it clear that if a statute was specific in forbidding the abuse of the American flag, the statute would be upheld.

Destruction of Draft Cards

The Supreme Court upheld a statute prohibiting the mutilation of a selective service certificate (draft card). A man arrested claimed that his destruction of the draft card was a form of expression and, therefore, was protected by the First Amendment. Rejecting that claim, the Supreme Court found that the government had sufficient interest to regulate the use of draft cards.

Freedom of Speech

The Supreme Court goes to great lengths to protect freedom of speech, even though such speech may be contrary to the public interest or tend to incite public disorder.

There was a case in Ohio in which a Ku Klux Klan leader advocated criminal action to advance the cause of white supremacy. He was subsequently convicted. His case was appealed to the Supreme Court, which held that where there was "no clear or present danger" but mere advocacy, the conviction was a violation of the free speech rights of the Ku Klux Klan leader.

Freedom of speech includes the right to dissent. However, dissent, for whatever cause, must be peaceful. When dissent reaches a violent stage and provokes riots, the government may step in to quell the riots.

An example of peaceful dissent is to be found in the remarks of Julian Bond in protest against the illegality of the Vietnam War. The Georgia legislature refused to seat Bond, though he had been duly elected, because of his anti-Vietnam War remarks. The Supreme Court held the action of the Georgia legislature improper and an invasion of Bond's right of free speech.

The courts have held that freedom of speech extends to speech in public forums, commercial advertising, labor picketing, door-to-door solicitation, and many other obvious situations. There are, of course, some restrictions on some types of speech such as obscenity, shouting "fire" in a crowded theater, and otherwise disturbing the peace.

Although the courts go far to protect freedom of the press, the Supreme Court stopped at protecting a newsman who asserted his privilege not to disclose the sources of his information.

Right to Bear Arms (Second Amendment)

The Second Amendment to the Constitution was tied to the ability of the states to maintain a militia and the right of persons to bear arms. The opponents of gun control argue that this limits the amendment to protecting the ability of today's national guardsman to carry firearms and therefore does not preclude regulation of private gun ownership. Gun control proponents say, in effect, "Can't you read?" The amendment language, "the right of each person to bear arms," is unequivocal.

The right to bear arms has had a long history. The 1789 Bill of Rights of the Articles of Confederation guaranteed certain fundamental principles, including the right to bear arms. At the time of the formation of the Constitution and of its Bill of Rights, ours was a citizen-army in the truest sense. If the community's way of life was threatened by domestic strife, it was assumed that all men would take up arms against the troublemaker. However, today the right to bear arms does not even guarantee the right to go deer hunting.

Police Power

An important part of constitutional law is called police power. This has very little to do with the "cop on the beat," but is concerned with the right and power of the government, generally through its legislature, to promote the general welfare, public health, public safety, public order, public morals, and to regulate occupations and professions.

Although police power rests in the government, state or federal, as a practical proposition the power is exercised by state governments.

For example, the Supreme Court upheld the power of the state to pass so-called Sunday closing laws or "blue laws" as within the police power of the state.

Due Process of Law

The U.S. Constitution provides that no person shall be deprived of life, liberty, or property without "due process of law."

Legal scholars say there is no brief comprehensive definition of the phrase "due process of law"; but the phrase requires multiple statements to explain its scope and ramifications.

If a person is to be deprived of life, liberty, or property, due process of law means that he or she must have the benefit of the process of law in a proper tribunal of justice after notice and full hearing.

"The due process of law" amendment, which is the Fifth Amendment to the Constitution, is probably one of the most important of the ten amendments. It is the counterpart of the Fourteenth Amendment, which limits state's activities. It has far-reaching interpretation.

For example, constitutional scholars disagree as to whether the right to "reproductive privacy" is protected by the Bill of Rights (the Fifth and Fourteenth Amendments). The extent to which the right also applies to minors is equally unclear.

Recently, the Supreme Court held that the Constitution does indeed apply to children and that students "do not shed their constitutional rights at the schoolhouse gate." There are exceptions: a minor's rights to use contraception and to obtain an abortion has been successfully restricted in several states. However, the Supreme Court recently held that a third party may not have an absolute say in a minor's ability to exercise her right to reproductive privacy.

The interrelationship of land use regulations and the Fifth Amendment guarantee of due process continues to be a source of litigation.

For example, an Environmental Protection Agency regulation holds that certain uses of land are prohibited. To that extent, it could involve a "taking," a *de facto* condemnation or appropriation, without giving the landowner just compensation.

For another example, the Supreme Court has held that a military decision to destroy American-owned oil refineries in a foreign land is an exercise of the "police power" and is not a "taking" in the meaning of the Fifth Amendment of the Constitution, entitling the owner of the property to compensation.

The framers of the U.S. Constitution added the Fifth Amendment to the Bill of Rights. It was a guarantee of individual rights, in reaction to the abuses of the arbitrary Star Chamber Courts in England. A little known provision of the Fifth Amendment states that "no person shall be held to answer for a capital, or otherwise infamous crime, unless on presentment or indictment of a grand jury, except in cases arising in the land or naval forces, or in the militia, when in actual service in time of war or public danger."

The mention of the grand jury comes first in the series of clauses that create four more of the precious protections of individual rights that Americans enjoy: protection against double jeopardy, against self-incrimination, against deprivation of life, liberty or property without due process and just compensation.

Right to Counsel

The Supreme Court held in the famous case of *Gideon v. Wainwright* (1963) that every defendant in a criminal case is entitled to counsel. Defendants who are indigent must be assigned counsel by the court.

Cruel and Unusual Punishment

The Eighth Amendment of the Constitution, prohibiting "excessive fines and cruel and unusual punishment, was adopted simply as an expression of the rights to which Americans felt they had through their birthright.

The principle has been invoked—sometimes successfully and sometimes unsuccessfully—in cases involving capital punishment (unsuccessfully), overcrowding in prisons (partially successfully), and so on.

The Fifteenth Amendment adopted in 1870 prohibits the United States or any state from denying the right of a United States citizen to vote on account of race, color, or previous condition of servitude, and the Nineteenth Amendment, adopted in 1920, prohibits the United States or any state from denying or abridging the right of any American citizen to vote "on account of sex."

It is clear that the text of the Constitution and the Bill of Rights extends to all United States citizens. The Supreme Court has held in numerous cases that certain of these protections also apply to aliens—whether in this country legally or illegally.

State Constitutions and Bills of Rights

Each state has its own constitution, and also many of the states also have bills of rights. However, some states' constitutions do not contain the protection afforded by the federal Constitutions' Bill of Rights. For example, initially, in 1790 the New York State Constitution had no bill of rights.

State constitutions are often wordy and deal with many minor problems. They are often the subject of debate; for example, the New York State Constitution, which was last exhaustively overhauled in 1938, has become increasingly obscure and outdated with the passage of time.

Therefore, the governor of the State of New York has requested a Constitutional Convention to consider revising and amending the New York State Constitution.

Loyalty Oaths

The courts have struck down some loyalty oaths as being too vague and an intrusion into government employees' thoughts and beliefs rather than their actions. However, the Supreme Court finally held that oaths to uphold and support the constitutions of the state and federal governments are valid.

The Exclusionary Rule

Over twenty years ago the Supreme Court established a set of principles which became known as the "exclusionary rule," which allowed the suppression or exclusion of evidence obtain by illegal means. Later, in the case of *U.S. v. Leon*, the same Court held that if the officer who obtained a warrant to search the defendant's premises acts in good faith, and where it turns out that the warrant is defective because of some technicality, the motion to suppress must be denied. In other words, the court put a restriction on the exclusionary rule to the effect that evidence obtained by an illegal warranty, although technically defective, may be admitted as long as the arresting officer acted in good faith.

The Court held that the university had created a forum for general use by students groups, and it was improper to limit its use to nonreligious organizations.

LAW OF DAMAGES

In law, damages are a means of compensating a person or corporation for an injury. When a person or thing is injured or a person's rights are violated and the person or thing cannot be replaced or restored to the condition that existed before the injury, the law does the next best thing and awards a sum of money as damages to compensate the injured party.

Where two or more people are jointly responsible for an injury, they are called *joint tort feasors*. If a person is injured by the negligence of several joint tort feasors and he settles his claim for damages against one of the tort feasors, such settlement releases his claim for damages against the other tort feasor or feasors. The effect of that rule is to prevent double damages for one injury; or to put it another way, there can only be one satisfaction for one damage claim.

John Jones, while riding as a passenger in an automobile owned and driven by Mary Smith, suffers injuries as a result of a collision of Smith's automobile with an automobile owned and driven by Tom Brown. The accident was caused by the joint negligence of Smith and Brown. If Jones settles his claim against Smith, such settlement releases his claim against Brown.

Different Kinds of Damages

General damages are damages that naturally result from any wrongful act. In a court of law it is not necessary to prove any amount of *general damages*.

John Jones, while crossing Avenue A in Bridgetown as a pedestrian, is struck by an automobile owned and driven by Howard Smith. Jones sustains a fractured arm as a result of the accident. Jones sues Smith for $500,000 general damages. A jury awards Jones $200,000 general damages.

Special damages are the dollars-and-cents loss suffered by the injured party and must be proved in a court of law.

John Doe, while driving his car on West Avenue in the village of Milltown, is struck by an automobile owned and driven by Richard Roe. Doe pays $7,000 doctors' bills as a result of permanent personal injuries that he sustained in the accident and pays $2,000 for the repair of his automobile, which was damaged in the accident. Doe sustains special damages of $7,000 doctors' bills and $2,000 automobile repair bills.

Nominal damages apply both to a case of breach of contract and to other wrongdoings. In the case of a breach of contract, if there is no actual damage sustained, then the party aggrieved by the other party may recover nominal damages.

Jack Jones agrees with Sam Smith to buy from Sam Smith a calf for $2,000. Smith fails to sell the calf as agreed. Jones is able to buy the same kind of calf from another person for $2,000, and hence he has sustained no actual damage as the result of Smith's breach of contract. However, Jones sues Smith for nominal damages. A jury awards Jones $1 nominal damages.

In the law that has come down to us from England (the Common Law) nominal damages are sometimes "six cents."

A debt or claim for liquidated damages results when a party to a transaction agrees to pay another person a fixed amount and then defaults in such payment, or when the parties to a transaction agree beforehand that a claim for damages resulting from a default or injury shall be in a fixed dollars-and-cents amount.

Howard Smith borrows $5,000 from John Doe and gives John Doe a promissory note for $5,000, payable in six months. At the end of six months, Howard Smith fails to pay John Doe $5,000. John Doe sues Howard Smith for $5,000 liquidated damages plus interest from the date of nonpayment.

John Smith collects antique automobiles. He makes an agreement with Howard Jones to buy a 1905 Pierce Arrow automobile for $50,000. In the agreement the parties agree that if Howard Jones fails to deliver the automobile by July 1,

Smith will have sustained liquidated damages in the sum of $10,000. Howard Jones fails to keep his agreement to sell John Smith a 1905 Pierce Arrow automobile. John Smith sues Howard Jones for $10,000 liquidated damages, the amount determined as liquidated damages in the agreement.

A claim for *unliquidated damages* exists when the amount of the claim is vague or undetermined when first presented.

John Smith is riding in an automobile of Herbert Brown and sustains a broken arm as a result of Brown's negligence. Smith's claim against Brown is $5,000, but the amount of the claim remains unliquidated until a jury, court, or other tribunal has fixed the amount of John Smith's damages.

Accord and Satisfaction

If the person who owes "unliquidated damages" tenders a lesser amount (than is in dispute), and signifies in writing that the amount is in full payment and discharge of the claim or debt, and the other party accepts the tender, then the debt is completely discharged.

Jones says Smith owes him $5,000 for home improvement work in 1992. Smith disputes the claim and says he only owes $2,000, bearing a legend "in full payment and discharge for home improvement work done in 1992." Jones cashes the check.

There has been an accord and satisfaction of an unliquidated claim and the debt is discharged.

Exemplary or punitive damages (sometimes called "smart money") are intended to serve as punishment to the wrongdoer or a deterrent against a repetition of the wrongdoing and often are recoverable when accompanied by malice, willful misconduct, fraud, gross negligence, or other gross wrongdoing. In most states exemplary or punitive damages are not generally allowable in contract cases. Before exemplary or punitive damages are allowed, the injured or aggrieved party must prove that he has sustained actual damages.

26

INSURANCE LAW

Insurance is a contract under which a company (called the insurer) agrees to indemnify another (called the insured) against specified losses.

KINDS OF INSURANCE

There are many kinds of insurance, including the following:

1) *Life insurance*, in which the insurer agrees to pay to a designated person a stipulated sum on the death of a named human being.
2) *Accident insurance*, in which the insurer agrees to indemnify the insured for specified expenses or lot is resulting from an accident causing physical injury to the insured.
3) *Sickness insurance*, in which the insurer agrees to pay the insured certain specified sums of money if the insured is disabled because of sickness.
4) *Fire and extended coverage*, in which the insurer agrees to indemnify the insured for loss or damage of a building resulting from fire, windstorm, hail, lightning, explosion, riot or civil commotion.
5) *Liability insurance*, whereby the insurer agrees to pay on behalf of the insured an amount equal to the insured's legal liability as a result of the death, personal injury, or property damages of a third person. Such liability insurance may result from the owner-

ship or operation of a particular automobile or the ownership or use of some other form of property.

6) *Workers' compensation insurance*, which insures employers for their liability to pay losses sustained by employees injured in the course of their employment.

7) *No-fault auto insurance*, which pays economic losses sustained by the insured, the occupants of insured's car, or pedestrians as a result of accident of the insured's car without regard to whose fault caused the accident. No-fault auto insurance has been the subject of widespread controversy. Over twenty states have adopted no-fault plans.

8) *Prepaid legal insurance*, under which the insurer pays the legal expense incurred by a member of a group insured by the insurer. Just as Blue Cross-Blue Shield or similar insurance applies to medical and hospital expenses, so prepaid legal insurance applies to legal expenses.

9) *Title insurance*, which indemnifies the insured against loss caused by defects of titles to real estate.

10) *Fidelity insurance*, which indemnifies an employer against loss due to employee dishonesty.

11) *Burglary and theft insurance*, which covers loss or damage to property caused by burglary, theft, or robbery.

12) *Reinsurance*, which is a contract made by an insurance company with another insurance company to share liability for loss occasioned by the original insurance.

13) *Annuity*, which provides monthly payments to the insured beginning at a fixed date and generally ending with the insured's death.

14) *Aircraft insurance*, which covers reimbursement for damage caused to an aircraft as a result of a forced or crash landing. Generally, in order for an aircraft to be covered, it must be piloted by a pilot who meets certain government qualifications.

15) *Group insurance*, which is coverage of a number of persons by means of a single blanket insurance policy. The "master policy" is issued to an employer, creditor, labor union, trustee, association, bank, or credit union. The individuals for whom the plan is formed make individual application, for which they receive certificates that refer to the master policy.

16) *Health insurance*, in which the insured is compensated for hospital and other medical expenses due to illness or accident.

17)   *Home owners' insurance*, which covers reimbursement for property damage to an individual's home and also personal liability insurance. The property damage coverage in home owners' insurance is generally broad and often includes damage by (a) fire and lightning; (b) windstorm and hail; (c) explosion; (d) riot and civil commotion; (e) vehicle or aircraft damage; (f) vandalism and malicious mischief; (g) smoke and heating or cooking; and (h) theft.

The broad form of such insurance generally covers residence (a) glass breakage, (b) rupture of steam and hot water systems, (c) water escape from heating or plumbing systems, (d) collapse of building, (e) damage from falling trees, (f) freezing of heating and plumbing systems, and (g) electrical damage.

Regulation and Control of Insurance

All states of the United States have insurance departments, insurance commissioners, or insurance superintendents. States rather than the federal government regulate and control insurance. State legislatures prescribe forms of insurance policies, rates, and so on.

The Insurance Contract

Because insurance is a contract and the terms and conditions of the contract are set forth in the policy, the policy is an all-important document. Some people speak disparagingly of the policy because it contains so much "fine print." Unless the fine print is ridiculously small and illegible, its provisions will be recognized by the courts and bind all parties. If any parts of an insurance policy are of doubtful meaning or ambiguous, those parts will be construed by the courts against the insurance company and more favorably to the insured.

Agents, Brokers and Adjusters

An insurance agent is an individual who solicits or procures applications for insurance policies. The question often arises whether a particular person is an agent of the insurance company or of the insured. An insurance agent is usually an agent of the company. A broker is generally an independent contractor who procures insurance on behalf of an insured. He is not an agent of the insurance company and has no power to bind the insurance company. An adjuster is a person who investigates, settles, or adjusts claims against insurance companies. An adjuster usually represents the interests of an insurance company. In some cases a public adjuster may represent an insured.

27

EVIDENCE

The subject of evidence is a broad one. It reaches into various other branches of the law, including contracts, torts, intentional harms, defamation of character, negligence, wills, estates of deceased persons, commercial paper, labor and management, corporations, partnerships, marriage and family law, divorce, separation and annulment, real property law, debtors and creditors, agency, criminal law and sales. Fundamentally, the law of evidence deals with the subject of whether certain statements or documents are properly admissible in the court of justice. The law of evidence has many facets. A brief list and definition of the major facets follows.

Relevancy. A fact is relevant if it goes to prove a material issue in a case; that is, if it is "probative." In some courts the requirement of "materiality" and "probativeness" are combined under the single definition of "relevancy." For example, under the Federal Rules of Procedure, "relevant evidence" means evidence tending to prove any fact of consequence to the action.

Character Evidence. Where a person's character itself is the ultimate issue in the case, "character evidence" must be admitted. However, evidence of character to prove the conduct of a person in the case itself is usually not admissible in a civil case. The general rule is that the prosecutor (in a criminal case) does not initiate evidence of bad character of the criminal defendant merely to show that he or she is more likely to have committed the crime of which he or she is accused.

However, the accused may admit evidence of his good character to show his innocence of the alleged crime.

Judicial Notice. Judicial notice is the recognition of a fact as true without formal presentation of evidence. For example, acquiring proof that Washington, D.C., is the capital of the United States would require unnecessary court time in a situation where any contrary conclusion would be ridiculous. Therefore, the court will take "judicial notice" of this fact and other matters of common knowledge in the community.

Dead Man's Act. Most states have statutes which disqualify a party or a person interested in the event to testify to a personal transaction or communication with the deceased. The reason for this statute is to protect estates from perjured claims. Death having silenced one party, the dead man statutes closes the mouth of the living party who, being interested in the litigation's outcome, wishes to testify on his or her behalf against the estate. In most cases, the bar to competency created by the dead man's statute applies only to civil cases and has no application in criminal cases.

Cross-Examination. Cross-examination of an adverse witness is a matter of right in every trial. It is recognized as the most efficacious truth-discovering device. It is governed by the rules of evidence.

The Hearsay Rule. Hearsay is a statement, other than one made by the declarant while testifying at a trial, offered in evidence as the truth of the matter at issue. The rule against hearsay is probably the most important exclusiary rule of evidence. There are many exceptions to it. Hearsay evidence can either be oral or written.

PRIVILEGED COMMUNICATIONS

The relationship between a husband and a wife is said to be confidential, thus not open to the public. If a husband or a wife tells his or her mate certain information, that information may not be repeated in a court of law without the mate's permission.

John Riggs was arrested for stealing some jewelry. The night of the robbery Riggs had told his wife that he had obtained the jewelry by trickery and it was kept in a secret hiding place. The wife cannot tell in court what her husband told her because it was confidential. Under the law of evidence, it is called a privileged communication between husband and wife.

The law is full of privileged communications and they are important to the law of evidence.

Lawyer-Client Privilege

Another example of a well-known rule of evidence is the evidentiary rule that statements made by a client to his lawyer in seeking legal advice are privileged and cannot be communicated to outsiders.

Under certain circumstances statements made by an officer or a key employee of a corporation to any attorney rendering legal advice on corporation matters may be privileged and not communicated to outsiders.

The lawyer-client privilege belongs to the client who can be an individual, a public officer, a corporation or other entity seeking legal services. That client has the privilege to refuse to disclose or permit others to disclose confidential communications. However, if the lawyer acted for both parties, then neither party can invoke the privilege of confidentiality.

There is no privilege if the services of the lawyer were sought or obtained as an aid in the planning or actual commission of something that client knew or should have known was a crime or a fraud.

Other Examples of the Privilege

The same statutory privilege exists in the doctor-patient relationship. If the confidential information is acquired during the course of the doctor attending the patient, the privilege applies, and only the patient can waive it.

The clergy-penitent privilege applies to members of the clergy, where the clergy acts in his capacity as a spiritual advisor. The clergy can be a minister, a priest, a rabbi, or other similar functionary of a religious organization, or someone reasonably believed to be so by the person consulting him. This common privilege is very similar in its operation to the attorney-client privilege discussed above.

Some states recognize by statute an accountant-client privilege, or a psychologist-psychotherapist/social worker-client privilege. In those states which do recognize such a privilege, the professional must be licensed or certified to act in the particular capacity and the communication must be confidential.

Although the U.S. Supreme Court has held that there is no constitutional protection for a professional journalist's source of information, and, therefore, there is no constitutional right to a confidential privilege, the existence of the privilege only exists where individual states have adopted statutes shielding the journalist. Less than half the states have enacted statutes protecting the journalists's source of information (sometimes called "shield laws"), and the protection ranges from an absolute privilege to one qualified by the need for disclosure in the public interest.

Polygraph Tests

Polygraphs are informally referred to as lie detector tests. Most courts refuse to admit results of polygraph tests, saying that scientific evidence has not yet produced a proven reliability of such test. A court within its discretion may allow the use of polygraph tests, but such cases are very infrequent.

Courts have repeatedly ruled on the admissibility of "scientific evidence" (such as DNA fingerprinting). The appellate courts have ruled in different ways.

Regardless of the outcome, the case throws into sharp relief the argument over the quality of science heard in the courtroom.

Rules of evidence change. In recent years the courts have allowed evidence of some scientific tests or experiments to be admissible in evidence if these scientific tests or experiments show that certain facts are true. For example, some courts have held that DNA tests are 100 percent reliable; others still hold DNA test results unreliable and inadmissible.

28

ENVIRONMENTAL LAW

Environmental law has fast become a part of almost all business life. Since 1969 and the "Earth Year," most state legislatures have vastly expanded the scope of laws protecting the environment.

The federal government also has accelerated the process. Congress enacted comprehensive laws governing pollution of all waters in the United States, which includes literally any water course in any state. Congress also authorized the division of each state into "air quality control regions." It extended federal wetlands permit controls to all wetlands in each state. Congress also enacted "cradle to grave" regulations of chemicals manufactured in, imported into, stored in, transported in or through, disposed of in, or used in each state. In addition to adding to the list of federal endangered species, the federal laws speak to pesticide laws, federal coastal zone management laws and flood plain management laws.

Although the administrations under Presidents Reagan and Bush have sought to encourage off-shore drilling, protection of the environment remains—to many—an important issue. President Clinton's administration appears to be more aggressive in enforcing the laws and regulations relating to environmental quality.

Whistle-Blowing: Environment Disclosures

Hazardous waste, as defined under the Resource Conservation and Recovery Act of 1976 (RCRA), and "hazardous substances," as defined under the Comprehensive Environment Response, Compensation and Liability Act of 1980 (CERCLA, also known as the Super Fund) may subject the officers, directors, employees—and perhaps their counsel—to criminal liability and perhaps liability to third persons.

Endangered Species

Species of plants and animals that are in danger of or threatened with extinction are directly protected under a variety of federal and state regulatory schemes. The Endangered Species Act, the Marine Mammal Protection Act, and various conventions on international trade in endangered species and plants are perceived to protect a variety of plants, animals, and habitats. In certain very limited exceptions, endangered species of fish and wildlife may not be hunted, fished, harvested, trapped, maimed, or shot. In addition to substantial penalties, federal law provides for forfeiture of personal property.

A 1993 analysis by an environmental group suggests that rare plants and animals are not added to the list of endangered species until their numbers are so low that extreme and expensive rescue measures are essential for their survival.

In 1960, there were an estimated 160,000 Steller sea lions in Alaska. By 1990, the number had shrunk to 25,000. Only after litigation was threatened by environmental groups was the breed added to the list.

The emphasis today appears to be shifting to saving a whole ecosystem (such as a parcel of old forest growth) rather than protecting a particular species or subspecies (such as the spotted owl).

Forest Preserves and National Parks

The federal government has set aside significant lands as national parks, and many states, which also have state parks, have forest preserve land. The distinction between these various categories of land and land use is important; in the western states, over half the land area is owned by the federal government.

The distinction between federal national parks and state forest preserve land lies principally in the constitutional prohibition that the land be kept "forever wild," and not be leased, sold, or exchanged, nor shall the timber thereon be sold, removed, or destroyed.

Many states also have adopted regulations governing private land that abuts state forest preserves, which many feel is too restrictive and amounts to the "confiscation or appropriation" of their private property.

Conservation and Environmental Organizations

For years such organizations as the Audubon Society and the Sierra Club have been in the forefront of environmental movement. The Supreme Court, in a landmark decision, held that any of these organizations which was directly affected by the proposed action had "standing" to enjoin the act of which it complained, be it polluting the environment, degrading water quality, limited the bird life through the use of pesticides, etc.

Negotiations Preempting Lawsuits

Traditionally, environmental protection agencies or state environmental agencies would promulgate regulations regarding the environment. These regulations would then be the subject of protracted lawsuits, either by businesses who felt they were adversely affected, or by environmental organizations who felt that the proposed regulations were not strict enough.

However, there has been a trend towards negotiations; federal environmental agencies have had the parties first sit down and hammer out regulations.

In 1990, the Environmental Protection Agency produced rules at the Grand Canyon through an agreement to reduce emissions of a cold-fired generating plant, which had been blamed for producing haze in the area. This agreement on the form of the regulations had been hammered out between the parties prior to the regulations being issued.

As part of the haze negotiations, it was agreed that neither the environmental groups nor the industry would sue to overturn the provisions which had been agreed to.

The Environmental Protection Agency hopes to conclude negotiations between environmental groups and the industries involved on rules governing everything from how to dispose of lead-acid batteries to how to glue down wall-to-wall carpeting.

Convention on International Trade in Endangered Species of Wild Fauna and Flora (CITES)

The United States and a number of other countries are convention signatories to the Treaty on International Trade in Endangered Species.

Periodically, the signatory nations to this international convention meet to add or subtract certain animals and plants which need protection. For example, the bluefin tuna, which is avidly sought in Japan for serving as sashimi, is possibly the first commercial fish proposed for the International Endangered Species list. Conservationists, led by the National Audubon Society, have petitioned to have the Western Atlantic bluefin declared endangered under the Convention. However, the National Marine Fisheries Service has recommended a delay of at least two years in any action by the United States, until the service can better determine whether existing controls on tuna fishing can be improved.

CITES has done a good job in world conservation, and is strongly supported by most concerned counties. However, unfortunately—often because of emotional influence—their efforts go too far.

In 1989, the CITES nations added elephant ivory to the prohibited list. This ban was documented only the disasters in certain East African nations, where the elephant has been poached practically to extinction. It specifically excluded the success of the Southern African states, where there is a surplus of elephants.

The Clean Air Act of 1990

Under this act, all industries which release emissions or pollute the air must either "upgrade" their plants or, for example, produce a car emitting a lower volume of pollutants. Target dates are set, and if a company can clean up its emissions more than is required under the new laws, it could sell its right to pollute (the excess) to another company. Although this "right" was meant to be an incentive, it has had an unintended side effect: the creation of a free market in pollution.

Federal Clean Waters Act

This act is the counterpart of the Clean Air Act, the Superfund of 1980, and amendments to the Resource Conservation and Recovery Act of 1984. Each of these acts was passed by Congress in response to the public's revulsion over the discovery of polluted waters and seeping chemicals in, for example, Love Canal.

29

THE UNITED STATES
SUPREME COURT—
THE HIGHEST COURT IN
THE LAND

Many people don't realize that the United States Supreme Court has played and is now playing an unsung and unheralded but crucial role in the history of our country. The strongest leader of the Supreme Court, often called "the great chief justice," John Marshall, brought strength, respect and stability to the Court. At a time when the infant republic was so weak that it was the ridicule and contempt of other nations, Marshall contributed so much to the Court that someone said he made the Court supreme.

In one of his first cases, *Marbury v. Madison* (1803), Marshall astutely found in favor of the Jefferson administration, but he annoyed Jefferson when he established in that case the power of the Supreme Court to pass on the constitutionality of acts of Congress.

So impressive were Marshall's character, intellect, and influence on the Court, that members of the Court of opposite political beliefs followed Marshall's thinking and reasoning. In *McCulloch v. Maryland* (1819), Marshall ruled on the superior power of the federal government over the power of a single state (Maryland). In the dramatic case of *Gibbons v. Ogden*, Marshall struck down New York's legislative attempt to control steamboat traffic on the waters of New York State and established the broad power of the Congress to regulate commerce. He thus broadened the economic life of the young nation. Many of Marshall's decisions (*Gibbons v. Ogden* was an exception) were unpopular, and there were times when Marshall was hung in effigy, but despite his temporary unpopularity, he changed the Court from a weak, uncertain body into a strong arm of the government, becoming an eminent tribunal with great traditions.

Marshall's successor as chief justice, Roger Taney, was a brilliant judge who served with distinction as head of the Supreme Court from 1806 until his death in 1864. Taney wrote many unpopular and historic decisions, chief among them the infamous Dred Scott decision, which held that blacks could not be citizens. The nation was sharply divided over slavery. The Dred Scott decision angered half the nation, and many people felt that it precipitated the Civil War. Even though most of Taney's decisions were not popular, however, as a judge he made an enduring contribution to the law of the land.

Despite the fact that Congress had passed a civil rights act that prohibited racial discrimination in public places, and despite the express language of the Fourteenth Amendment to the Constitution, the Supreme Court held in 1888 that this civil rights act was unconstitutional. Then the Court went a step further and held in 1896 that Louisiana's statute requiring "separate but equal" railroad accommodations for blacks (Jim Crow cars) was proper. That was the famous case of *Plessy v. Ferguson*, which virtually upheld the legality of Jim Crow cars. The case was renowned for the dissent of Justice John Marshall Harlan, whose grandson sat on the Court in the 1950s and 1960s. Justice Harlan in his dissent in *Plessy v. Ferguson* said, "Our Constitution is color blind." Justice Harlan, the grandson, must have been very proud when the Supreme Court in the 1950s repudiated *Plessy v. Ferguson* and established legal racial equality. (See *Brown v. Board of Education*, p. 364.)

Though the Supreme Court was at a low ebb during the late 1800s, it fostered industrialism in the American economy. The Court approved of due process for the protection of American business from the encroachments and restrictions of government. The protection of business became very important in developing the nation in those formative years. Protection of property and freedom of contract were special concerns of the courts in the latter half of the last century and the first quarter of the twentieth century. Regrettably, the Supreme Court disapproved of early workmen's compensation laws. The Court said, "Consider what the employer does. He invests his money. He takes all the risks of the venture. Now there is put upon him an immeasurable element that makes disaster inevitable." The Court held that workers' compensation would "stifle enterprise, produce discontent, strife, idleness, and pauperism." How wrong was the Supreme Court of those days. In the latter part of the last century and the first quarter of the twentieth century, the Supreme Court held unconstitutional over fifty national and over 200 state statutes. The Court invalidated all sorts of reform legislation, social welfare laws, and laws regulating hours of labor, prohibiting child labor, and establishing minimum wages. But workers' compensation was a plan whose time had come. In 1916 the Supreme Court finally came to its senses and upheld workers' compensation laws, which had spread from state to state throughout the nation. We had a reactionary Supreme Court in the second half of the past century and the first quarter of this century. Today we have a sensible court that has kept pace with modern legislation, a Court that construes the Constitution as a flexible document devised to serve the needs of the people.

Franklin Roosevelt's New Deal

We come to think of President Franklin Roosevelt as the great critic of the Supreme Court, but it was his cousin President Theodore Roosevelt who complained of the reckless power of the courts. Many critics of the Supreme Court said that the Court was going beyond its function in vetoing legislation, that the Court was acting as a superlegislature in establishing the rule of "government by judiciary."

Several decades later, along came Franklin Roosevelt's New Deal which attempted legislation and economic regulation to cure a serious economic depression. These efforts at economic regulation ran smack into a stone wall put up by the Supreme Court, which invalidated most of the important New Deal regulations. It was a terrific blow to Roosevelt, who said, "We must take action to save the Constitution from the Court." He was furious at the Supreme Court, which he said was made up of "nine old men." He proposed what became known as his "court-packing plan," under which the president would appoint a new

Supreme Court justice when an existing justice reached the age of seventy and failed to retire. Roosevelt's plan meant that as president he would have the power to appoint six new Supreme Court justices. The battle over the president's plan raged. Hearings were held, and pros and cons were debated. Roosevelt lost the battle. The American people were behind him on almost everything, but they would not stand for tampering with the Supreme Court.

Strangely enough, the Supreme Court thereafter seemed to reverse itself. From 1934 to 1936 the Court had held various pieces of New Deal legislation unconstitutional. Then starting in 1937, the Court, under the leadership of Chief Justice Charles Evans Hughes, started to uphold New Deal legislation that was only slightly revised from legislation that had been rejected by the Court. Some students of law believe that the reversal of the Supreme Court's attitude toward New Deal legislation was not due to slight changes in the legislation but to changes in the leading legal and judicial thinking and reasoning of those days. In any event, the trend represented a conversion to a more liberal attitude on legislation promoting social and economic welfare.

For example, in 1937 the Court approved a state minimum-wage law similar to the one it had previously rejected. A great victory for the New Deal was achieved when the Supreme Court approved the Wagner Act. This law gave employees the right to form unions and to bargain collectively and prohibited certain "unfair labor practices" of employers. The Supreme Court also upheld old-age and unemployment benefit laws.

Some people feared that the Social Security laws might meet the fate of early New Deal laws, but they were wrong. The Supreme Court was keeping abreast with social reform and the "welfare state." During the second quarter of the twentieth century, the Court's emphasis seemed to shift from property rights to personal rights, that is, those rights guaranteed to citizens by the Bill of Rights.

A revolution, if not an explosion, occurred in 1953, when President Eisenhower appointed Earl Warren, former governor of California, as chief justice of the Supreme Court. Chief Justice Warren had never been a judge. He had been a governor for ten years. He had been a Republican nominee for the vice-presidency. As chief justice he proved that he was not only a good judge but a statesman and a leader of men. Not since the days of John Marshall had the Supreme Court vitalized the law to fit the needs of humanity and of a nation as did the

"Warren Court." The Warren Court placed its emphasis on the protection of individual rights and liberties. The Court was solicitous for freedom of speech, freedom of religion, and the rights of the minorities. Some diehard conservatives resented the Warren Court's liberal attitude and launched a movement to impeach Warren. Such an idea was ridiculous. In fact, there is no doubt that the liberal attitude of the Court served a need: to respond to the demands of those seeking social justice for the poor and the disadvantaged. Among the decisions of the Warren Court were the case of *Mapp v. Ohio* (1963), which banned the use in a courtroom of illegally secured evidence; *Miranda v. Arizona* (1966), which imposed restrictions on police interrogation of alleged criminals and voluntary confessions of those accused of crime; and *Gideon v. Wainwright* (1963), in which an unknown and impoverished convict wrote a penciled petition to the Supreme Court telling his story and established with his case the right of poor people to have court-appointed legal counsel.

Although opponents of the Warren Court protested that the Court went too far, it was obvious that one of the Court's primary concerns was to protect the rights of those accused of crime. Many felt that the successor Court, headed by Chief Justice Warren Burger, would reverse decisions of the Warren Court Protecting the rights of those accused of crime, but the Burger Court respected the decisions of the Warren Court and on the whole stabilized the liberal doctrines of its predecessor. Often we hear some defeated litigant say that he or she will carry a case to the U.S. Supreme Court. Such a statement is meaningless, because only the Supreme Court can decide which cases it will hear. Each year the Court is asked to accept several thousand litigated cases, but it accepts fewer than 200 cases. The Court will accept only those cases that have an important public and constitutional concern.

During a term of Court, the justices meet about once each week. At the end of each conference, cases are assigned to the various justices for the writing of opinions. Cases are assigned by the chief justice, unless he is in the minority.

The president of the United States appoints the justices of the Supreme Court, subject to the "advice and consent" of the United States Senate. Over the years, a number of fine legal and judicial minds have been rejected by the Senate, based upon their perceived ideological "mindset."

30

DEVELOPMENTS IN THE LAW

The law changes, and there are some recent developments.

Law of Products Liability

It used to be that if a consumer or a customer wanted to sue a manufacturer, the plaintiff had the burden of showing that the manufacturer was negligent in the making of the product. Now, in practically every state, under the Law of Products Liability, it is not necessary to prove negligence, but it is required to prove that the product was defective and such defect caused an injury to the plaintiff. This rule of products liability is sometimes referred to as the Law of Strict Liability.

The only defenses to an action for products liability based upon the Doctrine of Strict Liability are assumption of risk and misuse of the product. The defenses are few and far between. Litigants were dissatisfied with customary rules of contract and court cases. Hence, the Products Liability Doctrine was developed.

Some courts have expanded liability in products liability cases.

In California, a suit was brought against a dozen drug manufacturers of a product commonly known as DES, which was supposed to be a miscarriage preventive. A plaintiff sued the dozen manufacturers, claiming that DES caused cancer in the plaintiff due to the use of DES by the mother. Proof was lacking as to which drug manufacturer supplied the DES that was used by the mother. Pharmacists filled prescriptions for DES from whatever supply of the product was on hand in the pharmacy. The plaintiff could not identify the particular drug manufacturer who produced the drug causing the plaintiff's injury. The California Supreme Court ruled that the defendants could be held liable collectively.

The Court developed the theory of liability based upon each defendant's share of the market. The plaintiff must only name enough defendants to constitute a "substantial" share of the market. The ruling of the California court is contrary to the traditional concept that a wrongdoer is liable for his own wrongdoing, but not for injuries caused by the group; however, this ruling is based on a theory of products liability and not ordinary torts. Whether the "market share liability" theory will be accepted by the courts of other states remains to be seen.

Recent products liability decisions, characterized by inconsistent holdings of various courts and judges in factually similar cases, reflect the uncertainty that permeates this area of law.

The Supreme Court noted that strict liability as set out in the Restatement of Torts refers to liability for injury to a consumer or his property.

Controversy has arisen between courts as to whether the Rule of Comparative Negligence should be applied in strict liability case. Some courts hold that the principles of fairness and justice require that the plaint give the defendant some credit for what amounts to the plaintiff's negligence. Other courts say that strict liability is a liability in and of itself, and comparative negligence has nothing to do with it.

The recently passed Product Liability Risk Retention Act of 1981 is evidence that the recovery of economic loss may be becoming more accepted. Congress recognized that this definition is broader than that in many jurisdictions, noting that most courts do not permit recovery of economic loss in tort. The rationale behind such a broad definition is to allow product sellers to protect themselves in jurisdictions where economic recovery is allowed or where the applicable law may change in the future.

Video Taping

The Supreme Court held, under the new Copyright Law, that the use of video taping in the home did not violate the Copyright Law and

Regulations. The Court held that when Congress passed the new Copyright Law, it did not intend to restrict home and noncommercial use of video tapes.

Social Welfare Laws, Lifestyle Laws and Zoning Laws

Business Regulation (although once viewed with suspicion) is now invariably sustained as a reasonable state action. Taxation is invariable sustained. However, discriminatory state taxes might still be invalidated.

Although there is no recognized right to lead a certain lifestyle, the courts uphold laws prohibiting use of drugs ("hard" or "soft"). The Supreme Court will not invalidate safety laws such as requiring motorcycle helmets (although a few state courts and legislatures have done so for a variety of reasons).

Zoning regulations regarding use and ownership of property have been liberally tolerated by the courts. However, statutes forbidding certain uses have been sustained. For example, the Supreme Court some years ago held that a Long Island suburb could zone out all groups consisting of three or more persons unrelated by blood, adoption or marriage. However, times change and today the courts would rule differently. The emphasis today is on "ownership" rather than "use" of property.

Sovereign Immunity

The doctrine of sovereign immunity, prohibiting suits against the government, was established by the kings of England centuries ago. This doctrine was transplanted to the colonies of this country. Each state had its own rule prohibiting a litigant from suing the sovereign.

This inequitable doctrine was part of the law of all states in the United States until in 1928, when Alfred E. Smith, governor of New York, recommended to the legislature that it enact a law creating a Court of Claims, which would pass on all claims against the State of New York. Many states followed New York's example and waived sovereign immunity in whole or in part, but still today more than half of the states of our union have sovereign immunity in one form or another.

The legislature of each state and the high court of each state possess the authority to abolish sovereign immunity. Congress got into the act by enacting the Federal Tort Claims Act (see Tort Claims Act, p. 21) by which the federal government waives sovereign immunity as to certain classes of claims and retains sovereign immunity as to other claims.

Foreign Sovereign Immunities Act

In 1993, the Supreme Court limited the scope of the Foreign Sovereign Immunities Act, which provides the only means of suing a foreign government in U.S. courts. That law holds that a foreign government is generally immune from suits instituted in United States courts, with the narrow exception of suits "based upon a commercial activity carried on in the United States by the foreign state."

The plaintiff, an American, was recruited in this country by an agent for the Saudi Hospital. He alleged that he had been mistreated, imprisoned and tortured by the Saudi police in retaliation for complaints about the hospital's system. However, the Supreme Court, in dismissing the complaint, said that a foreign government's exercise of its police power has long been understood to be "peculiarly sovereign in nature" and, therefore, immune from attack in a federal court under the 1976 law.

Limited Privacy—Caller ID System

The Federal Communications Commission (F.C.C.) has proposed that telephone customers have the limited ability to block caller ID, a service that displays the phone number of incoming calls before the person answers the telephone. Although telephone companies are heavily promoting the service as a way for people to identify unwanted callers, critics have argued that callers are entitled to privacy and should be allowed to conceal their identity if they choose.

The proposal of the F.C.C. pits the federal government against some state regulators, who advocate stricter protection for callers who want to conceal their identities when using the phone.

The advances in this type of technology challenge the law to its outer limits.

The Consumer Product Safety Commission

The Consumer Product Safety Commission is an independent federal agency that regulates the safety of all consumer products, other than cars, boats, drugs, and food, under the direction of Congress.

It has recently come under criticism for not being aggressive enough. For example, the commission determined that a popular portable heater might pose a fire risk, but it did not alert the public until twenty-one months later, after eight people had died in two fires allegedly started by faulty wiring in the heaters. Ride-on lawnmowers have also been the subject of investigation—for six years—to determine why they are liable to tip. This investigation has not been resolved.

Critics have said that the Consumer Product Safety Commission is a listless watchdog, while other agencies such as the Federal Food and Drug Administration and the Federal Trade Commission are far from listless. The Commission says that its problems relate to budget cuts.

VICTIMS OF RAPE

Victims of rape are turning to civil—as opposed to criminal—courts for help. There are two reasons why victims of rape often take this alternative:

In order to obtain a criminal conviction, a prosecutor must meet a higher standard of proof. This often results in a more intensive cross-examination of the rape victim, many times resulting in an acquittal because of lack of evidence. However, the standard of proof in a civil liability case is much lower.

Secondly, in a civil case (wherein the plaintiff seeks monetary damages) there usually is someone other than the rapist who was at fault. (Many times the accused rapist is "judgment proof," so that it is essential that there be other defendants.)

For example, a woman is raped in a housing authority complex. In addition to naming the rapist as a defendant, she also named the housing authority, the housing authority police, and the security service, for their failure to have secured the apartment building in which she was raped.

Sex-Offender Registration Laws

As of December 1991, twenty-two states (Alabama, Arizona, Arkansas, California, Colorado, Florida, Illinois, Louisiana, Maine, Minnesota, Montana, Nevada, New Hampshire, North Dakota, Ohio, Oklahoma, Oregon, Rhode Island, Tennessee, Texas, Utah, and Washington) have passed laws requiring sex criminals to register their address and other information as they are released from prison. The laws vary widely from state to state in their stringency. (The newest laws are the most stringent.)

Although civil libertarians have challenged the laws, proponents of the laws believe they deter sex offenders from repeating their crimes.

Family Leave and Maternity Act

In February 1993, Congress passed and the president signed the Family Leave and Maternity Act. This act requires any employer having fifty or more workers to grant to any employee up to twelve weeks unpaid leave (in any twelve-month period) for the birth or adoption of a child, to care for a child, spouse or parent with a serious health condition, or for the worker's own serious health condition that makes it impossible to perform the job.

The employee, who must have been with the employer for at least a year, must be returned to his or her old job (or an equivalent position) upon returning to work.

The act also allows an employer to deny leave to a salaried employee within the top 10 percent of its work force if the leave would create a "substantial and grievous injury" to the business operations.

This measure grants to American workers a benefit similar to those already enjoyed in Japan, Germany, and other industrialized countries.

Over twenty-five states and the District of Columbia also have some form of legislation of their own, and many employers presently have policies regarding unpaid maternity leave and other emergency leaves of absence. They say it has greatly increased employee loyalty.

GLOSSARY

Many other legal terms are defined in the text of the book. These are listed in the Index.

Abatement means reduction or decrease; when applied to the payment of claims from a fund which is insufficient to pay claims in full, it means a proportionate reduction of the claims.

Abduction (criminal law) is the offense of taking away a female or child by violence or fraud.

Abeyance is a state of being undetermined or held in suspension.

Ab initio (Latin, "from the beginning") signifies a transaction or document from its inception; thus, a marriage may be held to be unlawful *ab initio* or an insurance policy valid *ab initio*.

Abstract of title is a condensed history of a title to land.

Accord and satisfaction is an agreement between two persons that settles a claim or a lawsuit.

Acknowledgment is the certificate of a notary or another officer having the authority to administer oaths attesting that the person who executed a document declared that the document was his free act and deed.

Acquittal, in the law of contracts, means a release or discharge from an obligation; in the law of crimes, it means the deliverance of a person from a charge of guilt.

Act of God (also known as *force majeure*) is an event caused exclusively by the violence of nature, which people are powerless to prevent.

Ademption is the cancellation of a legacy because an act of the testator is interpreted as an intention to revoke the legacy.

Adjective law refers to rules of procedure or practice (see *substantive law*).

Adjudication ordinarily means the pronouncing of a judgment or decree in a litigated case. When used in bankruptcy proceedings the term refers to the order of a bankruptcy court declaring that the debtor is a bankrupt person.

Adjuster usually refers to a person who is employed to make a settlement; an adjuster is most frequently employed by an insurance company.

Administrative law is that branch of law which governs procedure before various agencies of the government.

Administrator or **administratrix** is the one who administers the estate of a person who dies without leaving a will.

Admiralty designates the branch of law which regulates maritime matters.

Adoption is (1) the act of one who takes another's child into his own family and treats him as his own (assuming all the responsibilities of parenthood and giving the child all the privileges of his own child) and (2) the act of a court which creates between two persons the relationship of parent and child.

Adultery, a crime in most states, is the voluntary sexual intercourse of a married person with a person other than the offender's husband or wife.

Adverse possession is a method of acquiring title to real estate by occupancy for a specified number of years; it is sometimes called "squatters title" (see Chapter 16, "Real Property Law").

Advocate refers to a lawyer who pleads for another person in court.

Affidavit is a written statement sworn to before a notary public or another officer having the authority to administer oaths.

Antitrust Laws are adopted by Congress to prevent perceived abuses by corporations monopolizing or conspiring to restrain trade.

Ambulance chasing refers to the unlawful and unethical conduct of a lawyer in the solicitation of claims arising out of personal injuries.

A mensa et thoro is a kind of divorce by means of which the parties are merely separated; it should be distinguished from a divorce *a vinculo,* which effects a complete dissolution of the marriage. Freely translated "a mensa et thoro" refers to a separation from bed and board; "a vinculo" means the breaking of the bonds or chains (of matrimony).

Amicus curiae (Latin, literally "a friend of the court") generally means a person who is not a party in a court proceeding but who is allowed by the court to introduce argument, authority, or evidence, because he has a corollary or collateral interest in the proceeding.

Arraignment is the bringing of a person accused of a crime before a court to be advised of the charge against him and to state his answer to the charge.

Arbitration means the submission for determination of a disputed matter to one or more unofficial persons (as distinguished from an official tribunal like a court) who make a decision or award with respect to the disputed matter. Arbitration is becoming a popular method of settling business disputes; the American Arbitration Association, a private organization, puts at the disposal of businessmen a panel of arbitrators whom the parties to a dispute may use to make an arbitration award or decision.

Arising out of and in the course of employment is a phrase used in connection with Workmen's Compensation Laws to classify an injury incident to employment.

Arrest is the act of depriving a person of his liberty by legal authority.

Arrest of judgment is the act of staying or postponing a judgment.

Arson is the crime of burning a building. In various states this crime is specifically defined as first-, second-, or third-degree arson. For example, in some states arson in the first degree involves setting fire at night to a house or other structure in which there is a human being. Arson in the second degree may be setting fire to a house during the day or setting fire at night to a building in which there is no human being. Arson in the third degree may be setting fire to a vessel, vehicle, or other structure or even setting fire to personal property valued at more than twenty-five dollars.

Articles of agreement consists of a written statement of the terms of an agreement.

Attachment is the act of seizing persons or property by means of legal writ, summons, or other judicial order.

Attestation of a will is the act of witnessing the execution of a will.

Attorney-at-law is an officer of the court and a member of the bar who is authorized to conduct legal proceedings in behalf of others and to give legal advice.

Attorney-in-fact identifies a person, not necessarily a member of the bar, authorized by another to act in his place and stead.

Averment is a statement of facts in legal pleadings.

Bail identifies a person who guarantees the appearance of a defendant in a criminal proceeding at a designated time and place or the security put up for this purpose.

Bail bond is a formal document, executed by an arrested person together with a surety or sureties, providing for the payment of money if the arrested person fails to appear to answer legal process.

Bailee names one to whom property is entrusted; it has nothing to do with criminal bail.

Bailiff usually refers to a sheriff or his deputy or a court attendant who is a representative of the sheriff's office.

Bailment is the delivery of personal property by one person in trust to another (a *bailee*) to carry out a special purpose and with the understanding that the goods will be redelivered when the purpose of the bailment is carried out.

Bench warrant is a process issued by a court in session for the arrest of a person.

Berne Convention is an international treaty among a number of developed nations—to which the United States just became a party—regarding protection of copyrights and certain other intellectual property.

Bigamy is the crime of knowingly contracting a second marriage while the first marriage to the knowledge of the offender is undissolved.

Bill is the formal declaration in a complaint or written statement; it is also the draft of a legislative act (before it becomes law).

Bill of attainder is a legislative act in which a person is pronounced guilty of crime, usually treason, without trial or conviction. It is prohibited by the Constitution of the United States.

Bill of costs is an itemized statement of expenses chargeable against the unsuccessful party to an action or suit.

Bill of indictment (same as *indictment*) is a formal written document accusing a person of having committed a crime.

Bill of lading is written evidence of a contract for delivery of goods by freight.

Bill of particulars is a written statement of the details of a claim for which a suit is brought.

Bill of Rights consists of the first ten amendments of the federal Constitution and guarantees rights and privileges to individuals.

Bill of sale is a written instrument by which one person transfers to another his rights in personal property.

Bill payable, in commercial parlance, is an obligation which is owed by the person keeping a ledger account.

Bill receivable, in commercial parlance, is an account owing to the person keeping the ledger account.

Blackmail is a term usually used as the equivalent of the term *extortion;* it is the extraction of money or something else of value in return for silence or for refraining from performing some act.

Bona fide (Latin) means "in good faith," without deceit or fraud.

Bond is a formal certificate or evidence of a debt.

Book value, applied to corporate stock, designates the value shown after deducting the liabilities from the assets.

Breach of the peace is a catchall phrase used in criminal law to describe the offense of disturbing the public peace by any riotous or unlawful act.

Bribery is a crime of offering, giving, or receiving anything of value to influence the action of a public official.

Brief is a written or printed document prepared by counsel and addressed to a court; it is a basis for an argument in support of a litigant's position.

Burden of proof is the duty to establish a fact in dispute in a lawsuit.

Burglary is the crime of breaking and entering the house of another at night with intent to commit a felony in the house. Various states have modified the foregoing common-law definition in order to cover breaking into and entering a house under different circumstances and have labelled burglary in various degrees. Thus, in some instances, the crime of burglary in the first degree is committed by the burglar who enters a house at night armed with a dangerous weapon or assisted by confederates; burglary in the second degree may be committed during the day by a person who simply breaks and enters a house of another; and burglary in the third degree may be committed by a person who commits the crime and then breaks out of the building (that is, he is already in the building and does not break in to commit the burglary, but he does break out of the building).

Bylaws are regulations, ordinances, rules, or laws adopted by an association or corporation for its internal government.

Calendar refers to a list of cases (sometimes called a "trial list") to be tried during a particular term of court.

Capias (Latin) is the general name for a class of writs which require a court officer to take (the body of) the defendant into custody, that is, arrest him.

Capital crime describes a crime for which the maximum penalty is death.

Capital stock describes the amount of stock authorized by a corporate charter.

Carnal knowledge is a phrase used in connection with criminal charges, such as rape, and signifies sexual intercourse.

Carrier, common, is one who undertakes to transport persons or property for hire.

Case law signifies that branch of law established by court decisions, as distinguished from statutes or other sources of law.

Causa mortis (Latin) means "in contemplation of approaching death."

Cause of action is a person's right to bring a lawsuit against another.

Caveat emptor (Latin) means "let the buyer beware."

Caveat venditor (Latin) means "let the seller beware."

Cease and desist is a type of order usually issued by federal regulatory agencies, such as the Federal Trade Commission, to require an individual or a firm to discontinue a practice which is considered objectionable. If the order is not obeyed, the government agency applies to a court for an order requiring the person to cease and desist and the violation of such a court order is punishable as a contempt of court.

Certificate of incorporation is the instrument by which a private corporation is formed. It is sometimes called a "charter," although originally a charter was a direct legislative grant which gave a corporation the right to exist.

Certiorari (Latin, "to be made certain") refers to a legal proceeding by which a court reviews the decision of a lower court or governmental agency.

Cestui que trust (Latin) means "the beneficiary of a trust."

Chambers refers to the private office of a judge.

Charter, see *certificate of incorporation.*

Chattel is an article of personal property.

Check-off system refers to the deduction of union dues by an employer from employees' pay.

Chose in action is the right to personal property which has not been reduced to possession. Most intangible property rights, such as checks, promissory notes, and claims for damage, are choses in action.

Circumstantial evidence is evidence of facts or circumstances from which the existence or nonexistence of a fact may be inferred. For example, if one of the points in issue in a lawsuit was whether John Jones was at a certain house at a certain time, the facts that his car was seen in front of the house and his gloves were found in the house subsequently might be considered circumstances from which the inference could be drawn that he was at the house at the time in question, even though there was no direct proof of his being seen there.

Citation is an order or notice by which a person is directed to appear in a proceeding.

Clean hands is an equitable doctrine that a person is not entitled to relief if he has been guilty of unjust or unfair conduct.

Clerk of court signifies an officer who has charge of the records and proceedings of court.

Client is the person who employs an attorney.

Code of Professional Responsibility is the successor to the Canons of Professional Ethics, the ethical guides for lawyers' conduct.

Codicil is a separate document which may modify or supplement a will. It must be executed with the same formalities as the will itself.

Collateral relatives refers to brothers, sisters, cousins, aunts, uncles, nephews, and nieces as distinguished from ancestors, such as parents or grandparents, and descendents, such as children and grandchildren.

Comity of states designates the practice or courtesy by which the courts of one state recognize the laws and judicial decisions of another state.

Commitment, in criminal law, is the act of sending a person to prison. The word may also refer to the warrant or order of the court which directs that a person be taken to a prison or another institution.

Committee of an incompetent person or a lunatic refers to a person who, by order of the court, is given the custody of the person and the estate of one who has been adjudged incompetent.

Common law refers to the ancient, unwritten law which originated in England. It also refers to that body of law in the United States which is derived from judicial decisions based on usage and customs of antiquity and on principles recognized in the English common law.

Common-law marriage is one not solemnized by ecclesiastical or civil ceremony but recognized in some jurisdictions as based on agreement between the parties.

Commutation, in criminal law, means a change from a greater to a lesser punishment.

Condemnation, in property law, is the taking by the government of the property of a private owner for public use.

Confidential communications refer to those which pass between persons who stand in a confidential or fiduciary relationship or who are under a special duty of secrecy, such as husband and wife, attorney and client, guardian and ward, and doctor and patient.

Conjugal rights are those which husband and wife have with respect to each other.

Consignment, broadly speaking, is the act of shipping goods, but in business it has come to mean an arrangement whereby the consignor, who sends goods to the consignee, remains the owner of the property until such time as the consignee sells the property to the ultimate consumer; at that time the consignee holds the proceeds of the sale in trust for the benefit of the consignor.

Conspiracy, in criminal law, refers to a combination or plan between two or more persons for the purpose of committing an unlawful act or an act which might be lawful if committed by one person alone but which becomes unlawful with the joint action of the conspirators.

Construction often refers to a court proceeding the purpose of which is to determine the true and real meaning of a legal document, such as a contract or a will.

Contempt of court is an act which is calculated to obstruct the administration of justice. There are two kinds of contempts of court: (1) those committed in the view and presence of the court and which are often punishable immediately by the court and (2) those which do not occur in the presence of the court, such as when a person fails to obey a court order to perform or refrain from performing certain acts.

Conveyance is a transfer of a right in property and most frequently refers to a transfer of an interest in real estate.

Coram nobis (Latin) is an ancient writ of error, recently revived, by which criminal proceedings are reviewed again by a court to determine whether or not there was an error in the proceedings.

Corpus delicti (Latin, "body of a crime"), as applied in criminal law, is the doctrine that there must be substantial proof of the fact that a crime has been committed.

Counterclaim is a claim presented by a defendant in a lawsuit which tends to defeat or to diminish the plaintiff's demand.

Creditor identifies a person to whom a debt is owing.

Crier signifies an officer of the court who makes announcements for the court.

Damages refers to compensation which may be recovered through the courts by any person who has sustained injury to his person, property, or rights, through the unlawful act of another.

Damnum absque injuria (Latin, "loss without injury"), applies to situations when a person has sustained harm without any breach of legal duty that would be the basis for an action for damages against the person causing the injury. An example is an unavoidable accident in which the person who may have been the immediate cause of the injury was guilty of no legal wrong.

Declaration is the first pleading for the plaintiff at common law and is a formal statement of facts and circumstances constituting the plaintiff's cause of action.

Decree is a final written judgment or determination of a court.

Deed is a conveyance of real estate, a written instrument signed by the owner whereby he transfers title to real estate to another person.

De facto (Latin) is used to characterize an officer, a corporation, a government, or a state of affairs that is accepted for all practical purposes although it may be illegal or illegitimate.

De jure (Latin) means "legitimate or lawful."

De minimis non curat lex (Latin) is a maxim meaning "the law does not take notice of small or trifling matters."

Default, in legal procedure, is a failure of a party to a legal proceeding to take a step or perform an act required by law.

Demise, in real estate law, refers to a lease or a conveyance; in probate law, the word means "death."

Demurrer is the formal common-law method of disputing the sufficiency in law of the written pleading of the opposing party in a lawsuit.

De novo (Latin) means "anew" a second time.

Deponent is one who makes a written statement under oath.

Deposition is the testimony of a witness taken not in open court but pursuant to law and under oath and reduced to writing.

Dicta are the statements of a judge in a particular case that are not essential to the determination of the court.

Disability is the absence of legal capability to perform an act. For example, an infant or a person who is mentally incompetent would be under a disability to perform legal acts.

Dividend, broadly speaking, means a fund to be divided. In corporate law, the term refers to a portion of the corporation's surplus profits set aside to be distributed proportionately to the stockholders. In bankruptcy law, dividends are proportionate payments to creditors out of the insolvent estate.

Docket designates a formal brief record of proceedings in court.

Domicile is the true and permanent home of a person as distinguished from a residence which may be only temporary.

Double jeopardy, prohibited by the federal Constitution, occurs when an accused is prosecuted or tried more than once for the same offense.

Draft, a common term for a bill of exchange, is an order for the payment of money drawn by one person on another.

Due process of law means following law according to prescribed forms through courts of justice; it is guaranteed by the federal Constitution.

Duress is the exercise of unlawful constraint whereby a person is forced to perform an act that he otherwise would not have done.

Easement is the right of the owner of one parcel of real estate, by virtue of his ownership, to use land of another for a special purpose.

Ejectment is the name of a common-law action which may be brought for the recovery of real estate.

Embezzlement is the fraudulent appropriation of property by a person to whom it has been entrusted.

Eminent domain is the power of the state to take private property for public use.

Emolument refers to profit arising from an office or employment.

Encroachment is something which legally intrudes or extends over or on the highway or the land of a neighbor, such as part of a house or building or fence.

Encumbrance is a claim, lien, or other burden on real or personal property which tends to diminish its value and affect its marketability. An encumbrance may be a mortgage, a mechanic's lien, or an easement.

Enjoin means to require a person or organization by a writ of injunction to perform or to desist from an act.

Entrapment refers to a procedure used by police officers in inducing a person to commit a crime so that they may institute a criminal prosecution against him.

Environmental Laws are laws which may have an impact on the quality of our life on earth, on the sea, in the air, or in outer space.

Equitable estoppel is the preclusion of a person by his acts or conduct from asserting rights which might otherwise have been his.

Equity of redemption is the right of a landowner to redeem land after the conditions of a mortgage have been broken. Modern laws cut off equity of redemption by foreclosure proceedings.

Escheat is the right of the state to take property or money when there are no heirs surviving.

Escrow is the delivery of property conditionally to a third person, not the owner, who holds it until the happening of an event and then redelivers the same property to the owner.

Estate refers to the kind of interest which a person has in property; it is a broad term with many gradations in meanings. It may also be used to refer to the property of a deceased person.

Et al. (Latin abbreviation of *et alii*) means "and others."

Et ux. (Latin abbreviation of *et uxor*) means "and wife."

Eviction is the act of depriving a person of possession of real property by process of law.

Ex parte means "on one side only." It is generally used in connection with an application to the court by one party to a proceeding.

Ex post facto law is one passed after the occurrence of an act that attempts retroactively to change the legal consequences of that act. Such laws are prohibited by the Constitution of the United States.

Exception, in legal procedure, is a formal objection to the action of a court.

Execution means the performance of all acts necessary to render a written instrument complete, such as signing, sealing, acknowledging, and delivering the instrument. It should be distinguished from the mere signing of an instrument which in and of itself may be *incomplete execution*. In court practice, execution refers to proceedings to enforce a judgment. In the case of a money judgment, it is a direction to the sheriff to take the necessary steps to collect the judgment.

Executory describes that which has yet to be executed or performed.

Exemplary damages, sometimes called "smart money," are punitive in nature and are intended to cover unusual situations in which the loss resulted from violence or wanton or wicked misconduct on the part of the defendant; such damages should be distinguished from ordinary damages which are sometimes called "actual damages," "compensatory damages," or "consequential damages."

Exemption is the right given the debtor to retain a portion of his property free from the claims of creditors.

Exhibit (noun) is a document or other item produced during a trial or a hearing which becomes part of the case.

Extortion involves obtaining property illegally from another by the wrongful use of force or fear.

Extradition is the surrender by one state to a second state of an individual accused or convicted of a criminal offense in the second state.

Falsus in uno, falsus in omnibus (Latin "false in one thing, false in everything") is the doctrine that if any part of the testimony of a witness is willfully false, the jury may disregard all his testimony.

Family car doctrine (also called "family purpose doctrine") is a law in some states that covers the use of the car owned by the head of the family by other family members. Under this doctrine, if the head of the family allows other members of his family to use the automobile for pleasure or convenience, each such member is his agent and the head of the family is, therefore, responsible for their negligence in the operation of the car.

Fee simple is the complete and absolute ownership of real property.

Felony is a crime of a more serious nature than a misdemeanor and is usually punishable by imprisonment or death.

Feme covert refers to a married woman.

Feme sole refers to a single woman.

Fiduciary (noun) is a person holding property for the benefit of another in a trust capacity, such as an executor, guardian, or trustee, As an adjective, "fiduciary" denotes the character of a personal relationship implying great confidence, trust, and good faith.

Fieri facias (Latin) is a writ of execution commanding the sheriff to levy on and to realize the amount of a judgment from the goods of the judgment debtor.

Fixture is something affixed to land or a building that becomes part and parcel of it and is ordinarily the property of the owner of the land.

Force majeure (French) is a superior force, generally an act of God.

Forceable entry is taking possession of land or dwelling place by force, against the will of those entitled to possession.

Forgery is the crime of fraudulently making or altering a writing to prejudice another person's right.

Franchise often refers to a special privilege, generally exclusive, conferred by the government on an individual or corporation to do certain things of a public nature. An example is the privilege (franchise) given by a state or a municipality to a public utility to construct and operate power or telephone lines or public transportation facilities.

Franchise tax is a tax on the right of a corporation to do business in a particular state.

Fraud is a deceitful act with intent to deprive another of his rights or to cause him injury.

Future interests are interests in property, possession or enjoyment of which begins in the future.

Garnishee is a form of execution against the property of a judgment debtor. In many states, a garnishee execution is a direction to an employer or other person who owes money to the judgment debtor to make periodical payments to the sheriff to be applied to and to reduce the money judgment (against the debtor).

Garnishment is a proceeding whereby a person's property is used to pay debts owing to another person.

Gift *causa mortis* describes a gift made in contemplation of death of the donor on the condition that the property shall belong to the donee on the expected death of the donor.

Gift *inter vivos* refers to an absolute gift made between living persons.

Grand jury is the jury of inquiry which is summoned to receive complaints and accusations in criminal cases and to decide if sufficient evidence exists for indictment.

Grand larceny, see *larceny.*

Ground rent originally meant a perpetual rent reserved by the owner of land when he sold the land to another. Today, ground rent is commonly a price paid to the owner of land for the use of land alone, either when the land is vacant or when the tenant has erected a building on the land owned by the landlord.

Guardian is a person charged by law with the duty of caring for the person of a minor child or the person of an incompetent and/or managing his property and rights.

Guardian *ad litem* is a guardian appointed by a court to prosecute or defend an action in behalf of a minor.

Habeas corpus (literally, "you have the body") is a writ requiring that the officer who has custody of a prisoner bring the prisoner before a court or judge for the purpose of determining whether the prisoner has been unlawfully detained.

Health Care Proxy is a written expression of one's desires regarding the extent of treatment to be given if that person becomes gravely ill or seriously injured.

Hearsay evidence is that which does not come from the personal knowledge of the witness but rather from what he heard others say.

Heir, at common law, originally was the designation of a person who inherited real or personal property. In some jurisdictions *heir* later became the designation of the person who inherited real estate, and the term *next-of-kin* sometimes designated only those persons who inherited personal property. To avoid confusion, some states adopted the term *distributee* to refer to a person who inherits real and personal property in the absence of a will.

Holding company refers to corporations whose primary business is to buy and hold the stock of other companies.

Holograph is a will written entirely in the handwriting of the person signing it.

Homicide is the killing of a human being. Homicide may be classified as justifiable or felonious. If "justifiable homicide," it is not usually a crime.

Ignorantia legis neminem excusat (Latin) means that "ignorance of the law excuses no one."

Impanel is the act of the clerk of the court in listing jurors for the trial of a case.

Incest is the crime of sexual intercourse between persons who are related to each other within the degrees of consanguinity prohibited by law.

Incompetency is the lack of legal qualification or ability to discharge a required duty; it is also the condition of a person who is mentally unable or unfit to manage his own affairs.

Incumbrance (see *encumbrance*) is a lien or charge against property.

Indemnity is an agreement by which one person promises to protect another from loss or damage.

Indenture designates a formal contract in which two persons obligate themselves to each other.

Indictment is a written accusation in which a grand jury charges a person with having committed a crime (see *bill of indictment*).

Infant describes a person under legal age, in most places, under eighteen years of age.

Information is a formal accusation charging a person with a criminal offense.

Injunction is a writ issued by a court; it forbids or commands a person to perform a particular act.

Inns of court are private educational associations, similar to colleges, founded in the fourteenth century in England and invested with the responsibility for educating and training barristers.

Inquest is a judicial inquiry. A "coroner's inquest" to determine the legal cause of a person's death is quite common.

Insurance involves a contract whereby a corporation usually called an "insurer" or "underwriter" undertakes to compensate another person usually called the "insured" for an agreed consideration called the "premium." The written contract is usually called a "policy." Such contracts may cover one or more various conditions or occurrences. Insurance may be classified as follows:

Accident insurance whereby the insurer undertakes to indemnify the insured against expense, loss of wages, and so on resulting from accidents which cause injury or death.

Automobile comprehensive insurance whereby the insurer agrees to pay the insured for loss of or damage to a motor vehicle caused by fire, wind, storm, theft, collision, and other similar hazards.

Burglary insurance which protects its owner against loss of property from burglary or theft.

Casualty insurance which protects its owner against one or more kinds of accidents.

Commercial insurance whereby the insurer guarantees parties to business arrangements against loss by breach of contractual obligations.

Fidelity insurance whereby the insurer undertakes to protect employers from the dishonesty (thefts) of officers, agents, or employees of the insured.

Fire insurance where the insurer agrees to reimburse the insured for losses resulting from fire damage to buildings, merchandise, or other forms of personal property.

Fraternal insurance is issued by fraternal organizations to their members as life or accident insurance.

Liability insurance whereby the insurer agrees to protect the insured against liability on account of injuries to the persons or property of another. (This differs from accident of indemnity insurance whereby the insurer pays for losses of the insured.)

Life insurance through which the insurer agrees to pay specified sums to a designated beneficiary on the death of the insured.

Marine insurance whereby the insurer undertakes to indemnify the insured for the perils of the sea or for other risks in connection with marine navigation.

Plate glass insurance through which the insurer agrees to reimburse the insured for loss from accidental breaking of glass.

Title insurance whereby the insurer protects the insured from loss or damage resulting from title defects to real estate.

Workmen's compensation insurance through which the insurer pays in behalf of employers awards to employees or their dependents for injuries sustained on the job.

Intent, an important term in the law of contracts, wills, and other documents, refers to the purpose or design of the person executing an instrument and is often determined by courts in construing the true meaning of an instrument.

International law is a system of rules and principles, founded on treaty, custom, and precedent which civilized nations are expected to recognize as binding upon them in their relationships with others.

Jeopardy is the danger of conviction and punishment which a prisoner faces when he is charged with a crime (see *double jeopardy*).

Judge advocate, in a military court-martial, is an officer who advises the court, but whose main duty is to act as prosecutor.

Judgment describes the official and authentic decision of a court of justice.

Judgment creditor designates one who has obtained a money judgment against his debtor.

Judgment debtor signifies one against whom a money judgment has been recovered.

Judgment lien is the charge of a court judgment against the real estate of a judgment debtor.

Judicial notice refers to the doctrine by which the court in conducting a trial or making its decision recognizes the truth of certain facts without demanding evidence. Facts of which a court may take judicial notice are: the laws of a state, international law, historical events, geography, and so on.

Judiciary refers to the system of courts.

Jurisdiction is the authority by which courts act.

Jurisprudence is the science that treats all the principles of law.

Jury, see *grand jury, petit jury*.

Justice of the peace is a judge of inferior rank whose duties are limited by law in each state.

Kidnapping, a felony, is the forceable abduction or stealing and carrying away of a person against his will. Taking a kidnapped person across state lines makes the crime a federal offense.

King (the) can do no wrong means that the king (and hence the government) is not legally responsible for acts of his representatives (see *sovereign immunity*).

Laches describes an undue delay which results in legal prejudice to another.

Larceny involves the unlawful taking and carrying away of another's personal property. In various jurisdictions, the crime is divided into grand and petit larceny, depending on the value of the property stolen. When the value of the goods stolen is considerable, for example, five hundred dollars, the crime is *grand larceny*. *Petit larceny* is committed when the value of the goods stolen is below that amount.

Last clear chance is a doctrine applied to a situation in which an injured person has been guilty of negligence but his helpless condition was realized by the person causing the injury. The person causing the injury would be held responsible if he could have avoided doing harm after discovering the predicament of the injured person.

Lateral support describes the right to have real property supported by adjoining real property (land or soil).

Leading question is one which suggests to a witness the answer desired by the person asking the question.

Lease is an agreement whereby a landlord rents property to a tenant. It may be written or verbal.

Legal ethics is comprised of the duties which members of the legal profession owe to the public, to the court, to their professional colleagues and to their clients.

Letters of administration is a document issued by a probate court; it gives a person authority to act as administrator of an estate.

Letters of guardianship designates a document, issued by the court, evidencing the authority of the guardian.

Letters rogatory is a request made by one court to another court that a witness be examined on written interrogatories.

Letters testamentary is a document, issued by a probate court, which empowers a person to act as executor of a will.

Levy describes the seizure and sale of property by a court officer to satisfy an execution or garnishment.

Lex fori (Latin) means the "law of the place where the litigation is tried."

Lex loci contractus (Latin) means the "law of the place where the contract was made."

Lex loci delictus (Latin) means the "law of the place where the crime or wrong took place."

Lex loci rei sitae (Latin) means "the law of the place where the subject matter is situated."

Libel of Public Figures refers to a person who defames another who, for example, is a celebrity, a politician or an office holder. This person may only be guilty of libel under certain limited circumstances.

Lien is a charge or encumbrance on property.

Life estate is an interest in property that is limited to the lifetime of an individual.

Life tenant designates one who holds an interest in property during the life estate.

Lis pendens (Latin, "pending suit") is commonly used as a notice warning those interested to examine the proceedings.

Living Will is an expression of one's desires regarding the extent of treatment to be given if that person becomes gravely ill or seriously injured.

Magistrate is a public officer, almost everywhere a judge of one of the lower courts.

Majority refers to full legal age; this is the age at which, by law, a person is entitled to manage his own affairs and enjoy all his civil rights.

Malfeasance is performing an act which is wrong and unlawful (see *misfeasance*).

Malicious mischief is the willful destruction of property.

Malicious prosecution involves instituting criminal proceedings without probable cause and for the purpose of injuring a defendant. The term applies only if the criminal proceeding terminates in favor of the person prosecuted.

Malpractice describes any professional misconduct or want of professional skill which results in injury to another. The term may be applied to physicians, surgeons, dentists, lawyers, engineers, and other professional people.

Malum in se refers to a thing that is evil in itself; a thing that is morally wrong.

Malum prohibitum refers to a thing that is wrong because it is prohibited by statute.

Mandamus is the name of a judicial writ, directed to a governmental officer or body and commanding the performance of an act.

Manslaughter is the killing of another without malice or deliberate intention.

Marital Deduction is a term used in estate planning and in estate tax law allowing a deduction under certain circumstances for the value of bequests to a surviving spouse.

Marshal is an officer in the federal judicial system with duties corresponding to those of a sheriff (see *sheriff*).

Marshaling of assets is the arrangement of assets and claims in an estate or in a bankruptcy or insolvency proceeding in order to secure the proper payment of the various claims, taking into consideration which claims have priority over others.

Mayhem is the crime of mutilating a human being or depriving him of a body member.

Mesne assignments are the intermediate assignments by which title to property is transferred.

. **Minor** is a person under the age of legal competence (in most places, eighteen years of age).

Misdemeanor is an act which violates public law, but which is not as serious as a felony. Such acts are generally punishable by fines or short terms of imprisonment.

Misfeasance is the improper performance of an act which a person has a right to do (see *malfeasance*).

Mistrial is a trial brought to a halt because of a procedural mistake.

Moot describes a subject for argument, a topic that is unsettled, undecided.

Moral Rights Laws refer to a legal doctrine that has been in effect in many European countries and that recently has been enacted by some states and by the Federal government giving some protection to the integrity of an artist's visual work. These laws give the artist the right of attribution and protecting the work from being defaced or changed to its detriment.

Motion is an application made to a court for an order.

Municipal law designates that which pertains to towns, cities, villages, and other political subdivisions. It is a highly specialized branch of the law, practiced by village and town attorneys and corporation counsels and certain attorneys in financial circles who approve bonds and other obligations issued by municipalities.

Murder is the killing with malice aforethought of one human being by another.

Mystic testament is in the law of Louisiana a closed or sealed will required by statute to be executed in a particular manner and to be signed on the outside of the envelope containing it by a notary public and seven witnesses.

Ne exeat signifies a decree or writ which forbids a person to leave the jurisdiction of the court.

Next-of-kin means those persons most nearly related to a decedent by blood, but in some jurisdictions it is used in the law of descent and distribution to designate those who inherit personal property only.

Nisi prius designates a court in which a case is tried before a jury; it differs from an appellate court in which a judge or tribunal decides the case.

Nolle pros. (abbreviation of the Latin phrase, *nolle prosequi*) is the plaintiff's declaration in a civil suit or the prosecutor's declaration in a criminal proceeding that he will no longer proceed in the action.

Nolo contendere (Latin, "I will not contest") in a criminal action is a plea that has the consequences of a plea of guilty, but it is not to be used as an admission of guilt or of liability elsewhere.

Non compos mentis means "not of sound mind" or insane.

Nonjoinder is a failure to include a person as a party to a legal proceeding when according to law he ought to have been made a party.

Nonsuit is the name of a judgment given against the plaintiff when he is unable to prove sufficient facts to constitute a cause of action against the defendant.

Notary public is a public officer whose duty it is to administer oaths, to take acknowledgments of deeds and other conveyances, and to perform certain other official acts, such as the protesting of negotiable instruments.

Novation is the substitution of a new debt, contract, or obligation for an existing one.

Nudum pactum (Latin, "a bare pact") is a pact unenforceable by action, that is, it is a voluntary promise or undertaking without legal obligation.

Nuisance is a legal wrong which arises from unreasonable or unlawful use by a person of his own property, or from improper, indecent, or unlawful personal conduct which works an injury to the right or property of another.

Nulla bona (Latin, "no goods") indicates that the judgment debtor has no property or which the sheriff can levy.

Nunc pro tunc (Latin, "now for then") applies to acts allowed to be performed after the time when they should have been, with a retroactive effect.

Oath is a solemn appeal to the Supreme Being in attestation of the truth of a statement.

Obiter dictum (Latin) is a statement in a court's opinion or a remark made by a judge that is incidental or collateral to the point at issue and that does not bear directly on the issue.

Obligee is the person in whose favor an obligation is contracted; for example, the person for whose benefit a bond is given is sometimes called the "obligee."

Obligor designates the person who has agreed to perform an obligation; for example, the person who gives a bond is sometimes called the "obligor."

Office frequently refers in law to a duty and power conferred on an individual by governmental authority and is sometimes used interchangeably for "public office."

Opinion evidence consists of a witness's opinions based on his background or experience. This kind of evidence is not admissible in court except in the testimony of experts such as coroners, ballistic experts, physicians, psychiatrists, and so on.

Option, in the law of contracts, is a privilege given to one person to purchase property from another at a specified price and within a specified time.

Order, in legal practice, is a written direction of a court or judge, other than a judgment.

Ordinance describes a local law passed by a municipality, such as a city, village, or town.

Overt act, in criminal law, is the first open motion or step taken to carry out a criminal plan. It is sometimes necessary to establish that this step has been made to commit a crime in order to justify a right of self-defense.

Oyer and terminer means literally "to hear and to determine"; hence, a judging on oral evidence. (Certain United States superior criminal courts are described as "courts of oyer and terminer.")

Oyez means "hear ye" and is a word used by court criers when about to make a proclamation.

Pardon, in criminal law, is the release of a person charged with crime from the entire punishment prescribed for the offense; it should be distinguished from a "parole," which conditionally releases the prisoner from the balance of his sentence.

Parol evidence rule provides that a contract cannot be modified or changed by oral testimony.

Parole, see *pardon.*

Particeps criminis (Latin) refers to a participant in a crime, an accomplice.

Partition is the division of lands held by joint tenants or tenants in common. When the owners themselves cannot agree, partition is used as a form of a legal action, whereby the court compels the land to be divided between the co-owners or directs that the land be sold and the proceeds of the sale be divided between or among the owners.

Party wall is a wall built partly on the land of one owner and partly on the land of another for the benefit of both.

Patent is both (1) a grant made by the government to an inventor giving him the exclusive right to make, use, and sell his invention for a specified period and (2) an instrument by which the government conveys public lands to an individual.

Pendente lite (Latin) means "pending the suit." It is used in connection with a temporary injunction and other orders issued in the course of a lawsuit.

Per capita (Latin, "by the head"), in the law of wills, denotes the method of dividing property by the number of individuals equally related to the decedent so each individual receives an equal share of the estate (see *per stirpes*).

Per curiam (Latin, "by the court") designates the opinion of the whole court rather than an opinion written by an individual judge.

Per stirpes (Latin, "by the root") is a means, in the law of wills, whereby a class or group takes the share which their ancestor would have taken (see *per capita*).

Perjury, in criminal law, is a willfully false statement given under oath.

Petition, in court practice, is an application in writing for an order of the court.

Petit jury refers to the ordinary jury of twelve (sometimes six) men and women, who serve at the trial of a civil or a criminal action. (The term *petit* [small] is used to distinguish it from the *grand* [large] *jury*.) Members of the petit jury are judges of the facts and make factual determinations, such as the truth or falsity of testimony, whether a contract has been broken, whether a person is guilty of negligence and damages. When a petit jury serves in the trial of a lawsuit the judge or justice presiding makes no determination of the facts, but only rules on the law. Sometimes in the trial of a case without jury, the justice or judge presiding is the judge of not only the law but also of the facts.

Petit larceny, see *larceny.*

Plagiarism is the act of appropriating the literary composition of another. It may constitute a crime in that it is stealing property rights which belong to another.

Pleading generally is the system whereby parties to a lawsuit present written statements of their respective contentions; a formal allegation of what is claimed by one side or denied by the other in a lawsuit. Pleadings in some courts may be oral.

Pledge is a transfer of possession or title to personal property to a creditor as security for a debt.

Power of appointment is a designation by one person in his deed or will of another person (or persons) who is to receive an interest in his property.

Power of attorney is an instrument authorizing another person to act as one's agent.

Preemptive right, in corporation law, is the privilege given to stockholders to purchase new stock issued by the corporation in proportion to their holdings, as stockholders, before the stock is offered to persons other than stockholders.

Presentment is an informal written statement made by the grand jury and representing to the court that a public offense has been committed, that it is triable in the county, and that there is ground for believing a particular individual has committed the crime. It lacks, however, the formality of a bill of indictment.

Presumption of innocence is a fundamental rule, in criminal law, which requires every accused person to be acquitted unless his guilt is established beyond a reasonable doubt.

Presumption of law is a rule requiring courts to draw a particular inference from certain evidence until the truth of such inference is disproved. For example, the courts will presume that an automobile which is registered in the name of a certain man is owned by that man until evidence is brought in to show that the automobile is actually owned by someone else.

Prima facie case is one sufficiently strong to establish a favorable finding for one side until contradicted by other evidence.

Prima facie evidence is that which is sufficient on its face, that is, sufficient to establish a given fact unless rebutted.

Probation, in criminal law, allows a person convicted of an offense to go free with a suspended sentence, during his good behavior, and usually under the supervision of a probation officer.

Process is a legal means, such as a summons, used to subject a defendant in a lawsuit to the jurisdiction of the court; in a broader sense it includes all other writs issued in the course of legal proceedings.

Professional Corporation is a type of corporation, allowing some limited liability, which may be availed of only by accountants, lawyers, doctors, etc.; sometimes known as a "professional association," "P.C.," or "P.A."

Promoters, in corporation law, are those persons who take the preliminary steps in the organization of a corporation and who issue prospectuses, procure subscriptions to stock, and obtain the certificate of incorporation.

Proof (legal) refers to evidence which is adduced at a trial or evidence that has some probative value in establishing the existence of a fact. Sometimes it signifies evidence which establishes the truth or falsehood of a fact.

Property is something which is of value to the individual who owns it. When a person has a property right in something, he has an interest in it. The word *property* is also used to describe anything which is the subject of ownership whether real or personal, tangible or intangible.

Proximate cause, in legal cases involving accidents and injuries, is that which in the ordinary course of events, unbroken by an intervening cause, produces an injury and without which the injury would not have occurred.

Proxy may be either a person or a written instrument. As a person a *proxy* is one deputized to represent another person at a meeting, such as a stockholders' meeting or a ceremony, such as marriage. When it is a written instrument, a proxy is a document which appoints a person to act at a meeting or similar event.

Publication, in the law of libel, is the act of communicating defamatory matter to one or more persons. In the law of wills, it is the formal declaration at the time of making a will whereby a testator states that the document is his will and testament. In legal procedure, in some states, it is the practice of serving notice or process by newspaper advertisement.

Public law is that branch of the law which is concerned with government in its political or sovereign capacity, including constitutional and administrative law; it should be distinguished from private law which is concerned with only the rights of individuals.

Putative means "commonly reputed": A man who is commonly known as the father of an illegitimate child is said to be the "putative father" of the child.

Quantum meruit (Latin, "as much as he deserved") is a form of pleading in which a plaintiff claims an amount not based on a contract but based on what he reasonably deserves to be paid.

Quash means to vacate or to annul.

Quasi-contract is an obligation which arises not from formal agreement, but from the relationship or the voluntary acts of the parties; it is sometimes referred to as an "implied contract."

Quasi-judicial refers to activities of public administrative officers who are required to investigate facts and draw legal conclusions from them.

Quitclaim deed conveys all interest which one has in a piece of real estate without warranty of title.

Quorum is the number of members of a body, such as a board of directors or stockholders or legislature or other public body, that is required to make the body competent to transact business in the absence of the other members.

Quo warranto (Latin, "by what authority") is a writ or proceeding which allows inquiry into the title of a corporation to a franchise or the right of an individual to hold a public or corporate office.

Rape is the crime committed by a man who has sexual intercourse with a woman (not his wife) without her consent. The crime of *statutory rape* refers to intercourse with a female under a stated age (for example, sixteen or eighteen or twenty-one), either with or without her consent.

Ratification is the confirmation of an act previously done. It either obligates, for the first time, the person doing the act or confirms the act's validity. When an agent performs an act without the authority of his principal, the ratification of the act may make it binding for the first time upon the principal. An infant's act, which is voidable because of his infancy, may be ratified by him after he reaches his majority, making the act binding upon the former infant.

Real estate (or real property) is land and everything growing or built on it.

Real evidence consists of the facts furnished by the things themselves, rather than from verbal testimony.

Recapitalization is the procedure by which stocks, bonds, or other corporation securities are altered in amount, income, or priority.

Receiver is a person appointed by the court to receive and preserve property pending the outcome of a legal proceeding.

Recidivist is a repeater, a habitual criminal.

Recorder is, in some states, a magistrate who has criminal jurisdiction similar to that of a police judge.

Referee is a person to whom the court refers a legal proceeding and who has authority to take testimony or other action, make a decision, or report back to the court.

Reformation is a remedy whereby written instruments may be changed to express the real agreement or intention of the parties.

Relator designates the person at whose instance a legal proceeding is brought but who is not the nominal party.

Release is the surrendering of a right, claim, or privilege by the person who owns the same.

Relevancy describes a quality of evidence which renders it properly applicable to determine the truth or falsity of the matter before the court.

Remainder, in the law of wills, signifies the balance of an estate after the payment of legacies. In property law, *remainder* refers to an interest in land or in a trust estate which takes effect at the termination of an estate for years or an estate for life. For example, Mr. X provides in his will that Mr. A should have the use of a certain piece of land during his lifetime; after Mr. A's death, Mr. B should have the life use of the land, and upon the death of Messrs. A and B the land should go to Mr. C. Mr. C would then have a remainder interest (see *reversion*).

Remand, in legal proceedings, occurs when a high court sends a case back to a lower court in order to have corrective action taken. It also means sending the prisoner back to custody pending a hearing.

Remedy is the means for enforcing a right or redressing an injury.

Remittitur of record is the return of a case record to the trial court by a court of appeal in order that the judgment of the appeal court may be carried out.

Replevin is a legal action brought in court to recover possession of goods unlawfully taken or detained.

Reprieve, in criminal law, is the suspension of execution of sentence for a period of time so a prisoner may carry out an instruction of the court.

Res (Latin, "a thing") refers to the subject matter of the action.

Res gestae (Latin, "things done") designates circumstances which are part of a particular incident. *Res gestae* is important in the law of evidence and procedure; when certain things are said and done as part of the particular transaction, they are considered to be exceptions to the hearsay rule.

Res inter alios acta (Latin, "transactions among others") refers to things done between third persons or strangers and hence not binding on the parties to litigation.

Res ipsa loquitur (Latin, "the thing speaks for itself") is the presumption that a person was responsible through negligence for an accident; it is based on proof that the instrumentality causing the accident was in the defendant's exclusive control and that the accident was one which ordinarily does not happen in the absence of negligence. If the doctrine of *res ipsa loquitur* is applicable, the plaintiff does not have to prove negligence.

Res judicata (Latin) is a controversial matter or dispute that has been settled by the judgment of the court.

Residuary estate is that part of a decedent's property which remains after the payment of his debts, expenses of estate administration, and legacies.

Respondeat superior (Latin, "let the master answer") signifies the doctrine that an employer is liable for the wrongful acts of his employees.

Respondent is the party who answers a petition in a court proceeding; he is also the party against whom an appeal is taken.

Restraint of trade refers to business activity or combinations which tend to eliminate competition or to result in a monopoly.

Retainer is the act of a client or the payment made by a client in employing an attorney.

Reversion is the future interest in land which a person retains for himself or for his heirs after giving possession of land to another for a term of years or for life. It differs from a remainder interest in that the remainder interest vests in someone other than the person who creates the interest, whereas the reversionary interest returns to the person who created it or to his heirs.

Right of way is a legal right to pass over land that belongs to another.

Riparian rights are those possessed by an owner of land on the bank of a body of water; they usually include rights to water for bathing and domestic uses and navigation, but may include rights to the soil and its contents (minerals and so on) under the specified area of water.

Robbery is the crime of taking property from another against his will by means of force or of intimidation.

Rule, in a court procedure, is a court order requiring a person to show why an act should not be performed.

Rule against perpetuities describes the doctrine specifying that no interest in property is valid unless title to the property vests in definite persons who will be alive after the death of certain persons living at the time the property interest is created.

Scienter (Latin, "knowingly," "willfully") refers to the defendant's previous knowledge of the fact which led to a wrongful injury.

Scintilla of evidence signifies the least particle of evidence.

Scire facias (Latin, "do you cause to know") designates a writ requiring a person to show why a record should not be annulled.

Seal is a particular sign or impression made to signify formally the execution of a written instrument.

Sealed instrument is a written instrument to which the party bound has affixed not only his name but also his seal. (The importance of sealed instruments has been gradually done away with by the legislatures in many jurisdictions.)

Search warrant identifies a written order issued by a judge or magistrate and directed to a sheriff, constable, or marshal; it commands one of the latter officers to search specified premises for personal property unlawfully held.

Secondary evidence describes that which is inferior to other evidence. For example, a copy of an instrument or verbal proof of its contents is secondary evidence of the instrument itself.

Seduction is the act of inducing a woman to unlawful sexual intercourse.

Seisin is the possession or the right to immediate possession of an interest in real estate.

Self-dealing refers to transactions in which one acting in a fiduciary capacity, such as a trustee, acts at the same time in his own self-interest. This happens when a man individually buys property for himself as trustee. Self-dealing is illegal and sometimes results in the voiding of entire transactions.

Sequestration is a court mandate ordering the sheriff to take over property of a defendant and to hold it until the decision in the suit.

Service of process is the delivery of a summons, subpoena, or other court paper to a person who is thereby officially notified of a court action or proceeding or to appear in court.

Set-off is a counterdemand.

Settlor is one who creates a trust.

Sheriff is an important county officer who is charged with the enforcement of civil and criminal law.

Situs (Latin, "location") is the place where a thing is considered to exist or to have happened.

Social security is a system, enacted by Congress, providing for old-age and disability benefits and unemployment insurance payable by the government from the fund contributed to by both employers and employees.

Sovereign immunity, a doctrine which dates from feudal times, exempts the government from suit at the hands of private individuals unless the government waives such immunity. The federal government has waived this immunity through the federal Tort Claims Act, enacted by Congress. Although many states have waived their sovereign immunity, others still rely on this ancient doctrine.

Spendthrift trust is one created to provide a fund only the income of which will be paid to the beneficiary; the purpose of such a fund is to support the beneficiary and, at the same time, protect him against his own improvidence.

Squatter, in real estate law, refers to one who settles on another's land without legal authority.

Stare decisis (Latin, "to stand by decided matters") refers to the courts' policy of following precedents.

Statute means an act of Congress or a state legislature.

Statute of frauds designates laws which provide that no suit or action shall be based on certain transactions unless there be a note or memorandum thereof in writing signed by the party to be charged with responsibility.

Statute of limitations prescribes that no suit shall be brought on a certain type of claim unless brought within a specified period after the claim accrues.

Stipulation, in court practice, is an agreement made by both parties.

Subordination of perjury, in criminal law, is the offense of procuring another to take a false oath which would constitute perjury.

Subpoena is a legal process commanding a witness to appear and give testimony.

Subpoena duces tecum (Latin) commands a witness to produce a document or property at the trial.

Subrogation acts to put a third person who has paid a debt in the place of the creditor to whom he has paid it, so that he may proceed against the debtor with all rights of the creditor.

Substantive law is the branch of the law that regulates rights; it is the opposite of *adjective law,* which prescribes remedies and procedure for enforcing rights.

Substituted service is the notice or delivery of legal process in a lawful manner other than by personal service (such as by publication or by mail).

Summons notifies a defendant in writing that an action has been commenced against him and that he is required to appear in court and answer it within a stated time.

Supersedeas (Latin) is a court writ that suspends legal proceedings.

Suretyship is the relationship created when one person formally contracts to be responsible for the obligations of another person.

Surrogate is the title of a judicial officer who has jurisdiction over the estates of deceased persons.

Talesman is a person summoned to act as a juror from among bystanders on the street or in the courtroom.

Testament is usually a will; strictly speaking it is a disposition of personal property to take place after a person's death.

Testamentary pertains to a will. It is often used in combination with other words—testamentary trustee, testamentary guardian, testamentary capacity.

Title, in the law of property, is the evidence of a person's right to possession and ownership of property.

Tort is a wrong committed upon the person or property of another, other than the violation of a contract.

Trade name is an appellation by which a person or persons are known in business; it functions as trade protection.

Treason, in criminal law, is the offense of attempting to overthrow the government or to betray the government into the hands of a foreign power.

Trespass is an unlawful injury to another's person or property by force or violence.

Trial is a judicial examination of a controversy.

True bill, in criminal law, is a bill of indictment handed down by a grand jury against an accused person, although technically it may be an endorsement of the bill of indictment by members of a grand jury and state that they are satisfied with the truth of the accusation.

Trust is the holding of property by one person for the benefit of another. The person who holds the property is called the *trustee;* the beneficiary is called the *cestui que trust.* A *constructive trust* is one arising out of operation of law. An *express trust* is usually in writing and definite in terms. An *implied trust* is created by implication of law. A *passive trust* is one in which the trustee has no active duties to perform. A *totten trust* is created by one person when he deposits money in a bank in his own name as trustee for another.

Trust ex maeficio is a type of constructive trust arising out of misconduct or breach of faith by a person entrusted with property.

Trust receipt is a written instrument whereby a lender who has advanced money for the purchase of property delivers possession of the property to the borrower on the agreement that the borrower will hold the property in trust for the lender until he is paid in full.

Ultra vires (Latin) describes the action of a corporation when it oversteps the powers conferred on it by its charter or by the statues under which it was incorporated.

Undertaking, in legal procedure, generally refers to a bond or other security which must, by law, be furnished before certain legal steps may be taken.

Undue influence is wrongful persuasion which overpowers a person's will and causes him to do something that he would not have done of his own volition.

Unemployment compensation is money paid to unemployed persons by the government from funds created in large part by employers' contributions.

Uniform laws are those which have been approved by the National Conference of Commissioners on Uniform State Laws and which have been adopted by all or some of the states.

Unilateral contract designates a legal agreement in which one party promises to do certain things without receiving in return any promise of performance from the other party. Such a contract differs from a bilateral contract through which both parties enter into mutual promises.

Unjust enrichment designates a situation by which one person profits unequitably at another's expense.

Unmarketable title refers to a substantially defective title to real estate which raises serious doubt that future purchasers would accept the title.

Usury consists of charging an illegal rate of interest.

Vagrancy is a minor criminal offense. It is a manner of living rather than a single act and consists of wandering from place to place without any apparent means of support.

Vendor is a person who sells real estate.

Venireman designates a member of a panel of jurors.

Venue is the place designated for the trial of a legal proceeding.

Verdict is the decision of a jury.

Verification, in legal pleadings, is an affidavit swearing that a writing is true.

Void designates that something is a nullity and has no legal effect; hence it cannot be confirmed or ratified.

Voidable refers to matter which may be declared void but which is valid until judicially found to be void.

Voting trust is an agreement among stockholders of a corporation that control of the stock shall be vested in a trustee.

Waiver is the relinquishing of a right. A waiver may be written or it may be inferred from a course of conduct which indicates that a person intends to abandon or surrender his legal rights.

Ward, in the law of guardianship, means an infant or person of unsound mind whose interest is represented and protected by a guardian.

Warehouse receipt is a written evidence of title given by a warehouseman for goods received by him for storage.

Warrant (verb) means to assure that certain facts are true.

Warrant (noun) is a document directing a public officer to perform certain acts (for example, make an arrest or a search).

Warranty is a promise that a certain statement of fact is true. An *express warranty* is one created by explicit statements. An *implied warranty* is one which the law infers from the nature of the transaction.

Waste is the destructive use of property by one in possession of it.

Witness may refer either to one who is present and observes a transaction (such as a witness to a will) or to one who observes an accident (an eyewitness). It may also refer to an individual who testifies in court.

Writ designates a court order directed to the sheriff or another public officer requiring the performance of a certain act.

Zoning is the division of a municipality into districts for governmental regulation of the use to which buildings or lands may be put.

INDEX

Note: Numbers followed by an *i* indicate illustrations;
those followed by a *t* indicate tables.